Turkey and the Soviet Union During World War II

Turkey and the Soviet Union During World War II

Diplomacy, Discord and International Relations

Onur İşçi

I.B. TAURIS
LONDON • NEW YORK • OXFORD • NEW DELHI • SYDNEY

I.B. TAURIS
Bloomsbury Publishing Plc
50 Bedford Square, London, WC1B 3DP, UK
1385 Broadway, New York, NY 10018, USA
29 Earlsfort Terrace, Dublin 2, Ireland

BLOOMSBURY, I.B. TAURIS and the I.B. Tauris logo
are trademarks of Bloomsbury Publishing Plc

First published in Great Britain 2020
Paperback edition first published 2021

Copyright © Onur İşçi, 2020

Onur İşçi has asserted his right under the Copyright,
Designs and Patents Act, 1988, to be identified as Author of this work.

For legal purposes the Acknowledgements on pp. x–xi constitute
an extension of this copyright page.

Cover design by Charlotte James
Cover image: Prime Minister İsmet İönü amongst Bolshevik leaders during a high-level
official visit to the Soviet Union in April 1932

All rights reserved. No part of this publication may be reproduced or
transmitted in any form or by any means, electronic or mechanical,
including photocopying, recording, or any information storage or retrieval
system, without prior permission in writing from the publishers.

Bloomsbury Publishing Plc does not have any control over, or responsibility for,
any third-party websites referred to or in this book. All internet addresses given
in this book were correct at the time of going to press. The author and publisher
regret any inconvenience caused if addresses have changed or sites have
ceased to exist, but can accept no responsibility for any such changes.

A catalogue record for this book is available from the British Library.

A catalog record for this book is available from the Library of Congress.

ISBN: HB: 978-1-7883-1134-2
PB: 978-0-7556-3662-4
ePDF: 978-1-7883-1780-1
eBook: 978-1-7883-1781-8

Series: Library of World War II Studies

Typeset by RefineCatch Ltd, Bungay, Suffolk NR35 1EF, UK

To find out more about our authors and books visit
www.bloomsbury.com and sign up for our newsletters.

For Defne and Yasemin.

Contents

List of Illustrations		viii
List of Abbreviations		ix
Acknowledgements		x
	Introduction	1
1	Things Thus Standing	11
2	Turkey's Eastern Question	37
3	The End of Soviet–Turkish Friendship	51
4	Of Enemies and Neighbours	73
5	The Barbarossa Bubble	99
6	Turanian Fantasies	123
7	When the Hurlyburly's Done	145
	Epilogue	165
Notes		177
Bibliography		219
Index		229

Illustrations

All images appear courtesy of the İnönü Foundation in Ankara. The author would like to thank Özden Toker, İsmet İnönü's daughter, for access to these photographs.

1.1 Turkish Prime Minister İsmet İnönü during an official visit to the Soviet Union in April 1932. 16

1.2 İnönü meeting prominent Bolshevik leaders in Moscow, April 1932. 16

1.3 İnönü and his Soviet counterpart, Vyacheslav Molotov, in Moscow, April 1932. 17

1.4 İnönü with Deputy Commissar for Foreign Affairs, Lev Karakhan, and Chairman of the Presidium of the Supreme Soviet of the USSR, Mikhail Kalinin. 18

1.5 İnönü in front of the Novodevichy Monastery with Mikhail Kalinin, Chairman of the Presidium of the Supreme Soviet of the USSR, April 1932 19

1.6 İnönü meets with Soviet Commissar for Defence Kliment Voroshilov. 20

1.7 İnönü and Kliment Voroshilov in front of the Turkish parliament in Ankara. 21

1.8 Seated next to İnönü, Kliment Voroshilov salutes Turkish spectators as they approach the Ankara hippodrome. 21

7.1 Winston Churchill and Anthony Eden are greeted by Turkish Foreign Minister Şükrü Saracoğlu in Yenice ahead of the Adana Conference. 148

7.2 İsmet İnönü arrives at the Yenice train station to attend the Adana Conference with Winston Churchill. 149

7.3 Turkish Foreign Minister Şükrü Saraçoğlu with Winston Churchill in Adana. 149

7.4 İnönü and Churchill in the train carriage that hosted the Adana Conference. 150

7.5 and 7.6 İnönü and Churchill during the Adana Conference. 151

7.7 İnönü and FDR at the Second Cairo Conference, December 1943. 154

7.8 and 7.9 İnönü with Churchill and FDR at the Second Cairo Conference. 155

Abbreviations

AVP-RF   Arkhiv vneshnei politiki Rossiiskoi Federatsii (The Foreign Policy Archive of the Russian Federation, Moscow).

BCA   Başbakanlık Cumhuriyet Arşivi (Prime Ministerial Archive of the Turkish Republic, Ankara).

TBMM   Türkiye Büyük Millet Meclisi Zabıt Ceridesi (Parliamentary Minutes of the Turkish Grand National Assembly, Ankara).

DBFP   Documents on British Foreign Policy, London.

DGFP   Documents on German Foreign Policy, Berlin.

DVP SSR   Dokumenty vneshnei politiki SSSR (Documents on Foreign Policy of the USSR, Moscow).

FRUS   Foreign Relations of the United States, Washington DC.

GPT   Dokumenty Ministerstva inostrannykh del. Germanii, vyp II: Germanskaia politika v Turtsii (German Policy in Turkey, Moscow).

PRO FO   Public Record Office – Foreign Office Archives, London.

RGASPI   Rossiiskii gosudarstvennyi arkhiv sotsial' no-politicheskoi istorii (Russian State Archive of Socio-Political History, Moscow.)

RGAE   Rossiiskii gosudarstvennyi arkhiv ekonomiki (Russian State Archive of the Economy, Moscow.)

RGVA   Rossiiskii gosudarstvennyi voennyi arkhiv (Russian State Military Archive, Moscow.)

TDA   Türk Diplomatik Arşivi (Turkish Diplomatic Archive, Ankara).

NA   The (US) National Archives, College Park.

A note on transliteration

For all Russian names and words, I have used the Library of Congress transliteration system, except in the case of a very few names for which different transliterations are seen recurrently in English-language sources (e.g. Trotsky instead of Trotskii). Likewise, for all Turkish names and words I have followed the modern Turkish spelling, with the exception of a few words that can be found commonly in English dictionaries (e.g. pasha not paşa). When writing about Turks in contexts before 1934, I have given their later surnames in parentheses only at the first instance.

Acknowledgements

The idea of writing about the Second World War's impact on Soviet-Turkish relations originated in a graduate colloquium offered by the late Professor Richard Stites. Shortly after I began my doctoral studies at Georgetown University, Richard asked me to produce a paper – a Quellenkunde as he called it – based on seized foreign records in the Smolensk collection at the National Archives. During one of our regular Tuesday meetings (usually at Martin's Tavern on Wisconsin Ave.), Richard agreed to supervise a dissertation on the subject but suggested adding a Turkish connection. To illustrate what he had in mind, he gave me a VHS copy of Joseph L. Mankiewicz's 1952 movie *5 Fingers*, which is based on a true espionage story in neutral Turkey during World War II. I was lucky to have the opportunity to write an earlier version of this book's first several pages under Richard's supervision before his untimely death in 2010.

Richard was a source of inspiration for many at the Hilltop and I feel very privileged to have been trained by his colleagues, whose critiques and comments have been most helpful. Mustafa Aksakal, who became my advisor, generously supported my belated introduction to Turkish scholarship and guided me through the twists and turns of my dissertation. David Goldfrank and Gabor Agoston conveyed a spirit of adventure in regards to linguistics and archives, and encouraged me to look for deeper transnational connections regarding our recent past. I owe special thanks to Catherine Evtuhov (now at Columbia University), who shaped my sense of direction in Russian history. Catherine recently invited me to the Harriman Institute to present a section of this book at a workshop on the Black Sea, which broadened my understanding of the region under review here. I also thank my previous mentor Steve Norris of the Havighurst Center at Miami University for passing on his excitement in regards to teaching.

At Bilkent, I am grateful to the late Professor Norman Stone (1941–2019), my mentor, adviser and great friend, who helped me immensely in the early stages of my education during the late 1990s. More than a decade later, when I joined Bilkent's International Relations Department as a faculty member, I was fortunate to find a second chance to work with Norman, who sadly died a few months before this book came out. At Bilkent, where I have taught since 2014, I have enjoyed the companionship of a remarkable group of scholars, especially my good friend Samuel J. Hirst, with his unparalleled knowledge of the field and nuanced interpretations of history. I am equally indebted to Erinç Yeldan for his constant support of my book at a time when high impact factor journal articles are more in demand.

While reworking the final version of my book, I was greatly helped by a number of dedicated professionals at the Turkish Diplomatic Archives (TDA). Special thanks to Ambassador Songül Ozan and Serkan Sönmez for providing me with hitherto untapped archival collections, which fundamentally altered my treatment of some of the issues I dealt with in my dissertation. Many thanks to the Scientific and Technological

Research Council of Turkey (TÜBİTAK), which funded my research in the Russian Federation. Part of Chapter 1 draws on a forthcoming article in *Kritika: Explorations in Russian and Eurasian History*, under the title 'Yardstick of Friendship: Soviet-Turkish Relations and the Montreux Convention of 1936'. Sections of Chapter 4 appeared in the *Journal of Contemporary History* (DOI: 10.1177/0022009419833443) in an article entitled 'The Massigli Affair: Turkish Foreign Policy after the Molotov-Ribbentrop Pact'. I am grateful to the editors and anonymous reviewers in these two journals who helped me phrase my arguments in this book more strongly.

Special thanks to Sean McMeekin and James Ryan for their subtle readings of Soviet and Turkish history, and for their thoughtful criticism on the final draft, which helped me tighten numerous arguments in the text. I am also grateful for the meticulous feedback I received from my copy-editor Lisa Carden, as well as my editors at I.B.Tauris/Bloomsbury, Thomas Hoskins and Nayiri Kendir, who made this project possible.

Parts of this manuscript were presented in several ASEEES conferences in Philadelphia, New Orleans, and Washington DC. I thank Peter Holquist and Michael Reynolds for their insightful comments. I am also thankful to Christine Philliou for giving me the opportunity to present at the 'Ottomans-Turks in Conflict' workshop at Columbia University in 2011. More recently, in 2018, Kate Fleet and Ebru Boyar kindly invited me to share my research at Cambridge University in an excellent workshop on human mobility during the interwar period. I thank them for allowing me to be part of this stimulating workshop.

The publication of a first book gives the opportunity to thank a great number of friends whose invaluable support helped me finalize it. In Washington DC, I was lucky to befriend Anton Fedyashin, Anita Kondoyanidi, Allison Block, Binio Binev, John Bowlus, Nicholas Danforth, Kelly Hammond, Emrah Safa Gürkan and Michael Polczynski. I am grateful to you for your unfailing encouragement and friendship. In Istanbul, I thank Marc and Rana Hoffman, Suzy Hansen, Arda Suner, Zeynep Güven, Cüneyt Başar, Hüma Arslaner, Behçet Güleryüz, Serkan and Hakan Ertekin. I thank each one of you for your compassion and presence in my life. In Ankara, I am grateful to Dimitris Tsarouhas, Anna Pavlova, Owen Miller, Eliza Gheorge, Tore Fougner, Jeremy Salt, Hakan Kırımlı, Özgür Özdamar, Berk Esen, Selver Şahin, Pınar İpek, İlker Aytürk, Barın Kayaoğlu and Taylan Gürbüz for inspiring me with their intellectual skills.

Last but never the least, I would like to thank my mother, Prof. Gunseli Sonmez-Isci, and my father, Prof. Sedat Isci. Words cannot express my gratitude to you and to all of the sacrifices that you have made on my behalf. It is your encouragement and guidance (both academic and otherwise) that has sustained me thus far. Likewise, I am indebted to my grandparents, Prof. Resit and Sabahat Sönmez, who inspired me with a familial devotion to knowledge.

Most of all, I thank my wife, Gamze Ergür İşçi. She accompanied this project from research to publication and gave birth to our daughters, Yasemin and Defne, to whom this work is dedicated. It has been a better life than I could ever ask for, and to all of you I will forever be grateful.

Introduction

On 27 March 1943, the shocking news that a Soviet reconnaissance plane had crashed in Turkey reached military headquarters in Ankara. From Eastern Anatolia, the commanding officer in Kars reported that a Turkish patrol had spotted two Soviet planes flying at low altitude near the border earlier that morning. The Turkish officer ruefully admitted that one of the soldiers on his watch later confessed to firing six or seven rounds of warning shots. The first plane had apparently been caught off guard and made a sudden manoeuvre leftwards, whereupon the second plane hurtled on towards a jagged hill, killing the two Russian pilots on board. Subsequent inquiries at the crash site revealed that Kurdish peasants in nearby villages witnessed the event, informing the gendarmerie that not one but two Turkish patrols had actually fired against the planes. To make matters worse, it turned out the plane had no ammunition on board.[1]

The downing of the Russian plane erupted like a bombshell among Turkey's policymakers, for it would now be much more difficult to defend their continued neutrality in the midst of World War II. Despite his outwardly unruffled demeanour, a dreadful uncertainty haunted President İsmet İnönü for several weeks as he struggled to pull through an increasingly hostile Soviet reaction in the form of radio broadcasts and newspaper articles. From the Soviet perspective, Turks had been cashing in on both belligerent blocs by sitting on the fence, and they deliberately pursued this policy at a time when their northern neighbour was in dire straits. The downing of the Russian plane, which came a fortnight after the Soviet victory in Stalingrad, gave substance to Stalin's qualms about Turkey's peculiar neutrality. Although the crisis did not effectively amount to a state of war between Turkey and the Soviet Union, it was another low in a relationship that had been deteriorating since 1939.

Two years after the incident in Kars, the Union of Soviet Socialist Republics (USSR) threatened Turkey, demanding concessions on the Black Sea Straits and the repatriation of Kars – as well as two other frontier provinces in Eastern Anatolia – which the Russian Empire had annexed in 1878 and Lenin had returned to Mustafa Kemal's nascent state after Brest-Litovsk.[2] Among the several fault lines of Russo-Turkish relations, the Straits question always loomed large; thus, Stalin's bid for Soviet bases after the Yalta Conference in 1945 deepened Ankara's fear that Moscow would soon resurrect the Eastern Question. By simultaneously probing the frontier in the borderlands of Eastern Anatolia, the Soviet Union also created the impression that it was returning to the imperial partitioning policy that doomed the Ottoman state.

Looking at Stalin's post-war quest to lock in the spoils of war, many accounts maintain that the Soviet Union played a significant role in the development of the Cold War in the Near East. In many ways, it was indeed Stalin who disrupted the Yalta scheme by orchestrating regional crises, now in Turkey, then in Iran.[3] Yet, Turkey's downing of the Russian plane in 1943 suggests that the antagonism in Soviet–Turkish relations did not begin at the Livadia Palace in Yalta and that it may not have been as one-sided as the emphasis on Moscow's imperial ambitions implies.

This book investigates the crucible of Soviet–Turkish relations during World War II, when a renewed fear of Russia – with a distinctly anti-Soviet spin – returned to the forefront of Turkish politics. The wartime exchanges between Moscow and Ankara invite us to consider the ways in which the Turkish government struggled to confront what it came to perceive as an imminent Soviet threat. Seen from this perspective, Ankara's ordeal to find for itself a place in the transatlantic community does not appear as a post-war addendum, but as a defining moment in Turkish history when fundamental principles of early republican diplomacy were reversed and a new course was established. The incident in Kars, when put in context, suggests a broader narrative that helps us understand the roots of the Soviet–Turkish animosity that emerged during World War II, and which sharply contrasted with the cordial atmosphere of the interwar period.

Roughly four years before Turkey's downing of the Russian plane in 1943, nothing suggested that relations between Moscow and Ankara could become so strained. Beginning in 1920, bitterness against the post-war international order drove Soviet–Turkish relations. Nationalist Turks and internationalist Bolsheviks laid to rest four centuries of rivalry between their imperial predecessors as they found themselves in a convergence that each side defined as anti-imperialist. At the heart of their cooperation was a geopolitical alignment, which sought to shield the greater Black Sea region from Western intrusions. Equally, both sides shared a commitment to the creation of modern states. This interwar exchange between Ankara and Moscow has aptly been called anti-Westernism on the European periphery; it was a meaningful partnership.[4] Right up to the final hours of peace in 1939, the first principle that guided Turkish diplomacy was good neighbourly relations with Moscow in the context of friendship rather than subordination. Turkey's leaders repeatedly stressed that they perceived all other alliances as complementary to 'Turkey's anti-imperialist coalition with Russia'.[5]

Soviet–Turkish tension during and after World War II, however, contributed to a widely held view that the default nature of the two states' relationship was chronically hostile and inherently destabilizing. In the context of the previous centuries of struggle, there is a certain logic to the portrayal of the interwar friendship between Ankara and Moscow as a short-lived pragmatic alignment in an otherwise conflict-prone affair that resumed after 1945. Thus, before the Soviet and – much more recently – Turkish archives became accessible, the scholars who approached Soviet–Turkish relations during the interwar period treated their political meaning in terms defined narrowly by geopolitics – a pragmatic alignment at odds with the broader visions of each government.[6] As a corollary to this belief, many accounts maintain that friendly Soviet–Turkish relations ended, rather predictably, at the Montreux Convention of 1936, when an age-old geopolitical dispute over the ownership and control of the Straits reemerged and drove a wedge between two natural enemies.

Yet such notions of historic enmity exist more in the works of scholars than in the words of historical actors. Scores of Turkish diplomatic records, which are currently being declassified, show that Soviet-Turkish partnership remained intact after Montreux. The question then remains: if Soviet-Turkish convergence during the interwar period was only a temporary geopolitical alignment, then how could Moscow and Ankara disagree over the principal strategic challenge – the Straits – and continue to talk about joint anti-imperialist endeavours? Key holdings from Russia's and Turkey's foreign ministry archives, the second of which is not yet officially open to researchers, demonstrate how Turkish and Soviet leaders imagined they could reconcile their strategic problems all the way until the final hours of peace in 1939. They also show that after Montreux there was even a slim ray of hope for a bilateral military pact on the Black Sea that would 'ward off imperialist penetration'.[7] Ultimately, more significant cooperation was achieved in the economic sphere. These activities demonstrate that a Black Sea logic was central in Turkish thinking, that Mustafa Kemal Atatürk's and İsmet İnönü's insistence on friendship with the Soviet Union as the primary goal of their foreign policy needs to be taken seriously. The Soviet Union, in turn, courted Turkey as an ally, including after Montreux. Continued cooperation after 1936 shows that, much more than a pragmatic alignment, Moscow and Ankara saw partnership on the Black Sea as a key response to imperialist threats from without.

A critical question for early republican Turkish diplomacy concerned the fate of the Straits, which served as the key trading route for Black Sea littoral states and as a passage for their navies. The Straits Question had long been an intrinsic part of the larger problem known as the Eastern Question, encompassing a strategic fault line that stretched out from the Mediterranean to the Black Sea. On the eve of the Republic's establishment, Ankara was vexed about the existing regime of naval passage through the Dardanelles and the Bosphorus – as that passage took foreign navies through the heart of İstanbul – but there were other priorities and problems to resolve, such as the annulment of the Ottoman capitulations granted to Western powers and the recognition of Turkey's sovereignty rights in Eastern Thrace and Asia Minor. Hence, at the Lausanne Conference in 1922–3, which replaced the 1920 Treaty of Sèvres, Turkey agreed to demilitarize the Straits and transfer their control to an international convention. Once again, behind Turkey's reconciliatory attitude regarding the Lausanne Convention of the Straits was friendly relations with the Soviet Union. Until the mid-1930s, when revisionism in Europe compelled Turkish leaders to mend fences with Western powers, strong relations with the Soviet Union safeguarded Turkey's security on its long eastern border and in the Black Sea.

Turkey's admission to the League of Nations in 1932 occurred at a critical interwar conjuncture when relations with Moscow had reached their climax, but a different source had produced apprehension in Ankara.[8] With Italian revisionism appearing increasingly threatening, Turkey shifted its attention to the Mediterranean from the Black Sea. Bitter memories of Italian claims to territory in southwestern Anatolia during the First World War, which had subsequently been disclosed at Brest-Litovsk, convinced Turkey's leaders that Rome would eventually seek to expand its sphere of influence towards the Aegean Sea, where no substantial Turkish naval defence structure was allowed under the existing Lausanne regime.⁹ Turkey's interwar relations with Italy had shown symptoms of bipolar disorder until 1935, with constant shifts between antagonism and amity. Recent scholarship suggests that aversion and friendship often coexisted in a peculiar way, leading French observers to label diplomacy between Ankara and Rome as *'amiadversion'* (amity-adversity).¹⁰ By 1936, Turkey's growing concerns over the status of the Straits demonstrated the need to revise the relevant clauses of the Lausanne regime, which had become more detrimental to Turkish national security. Consequently, Turkey had to change its own view of Great Britain, and established closer relations with London to remilitarize the Straits in 1936. The one obvious caveat of this strategy was that what now seemed like Turkey's own revisionism could easily have been misinterpreted by the Soviet Union. It was no coincidence, that during the course of 1936–9, Turkish leaders often made one last stop in Moscow before ending their diplomatic tours in Europe, because they knew only too well that their Soviet friends would be somewhat irked by this shift in their foreign policy.

After Montreux, Soviet and Turkish leaders did indeed lament that 'the whole world' seemed to have become 'aware of their dwindling attachment'.¹¹ Yet both the Soviet and Turkish governments also sought to address that tension, and took dramatic steps in the late 1930s to prolong cooperation, particularly in the economic sphere. These attempts to maintain the partnership after the challenge of Montreux reveal much about the nature of the Soviet–Turkish relationship. New research on Russo-Turkish relations confirms that by the beginning of the twentieth century, the major powers on either side of the Black Sea had increasingly begun to see convergence as the basis of their relationship.¹² Until 1939, when the Molotov–Ribbentrop Pact demonstrated that one party had aligned with an expansionist power outside the region, Moscow and Ankara shared a sense that their interests overlapped in defence of the Black Sea. But the Soviet Union's alignment with Nazi Germany challenged the very logic of the Soviet–Turkish relationship.

The Soviet–German reconciliation came as a tremendous shock for Turks because they had been at pains to respond to Soviet fear of Germany throughout the late 1930s. When, for example, Ambassador Lev Karakhan inquired about 'the unfortunate pro-German tendencies of certain top-ranking Turkish generals', President İnönü soothed his apprehension by sending the Turkish chief of general staff with a delegation to observe Red Army manoeuvres in Ukraine.¹³ During the Montreux Conference, the Turkish foreign minister assured his counterpart that 'not only was a German–Turkish rapprochement implausible, but that Turkey would be willing to participate in a coalition against German aggression'.¹⁴ Turkish leaders even sought unusual forms of diplomatic cooperation, and expressed their 'discontent over the surge of German specialists infiltrating Turkey's cultural institutions' to plead for more 'Soviet experts and cultural figures to work in Turkey'.¹⁵ Less than a year before the signing of the Molotov–Ribbentrop Pact, the Turkish ambassador in Moscow reported that, despite Ankara's assurances, the Soviets were still anxious about the breadth of German 'infiltration' in Turkey, and were probing him about possible ways to enhance the Soviet Union's sphere of influence by improving trade relations and cultural exchange.¹⁶

The 1939 agreement between Nazi Germany and the Soviet Union played a crucial role in shaping Turkey's wartime neutrality. Ankara's new leaders were animated by a strong desire to remain aloof from what they now perceived as a European politics characterized by imperialism on all sides. On the other hand, they needed allies because rapprochement between two colossi that had previously been at each other's throats made it difficult to play one against the other. President İnönü defined his government's only goal as the nation's uncompromised sovereignty and rebuffed the sort of imperialist designs that once trapped the Ottoman Empire. Parliamentary minutes during this period are full of Kemalist aphorisms such as 'anti-imperialism' and 'independence', but, while in the Kemalist years national sovereignty was used exclusively in conjunction with Western imperialism, under President İnönü's leadership the term acquired a new meaning and reflected Turkey's apprehension vis-à-vis Soviet Russian imperialism. Between 1939 and 1945, Soviet-Turkish cooperation came to a spectacular end, and the rapidity of its collapse must surely explain why it has received so little attention in historical scholarship.

Turkish neutrality

Much of the newer literature on World War II has begun to compensate for earlier accounts that overlooked neutral powers, but Turkey has only recently begun to achieve attention as a regional actor. In his influential 1989 book on Turkish foreign policy during the Second World War, Selim Deringil described Ankara's diplomacy as one of 'active neutrality', and cemented the vision of a neutral but ambitious Turkey in the historiography.[17] Deringil challenged previous notions of Turkish war-profiteering and argued that the principal reason behind Turkey's non-belligerence was its leaders' shared perception of the war as a mainly European imperialist conflict, unrelated to its basic security and vital interests. Nonetheless, there was a certain continuity with the labels used by previous historians – evasive, benevolent, cunning etc – all of which suggest a proactive Turkish leadership; they also all do more to describe neutrality than they do to explain it.[18] Indeed, the scholarship sometimes sounds like the journalists of that time, who depicted a Turkish leadership that abruptly transformed from rigid caution and even timidity at the outbreak of war to behaviour befitting the 'heirs of the wily traditions of the Sublime Porte', with the 'methods of the old viziers, who brought the pluck and nerve of the modern gambler'.[19] These descriptions reflect foreign observers' perceptions more strongly than those of Turkey's own historical actors.

A succession of more recent publications has offered new perspectives on Turkey's relations with the Soviet Union during World War II.[20] Given the restricted access to Turkey's own archives, however, the mindset of the country's historical actors has been largely a matter of speculation. The hitherto untapped holdings of the Turkish Diplomatic Archives (TDA) contain scores of diplomatic cables, intelligence reports and policy papers that offer a much fuller understanding of Turkey's *Weltanschauung*. Likewise, records of the Turkish Prime Ministerial Archives (BCA) demonstrate a consistent fear of Soviet Russia coupled with an apprehension about Nazi encirclement that allow us to account for the factors that shaped Ankara's diplomacy between 1939 and 1945.

Correspondence between Turkish missions and the Ministry of Foreign Affairs reveals that after the eruption of hostilities in Europe, Turkey's 'neutrality' was, in fact, an attempt to maintain relations with both Britain and the Third Reich, as possible allies against Soviet aggression. President İsmet İnönü, for instance, purchased three Neptune-class vessels from the British Royal Navy to offset the three *Germaniawerft* submarines he had received from the *Kriegsmarine* earlier that year. İnönü tried to keep the same equidistance during the war and ordered three more from each country, even though the findings report indicated that Nazi Germany could deliver its portion in half the time (in twelve months as opposed to Britain, which promised twenty-four months) and at a lower cost (£223,000 as opposed to Britain's £225,000).[21] In their private conversations with British diplomats, leading members of President İsmet İnönü's cabinet were vocal about their hope for Britain's ultimate success, but they also alluded to the need for a strong Germany in the centre of Europe to check Soviet expansion. As much as Turkey's leaders hoped to see Britain emerge triumphant, they feared that 'if the war ended with the total destruction of Germany, then a tremendous abyss will open in Europe, a whirlpool into which Turkey will also be swept'.[22] In other words, Turkey did have sympathies for both sides, but those sympathies were not equal. After France succumbed to Hitler's armies in June 1940, Ankara began hedging its bets for two separate wars involving Nazi Germany, conducted independently by Britain and the USSR. On the eve of the impending Nazi–Soviet War, fear of the Soviet Union was so strong that Ankara hoped for a Nazi victory over the Soviet Union, provided that Britain was then able to check the Third Reich, which encircled Turkey via Romania, Bulgaria and Greece.

Turkey's unusual phased-thinking has often been misconstrued as pro-Axis neutrality, given the country's impressive trade volume and historic relations with Nazi Germany.[23] A closer look into Turkish records, however, reveals a different story. İnönü was, in fact, deeply disturbed by Turkey's levels of trade with the Third Reich. He carefully appointed pro-German men of the old order to negotiate with the Nazis, but he worked hard to contain that spirit at home. When, in 1940, Ambassador Hüsrev Gerede in Berlin made his pro-Nazi tendencies too explicit and implied that Turkey's leaders 'still belonged to the previous generation who fought alongside Germany' in the First World War, he was reprimanded not once but twice.[24] In August 1941, Gerede was recalled to Ankara for delivering a public speech 'leaning too far in the Nazi direction' and in 1942 he was dismissed after publishing an article that celebrated Germany and Turkey's cooperation in the Great War.[25] İnönü clearly had no tolerance for rhetoric that indicated a historical conditioning of German–Turkish relationship, especially in light of the Molotov–Ribbentrop Pact.

It did not take too long before Nazi Germany realized that the very idea of a prolonged war was a nightmare for the Turks. Perhaps it seemed possible that Turkey would appeal to Germany to defend itself against a Russian attack, just as it did in the previous World War. But unlike contemporary historians, the Third Reich's ambassador in Ankara, Franz von Papen, knew that Turkey was not 'wavering between Germany and England like a shopper in the bazaars in order to see with whom she can make a better deal'.²⁶ It was clear to von Papen that Turkey was a silent ally of Great Britain and inconspicuously desired to see that country emerge triumphant.²⁷ But von Papen was equally aware that the mere prospect of a Russian alliance was distinctly displeasing to Turkey, and that a Soviet threat would eclipse all other considerations. From that point onwards, Germany did everything in its capacity to orchestrate anti-Soviet propaganda in Turkey.

With Hitler's unleashing of Operation Barbarossa, another contingency began to shape Turkish diplomacy. A series of cables communicated between the Ministry in Ankara and various Turkish diplomatic missions demonstrates that Turkey was less than enthusiastic about the coming into being of an Anglo-Soviet coalition against Nazi Germany, which now made it even more difficult to retain close relations with Britain without factoring in the Soviet element in the equilibrium.²⁸ As relations between Ankara and Moscow grew frostier through the fog and filthy air of 1942–3, Turkey began fast reverting to its old imperial attitude, when the Porte's foreign policy had been dictated chiefly by the Sultan's fear of Russia. This was so much the case that the British ambassador noted: 'once again, Turkey's foreign policy [was] governed by that of Russia – the hereditary enemy, whose age-long ambition is to wrest the Straits from Turkey . . . whatever country is opposed to Russia is, ipso facto, favored by Turkey'.²⁹

Naturally, Nazi Germany was only too willing to detach Turkey from its existing neutrality and set itself up once again as the protector of Turkey and the Near East against Anglo-Soviet domination. With the outbreak of Nazi–Soviet War, Hitler decided not to cajole the Ankara government into a full-fledged wartime alliance, but rather advocated a strategy of benevolent neutrality for Turkey. The argument, then, is in keeping with newer literature on World War II that focuses on neutral powers.³⁰ Looking at the objectives of Nazi activities in other neutral states, it would be fair to suggest that propaganda aimed at more than just obtaining them as belligerent allies – hence its broad impact. German records demonstrate a similar dynamic in the dispute between Ribbentrop and ambassador to Ankara, Franz von Papen, about Turkey's role in the Nazis' impending war against the Soviet Union. In response to von Papen's attempts to incite Turkey, Ribbentrop instructed him to refrain from using language that could be misconstrued as a military alliance, as Germany's sole objective was to guarantee Turkey's neutrality.³¹ But Ribbentrop's instructions did not indicate a lack of ambition. German propaganda in Turkey had aims beyond cajoling the Turks into a belligerent stance and concentrated on strengthening the ideological and economic links between Berlin and Ankara. The effects of these efforts outlived Nazi Germany's defeat, for Russophobia continued to be a defining feature of Turkish foreign policy long after 1945.

Beginning with the Soviet victory in Stalingrad, wartime neutrality became a boring dilemma for the İnönü administration. Turkey's continued policy of sitting on the fence was repeatedly called into question by Great Britain after the Adana Conference between Churchill and İnönü. As Ankara delayed the moment of entering the war, London made its dissatisfaction more explicit. In addition to Britain's grievances as to the open advocacy of neutrality, the question of Turkey's position in the post-war world turned upon two factors: its position vis-à-vis the victorious powers; and its relations with the Soviet Union. Turkish policy-makers were forced to play the role of Hamlet in their indecisiveness until February 1945, because Great Britain did not truly appreciate Turkey's chronic mistrust and fear of Soviet Russia, which, in return poisoned Anglo-Turkish relations. War-related problems and Turkey's revived Russophobia rendered only a single safe course for Turkey to enter the war: to align itself with the United Nations before Soviet dissatisfaction found expression. The Turkish point of view was such that if the country *were* to enter the war, such a move would merely weaken its already inadequate forces and increase the danger of becoming a satellite of Soviet Russia – like Poland. In some ways, Great Britain understood Turkey's thinking and admitted that 'she had to keep her powder dry against the day when Russian imperialism will inevitably revive', but the Turks' fear of Russia, in the British mind, was never completely justified.[32]

Regardless of the root cause of Soviet–Turkish tension, plans for a sustainable, if not cordial, relationship failed following World War II. In places like Turkey, the post-war international order looked far grimmer than before. The Second World War decisively put an end to any Turkish belief that the Bolshevik regime was substantively different than the Tsarist Empire, which had been a constant threat to the Ottoman sultans. Beginning with the Molotov–Ribbentrop Pact, Turkey had already reverted to an understanding of the USSR in terms of older (ie, Bismarckian) realpolitik. Confronting an imminent Soviet threat, Turkey could not maintain its precarious neutrality and began negotiating a stronger alliance with the West. From the wartime conferences among the Allies, two factors stood out as sources of apprehension for the Turks: the exigencies of war against the Axis; and the historic rivalry between Britain and Russia in the Eastern Mediterranean. In this rivalry between the two imperialist powers, it was the Soviet Union that the Turkish ruling elite now feared. This explains the transports of joy with which the Ankara government embraced President Truman's proclamation of 'American determination to uphold by whatever means necessary the integrity of states endangered by communist subversion'.[33]

This book's structure

The organization of chapters is largely chronological, although each has a thematic focus as well. Rather than a broad survey of Turkey's bilateral relations with the Soviet Union during World War II, the present work explores the main fault lines that radically transformed Soviet–Turkish relations. Hence, instead of focusing on wartime exchanges in isolation, this book puts certain episodes in context, covering events that preceded the outbreak of war in 1939 as well as those that outlived 1945. To fully illustrate when and how the Soviet Union turned from friend to foe in the Turkish mind, I have chosen to cover the late interwar period more extensively in Chapters 1 and 2. Together, these two chapters probe the changing international equilibrium surrounding Soviet–Turkish relations after the Montreux Straits Convention of 1936 until the outbreak of war in 1939. I argue that two interrelated policy considerations – involving Turkey's problematic relations with Italy and Syria – led to its abandonment of the Lausanne status quo and shift from a position of non-alignment to one where it reluctantly clung to the Anglo-French power bloc. On the eve of World War II, Turkey's rapprochement with Western powers came at the expense of a predictable apprehension in Moscow. But, as these two chapters demonstrate, even as the post-war environment became more perilous between 1936 and 1939, both states were determined to isolate the post-imperial space they shared from the pressures of an international order that was dictated by what they often referred to as imperialism.[34]

Chapter 3 deals with Turkey at the outbreak of war and looks at the period from the conclusion of the Anglo-Turkish declaration in May 1939 until the summer of 1940, when France succumbed to Hitler's armies. A central episode in this chapter is the Molotov–Ribbentrop Pact, when the interwar friendship between Ankara and Moscow came to an end. Looking at Russian and Turkish diplomatic records, I investigate how and why Soviet and Turkish attempts failed to put their relations on a friendlier footing during the Moscow talks in September 1939. From the Soviet point of view, among Turkey's ruling classes, supporters of the Anglo-French bloc held the upper hand, advocating the well-known Munich policy of appeasement, pushing Hitlerite aggression and fascism to the East. Conversely, İnönü contended that negotiations with Moscow broke down because the Soviet Government had made demands which ran counter to the two fundamental rules which the Turkish Government had laid down: first, that Turkey should not in any way interfere with the normal working of the Montreux Convention; and second, that Turkey should agree to nothing that would weaken the operation of the treaty which she contemplated with Great Britain and France. There was hardly a moment in the second half of 1939 when serious hope of a permanent improvement in Soviet–Turkish affairs could have been entertained.

In Chapter 4, I explain how the Nazis' sweeping anti-Soviet propaganda – from diplomatic manoeuvres to pro-Nazi organizations and social clubs – contributed to the revival of the image of an evil Russia in Turkey. Between the Molotov–Ribbentrop Pact and Hitler's unleashing of Operation Barbarossa, the Third Reich attempted to cultivate Turkey's historic fear of Russia, which had a new, distinctly anti-Soviet hue. These efforts also created, however, a deep reserve – even fear – in Ankara toward Berlin. This chapter focuses on the Massigli Affair as a case study that – when put in context – reveals how fear of Nazi power and even greater fear of the Soviet Union created in Turkey a complex view of a desired outcome from World War II. In July 1940, this now forgotten episode marked the nadir of Turkish–Soviet relations. The Nazis leaked confidential cables that implicated Turkey in a conspiracy against the Soviet Union and Ankara watched with trepidation as the Soviet Union mobilized troops in the Caucasus.[35] The last part of this chapter takes the narrative into the period between the Massigli Affair and the outbreak of Nazi–Soviet War. Stalin's response to the Nazi plot was harsh and paved the way for 'countless rumors' that a Soviet advance towards the Straits was in the offing. For Hitler, Turkey was necessary as a buffer zone against the Allies, mainly because Romanian oil destined for Nazi Germany was shipped via the Straits to Italian ports.[36] The Third Reich decided not to entice the Ankara government into a fully-fledged wartime alliance, but instead advocated a strategy of benevolent neutrality for Turkey, and in so doing continued to stoke Turkey's fear of the USSR.

Chapters 5 and 6 tie together and explore Turkish diplomacy from Hitler's unleashing of Operation Barbarossa until the Soviet victory in Stalingrad. The fifth chapter covers one of the largest sources of friction in wartime Soviet–Turkish relations and explores the impact of Nazi–Turkish Non-Aggression Pact, signed only days before the Wehrmacht's march on the USSR. It would be safe to suggest that Nazi Germany's anti-Soviet propaganda met with considerable approval in Ankara, particularly after the Anglo-Soviet occupation of Iran. Operation Countenance created the impression among Ankara's ruling elite that Great Britain was returning to the Anglo-Russian partition policy of 1907. It was inevitable that the Turks were to become nervous when they saw Britain and the Soviet Union putting pressure on Iran in these conditions. It is equally fair to argue that in the aftermath of the Soviet occupation of Iranian Azerbaijan, Nazi Germany revived and propagated the 'evil Russia' trope in Turkey. But Stalin's own blunders, which aggravated Turkey's Russophobia, played an equally important role. The two main incidents that marred Soviet–Turkish affairs during this period were the failed assassination attempt on Franz von Papen by Soviet agents in Ankara, and the sinking of the SS *Struma* on the same day. Several hours before the von Papen Affair, a Soviet Submarine (Shch 213) attacked the SS *Struma* in Turkish territorial waters, which was chartered to carry Jewish refugees from Axis-allied Romania to British-controlled Palestine.[37] In this chapter, I demonstrate how the ominous incidents of 24 February 1942 left Turkish–Soviet relations irreparably damaged.

Chapter 6 looks at an entirely overlooked aspect of wartime Soviet–Turkish relations and explains the role of pan-Turkists in Turkey, who found a reinvigorated zeal in the Crimean Tatar cause and facilitated the Tatar–Nazi collaboration. Here, I examine the triangular relations between the Turks, Tatars and Nazis, in order to explain whether it was the Turkish government (as the Soviets claimed) or independent pan-Turkist groups in Turkey that collaborated with the Tatars in a vehemently anti-Soviet campaign. Second, I seek answers to the role of Nazi Germany in bolstering Turks' and Tatars' hopes for the so-called grand scheme of Soviet encirclement. I demonstrate the public consequences of Nazi Germany's efforts to orchestrate nationalist and fascist circles in Turkey.

Chapter 7 takes the narrative firmly into the latter part of World War II and looks at the events that transpired after the Soviet triumph in Stalingrad. This is a probe into an intense period of negotiations between the Anglo-Soviet bloc and Turkey, which determined the latter's fate in the immediate post-war years. Looking at recently declassified Turkish diplomatic records, I analyse the conferences held in Adana, Tehran, Cairo and Yalta, and demonstrate the reasons behind Turkey's quixotic neutrality in the face of growing pressure from Moscow and London to drag Ankara into the battlefield. As such, the epilogue of this book deals with the immediate aftermath of World War II and Turkey's response to an increasingly menacing Soviet attitude. Stalin's demands for Soviet bases on the Turkish Straits and the repatriation of three Eastern Anatolian provinces continue to be a source of controversy among Turkish historians. In its final pages, this book illustrates how the culmination of wartime Soviet–Turkish antagonism ushered in a new era when Stalin embarked on his odyssey to provide absolute security for the Soviet Union and the broader implications of Turkey's post-war response to a renewed Russian threat by establishing closer ties with the United States.

1

Things Thus Standing

Like a prism that scatters rays of light, the Ankara Central railway station reveals a wide range of issues regarding Turkey's recent past. Commissioned in 1935, it replaced a dilapidated eastern terminal of the Anatolian Railway. On the outside, the building sports an art deco clock tower and a window-covered façade with neoclassical columns that reflect the revolutionary dreams and great expectations of early Kemalism. By contrast, its aging marble floors and gloomy stone walls still echo with the bitter quarrels of Ankara's political leaders who followed Mustafa Kemal after his death in 1938. More than 10,000 tons of concrete and sandstone were brought from nearby quarries to complete the project between 1935 and 1937.[1] Its chief architect, Şekip Akalın, was a 25-year-old desk officer at the Ministry of Public Works. He was sent to Europe for an inspiration tour in 1934 and was asked to produce something that would mirror the achievements of the bourgeoning republic. Akalın's moment of revelation, perhaps unsurprisingly, arrived in the Third Reich, and he returned home to imitate the Stuttgart Hauptbahnhof. When Ankara's new station was finally inaugurated in October 1937, it stood thirty-two metres high, extended 150 metres wide, and quickly became an iconic monument of the country's new capital.

A fortnight after his election to the office, it was Prime Minister Celal Bayar who attended a carefully timed ribbon cutting ceremony, which took place on the fourteenth anniversary of the republic's foundation.[2] For Bayar, two decades after the loss of the Hejaz railway to Syria, Ankara's new terminal came to symbolize the proud creation of a modern state, moving Turkey's heart closer to its margins and beyond. Connecting 2,800 kilometres of new railway tracks laid since 1923, Ankara Central station was the perfect foil to display the modernity of an otherwise poor and small Anatolian town.[3] Compared to the staggering beauty of the imperial capital in İstanbul, Ankara was less charming and more isolated from its western neighbours, metaphorically as much as physically. Until the 1930s, many European states maintained their embassies in İstanbul, feeding Turkey's conviction that Ankara was being boycotted by the West. Equally marginalized after the Great War, Germany played a key role in crafting Turkey's new face, including the first city blueprints for Ankara and numerous early-republican buildings.[4] But distancing the nascent republic from the Ottoman political order also meant a separation from Germany in the international sphere. This underlying motive is crucial for understanding Turkey's priorities during the interwar period and why Ankara turned to Moscow as an alternate source of support.

When Turkey's new leaders looked at their truncated country and the world around it, they did so with hope but also with restraint. In 1938, Ambassador Percy Loraine captured this tension when he said of Ankara: 'the Sick Man ... has left behind a number of lusty children, who were acutely aware of their limitations.'[5] Throughout the 1920s and early 1930s, Turkish diplomats preoccupied themselves with issues that were left unresolved on the table at the Lausanne Conference in 1922–3. At the outset, Turkey had problems with all of its neighbours, from the Balkans to the Middle East, and, as a balancing act, relied almost exclusively on its friendship with the Soviet Union. In turn, Moscow courted Ankara as an ally against Western imperialism and British efforts to isolate the Soviet Union behind a cordon sanitaire of anti-communist states. The two defeated countries, which were really revolutionized after the Great War – Turkey and the Soviet Union – became what Eric Hobsbawm called 'forces for stability' in the 1920s and 30s.[6] With the advent of fascism and the ensuing surge of revisionism in Europe, Ankara and Moscow were destined to mend fences with Western powers but, all the way up to the outbreak of World War II, they tried to maintain a close partnership that transcended diplomatic routines.

By the time Ankara's new train station was inaugurated in 1937, the Soviets were not the only pebble on the Turkish beach; several European states relocated their diplomatic missions to the new capital, reinstituting friendly relations with the Kemalists. The Turkish popular press, including state-sponsored papers, employed editorial lines that were at once favourable to the Soviet Union *and* pro-Western. On the eve of World War II, the Turkish government seemed to enjoy its new image as a 'bridge between the East and the West, safeguarding peace and harmony in its region.'[7] Among the architectural metaphors that define Turkish leaders' imagining of their country's diplomacy, 'bridge' has probably been the most prevalent. Yet, in Turkish journalists' aphorism, peace and harmony were not merely linguistic ornaments but a direct adaptation of one of Atatürk's many dictums that became popular in the 1930s. During a campaign speech for the 1931 elections, Mustafa Kemal had succinctly laid out his party's agenda as 'Peace at Home, Peace in the World' (*Yurtta Sulh, Cihanda Sulh*) – a phrase that was later adopted by the constitution as 'the core principle on which Turkish diplomacy shall operate'.[8]

Looking at early republican monuments and official statements of Kemalist apparatchiks, historians have long held that, under the surface of Atatürk's pacifist rhetoric throughout the latter half of the 1930s, what guided the Turkish state and diplomacy was a quest to maintain domestic and regional status quo. It is often argued that through curbing adventurism and revisionism – common goals in most successor states to the Great War's crumbled empires – Atatürk sought to eliminate any military or diplomatic undertaking that could easily destabilize the budding republic. As a corollary to this argument, scholars frequently looked at the conflict-prone European periphery, where revisionist powers were establishing their own spheres of influence, and suggested that Turks successfully isolated themselves from their past, thereby anchoring their state firmly in the Western order. Consequently, the status quo has become the defining framework for the Kemalist period, both in foreign and domestic affairs, and the term has been mistakenly conflated with a pacifist agenda.[9]

In reality, however, Turkish diplomacy went through a remarkable metamorphosis in the second half of the 1930s, adopting a highly revisionist spin. Behind Ankara's changing motives and attempts to reformulate its regional diplomacy anew, the Italian threat played the greatest role. With Benito Mussolini's menacing attitude towards Turkey and aggressive militarization of the Dodecanese islands – only a few miles off the Aegean coastline – Turkey began to change its own conceptions of Great Britain and established closer relations with London to remilitarize the Straits in 1936. After long hours of heated debates at the international conference summoned in Montreux, the new convention replaced the Lausanne regime and reinstated 'Turkey's full sovereignty over the Straits in times of war and when she feels an imminent possibility of war'.[10] This became a source of apprehension for the Soviet Union since the sovereignty clause included Turkey's freedom to remilitarize the Dardanelles and to close or open the Straits to the free passage of warships of all sizes whenever and to whomever it thought necessary.[11] But, even then, Turkey did not turn from friend to foe; the Soviet government tried to keep things in perspective and continued to work with the Kemalists.

A second development in the latter half of the 1930s was a surge in Syria's support of Kurdish provocations in Alexandretta, bordering Turkey's southernmost frontier. The provisional French mandate, which had been governing Alexandretta as part of Syria since the 1921 Franco-Turkish Armistice Treaty, expired in 1935.[12] Between 1936 and 1939, the Syrian administration in Alexandretta failed to check, and at times directly sponsored, regional Kurdish tribes who had their strong disagreements with Turkey – some lingering from past imperial conflicts, some pertaining to the new regime's strong centralism. Kurdish chieftains, along with local Armenian community leaders, stirred up incipient rebellions in Turkey's southern provinces through Syria during the course of 1920s and 30s. Thus Turkey's annexation of Alexandretta, which occurred in stages between 1937–9, paved the way for an equally striking rapprochement between Turkey and France.

As Great Power rivalry intensified in Europe after Nazi Germany's repudiation of its Locarno liabilities, Turkey's disputes with Italy and Syria became two merging tectonic plates, creating a fault line stretching out from the Middle East looming over the Mediterranean. Wedged between two security considerations – with Italy on the one hand and Syria on the other – Turkey adopted a strategy of revisionism, effectively changing the status of the Straits and Alexandretta to its advantage after 1936. But, establishing a proper defence structure of such magnitude was a bigger undertaking than what Turkey could manage on its own and required a broader security agreement. From this perspective, Mustafa Kemal's frequently cited dictum – Peace at Home, Peace in the World – should not be taken as a pacifist policy but, rather as a guarantee extended by the Turkish state to its new-found partners in the West, signalling a phase of revisionism that would run parallel to British and French interests. The Soviets were less vocal about Turkey's alignment with the French, but Ankara's attempts to improve relations with Britain came at the expense of a predictable anxiety in Moscow.

The ambivalence of the 1936–9 period was on display during Mustafa Kemal Atatürk's visit to the Soviet embassy's celebrations of the thirteenth anniversary of the establishment of the Turkish Republic.[13] On 29 October 1936, just three months after the Montreux Convention had been signed, Atatürk arrived at the Soviet embassy on his state's most important holiday. In some sense, his visit was not particularly unusual.

During the peak of Soviet–Turkish collaboration, the Soviet embassy was a mecca for Ankara's new leaders, and one of the regular participants recalled that 'rather unlimited amounts of vodka and caviar were served over politics'.[14] For the 1936 celebrations, Ambassador Lev Karakhan had as usual secured the attendance of Turkey's political elite, including Prime Minister İsmet İnönü and Foreign Minister Tevfik Rüştü Aras. Atatürk was not an expected guest; he turned up at half past two in the morning, already in high spirits. With relations as they were, the nocturnal conversations proved awkward.

Atatürk's behaviour suggested that he was frustrated with his Soviet hosts, but also that he wanted to put these frustrations behind him. He took Karakhan aside and demanded to know why Stalin had not met with him personally after so many years: 'Is Stalin indifferent to such a meeting or deliberately ignoring me?' He claimed to be offended that, instead of the leader of the Soviet Union, 'Comrade Kalinin' had sent him a laconic congratulatory telegram on the anniversary of Turkey's independence. Karakhan reported that Atatürk was visibly irritated as he insisted that he was a friend of the Soviet Union, that this friendship would exist as long as he lived, but that he could maintain this friendship only on reciprocal grounds.[15] Karakhan promised to arrange a meeting with Stalin, but, far from mollified, Atatürk reiterated resentment for recent insolence, albeit with a further proclamation of loyalty. Amidst these vacillations of mood, Atatürk let slip that he respected Russia with its strong, disciplined and mechanized army, but that he was not afraid of anyone, as there were 18 million Turks behind him.[16] His tirade continued with further exhortations about the need for a continued alliance between Ankara and Moscow until, finally, he alluded to the elephant in the room – the recent quarrel at Montreux. Atatürk knew that the Soviets were unhappy with some of the clauses in a new Straits regime that introduced Turkey's full sovereignty over the Bosphorus and Dardanelles, as well as precise limitations on naval tonnage in the Black Sea for littoral and non-littoral powers. He referred to the latter limitations as a yardstick, and ran with the metaphor. Figuratively, he told Karakhan, collaboration across the Black Sea was a much more meaningful yardstick for appraising Soviet–Turkish friendship than any of the Montreux clauses.[17]

Atatürk's visit thus demonstrated the tension that emerged after Montreux, but also Montreux's place within a broader context. Karakhan immediately transmitted his record of the conversation, shortly after Atatürk had retired with his entourage at 7 a.m. and the orchestra had stopped playing. A few months later, Stalin took an interest in the report and had it circulated to the Soviet political elite, with the suggestion that they would find interesting the words of their '"friend"' Atatürk.[18] The cynicism of Stalin's quotation marks around the word friend matched that visible in Atatürk's reference to the strength of his army. Yet Stalin's description of Atatürk as friend also alluded to a momentum that Montreux alone was not enough to break. It would be wrong to misconstrue this meeting at the Soviet embassy as evidence that Ankara and Moscow's honeymoon had ended. In 1937, Atatürk quietly observed that 'even the happiest families have minor spats, but that does not lead them to fall apart'.[19] In the face of a widening gap over the Straits, Turkish and Soviet diplomats desperately tried to maintain the anti-imperialist understanding of the Black Sea that had once united them.

Soviet-Turkish friendship

During the interwar years, the two young states sought to challenge what they referred to as imperialism while at the same time coping with similar problems bequeathed to them by the collapsed Houses of Romanov and Osman. In the 1920s and early 1930s, when Turkish and Soviet leaders spoke of international relations, they did so in the context of a struggle between imperial metropoles, which used to include İstanbul and St Petersburg. In effect, Ankara and Moscow framed their convergence in anti-imperialist terms, which was an unusual form of bilateral diplomacy beyond the confines of conventional realpolitik. Kemalists and Bolsheviks were a mental world apart from each other in ideological terms and they disagreed over major geo-strategic issues. Yet, they reconciled some of their differences, overlooked others, and inter-state exchange continued all the way until World War II. In other words, Soviet and Turkish motives behind harmonizing their divergent security interests were not divorced from domestic ideological constraints. On the contrary, Soviet-Turkish bilateral diplomacy was shaped by a shared understanding of the post-war international structure.

The groundwork for Soviet policy toward Turkey in the early 1920s was laid by Georgii Chicherin, Commissar of Foreign Affairs, who, in the midst of the Russian Civil War, offered guns, gold and grain to Mustafa Kemal's army against foreign interference and imperialism.[20] Soviet ambassador Semen Aralov, who was received in Ankara as the first foreign chief of mission, seconded Chicherin's complex and interconnected policies and, in the face of growing Politburo opposition, supported Chicherin's idea of assisting Kemalists. In return, Turkish leaders courted the Bolsheviks and argued that, although certain aspects of communism were unsuitable for Turkish nationalism, their alliance with the Soviet Union was at the heart of Ankara's politics. Ultimately, more remarkable results were attained in the economic sphere. According to Stefanos Yerasimos' calculations, the Bolsheviks provided the Ankara government with more than eleven million rubles in less than two years, which was equivalent to slightly more than the Turkish national budget for 1921 and 1922.[21]

Soviet-Turkish cooperation in the 1920s never amounted to a military alliance that Chicherin had hoped to see, but what was once a doubtful combination ushered in a new era in the early 1930s. Following a round of reciprocal visits at the foreign ministerial level – by Tevfik Rüştü and Maxim Litvinov in 1930 and 1931 respectively – the relationship between Ankara and Moscow was labelled by Turkish newspapers as 'a strong fortress against world imperialism, the sole purpose of which is to subdue and colonize weak states and rob them of their national pride and resources, as witnessed in China and other civilizations that succumbed to imperial powers'.[22] Similar voices were echoed during Litvinov's week-long visit in 1931, when he met with Mustafa Kemal and İsmet İnönü, devising strategies to diversify Soviet-Turkish exchange in trade and culture. Speaking to Turkish journalists at the Pera Palace in İstanbul before his departure to Ankara, Litvinov drew strong parallels between Soviet collectivization and Turkey's struggle to build its own sovereign industry and national economy.[23] In Ankara, Litvinov attended the eighth anniversary of the Turkish Republic, renewed the Soviet-Turkish Friendship Treaty for another five-year period and passed on Stalin's invitation to host Turkish leaders in Moscow for a deeper round of exploratory talks in the spring.

Figure 1.1 Turkish Prime Minister İsmet İnönü (centre) during an official visit to the Soviet Union in April 1932. İnönü is surrounded by prominent Bolsheviks, including (from left to right) Soviet ambassador in Ankara Yakov Suritz; Soviet Commissar for Foreign Affairs Maxime Litvinov; Deputy Commissar for Foreign Affairs Lev Karakhan; Soviet Premier Vyacheslav Molotov; Turkish Foreign Minister Tevfik Rüştü Aras; and Marshal Semyon Mikhailovich Budyonny.

Figure 1.2 İnönü (centre) in Moscow in April 1932. İnönü is amongst prominent Bolshevik leaders, including (from left to right) Soviet Commissar for Foreign Affairs, Vyacheslav Molotov; Commissar for Defence, Kliment Voroshilov; Soviet Commissar for Foreign Affairs, Maxime Litvinov; and Turkish Foreign Minister, Tevfik Rüştü Aras.

Things Thus Standing 17

Figure 1.3 İnönü and his Soviet counterpart, Vyacheslav Molotov, in Moscow, April 1932. Foreign Minister Tevfik Rüştü Aras and Marshall Semyon Mikhailovich Budyonny appear in the background.

When, in April 1932, Prime Minister İsmet İnönü led a large Turkish delegation to the Soviet Union, it was in the context of Turkey's membership to the League of Nations and to discuss the possibility of Soviet support for Turkish industrialization. As İnönü sailed across the Black Sea aboard the SS *Grouzia*, he brainstormed with his ministers and journalists, formulating a cohesive proposal to present to Stalin. In İnönü's mind, the lands and peoples that comprised the post-imperial space could be conjoined through carefully designed vectors of political, economic and cultural exchange. He was rightfully convinced that his mission would give impetus for this convergence, and told the Soviet reporters in Odessa that this was the right moment.[24] Admittedly, when the Turkish delegation arrived in Moscow from Ukraine, they were taken by surprise to see the 'grand reception given in their honor', which to some elder journalists was reminiscent of Tsarist balls.[25]

During the two weeks İnönü spent in the Soviet Union, as he visited Moscow factories, collective farms and army units, *Izvestiia*, *Pravda* and other major Soviet papers gave extensive coverage of the Turkish delegation's visits on their front pages.[26] İnönü was the guest of honour in the First of May celebrations and barely had time to rest in between his meeting with Stalin, Molotov and several other leading Bolsheviks. As for the rest of the delegation, which included famous Turkish writers and journalists, they were 'shocked' by the number of lavish receptions thrown by the Soviets: Vala Nureddin (Va-nu), who was a close friend of Nazim Hikmet, recorded that beyond the

Figure 1.4 İnönü appears with Deputy Commissar for Foreign Affairs Lev Karakhan (centre) and Chairman of the Presidium of the Supreme Soviet of the USSR, Mikhail Kalinin. This picture was taken during İnönü's official visit to the USSR in April–May 1932.

numerous meals, each lasting for two hours, the Soviets spoiled them with unlimited amounts of cigarettes, alcohol and caviar – 'this was truly a socialist paradise'.[27] Hospitality aside, Soviet and Turkish leaders both approached İnönü's 1932 visit as an opportunity to transfer Soviet models of 'state-development' and 'cultural modernity' that transcended 'ideological constraints' with a strong emphasis on sovereignty.[28]

In October 1933, roughly eighteen months after İnönü's trip to the Soviet Union, Kliment Voroshilov, head of the Soviet army and navy, travelled with his entourage to Turkey for the tenth anniversary of the Turkish Republic. Molotov excused himself for health reasons and Litvinov was in Geneva, but Voroshilov was accompanied by several high-ranking Soviet officials, journalists and artists.[29] A few days before the arrival of the Soviet delegation, Tevfik Rüştü had already made arrangements for a memorable scene – he asked for two Soviet vessels to flank the Turkish ship *İzmir*, which would bring the Soviet delegation to İstanbul, and dispatched aerobatic aircraft and dozens of smaller boats to greet them as *İzmir* docked in the Bosphorus.[30] Given recent memories of Russo-Ottoman warfare, indeed it turned out to be a remarkable scene that inspired the two famous film directors on board – Sergei Yutkevich and Lev Oskarovich Arnshtam. Mirroring the friendship between two historical adversaries and the achievements of the new and secular Turkey, Yutkevich and Arnshtam shot a documentary film pertinently entitled 'Ankara: The Heart of Turkey' (*Ankara-Serdtse Turtsii*).

Things Thus Standing 19

Figure 1.5 İnönü in front of the Novodevichy Monastery with Mikhail Kalinin, Chairman of the Presidium of the Supreme Soviet of the USSR, April 1932.

The most significant aspect of this visit was that Voroshilov brought with him a Soviet loan equivalent to $8 million, as Stalin had promised İnönü earlier in April 1932.[31] Aside from army modernization, the much-needed Soviet credit was used to finance Turkey's First Five-Year Industrialization Plan (Birinci Beş Yıllık Sanayi Planı), which was based on an import-substitution model, reducing the country's foreign dependency through the local production of industrialized products. In less than two years, the Turkish minister of finance was once again in Moscow, probing the possibility of another Soviet credit (approximately $20 million) to sponsor the Second Five-Year Plan as well as a $2 million credit for military and defence expenses. What made the ongoing Soviet–Turkish talks for the latter's modernization so remarkable was that negotiations continued *despite* a plethora of strategic problems. Between 1933 and 1936, Turkey's qualms about Moscow's relationship with fascist Italy were matched by Soviet reservations about Ankara's role in the Balkan Pact.

After the signing of the Four-Power Pact between Great Britain, France, Italy and Germany, Turkey's leaders looked at the Soviet Union not only as a regional partner

Figure 1.6 İnönü meets with Soviet Commissar for Defence Kliment Voroshilov during his official trip to the Soviet Union in April 1932. İnönü secured an $8 million Soviet credit and technical assistance for Turkey's industrialization efforts after this meeting.

but also as an ally to counter-balance hostile combinations in Europe – hence, Moscow's association with Italy constituted somewhat of a conundrum. Even before the Soviet delegation's arrival in Ankara, Litvinov had been negotiating for an Italo-Soviet Pact, but, mindful of Ankara's protests, he had kept the Turkish ambassador in Moscow in the loop, 'sharing the smallest details about their talks with Mussolini'.[32] Turkey returned the favour by involving Lev Karakhan in their negotiations with their Balkan neighbours on the eve of the Balkan Pact's foundation.[33] While these gestures were taken by both governments as signs of 'endless affection', the Turks were vexed by the Soviets' rapprochement with Italy. During his regular meetings with the Turkish ambassador, Litvinov repeatedly asserted that a 'genuine alliance' with the fascist government in Rome was 'improbable' due to the two states' irreconcilable ideological differences and that the Soviet Union would be willing to commit itself to Turkey's defence against a possible Italian naval attack.[34] The only caveat was the Balkan Pact, through which the Turks could be 'pulled into the landlocked valleys of Southeastern Europe against a battle with Italy, dragging Moscow along' – a scenario which Litvinov was trying to avoid. Litvinov was also vexed about Bulgarian revisionism but more disturbed with the prospect of a collective Balkan reaction against Sofia.

Contrarily, one of the main objectives of Turkish diplomats was to keep the conflict from spreading to the Balkans, which had been an historical zone of conflict amongst

Figure 1.7 İnönü and Kliment Voroshilov in front of the Turkish parliament in Ankara. Voroshilov headed a large Soviet delegation in October 1933 to commemorate the tenth anniversary of the Turkish Republic.

Figure 1.8 Seated next to İnönü, Kliment Voroshilov salutes Turkish spectators as they approach the Ankara hippodrome, where an official ceremony was held on 29 October 1933.

Turkey's Balkan neighbours. A major source of security concern for Ankara was its disadvantageous position in a potential war with Greece or Bulgaria, particularly if these two were supported by Italy. Therefore, Turkish diplomats intensely lobbied in the early 1930s to cast an alliance with one of these two neighboring Balkan states, preferably with both. Thus came into being the 1933 Greek-Turkish *Entente Cordiale*, which guaranteed an agreed frontier in the Thrace as well as a mutually benevolent neutrality between Athens and Ankara. Meanwhile, Turkey's negotiations with Romania and Yugoslavia turned out to be fruitful and produced solid bilateral agreements between the respective governments. In 1934, the four states – Greece, Turkey, Romania and Yugoslavia – agreed to establish a collective security organization, which came to be known as the Balkan Entente. From the Turkish viewpoint, the exclusion of Bulgaria from the pact over a dreary headache like Macedonia constituted a problem, but, overall, the Turks looked at the Balkan pact as a successful achievement.

In response to Soviet reservations, Turkey extended guarantees toward Bulgaria and emphasized their general policy of non-interventionism. The Turkish ambassador in Moscow took a step forward and proposed a secret Soviet-Turkish reassurance treaty.[35] Given the exigencies of revisionism in Europe, Turkey's proposal appears even more remarkable and shows the extent of diplomatic cooperation between the two states. In a similar vein, when the Soviet Union entered into negotiations with France for a mutual assistance treaty in 1935, Litvinov arranged a meeting in Geneva with his Turkish counterpart, Tevfik Rüştü Aras, to discuss terms of a corresponding alignment with Turkey at the League of Nations.[36] The Turkish government knew that Litvinov faced severe criticism from many Politburo members for pursuing an openly hostile policy towards the German Reich and that one of his leading critics was Lev Karakhan, who argued that the Soviet Commissar was giving too many concessions to the French government to contain Nazi Germany.[37] In effect, the popular surge of revisionism in Europe was pushing the Soviet and Turkish governments in search for competing alignments, while the two states desperately tried to resist the pressure and maintain harmonized strategic interests.

Mare Nostrum

The Straits question, which had been dormant since Lausanne, reemerged in the context of a Europe whose map was changing. Hitler's remilitarization of the Rhineland in March 1936 demonstrated that Western Europe remained hesitant to confront the German desire to revise that map. From the Turkish perspective, however, Italian revisionism was an even greater threat.[38] For the greater part of the 1920s, there was a prevalent sense of bitterness and resentment between Italy and Turkey, and the situation owed more to Mussolini's treatment of Turkey as an ephemeral geographic entity and a potential area of future expansion rather than a sovereign state or partner.[39] Yet, in 1928, political exchange between Mussolini and Atatürk suddenly recovered and culminated in the Treaty of Neutrality and Reconciliation following Foreign Minister Tevfik Rüştü Aras's official visit to Rome. Thus came into being a momentary episode in Italo-Turkish relations when more cordial prospects seemed possible. On 24

May 1932, Prime Minister İnönü paid a high-level visit to Italy and was given a warm welcome at the port of Brindisi, as his ship (SS *Tevere*) anchored amidst aerobatic shows, steamboats, and a military band performing the Turkish national anthem.[40] İnönü's visit marked the climax of interwar relations between Turkey and Italy, when the latter considered extending a 300 million Italian lira loan with 6.5 per cent interest. But Turkey and Italy were destined to drift apart as Italian territorial claims over Yugoslavia became more vocal. Ultimately, Turkey decided to accept a Soviet loan of $8 million with 0 per cent interest rate.[41]

Only three years after İnönü's visit, Italy was well on its way to become a regional power. Wedged between the *Regio Esercito*, which loomed over the Balkans, and the *Regia Marina* over the Aegean, a prevalent sense of encirclement set the stage for Turkey to seek for its own course of revisionism. Between late 1935 and early 1936, the Turkish ambassador in Rome dispatched a series of detailed reports on the strength and operational capabilities of the Italian Royal Army and the role of the Dodecanese in Italy's new naval policy.[42] Citing Benito Mussolini's official statements published in the Italian popular press as well as the ambassador's personal interviews with Italian authorities, these reports indicated a serious increase in Italian fortifications in Leros and Kastelorizo – the two main naval bases of the *Regia Marina* in the Aegean Sea. Clearly, Mussolini had a cunning scheme in mind – one that aimed at containing the French dominance in the Mediterranean from the east, through the Aegean islands – which fell in sharp contrast with his earlier assurances on using the Dodecanese mainly as a trading hub. The ongoing animosity was further exacerbated by Mussolini's anti-Turkish statements, which were publicized in the Turkish press. In October 1935, when the *Bersaglieri* battalions began the invasion of Ethiopia, the Turkish government passed their concerns to Italian authorities, to which Mussolini responded with assurances that the invasion should by no means trouble Turkey.[43] Yet, this was hardly a relief for the Turkish leadership, as they watched with trepidation Italian expansionism in the Mediterranean, which Mussolini kept referring to as *Mare Nostrum* (our sea).

In December 1935, the French media leaked the infamous Hoare–Laval secret deal, which aimed at ending the Second Italo-Abyssinian war by simply allowing Italy to swallow large areas of Ethiopia.[44] What credibility the Italian government had hitherto had in the eyes of the Turkish state, or the League of Nations for that matter, ceased after the Hoare–Laval plan became public.[45] In January 1936, when the Turkish Chief of General Staff carried out a discreet inspection tour of the Aegean regiments along the coast, he logged in remorse that dark prospects were in the offing. He told the 4th Army commander in Izmir that in the likelihood of an Anglo-Italian naval battle in the Mediterranean, the British Royal Navy would lack the resources to engage with the *Regia Marina* on the Dodecanese and would focus on Egypt instead.[46] Consequently, Turkey decided to reinforce its land forces in the Aegean, dispatched the majority of new conscripts to the region, and purchased modern anti-aircraft guns from Great Britain and the Soviet Union. But these precautions could not address Turkey's main concern – the Straits – which remained demilitarized according to the Lausanne agreement.

In March 1936, a few days after the German reoccupation of the Rhineland, Turkish Foreign Minister Tevfik Rüştü Aras decided to propose a motion for the resolution of the Straits problem at the League of Nations, based on the principle *rebus sic stantibus* (things thus standing). The Turkish case, which Tevfik Aras sought to establish, was that conditions had substantially changed – and to the detriment of the security of Turkish territory – since the Straits Convention was signed in 1923. Aras claimed:

1. that the feeling of general insecurity was deepening, as a natural result of the issues raised by the Italo-Abyssinian conflict; by Germany's repudiation of the Treaty of Locarno and her unilateral action in reoccupying the Rhineland; by Austria's practical and unilateral denunciation of the military clauses in the Treaty of Saint-Germain; by the general process of rearmament; and by the development of events in the Far East.
2. that there was a perceptible danger of European war.
3. that the Italians had altered the position in the Mediterranean by fortifying the islands of the Dodecanese.
4. that the guarantee afforded to Turkey by Article 18 of the 1923 Straits Convention was seriously vitiated by the facts that (a) Japan, who had been one of the signatories, left the League of Nations, and (b) Italy refused to regard herself as bound by international law.
5. that the habit of unilateral repudiation of international obligations was spreading.[47]

The Montreux Convention represented the first peacefully negotiated revision of the post-First World War peace treaties. At the Lausanne Conference in 1923, Turkey had taken a conciliatory position on the Straits in return for Allied concessions on other issues. Ankara agreed to demilitarization in the Straits and a right of passage determined by international agreement rather than by the Turkish government. At Montreux, with a position strengthened by post-war recovery, Turkey asserted its sovereignty over the Straits, claiming the right to develop fortifications in the area and take control of passage into its own hands. Ironically, Moscow had pushed harder for Turkish sovereignty at Lausanne than Turkey itself, but was nonetheless disappointed by the negotiations at Montreux. The crux of the Soviet–Turkish disagreement lay in the relationship of each side with Great Britain, the power pushing most forcefully for an open Straits regime at Lausanne and at Montreux. The Soviet Union sought to have the Straits permanently closed to ships of war, thus offering protection to the Soviet coastline in Ukraine, Southern Russia and Georgia. Turkey, however, was anxious about a growing Italian threat, and sought to alienate neither the Soviet Union nor Great Britain.

On the eve of the conference, Aras's primary challenge was to harmonize diametrically opposed British and Soviet positions. While Turkey easily attracted Britain's attention, it was unclear if the Soviets would endorse Turkey's decision to formally raise the issue of revising the Lausanne agreement. During his preliminary negotiations with his British and Soviet counterparts, Anthony Eden and Maxim Litvinov, Aras made the Turkish government's logic clear. He pointed to Italian fortification of the Dodecanese, and, by calling the islands 'the Heligoland of the Eastern Mediterranean', compared them to Germany's main naval base and pointed to the revisionist context.[48] Aras stressed that such a base could only serve two purposes:

to control the Suez Canal; and to dominate the Dardanelles. The former peril, Aras hoped, would induce Britain to assist Turkey, while the latter would persuade the Soviets. In any case, he argued that if Italy had highly fortified islands within a few hours' sail of the Dardanelles, Turkey could not be forbidden the right to keep garrisons in self-defence. Aras pleaded that the step he proposed was the only way of forestalling a possible Italian *coup de main* on the Straits.

Although Eden and Litvinov both sympathized with Aras's logic, they disagreed on the best course of action. Given recent convention breaches in Europe, Eden was unsure about the timing, but he was favourably disposed to the idea of renegotiating the Straits problem for two reasons: to relieve the Royal Navy from the burden of assisting Turkey's defence of the Dardanelles; and to dislodge Turkey from its interwar connection to the Soviets.[49] By contrast, Litvinov was strongly opposed to any renegotiation that included non-littoral powers. The Soviet Union had long held that the Black Sea constituted a *Mare Clausum* that differed from internationalized waterways like the Suez and Panama Canals. Litvinov told Aras that the Soviet position had undergone no change since the Lausanne Convention of 1922–3, and that they had always been supportive of Turkey's sovereignty and its desire to remilitarize the Straits.[50] Indeed, it was Georgii Chicherin, head of the Soviet delegation at Lausanne, who had argued against the demilitarization of the Straits much more strongly than the Turks themselves.[51] Hence, the Soviet government understood 'Turkey's legitimate concerns regarding the insecurity of peace and the grave danger of the outbreak of war', but continued to be categorically against the inclusion of non-littoral powers in any negotiation.[52]

Aras seems to have been overly confident in his ability to serve as a bridge between London and Moscow. Given his assurance to Litvinov that Ankara would confer with the Soviets before taking action, the Soviets responded with understandable outrage when, on 11 April 1936, the Turkish government raised the issue before the League of Nations without having informed Moscow. When Karakhan informed the Soviet foreign ministry about this fait accompli, he was told that Turkey's timing was 'terrible' – only days after the Wehrmacht's march into the Rhineland, it suggested silent approval of German revisionism. Despite private misgivings, in public the Soviet Union tried to maintain the appearance of Soviet–Turkish solidarity. In their newspaper coverage, Soviet columnists took pains 'to paint the Turkish move in a light that it did not have'. Explaining the rationale for this position, the Soviet foreign ministry, like Atatürk, adopted a marital metaphor for the relationship: 'we, of course, have decided not to take the argument out of the Soviet–Turkish hearth.'[53] The Soviets lobbied in vein to dissuade the Turks from going forward with procedures in the League, not because they disagreed with the goal, but 'in order to give Turkey a free hand'.[54] Much to Moscow's dismay, the international conference convened in Montreux on 22 June to discuss the fate of the Straits. It is hard to overstate Moscow's scorn for Aras, whom they found to be duplicitous and personally responsible for some of the challenges to the Soviet–Turkish relationship.

To make matters worse, during preparations Aras had repeatedly insisted to the British delegation that the Soviet Government were in complete agreement with the Turkish position, and that Turkey's proposals would meet with no difficulty from that quarter.⁵⁵ When, however, the Turkish draft was eventually presented at Montreux on 22 June, it emerged that Aras's claims about Soviet endorsement were unfounded. There were a number of issues that the Soviets sanctioned: for instance, it was more or less established that unhindered commercial traffic, both in peace and war, would be guaranteed, and that Turkey would have the right to remilitarize the Straits.⁵⁶ What was disturbing for the Soviet Union in the draft treaty was the inclusion of the Turkish sovereignty clause, which meant that Turkey would have the right to open or close the Straits to warships. Secondly, Litvinov was aware of Britain's desire to drive a wedge between Ankara and Moscow, and viewed Aras's repeated attempts to satisfy England with revulsion. So incensed was Litvinov that the Soviet delegation was prepared to leave the conference. They stayed not despite but because of Aras's 'pointless Anglophilism', which some in Moscow thought might not be fully representative of the official Turkish position.⁵⁷ Deputy Commissar of Foreign Affairs Boris Stomonyakov, for example, told Karakhan that when he broached the subject of Soviets' discontent with Aras at Montreux, the Turkish ambassador in Moscow, Zekai Apaydın, 'blamed everything on Aras, with whom everyone knew he had terrible relations'.⁵⁸ Stomonyakov thought that Aras undoubtedly related to the Soviets worse than İnönü and Atatürk, and apparently, 'being impelled by his feelings and desire to curry favor before the British', went much further than what İnönü and Atatürk had in mind.⁵⁹ In his response, Karakhan concurred, and said that the position taken by Aras, who was junketing between British and Soviet receptions, did not correspond to the content and tone of traditional Soviet–Turkish relations. Nonetheless, he admitted Aras was not entirely alone, and that a role in the general worsening of relations was played by Soviet intransigence. They were 'guilty of much' in the Turks' growing coldness towards Moscow.⁶⁰

Mare Clausum

In the context of worsening relations, Litvinov and Aras met in Geneva on 29 June to reconcile their differences and repair some of the damage of Montreux. Aras sought to ease Moscow's apprehension by offering a separate, albeit less binding, bilateral treaty – one that would supplement the soon-to-be concluded general accord at Montreux. Litvinov received the offer with amused surprise and reminded Aras that as early as 1934, there had been discussions of a Soviet–Turkish pact for defence of the Straits in case of naval assault. In other words, Litvinov pointed to a solution to Turkey's security problems that did not involve non-Black Sea powers. Of course, the Soviet Union stood to gain, for 'in return for Soviet assistance, Turkey had offered to close the Straits in case the Soviet Union was attacked'.⁶¹ The Turkish foreign minister, however, seemed to have a different recollection of their talks in 1934. His offer to negotiate a supplementary treaty with the Soviet Union was, in reality, something of an empty gesture. Aras saw it primarily as a concession to the Soviets and of little real meaning. From his perspective, the momentum of Soviet–Turkish cooperation was sufficient. 'Why was the 1925 Soviet–Turkish Treaty of Friendship not enough?,' he repeatedly asked Litvinov, and appealed to Chicherin's pledges of mutual assistance in case of attack. Back in 1925,

Aras had pushed for a clause guaranteeing 'friendly neutrality' in case either the Soviet Union or Turkey was at war with a third party, but the Politburo had ordered Chicherin to exclude this term 'because it had no clear meaning'.[62]

Chicherin's compromise was a secret letter attached to each copy of the pact, in which each side promised that the 'genuine friendship' that existed between them would be preserved in the event of an attack by a third party on the other. From the Soviet perspective in 1936, this was hardly a formal commitment. Karakhan challenged Aras, and pointed out that in the 1934 negotiations Turkey had also seemed to think that more formal mutual commitments were necessary, and that there had even been discussion of stationing a Soviet fleet on the Aegean near the port of İzmir.[63] Caught off guard, Aras backtracked, and said that he had yet to receive authorization to put in writing anything that would produce binding obligations.[64] In view of the exacerbating tensions, Soviet newspaper editorials could no longer remain aloof. On 2 July 1936, *Izvestiia* published a succinct but accusatory account of the whole affair in Geneva, which prompted the Turkish government to respond with a diplomatic note.[65] Despite Turkey's insistence on continued loyalty, the Soviet Union was frustrated that that loyalty was not exclusive.

Litvinov's increasing resentment towards Aras and the very idea of Montreux notwithstanding, he tried to ensure that the new Straits regime would be as beneficial towards the Soviet Union as possible. Litvinov announced that his government would support the Turkish thesis provided that non-littoral use of the Straits would be 'for specific purposes and within specific limitations'.[66] In its final amendments, Article 10 of the Montreux Convention introduced the kind of specific limitations Litvinov sought, and expressed exactly when and how non-littoral powers could pass through the gates of the Black Sea. Additionally, Article 12 gave Black Sea-littoral countries privileged access to the Straits and the right to dispatch their respective fleets for purposes of rejoining their base outside the Black Sea with adequate notice.[67] Finally, Article 18 curbed the aggregate tonnage of non-littoral states in the Black Sea in times of peace, and stipulated that 'their vessels of war may not remain in the Black Sea more than twenty-one days, whatever be the object of their presence there'.[68] In other words, Soviet conditions were almost entirely met in the new accord. The only clause of concern to Moscow related to times of war, when the passage of warships was left entirely to the discretion of the Turkish government, provided that it remained neutral.[69]

Given the impending war in Europe, the Soviets were understandably irritated that Black Sea security now relied exclusively on good neighbourly relations with the Turkish government. Although this was a significant issue, serious concessions had been made to Soviet concerns. The so-called 'Black Sea yardstick' clause, which Aras had introduced in the final draft of the treaty, limited non-littoral powers to a fixed tonnage of 30,000 tons with a limited period of stay in the Black Sea. There was a clause allowing a one-off increase in tonnage to 45,000, if the Soviet fleet was further expanded. Nonetheless, this was a much more stringent limitation than anything in the Lausanne Convention, and, given the Soviet Black Sea fleet had a known tonnage of 60,000 tons, beneficial to the Soviet Union. The Soviets accepted the yardstick clause and agreed to sign the convention, which replaced the Lausanne regime on 20 July

1936 and reinstated 'Turkey's full sovereignty over the Straits in times of war and when she feels an imminent possibility of war'.[70] All the Lausanne signatories were present except Italy, who refused to send a delegation due to Anglo-French orchestrated sanctions through the League.

The Montreux Convention was a clear victory for Turkey and for its allies in the region. Turkey had peacefully negotiated a revision to the Straits regime agreed to in the aftermath of the First World War, achieving sovereignty over the Straits and the right to militarize them. Germany, and even more so Italy, were the main losers, since the anti-Italian group in the Mediterranean was reinforced. As for Moscow's gains, however, there were competing assessments. Some thought that Soviet Russia, closely associated with Turkey and recently allied to both France and Czechoslovakia, received an equally valuable prize. The Soviets could now dispatch their fleet into the Mediterranean in times of peace without restrictions, while all non-littoral Powers were limited to 45,000 tons in the opposite direction.[71] Despite Eden's attempts to put a good face on the new Convention, Britain feared that 'should Turkey adhere to the Franco-Russian pact, the French and Russian fleets might utilize the Black Sea as a base for naval operations in the Mediterranean'.[72] Despite Soviet accusations that Turkey had sided with Britain, Britain's sponsorship of the Oriental Entente less than two years later demonstrated London's recognition that its position in the Eastern Mediterranean had weakened.

While most signatories at Montreux thought that the Soviet Union would now enjoy a more favourable position than it had occupied since 1923, for months Moscow's attitude towards Turkey remained puzzlingly sour. İnönü tried probing his Soviet counterparts about Moscow's lingering pessimism. 'Was it really in Stalin's best interest,' he asked, 'to risk the collapse of a friendship so cautiously protected for decades from the most intransigent powers of imperialism?'[73] Three months after Litvinov and Aras parted ways acerbically at Montreux, İnönü took the initiative and apologized to Litvinov for the confusion in Switzerland. 'If something was necessary to prove Turkey's continued friendship,' İnönü told him, the Turkish government was ready to sign an agreement with the Soviets about the defence of the Straits in case of Italian aggression 'despite a legitimate fear of economic retaliation from the Germans'.[74] At first, the meeting between Litvinov and Ambassador Apaydın, who was communicating İnönü's message, revealed a marked sense of bitterness, which the Soviets continued to hold against Aras. Litvinov disdainfully asked whether İnönü was offering this belated apology 'out of pity for the Soviet Union'.[75] Apaydın's minutes of the meeting demonstrate an even harsher language than what Litvinov recorded for Soviet accounts, and the Turkish ambassador seems to have been cajoling his government into action. Apaydın told Ankara that Litvinov's impression of Turkey had been reduced to naught by Aras's frivolity and that 'Turkey was no longer the master of its own foreign policy'.[76]

Hope emerged as Litvinov began probing the possibility of a formal agreement. Although the Turks still maintained the existing treaty and its annexes were 'one of the constituent documents of the republic, obviating all requisites for additional accords', Litvinov cherished hopes of forging a military alliance more binding than the 1925 Treaty.[77] Confronted by Litvinov's persistence, Apaydın suggested that Turkey had considered Soviet–Turkish relations since the early 1920s within the framework defined by Chicherin in his famous letters. But if the Soviets now hoped for a less ambiguous statement of that framework, Apaydın said his government would be willing to reformulate it in writing. Litvinov seemed intrigued; he rummaged through the pile of documents on his desk and found Chicherin's letters, which the two then proceeded to interpret. Later that evening, Apaydın reported to İnönü that the most viable option to rejuvenate their relations with Moscow was to rearticulate Aras's proposal for a separate treaty in Soviet language.

Litvinov had no doubt of the appeal of reinforcing Moscow's relations with Ankara and informed the Politburo on 25 October: 'It is not so much the assistance that Turkey would be able to provide us in the event of war, but the political effect of such a pact, which will do something to prevent Turkey's drift away from us'.[78] For the Soviets, the exigencies of the impending war in Europe necessitated a much more binding treaty, particularly after what happened in Montreux, 'if only for purposes of more clearly defined allegiances'. He was equally aware that Aras would 'no doubt seek Britain's consent first' and would 'try not to disobey their orders'; but he still believed that if Turkey fully disclosed its cards and formulated the promised treaty, it would be of great interest to the Kremlin, 'however little it gives us from a geostrategic point of view'.[79] Evidently, Litvinov thought of Soviet–Turkish relations in political terms more than strategic, for he advised the Politburo to accept the Turkish proposal and to ask Arkady Rosengolts, Commissar for Foreign Trade, to present his views on expanding trade relations with Turkey.

Much to Apaydın's dismay, Ankara did not concur with its ambassador's appraisal of the situation and showed little eagerness to enact a treaty with the Soviet Union. Aras told him to 'stop negotiating until further notice',[80] and to simply communicate Atatürk's friendly but ceremonial note of gratitude to Stalin.[81] Turkey's volte-face came on 28 October, just hours before the Republic Day reception at the Soviet Embassy in Ankara, where Atatürk made his surprising appearance and added more confusion to Soviet–Turkish relations. Apaydın himself was perplexed and bluntly told Aras that 'he could not grasp exactly what it is that Aras wanted him to do'.[82] Bearing the burden of delivering his government's message, Apaydın certainly did not expect Litvinov to respond favourably. Yet, Litvinov's response was even more shocking that he could have imagined, for Litvinov told him that 'Turkey has definitely adopted a new orientation' and that the Soviet Union saw 'nothing positive' in it.[83]

Whatever Apaydın hoped to gain negotiating a treaty with the Soviets, it was not Litvinov's esteem. But, unhappy with the failure of his initiative, he revealed his personal problems with Aras and fed Litvinov's suspicions that Aras was personally responsible for the more anti-Soviet turns in Turkey's recent policy. Litvinov considered Apaydın's offer to be the one that Aras had already made to him earlier in Geneva and now had taken back. Litvinov claimed that 'he knew for sure that Aras reneged because of British pressure', and that, 'he had information that Aras even thanked the British for their advice'.[84] For the Soviets, the failure of Apaydın's latest approach in Moscow, three months after Montreux, was the nail in the coffin. In a snappy telegram, Litvinov instructed Karakhan 'not to talk with the Turks anymore about pacts'.[85] When Aras paid a visit to the Soviet Embassy in Ankara the next day, he tried to smooth things over, but Karakhan told him: 'nothing changes the fact that Turks preferred the English to the Soviets, and were now more loyal to that camp'.[86]

British diplomatic records illustrate that the Soviets were right about Anthony Eden's role in obstructing the Soviet–Turkish Pact and that Litvinov's fears of an emerging Anglo-Turkish Spring had some basis. But they also attest to Soviet exaggeration of the British threat and a sense of insecurity that haunted Litvinov's decisions for months after Montreux. Several meetings between Anthony Eden and Turkey's ambassador in London, Fethi Okyar, demonstrate that Aras was in fact pleading incessantly for British acceptance of a Russian guarantee to Turkey. Eden told Okyar that a Soviet–Turkish Pact 'would be extremely dangerous and open to grave political objections', given the situation in Europe. But Aras kept pushing to bring the Soviet Union to the table as a guarantor of Turkey's Black Sea coasts.[87] Ankara was only willing to move so far in London's direction. Aras's attempts to harmonize Soviet and British positions irritated Okyar so much, that the latter seemed to the British 'distinctly embarrassed by Aras, of whom he had a poor opinion'.[88]

It was, in fact, Okyar and not Aras who 'thanked' Eden for his advice. This was to be expected, for Okyar was an ardent supporter of liberal economics known for his Anglophile tendencies. Because Aras sought to balance Moscow and London, the pro-British Okyar was now levelling the same accusations against Aras for exactly the opposite reasons that Ambassador Apaydın had in Moscow. Although he caught flak from both sides, Aras did have a firm position. He described the state of affairs between Ankara and Moscow as 'an insidious rift' that needed to be dispelled.[89] In October 1936, Aras informed Okyar that, even though a Soviet–Turkish Pact did not seem in the offing, his rejection would not be brusque, as it was important to give Russia a soft answer 'because Turkey wished to do nothing that might jeopardize friendship with Russia, which was the corner-stone of Turkish policy – both at home and abroad'.[90] Turkey's goal was to remain free and unaligned, but favourably disposed to the Soviet Union.

Events at Montreux and in its aftermath did introduce new tensions into the Soviet–Turkish relationship, despite the fact that the actual terms of Montreux were more beneficial to the Soviet Union than the Lausanne agreement that it replaced. The crux of the disagreement was Moscow's desire to close the Black Sea to non-littoral powers, and the consequent need for Turkey to enter into an exclusive relationship with the Soviet Union. Turkey refused and sought to maintain Britain's support in case of problems with Italy in the Mediterranean. Nonetheless, Turkey strove to satisfy as many of the Soviet Union's Black Sea concerns as possible. At no point did Montreux represent a clean break in Soviet–Turkish relations. Indeed, the strength of the Soviet–Turkish understanding of their partnership as crucial to the politics of the Black Sea is visible in both sides' efforts to rekindle relations in other spheres after Montreux.

Beyond pragmatism: Economic preferences across the Black Sea

While Italian activities in the late 1930s were Ankara's primary concern in the military sphere, Germany was a source of a different kind of anxiety. Germany had come to dominate Turkey's foreign trade, and was doing so in an increasingly dramatic way. 'Dependence on Germany' was a common refrain among the Turkish political elite, and, given the memory of the Ottoman Empire's economic fate, these were words spoken with a particular anxiety. Here, the Soviet Union offered an attractive alternative, because it was a source of some of the goods that Ankara sought. Indeed, after Montreux the Turkish government continued to seek Soviet support in its attempts to industrialize. Turkey looked to the Soviet Union, Moscow sought to oblige, and both hoped to develop bilateral trade in order to lessen Turkish dependence upon Germany and make a Black Sea partnership work.

In Moscow, at the nineteenth anniversary celebrations of the Bolshevik Revolution, Apaydın was surprised by Litvinov's friendly welcome. This was just a week after Atatürk's performance at the Soviet embassy in Ankara, and he was greeted before even the British ambassador, with whom he had arrived at the same time. Taking Apaydın aside, Litvinov immediately began showering him with questions about Atatürk's visit. He told Apaydın that Stalin knew and appreciated Atatürk's genuine feelings towards the Soviet Union.[91] After alluding to Turkey's economic problems and its over-reliance on Nazi Germany, Apaydın said that 'the nature of Soviet–Turkish collaboration has always been based in politics and economics', and that the two states would be better served by the expansion of trade relations than by rehashing trivial disputes. Apaydın's response, unvarnished as it was, did come with a couched criticism of the Soviets' disregard for Turkey's more fundamental economic difficulties. He did not avoid a delicate subject, and expressed regret that the total volume of trade between Ankara and Moscow had fallen from 20 million Turkish liras in 1930 to just 8.5 million liras in less than six years.[92] In the discussion that ensued, Litvinov proclaimed that the Soviet Union was, 'of course, willing' to relieve Turkey of its troubles by purchasing the agricultural products or 'whatever it is that the Germans were buying from Turkey'.[93] There was an element of bombast here, for the Soviet Union could not truly compete with Germany, but there was also a sincere declaration of an attempt to try.

Apaydın's comments were not the first Moscow had heard of Turkey's foreign trade problems. Litvinov was well aware of Turkey's soaring trade volume with Nazi Germany, for Soviet reports showed that Turkey's leading trading partner in 1935 was Germany (35.5 million Turkish liras for German imports versus 39.2 million for Turkish exports), dwarfing England (8.7 million/5.2 million) and the Soviet Union (4.32 million/4.15 million) combined.[94] The Soviet Union had further cause for worry, because in 1936 the total volume of trade between Turkey and the USSR (9 million liras) was again significantly lower than the Turkish–German exchange (102 million liras),[95] and, in its trade with the Soviet Union, Turkey ran a deficit of just over 1 million liras. Thus, with discernible haste the Soviet Foreign Commissariat called Apaydın the morning after he broached the subject and informed him that Stalin approved the commencement of a new round of negotiations in Ankara for the expansion of Soviet–Turkish trade and to replace the commercial treaty of 1931.[96]

Nazi Germany's 'export empire', which stretched out from Hungary to Turkey and Iran, was difficult to compete with.[97] In a private letter to Kliment Voroshilov, Karakhan aptly noted that Nazi–Turkish trade had been accompanied by exponential growth of Berlin's propaganda network in Turkey. This is 'ultimately a question of preparing for war', he wrote, 'and the Germans are doing this well'.[98] Karakhan knew that the rapid advance of Nazi–Turkish commercial exchange had not been solely a product of mutual benefits, but due to growing Turkish demand for goods such as iron and steel, locomotives and trucks, and machinery, mainly owing to Turkey's railway construction programme.[99] Since Turkey's main railway system had been built according to German standards before the First World War, most of its rolling stock was of German origin and most of its technical employees had been trained in Berlin. Additionally, however, both Ankara and Berlin faced similar economic policy challenges after the Great Depression, and cooperation was facilitated by an effective policy that limited the outflow of coveted hard currency for either. Agreements between the *Reichsbank* and the Central Bank of Turkey in 1934 and 1935 established a clearing system, and a stipulated margin guaranteed that any Turkish debts to the Third Reich would be paid.[100] According to Turkish statistics, Nazi Germany absorbed 48.7 per cent of Turkey's total exports in 1935, up from 36.6 per cent in 1934.[101] The exponential advance was, in part, a result of the net-balance system.[102] By 1939, despite the slight decrease in Turkey's volume of trade with countries that fell under Nazi occupation, the value of all imports from Nazi Germany rose to an astounding £20,946,837 (55.3 per cent of all imports into Turkey for that year). Likewise, the level of exports to the Third Reich rose to an unprecedented £11,860,968 (43.75 per cent of Turkey's entire export market).[103]

If Nazi Germany provided Turkey with necessary industrial goods in a fashion that prevented Turkish accumulation of a trade deficit, then why did İnönü relentlessly plead with the Soviets to counterbalance the Third Reich's share? In 1936, the message İnönü conveyed during his meetings with the Soviets was that, despite the impressive trade volume between Ankara and Berlin, the reality did not match what the numbers suggested. Turkey had become caught, he argued, 'in the webs of a trade system that placed her in the hands of Germany'.[104] Despite the clearing agreements, Turkey was rapidly accumulating a foreign trade deficit.[105] Turkey's purchase of war materiel was growing and becoming ever harder to be paid off with the sale of Turkey's chief exports. Part of the difficulty, according to İnönü, was that, as Turkey had become more and more dependent upon Nazi Germany, Turkey's outside markets had been lost while the Soviets were looking elsewhere. It was presumably understood that he lamented the loss of other export markets as well, but it was a clear plea to the Soviet Union to step in. İnönü made it clear that Turkey's conundrum was fundamentally a political one that reflected its political preferences.

The scope of the trade negotiations that began in December 1936, reveals how closely Turkey was prepared to align itself with the Soviet Union in economic terms. During preliminary talks in Moscow, Apaydın asked for 100 million US dollars from the USSR in a five-year instalment plan for the purchase of military equipment, the establishment of two new industrial plants, agricultural development, and the improvement of Black Sea ports for coastal trade. This loan, Apaydın proposed, would ideally be repaid in ten years in the form of agricultural produce totalling US$112.5 million, including interest. As in previous Soviet–Turkish commercial agreements, Apaydın imagined a state-sponsored Turkish enterprise to partner with the Soviet trust *Turkstroi* (see below) to facilitate future ventures.[106] Stomonyakov, like other Soviet officials, balked at Apaydın's figure, and thought that even half of this amount would require Moscow to purchase too many consumer goods.[107] Nevertheless, he thought that the Soviet Union could achieve a significant increase in their trade with Turkey. Given the Soviet Union's wariness about importing consumer goods, it is all the more striking that Stomonyakov hoped that the Soviet Union should challenge Germany for the import of Turkish 'raisins and figs'. In his response to a draft letter by the People's Commissariat of Foreign Trade (NKVT), which recommended 7.5 million liras for imports from Turkey in 1937, Stomonyakov firmly pushed for 15 million.[108] Karakhan agreed with Stomonyakov's course of action and acknowledged that the expansion of trade with Turkey was hardly in the Soviet Union's economic interests, that the decision would be made 'for exclusively political considerations'.[109] In a private letter to Kliment Voroshilov, Karakhan fleshed out some of those political considerations. He argued that Nazi–Turkish trade had been accompanied by exponential growth of the German propaganda network in Turkey. This is 'ultimately a question of preparing for war', he wrote, 'and the Germans are doing this well'.[110] In other words, Karakhan was pushing for economic and cultural exchange to keep Turkey as a potential ally, despite the fallout at Montreux.

In the end, the Soviet Union did not offer Turkey a large loan, but 1937 saw a marked upswing in economic relations. A new trade agreement was signed in 1937, with a subsequent increase in the volume of exchange. Most importantly from Ankara's perspective, Soviet purchases of Turkish exports increased from 3,900,000 liras to 6,500,000 liras.[111] The two sides almost attained a net-balance in their bilateral trade. Additionally, Turkey's industrial plans for 1937 were devised under the aegis of the Soviet Union. In previous collaboration, Turkey had worked with *Turkstroi*, a subsidiary organization of the Soviet People's Commissariat of Heavy Industry (NKTP) dedicated to the export and installation of industrial equipment in Turkey.[112] Ankara was disappointed to see *Turkstroi* folded into a larger organization that dealt with the export of industrial equipment to 'the East', but they put aside any reservations.[113]

Soviet support for Turkish industrialization ultimately had mixed results. The upswing in 1937 was part of a larger Soviet commitment that had helped Ankara launch its first Five-Year Plan (1932–7). Turkey had already been receiving substantial support for years, but 1937 seemed a showcase year for collaboration. In that year alone, Turkey completed three factories, all equipped to varying degrees with Soviet-sponsored machinery: a cotton mill in Nazilli; a merino-processing factory in Bursa; and an artificial silk factory in Gemlik. The Nazilli plant was Turkey's fourth and largest textile mill, with a production capacity of 20 million metres (1,800,000 kg) of coarse cotton fabrics for peasants as well as fine fabrics for urban consumers. Much of the construction work for Turkey's textile industry was financed by *Eksportstroi*'s Turkish counterpart, Sumer Bank, and this development brought new life into remote towns, triggering an influx of people looking for much-needed jobs, housing, schools for their children, and a cultural environment. But there were also setbacks, many stemming from *Eksportstroi* and Sumer Bank's failure to fully harmonize their efforts, with consequent interruptions in work.[114] After its opening, it took another eight months for the Nazilli plant to reach full capacity, delaying the 8 million rubles' worth of textile products that were to be exported to the Soviet Union. Equally, however, collaboration suffered from the two sides' ambition. Moscow and Ankara were frequently overzealous, commencing ventures with no specific deadline, cost, or technical specifications. The planned construction of a short-wave national radio station in Ankara, for example, was ultimately aborted, along with several other local stations in the Aegean. For Karakhan and others concerned about German propaganda, this was a particularly frustrating failure, since this was a project in which the Soviet economic and cultural challenge to German influence in Turkey had been particularly entwined.[115]

Despite hindrances, Soviet–Turkish interactions in 1937 permeated the Black Sea, where the two states looked beyond their geopolitical differences and focused on state-sponsored ventures. These developments fell in stark contrast to what British and German observers had hoped for only a year ago at Montreux. This was so much the case that the British government watched with trepidation when Tevfik Rüştü entered into negotiations with Ion Antonescu of Romania for a Black Sea Pact that would have included the Soviet Union.[116] Even though the proposed Black Sea Pact was not much more than a gesture to the good, the British ambassador in Ankara voiced his concerns about the support they had given Turkey at Montreux and questioned whether it would backfire.

Indeed, the Soviet Union had significantly more interest in the Black Sea coast line than it did in the ice-bound Baltic or the Barents Sea, which were easily threatened by the German navy. The Black Sea had well-equipped commercial ports, proximity to valuable manganese, oil, wheat, coal and steel hubs, and developed canal systems. Another auxiliary aspect of the question of a Black Sea Pact was also evident in the matter of inter-state trade amongst its littorals. Turkey, Romania and Bulgaria were all customers of the Soviet Union, where water-borne merchandise passed through the Black Sea to the Danube, and was then reshipped to İstanbul and to other Black Sea ports. Given the centrality of this area for Soviet trade outlets and routes, the British government was concerned about a more privileged partnership between Ankara and Moscow, which they had so carefully sought to circumvent at Montreux.[117]

In July 1937, when Tevfik Rüştü Aras paid an official visit to the Soviet Union, nothing seemed to herald a setback in the calm that had characterized Moscow–Ankara relations since Montreux. As previously, İnönü carefully selected a Turkish delegation whose stature would match the previous delegations that had visited Moscow. Şükrü Kaya, minister of the interior, accompanied Aras and made frequent references to the two states' 'heroic struggle against foreign enslavement' and 'the oppression of European aggressors'.[118] The Soviet press dutifully translated Kaya's proclamations in a way that emphasized the two states' shared values. *Izvestiia*, for instance, suggested that Kaya's remarks were a warning against European imperialists, who incessantly tried to separate Turkey from its connection to the Bolsheviks.[119] In his exchanges with the Soviets during his stay, Aras stressed that Turkey's amicable feelings for Russia were genuine and that, whether or not the proposed Black Sea Pact would materialize, Turkey would scrupulously fulfil its obligations to the Soviet Union. His carefully worded speech in Moscow on 13 July, when he proclaimed that 'the friends and enemies of Russia were *ipso facto* the friends and enemies of Turkey', was meant to convey that even without a pact Turkey was prepared to think of itself in alignment with the Soviet Union.[120]

In Moscow, Aras shed his earlier image of a mediator and embraced a different role. He referred to himself as one of the architects of Soviet–Turkish friendship and celebrated his tenure in Moscow in 1920-1 as the representative of the Turkish Communist Party (or 'the Left party', as he now labelled it) and 'a figure of the Comintern'.[121] Aras's mission in Moscow was to dispel all negative rumours that had arisen since Montreux, and to convince Stalin that 'the two states could not remain indifferent to each other's fate, with or without contractual agreements and military obligations'.[122] In a letter addressed to the Soviet people, İnönü wrote that 'of all the desiderata shaping Turkish diplomacy, friendship with the Soviet Union was a permanent and vital element, particularly in the Black Sea Basin, and that no aggressor can expect any help or support from the Turkish side'.[123] Returning to the yardstick metaphor Atatürk had used at the Soviet reception a year earlier, Aras and Kaya proclaimed that Turkey's historic amity towards the Soviet Union permeated the Black Sea beyond naval measures, that it represented the truth, 'nothing more nor less', and that 'there was no empty phraseology in it'.[124] More than a year after Montreux, Turkey still clearly staked its position in the Black Sea – and, indeed, its diplomacy more broadly – to a strong relationship with the Soviet Union.

2

Turkey's Eastern Question

Commensurate with great power interests in the region, historians working on Soviet–Turkish relations have a tendency to focus on the Straits question in isolation.¹ There is an element of truth in this prevailing argument insofar as Turkey's remilitarization of the Straits led to momentary episodes of distress when, for instance, the Soviets ordered their two submarines (Tashkent and Dimitiev) in 1937 not to leave the Dardanelles until further notice, irritating the Turkish naval command.² But as Soviet and Turkish records demonstrate, both countries looked past their differences at Montreux, with a shared commitment for cooperation in areas beyond the Straits. An obvious place to look for signs of Turkey's continued convergence with the Soviet Union is the permeable eastern frontier, where the Ottoman state had waged a life and death struggle over the borderlands of the Caucasus. The absence of a Russian threat in this region and the Soviet Union's conspicuous silence during the Kurdish uprisings against the Ankara government in the 1920s and 30s was more than a sequential step in Soviet–Turkish relations and illustrates the nature of Soviet foreign policy, which fell at odds with the global trend of antagonistic groupings elsewhere.

Eastern Anatolia – the area surrounding present-day Kars – provides an unusually revealing case through which to study the fate of post-imperial borderlands in the hands of ideologically different systems.³ This territory had become a formal part of the Russian Empire after the Russo-Ottoman War of 1877–8, and was merged into the greater Karskaia Oblast.⁴ In his magisterial account on the imperial struggle between the Romanovs and Ottomans, Michael Reynolds demonstrates how 'fear of partition led the Ottoman state to destroy its imperial order, whereas the compulsive desire for greater security ... spurred the Russian state to press beyond its capacity and thereby precipitate its own collapse'.⁵ In 1921, the Bolsheviks ceded this territory back to the Ankara government, signalling a radical reversal in centuries of Russo–Turkish conflict. Looking at interwar territoriality in Europe, which was one of the spokes radiating out from a capital to the state's margins, we can see that right up to World War II this model did not fit eastern Anatolia, a borderland that was as yet untangled, as the Soviet–Turkish cross-border exchange reveals.

The border between Turkey and the Soviet republics of the Caucasus was defined by the Treaty of Kars in October 1921, which succeeded an agreement signed in Moscow earlier that year. For physical reasons, demarcation proved to be extremely difficult due to the ongoing war in Central Anatolia and a landscape that was at times inaccessible. When groundwork was finally completed in 1926, the Soviet–Turkish boundary followed an irregular course for about 367 miles across the area east of the Black Sea. From west to east it traversed three distinct terrains: the rugged mountainous area along the Georgian highlands; a high, dissected plateau along the Akhurian River that divides Soviet Armenia and Northeastern Anatolia; and the greater valley of the Aras River.[6] This complex pattern is especially notable between the towns of Kiti (present-day Çalpala) and Serbarabad, where in 1927 the Turkish and Soviet governments completed an irrigation agreement, providing for the construction of a dam.[7] The culmination of these efforts was the 1928 Border Agreement, which set up a perimeter of 10 kilometres on either side of the frontier to facilitate further commercial exchange between the inhabitants of neighbouring townships. Interstate cooperation, joint ventures and cross-border trade paved the way for engineers and workers from either side of the river to build more dams, canals and irrigation facilities, ultimately remaking the borderlands that they shared.

As late as 1937, the Turkish Ministry of Public Works relied almost exclusively on *Exportstroi* for ongoing construction projects in Eastern Anatolia – such as the building of a tunnel on the Aras River and a dam in Serdar'abad.[8] Soviet and Turkish engineers were exchanged to complete these projects as well as several irrigation facilities near the Igdir Valley.[9] By March 1937, *Eksportstroi* intensified its efforts to promote Soviet experts to be employed as technicians and engineers in Turkey's eastern provinces. Located in the immediate vicinity of Soviet Transcaucasia, the snow-capped villages near Kars and Igdir witnessed a surge of Soviet mechanics (300–400 people a day at the construction stage), who worked on water-pipeline projects.[10] Meanwhile, Ambassador Apaydın was haggling over the price of new projects, over whether the cost of the labour was to be provided by the Turkish government in advance or included in the estimated total budget.[11] In early June, when the Chief Engineer of *Eksportstroi* returned to Moscow, about 70 per cent of the installation work was completed and Celal Bayar, the Turkish minister of economy, anticipated that most Soviet-sponsored facilities would be up and running by the year's end.[12]

Soviet–Turkish cooperation along the Aras river yielded more significant results in cross-border trade, which obscured territorial demarcations and fell in stark contrast with an otherwise territorializing world. In that sense, the Border Treaty of 1928 was the product of a shared desire to regulate bilateral commerce as much as it was about transforming the borderlands. Through joint patrolling of the border, Turkish and Soviet governments took concrete precautions against cross-border smuggling of material goods and trafficking of arms. The Ankara government benefitted from this convergence in a different way; as the Soviet–Turkish exchange along the border had a negative impact on local Kurdish tribes, whose struggle for autonomy rested on porous frontiers. From the very onset of the republic's proclamation, Kurdish insurgency constituted the most significant concern in Turkey's eastern policy. A retrospective analysis of the three main Kurdish rebellions (Sheikh Said, Ararat and Dersim) during this period reveals that the underlying reason behind Turkey's success in consolidating central authority in its eastern provinces was the absence of a Russian threat.

Although historians have recently begun to explore different aspects of the Soviet–Turkish alliance on Europe's margins in the 1920s and early 1930s, the Soviet factor in Turkey's Kurdish problem during the late interwar period remains terra incognita.[13]

While the Russian Empire incessantly pursued local and temporary alliances with Kurdish notables and tribes in order to exploit their grievances against the Ottoman state, the Soviet Union consistently remained aloof to the Kurdish question. In 1927, Soviet ambassador Yakov Suritz openly told Turkish foreign minister Tevfik Rüştü that the USSR would stick to its principle of non-interference vis-à-vis the Kurdish issue, but that Turkey needed to be careful as Moscow was aware of British designs for an independent Kurdistan.[14] Looking at Soviet records, it would be fair to suggest that Stalin perceived Kurdish nationalism as a feudal movement open to exploitation by Western imperialism. On the rare occasions that Soviet newspapers wrote about Kurdistan, they referred to a tribal nation, which was separated by the impassable mountainous terrains of greater Mesopotamia.[15]

Kurds and Bolsheviks

Inspired by the earlier successes of Turkish nationalists and driven into desperation by its own failure, Kurdish nationalism grew steadily radical and doctrinaire throughout the early twentieth century.[16] In fact, the Turks themselves, fearful of losing their eastern provinces to the Armenians before and during the Great War, had done much to bolster Kurdish nationalist aspirations.[17] Once the triumphant Kemalist regime proclaimed the republic in 1923, however, Turkey's new leaders first discouraged and later circumscribed Kurdish nationalism.[18]

Throughout the second half of the 1920s, two major Kurdish rebellions broke out – Sheikh Said and Ararat (*Ağrı Dağı İsyanı*) in 1925 and 1930, respectively – acting as reminders of Turkey's overambitious nationalist objectives in the Eastern provinces. Within less than a year of the republic's proclamation, Kurds began to express their bitterness against Ankara's vigorous attempts to homogenize Asia Minor through exiling Kurdish notables to Western provinces and prohibiting the usage of Kurdish language. In 1925, the Turkish government sought to resettle the Kurdish population, which constituted the second-largest ethnicity in the country, based on a comprehensive Reform Plan for the East (*Şark Islahat Planı*). The Kurds denounced the plan, and, in the spring of 1925, Sheikh Said of Piran, a leader of the Naqshibandi order of Dervishes, rose against the Turkish government.[19] Having acquired almost the entire Kurdish popular support behind his movement through matrimonial alliances with the neighbouring chieftains, particularly the Zaza of Dersim highlands, Sheikh Said's army quickly advanced towards Diyarbakir, briefly capturing a few important towns including Harput.[20] Said was ultimately defeated by a Turkish counteroffensive that was unleashed against the insurgents in several locations, but it took the Turkish army almost three weeks to capture him.

The suppression of the rebellion, accompanied by summary trials, mass deportations and punitive measures, failed to break the spirit of Kurdish resistance or to extirpate the last vestiges of opposition to Turkish rule. In their quest for absolute security, the Turkish state was driven into more isolation except for continued convergence with the Soviet Union. On 5 March 1925, when the Sheikh Said rebellion reached its climax, the Soviet ambassador in Ankara, Yakov Suritz, delivered his government's friendly note to Mustafa

Kemal, extending the USSR's full sympathy and support for the Turkish government vis-à-vis the Kurdish problem. In response, Mustafa Kemal conveyed his gratitude for Georgii Chicherin and Maxim Litvinov, noting that he already had strong faith in the loyalty of the Soviet Union, 'especially in light of the pro-Turkish Soviet position vis-à-vis Turkey's recent conflict with the Greeks'.[21] What the Turkish government found most remarkable, however, was the Soviet decision to remove all military units from their side of the border during Said's rebellion as a gesture to Ankara.

The Turkish government held the Kurdish problem under close scrutiny after the Sheikh Said rebellion, and commissioned two parliamentary research groups under Abdülhalık Renda, who was Speaker of the Turkish National Assembly, and Cemil Ubaydın, who was serving as minister of the interior.[22] In 1931, Prime Minister İnönü received several surveys of the Kurdish question from public security authorities in the southeastern provinces.[23] Looking at these reports, which clearly summarized the Turkish government's perspective, three factors stand out as important considerations behind the Sheikh Said uprising. First, the mutineers were almost exclusively portrayed as retrograde counterrevolutionaries led by obscurantist and primitive tribal leaders, rather than nationalist reactionaries. Second, it seemed hardly spontaneous and coincidental that the revolution broke out when the British government was putting pressure on the League of Nations to pass a resolution that would award the Kingdom of Iraq with the strategic oil-rich province of Mosul, where the Kurds were headquartered in their attacks against Turkey.[24] Finally, strategic and logistical findings of all military reports pointed to the necessity to finding access to rebel territory, which was blocked by mountainous terrain. The only possible entry to the region was through the Baghdad Railway, which now lay in the Syrian portion under French administration stationed in Alexandretta. Although France granted permission to transit Turkish troops and supplies in accordance with Article 10 of the 1921 Franco-Turkish Agreement, Syrian authorities were making it difficult to utilize the station as a Turkish military garrison, which ultimately hindered the Turks' original plan of mass encirclement and provided the Kurds opportunity to disperse easily, ultimately turning the operation into a prolonged guerilla warfare.[25]

In 1927, a Kurdish National Congress was summoned with the initiative of Kurdish nationalists in Syria. At this conference, which was properly entitled *Khoybun* (Independence), representatives of various Kurdish tribes decided to put an end to all Kurdish–Armenian or Kurdish–Persian differences and designate Ararat as the provisional capital of the Khoybun, dissolving all other existing Kurdish nationalist organizations into one. Through subsequent conferences in Beirut and Alexandretta within the next several years, the Khoybun grew from a miniature provisional government to a well-organized state structure with a substantial army, supported by the French mandate.[26] Mindful of the perilous and costly suppression of the previous Sheikh Said rebellion, the Turks initially sought to negotiate with the Khoybun, declaring general amnesty for those who laid down their arms within three months, and allowed all deportees to return to their homes. To reach an amicable settlement, the governor of Doğu Beyazıd was authorized to open up an even larger window for negotiations with local Kurdish chieftains, while the Ankara government approached İhsan Nuri Pasha, a former sergeant in the Turkish army and the new leader of the Khoybun.

In a detailed report dated January 1928, Yakov Suritz shared his observations on Turkey's 'Eastern Question', arguing that, in fact, the Turkish government had pursued an effective strategy to fight clericalism in these areas. Suritz wrote that Turkey's most obvious strategy was to knock out the economic base from under the feudal lords and the clergy.[27] That is why the political and repressive struggle was going on in parallel with the confiscation of land from the compromised beys, and the repression was mainly reduced to their expulsion from the families of the eastern vilayets. This campaign, however, did not produce the desired results. For Suritz, this was partly because the Turkish government did not show sufficient determination on the issue of disposing of confiscated lands (they were hesitant to give land to the Kurdish peasantry free of charge), and partly because the expulsion took place unsystematically without a premeditated plan. 'It touched many innocent people and led to a deepening of discontent on the part of the population', he wrote, explaining why in the summer of 1927, local discontent came to the brink of a regular uprising.[28] As Turkey's clash with Kurdish chieftains sharply escalated on the Persian border, which led to an aggravation of relations with Persia and the unceasing growth of banditry in the greater Kurdistan region, the Ankara government was forced to reconsider its 'Kurdish policy' and move from a purely military regime to some normalization. But Suritz was not optimistic.

Indeed, in the midst of the Mutki Rebellion (May–August 1927), Şükrü Kaya had 'a sincere and friendly' conversation with Suritz, when he let slip that Turks themselves had little understanding of the Kurdish psychology. For Şükrü, 'these small, cunning traffickers who blackmail even their own weak ones', constituted the main obstacle to regional peace.[29] Until the Turks had the opportunity to operate on the other side of Ararat, and until the Kurdish nest was uprooted in this area, he told Suritz that the situation would never calm down beyond the adjacent vilayats. He said that he knew Suritz would not be convinced, but that he wanted the Soviets to understand his reasoning. It was not that Turks were seeking territorial aggrandizement – they would be willing to give up much more in exchange for the other side of Ararat. He just wished that 'all Kurdish separatists were rooted out'.[30]

Ultimately, a peaceful settlement of the dispute was rendered impossible with Kurdish leaders' demands for regional autonomy, for which the Turks had simply zero tolerance. Ankara, once again, resorted to arms for settling the problem, which in return culminated in the form of a full-blown rebellion in Ararat.[31] The 4th and 6th Army Corps under General Salih Pasha's command unleashed an offensive in May 1930 against Kurdish insurgents in Ararat, but failed to contain the uprising, which quickly spread into neighbouring provinces of Van, Bitlis, Iğdır and Diyarbakır. Throughout the summer of 1930, a state of war existed between the Turkish army and Kurdish rebels with intermittent fighting in Mardin, Siirt and Urfa. When the Kurdish forces, having exhausted their local remedies and initial impetus, ultimately surrendered, Ankara saw the solution in further centralization, and enacted on 5 May 1932 the Public Inspectorships Law (*Umum Müfettişlik Kanunu*), followed by the Resettlement Law (*İskan Kanunu*) in 1934.[32]

With its snowcapped mountains and narrow valleys at the heart of Eastern Anatolia, Dersim remained to be the last autonomous enclave that the Turkish state failed to consolidate into central government control by the mid-1930s.[33] Inhabited by a large number of small tribes, which had always enjoyed quasi-independence since the Sultanate of Rum, Dersim was a culturally distinct part of Kurdistan with its ethno-religious and linguistic peculiarities.[34] Approximately 65,000 people lived in Dersim at the time, almost exclusively adhering to the heterodox Alevi sect of Anatolian Shi'ism (as opposed to Sunni Kurds), speaking in a different vernacular known as Zaza. Despite the perpetual conflicts among the tribesmen, which often turned into protracted feuds, established norms of Zaza customary law provided fertile ground for commoners to form an ostensible polity that refused to pay taxes and evaded conscription.

In 1936, a state of martial law was proclaimed (*1936 Dersim Kanunu*) with an explicit goal to pacify and civilize the Zaza.[35] Within twelve months, Turkish authorities launched a military campaign to preempt an imminent rebellion in Dersim, the chief conspirator of which was an 82-year-old religious leader, Seyit Riza.[36] Military operations to subdue the rebellion, despite a more resolved and better-equipped Turkish army, continued throughout the summer of 1937.[37] Even after Seyit Riza's surrender, summary trial and execution accompanied by that of several other conspirators, the insurgency resumed on a greater scale prolonging the war into the spring of 1938 with the arrival of new reinforcements from Syria.[38] A significant consequence of the previous Kurdish rebellions had been the emergence of Turco-Persian and Turco-Syrian conflicts in the late 1920s and early 1930s, with mutual recriminations over the Kurdish question. The Turks had accused the Persian and Syrian governments of explicitly aiding the Kurdish rebels and allowing them to use their territories as bases for attacks against Turkey. With regards to Iran, in the early 1930s, the Soviet Union had offered its services as a mediator between Ankara and Tehran, successfully resolving the dispute between the two, which would later be cemented by the Sa'dabad Pact in 1937.[39] The irreconcilable differences between Ankara and Damascus, however, lingered on throughout the latter half of the 1930s, and the Kurdish encampments in Syria became the backbone of contention between the two nations in the Dersim Rebellion of 1937–8. The state of crisis that emerged during the Dersim Rebellion culminated in the form of mutual hostility on the eve of World War II, and led to Turkey's annexation of Hatay in 1939.

What began in the early 1930s as low intensity conflicts across the Syrian border between Turks and the Kurdish-Armenian bands of several hundred insurgents gradually became larger skirmishes.[40] In 1933, Turkish intelligence reports indicated that several of the defeated Kurdish rebels' sons and relatives defected to Syria in pursuit of running the resistance movement from Aleppo, Beirut and Alexandretta. Among them were men of certain reputation, such as Kürt Cemil Pasha's sons Mehmet Ferit, Bedri and Kadri, who reportedly offered their services to the French Deuxième Bureau.[41] In November 1935, a series of joint Kurdo-Armenian conferences were held in Aleppo and Alexandretta under the aegis of the Italian embassy. Co-chaired by Mustafa Şahin, the Kurdish member of the Syrian parliament, and Balyan Papazyan, editor-in-chief of the Armenian newspaper *Astane*, the conference reached important decisions with regards to the future of anti-Turkish resistance in Syria and laid out the blueprints of a new assistance network for Dersim.[42] Turkish intelligence in Syria monitored Kurdish conferences and compiled detailed accounts of the supplies smuggled into Turkey, including guns, bullets, bombs, poems and propaganda materials. These were later apprehended by Turkish authorities before reaching their destination.⁴³

It was at this point that a big Kurdology Conference was convened in the Armenian SSR, which caused great excitement in Turkish circles. Although this conference did not pursue any political goals, and was simply devoted to the creation of a new Kurdish alphabet to fight illiteracy among the Kurdish population of the USSR, the Turks saw in it a big threat to their policy of denationalizing the Kurds.⁴⁴ The Ankara government expressed their doubts that, under the veil of linguistic scholarship, a political action could ignite feelings of unification amongst the Kurds inhabiting various neighbouring countries. In response, the Soviet government took measures to ensure that the conference was strictly limited to a Soviet Kurdish audience and aimed at 'improving the Kurds' native language and culture without jeopardizing the Soviet nationality policy'.⁴⁵ Although the Turkish government was not entirely mollified, Soviet policy toward the Kurds of Armenia was, to a certain degree, tolerated until World War II.

In June of 1937, as the Dersim rebellion was at its apex, the Turkish consulate in Beirut reported that several hundred Kurdish insurgents, who had sought asylum in the Soviet Union after the Ararat uprising, were forced out and returned to frontier towns in northern Alexandretta, closer to the Turkish frontier.⁴⁶ Throughout the summer of 1937, the Turkish Prime Ministry received similar reports, alerting the Turkish government to incoming waves of insurgents, who caused public disturbance and obstructed security forces. The straw that broke the camel's back came on 30 August 1937; after receiving another such consular telegram from Damascus, the Turkish government raided a convoy in Alexandretta and captured the new Khoybun leader and youngest son of Sheikh Said – Haco Mehmed – whose car was driven by a Syrian MP of Armenian descent.⁴⁷ The Turkish government delivered several diplomatic notes to Damascus during the course of 1937–8, accusing both the French and Syrian authorities of openly abetting Kurdish separatists in Turkey.⁴⁸

From Alexandretta to Sa'dabad

As Turkey's relations with Syria gradually worsened during the late 1930s, France began negotiating with the Syrians on their independence, including a change in the status of the Sanjak of Alexandretta. Turkey immediately put pressure on the French government to implement the 1921 Ankara Treaty clause concerning the inclusion of the Sanjak within Turkish borders. The Gulf of Alexandretta, located on the easternmost tip of the Mediterranean, had a vital geostrategic value but beyond that, it took on a new symbolic meaning after the loss of Mosul in 1925. Both Mosul and Alexandretta were included in the National Pact (*Misak-ı Milli*) of 1920, which emphasized the indivisibility of Anatolia against imperial designs, but was left unresolved at the diplomacy table in Lausanne. With an independent Syria in the offing, and bitter memories of the Mosul dispute not quite forgotten, Alexandretta became a priority for Turkey's ailing leader in his remaining years.

Turkey's annexation of Alexandretta, which occurred in stages between 1936 and 1939, was a peculiar episode in international relations.⁴⁹ What triggered the dispute over the status of the Sanjak, or district, was the signing of the Franco-Syrian Treaty of Alliance on 9 September 1936, which guaranteed the independence of Syria within three years. Alexandretta, however, had been governed by a different administrative regime based on the Franco-Turkish Ankara agreement of 20 October 1921, where the two signatories agreed that Turkey would also be a guarantor state within a broader French mandated Syrian territory. The Franco-Syrian Treaty of 1936 made little mention of the Sanjak's status, but simply indicated that the safeguarding mechanisms of the Ankara agreement would be preserved under independent Syria.[50] When the draft Treaty was published on 10 September the Turkish representative at the League expressed his government's apprehension with regards to Alexandretta's Turkish population and stated that while the safeguarding clauses had been adequate in 1921, France must now sign a separate agreement with Turkey based on 'changing circumstances' (*rebus sic stantibus*) and transform the Sanjak into a separate demilitarized zone with its own Statute and internal autonomy.[51]

Initially, France rejected this proposal on grounds that this would be an unjustifiable dismemberment of Syria and left it to the League to resolve the problem. During the course of the next few months, Turkish and French authorities intermittently discussed this matter, while the League agreed to send a special *rapporteur* to Alexandretta for conducting research on the Turkish claims, particularly on those pertaining to demographics. In January 1937 a second round of Franco-Turkish talks opened in Geneva and produced a draft resolution that granted Turkey special rights in the Gulf of Alexandretta; changed the Sanjak's official language from Arabic to Turkish; established a tripartite Franco-Turkish-Syrian Treaty mechanism to safeguard tranquillity; accepted existing demarcation lines as the Sanjak's official frontiers; and determined a provisional Statute that would engineer Alexandretta's internal autonomy on issues such as local currency, constitution, and parliament.[52] Amidst heated Arab demonstrations, preparations for the establishment of a Provisional Government were taking place in Alexandretta, which became a distinct but not separate entity from Syria. The new regime was finally announced in November 1937.

In December 1937, Ankara made a further move, after docking a steamer in the Gulf, opening up a bank, and repudiating the former Syrian constitution, replacing it with a Turkish draft.[53] The Turkish foreign minister, who was visiting Geneva, protested the Syrian government's refusal to accept the electors' own expressed choice of community in voter registrations.[54] Turkey demanded new demographic studies to be conducted (existing ones still fell short of showing the Turks as a majority) and during the spring of 1938 an ethnicity-based voter registration system was put in place by Turkish and French Authorities.[55] On 4 July 1938, the Franco-Turkish Friendship Treaty was signed, signalling the coming into being of the final interbellum state.[56] The new Hatay State replaced the Sanjak of Alexandretta on 7 September 1938, two months before Mustafa Kemal's death. During a parliamentary session on 29 June 1939, the short-lived independent Hatay State reached a unanimous decision to become a part of the Turkish Republic.

In Western scholarship, the whole incident was generally portrayed as a 'crude example of power politics by Turkey, a regrettable yielding by France of Syria's rights in her own interest, and a resented blow to Syria', whose claims were overridden and weakness abused.⁵⁷ Yet for Western historical actors involved in the affair at the time, such were the grim exigencies of the period; Turkey's friendship for France had been too valuable to risk in return for gaining Syrians' respect by defending their territorial integrity. Hence, Western public opinion was divided as newspapers debated whether the Sanjak affair meant an unnecessary dismemberment of Syria, or a justifiable act by Turkey to protect the Turks of Alexandretta, which constituted an ethnic majority. What led to this confusion was perhaps Turkey's precautious diplomacy of resolving the dispute by strictly following the legal procedures and devices provided by the Covenant of the League of Nations.

Admittedly, relations between the Turkish Republic and Syria during the French mandate had never been friendly and still bore the scars of the Great War. But the Alexandretta dispute dominated Syrian political thinking and emotion throughout World War II, agitated youth movements in the country and the League for National Action, and gave cause for bitter disputes from within Damascus politics with mutual accusations of half-heartedness. The League for National Action propagated rumours through party newspapers that Turkey would eventually attempt to invade the entire Syrian state, either through an alliance with Nazi Germany or simply by the Anglo-French bloc's ineptitude and disregard, as witnessed in the case of Czechoslovakia.⁵⁸ Under these circumstances, there was a growing sense of sympathy for *fasci di combattimento* among the young Arabs, as Mussolini reached out to Syria with a rhetoric indulgent of Arab nationalism.⁵⁹

In order to shield its prize, Turkey thus turned to Iran and Iraq as potential partners for a regional security structure, and to Great Britain and the Soviet Union as potential sponsors.⁶⁰ The result was the Sa'dabad Pact of 1937, otherwise known as the Oriental Entente, which turned out to be another source of friction between Ankara and Moscow.⁶¹ What facilitated the Pact's success was Turkey's diplomatic sondage in the Middle East, particularly with Iran in the early 1930s. There was much in common between the centralizing governments of Turkey and Iran. Scholars have long held the view that both Mustafa Kemal and Reza Shah's modernizing policies, as well as their means of implementation, were in a sense a reaction to a widely felt need for authoritarian reform.⁶² The process of political and cultural centralization, which was flavoured with secularism, Westernism and meritocratism, generally enjoyed the support of many members of the Turkish and Persian intelligentsia, especially those with progressive and left-wing leanings. The ideological overlap between Iran and Turkey certainly had a positive impact on their diplomatic exchange, which became closer throughout the 1930s.

As far as Iraq is concerned, having cleansed itself from the Mosul trauma, it had enjoyed good relations with Turkey since June 1926, when King Faisal visited Mustafa Kemal to sign the Iraqi border treaty and gave assurances for curbing Kurdish insurgency in Iraq. Turkey continued to expand its network around the Iraqi border through official visits by Imam Yahya of Yemen and Ibn Saud of Nejd and Hejaz in 1927 and 1928 respectively.⁶³ In February 1929, representatives of Ibn Saud visited Turkey and agreed to sign a treaty of good neighbourly relations. Turkey also exercised a strong influence in Afghanistan, sending teachers and a military mission there and receiving Afghan students.⁶⁴ A turning point in Turkish–Iraqi relations came in 1930, when Iraq signed a treaty with Great Britain, which would end the British Mandate within two years. The wording of the agreement was drafted with caution, securing the latter's rights in Iraq by keeping the RAF bases intact.[65] Britain was also bound to come to Iraq's aid in case of war, and Iraq pledged to consult with Britain on foreign policy issues. In 1932, when Iraq gained formal independence and was admitted to the League of Nations, these diplomatic and military privileges granted to Britain became a problem and nationalist opposition in Iraq flared up. Consequently, Prime Minister Nuri al-Said and King Feisal sought to reduce Iraq's dependency on Britain by improving their diplomatic ties with Turkey and Iran.[66] Under such circumstances the king and his prime minister visited Turkey in July 1932, which opened up an extended round of foreign ministerial talks that would take place at the League of Nations in Geneva between 1932 and 1936.

Nevertheless, there were three problems that postponed the signing of a tripartite security alliance between Turkey, Iraq and Iran. First, the border dispute between Iran and Iraq over Shatt al-Arab became a protracted headache that Turkish diplomats found too exhausting to mediate. Second, the Turks were acutely aware that the absence of British involvement would render the treaty practically ineffective, which was diametrically opposed to what the Iraqi government had in mind. Third, the Turkish diplomats frequently consulted with their Soviet counterparts to preempt their possible objections and, at times, even encouraged their participation, which seemed unacceptable for Iran. Regarding the third obstacle, the Turkish government was more eager and more involved for reasons that ran parallel to their alliance with the Soviets.

The Soviet ambassador to Turkey, Yakov Suritz, remarked during a conversation with his successor Lev Karakhan in 1932 that the Turks regretted the difficulties between the USSR and Iran. It was such a pity, he said, that relations could not be as close as they were with the Turkish nation.[67] In reply, Karakhan observed that 'the Persians, I'm afraid, have a much harder time dealing with us than the independent Turks ... You see, Mr. Minister, the English carry much more weight in Iran than you think'.[68] The Soviet leadership had gone to great lengths in seeking support of Ankara, to nudge Tehran closer to the USSR. At one point, Foreign Minister Tevfik Aras himself coaxed the Persian leaders into concluding the same sort of political protocol with Moscow, which the Kemalist government had signed.[69] 'Relations between Iran and the Soviet Union', Aras argued in Tehran, 'ought to be as those existing between Turkey and the Soviet Union. Iran should relate to the USSR with more trust'.[70] Much to Aras's dismay, however, relations between the Soviet Union and Iran deteriorated, if anything, with armed conflicts in the Soviet–Iranian border.

In December 1933, Turkish and Soviet diplomats probed possible scenarios for a Near Eastern Non-Aggression Pact (*Yakın Şark Ademi Tecavüz Misakı*) together with Iran, Iraq and Afghanistan. The project failed as the Iraqi government insisted on the inclusion of Great Britain, which was reluctant, claiming that a possible Soviet–Japanese conflict in the Far East might drive home unwarranted results.[71] But in 1937, as the conclusion of a security alliance in the Middle East became a matter more of necessity than of prestige, the Turkish foreign minister set out to mediate the border disputes between Iraq and Iran as well as those between Iran and the USSR more vigorously. He knew only too well that the answer for both of these third party disputes was to force the Shah's hand for concessions. Subsequently, Tehran became his frequent destination in 1936.

In the aftermath of Aras's successful mediation of the Iran–Iraq border dispute, the three countries decided to invite both the Soviets and the British to join the pact, hoping that their conflicting threat perceptions would balance out. While the Soviet government indicated its willingness to enter into the pact, Britain was reluctant to go forward with it. Ultimately, it was decided that neither of the two Great Powers would be invited to take part in the pact, with a last-minute inclusion of Afghanistan on Turkey's request. Yet, Turkey was careful to show that the pact was not directed against the interests of the Great Powers. This concern was reflected in Aras's speech at the Parliament in June 1938, as he made it clear that the draft treaty for the Oriental Entente had in fact been concluded 'with the assent and support of both Soviet Russia and the British Empire'.[72] On 8 July 1937, the foreign ministers of Iran, Iraq, Afghanistan and Turkey signed the alliance treaty at the palace of Sa'dabad, in Tehran.

In geopolitical terms, the four states that made up the Oriental Entente all lay on a thin grey line that separated the respective spheres of influence projected by the Soviet Union, a continental power, and Great Britain, a naval power. As a chunk of earlier Soviet security designs against Britain, which broke away from its origins and launched out on its own, the Pact became a precursor to the Northern Tier of the Cold War. Strictly from the signatories' perspective, the Pact would be governed in theory by ideas of non-interventionism. In practice, however, this proved to be too quixotic a goal to achieve collectively since all four of the signatories had different policy considerations that separated them. A second problem, which became clear at the onset of World War II, was that members of the Pact lacked the necessary military power, even with their forces combined, to undertake commitments to each another in the case of an attack, for instance, by a Great Power. While the Oriental Entente possessed little credibility in practice, it nevertheless had such merits as freezing border disputes among the member states and providing breathing space within the Middle East by successfully concealing wartime troubles in each member state from spreading out. Leaving aside minor customs violations and smuggling, the Pact helped the Turkish state maintain friendly relations with Iraq and Iran during World War II.

From the Soviet perspective, however, the consummation of the Oriental Entente without its full consent became a forebear of the ill-fated Baghdad Pact of 1955. The stark realization of a westward-moving Turkey darkened the already pessimistic picture in Moscow. Although the Sa'dabad Pact did not really amount to an imminent threat against the Soviet Union, Stalin was acutely aware of Great Britain's underlying desire to contain the Soviet sphere of influence on their southern frontier.[73] Stalin saw Turkey's new role and active diplomacy in the Middle East as a direct extension of Mustafa Kemal's revisionism that had surfaced in Montreux. While the Soviet printed press initially sought to put a good face on Turkey's position during the Sa'dabad negotiations and emphasized 'Mustafa Kemal's respect for the Kellogg-Briand Pact of 1928', Stalin was perplexed by Prime Minister İsmet İnönü's resignation barely two months after the signing of the Oriental Entente.[74] In October 1937, two weeks before the inauguration of the Ankara train station, Mustafa Kemal and İsmet İnönü had a heated exchange, which resulted in the latter's resignation. Turkish newspapers began circulating rumours of a dispute over Turkey's foreign policy orientation as the main reason behind their quarrel. Apparently, İnönü had strong reservations about Turkey's new security agreement with Great Britain in the Middle East and abandonment of their benevolent partnership with the USSR.[75] Ever since the 1932 Soviet–Turkish exchange, İnönü was regarded as a closer friend of the Bolsheviks; therefore, Stalin considered his resignation as a bad omen for bilateral affairs.[76]

Sailing towards war

As World War II approached, it became increasingly hard for Moscow and Ankara to maintain their interwar friendship. Aras's 1937 Moscow visit did not cement inter-state cooperation in the ways that each side hoped, and in some ways, it was plagued by the same tensions that had been present since Montreux. Moscow continued to insist that a contractual and more committed relationship was needed. Ankara, in its new position as sole custodian of the Straits, refused to pledge itself to an open-ended military defence of the Black Sea, whereby Turkey would be charged with the heaviest burden and other littoral states would reap the benefits.[77] But Turkey's reluctance to sign a pact did not negate hopes that the Moscow visit would improve relations. Soviet internal correspondence reveals that Aras was active – he spoke 'incessantly for a period of three days' and 'consumed cognac in immoderate amounts'. The Soviets, however, saw this talk as empty rhetoric, doing little more than confirm the basic principles of Soviet–Turkish friendship.[78] Moscow's impatience did not breed implicit or explicit anti-Soviet feelings in Turkey, but it did create frustration. Soviet pressure for a written Turkish guarantee seemed particularly counterproductive because the Turks could not understand why the Soviets needed it after nearly two decades of friendship and recent Soviet-sponsored Turkish industrialization.

The optimism with which Turkey had prepared for Aras's Moscow trip was matched by the pessimism with which he and Kaya returned. On their journey home, the Turkish representatives did not hide their gloomy mood, and sat locked up in a cabin, barely speaking to the Soviet representative who accompanied them. Upon arrival in Ankara, the Turkish ministers asserted that the whole purpose of their visit had been 'to speak frankly with the leaders of the Soviet state', and that 'their inability to see Stalin, notwithstanding an undertaking by the Soviet ambassador in Ankara that was publicized in Turkish papers' was the crux of their resentment.[79] For several weeks after his trip, Aras barely saw Soviet officials, and on those rare occasions, he reminded them that Turkey now represented the interests of 100 million people, from the Dniester to the Himalayas, in which capacity it needed to be treated like a great power.[80] The extremes of this conversation were remarkably similar to the discussion surrounding Atatürk's visit to the Soviet embassy a year earlier – the sense that if only Turkey were treated by Stalin with the respect due, all would be fine – while hinting at a military threat should that respect not be accorded.

Yet in 1937, this was not merely a repetition of the earlier scenario. Soviet–Turkish interaction during the fall of 1937 was hampered by the appalling transformation in Moscow's political and diplomatic leadership. The Great Terror saw almost all of

Moscow's notable experts on Turkey purged, imprisoned or executed. In less than four months, the host of men with whom Ankara had been intimately acquainted but were now disgraced included Lev Karakhan, recalled from his position as ambassador in Ankara, and Andrei Bubnov, who had accompanied Voroshilov in the famous Soviet grand delegation to Ankara in 1933. Atatürk was deeply resentful of the treatment of people to whom he had shown personal favour in Ankara's *corps diplomatique* for nearly two decades. When he received the new Soviet ambassador Karskii, only weeks after Lev Karakhan's execution in September 1937, Atatürk told Litvinov that one after another, the Soviet officials who were recommended to him as persons deserving Turkey's confidence and esteem had been either disgraced or executed as persons inimical to the very government that entrusted them with their missions. 'Who, therefore, can I trust?' he asked Litvinov tersely.[81]

Even as the sources of tension grew, Moscow and Ankara managed to maintain something of the balance that had been achieved after Montreux. The Soviet Union responded with delight when İnönü ascended to the presidency in November 1938, immediately after Atatürk's death.[82] İnönü's pictures and biography appeared on the front pages of *Izvestiia* and *Pravda*, which published a series of laudatory blurbs on İnönü's statesmanship and heroic career as a general.[83] A fortnight after his election to the office, İnönü reshuffled the cabinet and replaced Aras with Şükrü Saraçoğlu as foreign minister, which was taken as another sign of İnönü's eagerness to rekindle Soviet friendship. Foreign observers did not fail to notice the continued improvement in Soviet-Turkish trade in 1938-9, when Turkish diplomacy progressively became more cordial towards the Bolsheviks.[84] Although the total volume of trade dropped from 13 million Turkish liras in 1937 to 11 million in 1938, Ankara and Moscow maintained the targeted net balance, while Turkey's exports to Germany fell 8 million lira short of imports.[85] In late 1938, Litvinov invited the Turkish Admiralty to visit Sevastopol and nearby Soviet ports as a sign of collaboration across the Black Sea.[86] Meanwhile, Ambassador Apaydın in Moscow was renegotiating the purchase of a squadron of bombers and fuel tanks for the army.[97] This deal was striking, as Turkey had asked for a similar transaction the year before, only for Stomonyakov to tell Apaydın that the Red Army was busy improving its own stockpile. Faced with Soviet refusal, the Turkish government had turned to Germany, but returned to the Soviet Union as soon as the latter was prepared to supply. İnönü yet again demonstrated his preference for Soviet connections over German dependency.

Remarkably, these struggles to make Soviet-Turkish cooperation work were undertaken by two governments that were a world apart in ideological terms. In private conversations with Turkish counterparts, Soviet leadership contended that, while Moscow would welcome any revolutionary state or reformist government in the Middle East, they would refrain from communist propaganda or agitation in those countries. The Soviet ambassador in Paris told Saraçoğlu that if, for example, the Bolsheviks wanted to, 'they could have easily converted the small Mongolian government in two days, but they did no such thing'.[88] Neither did the Turkish state hide its politics – it was harsh on communism, imprisoning prominent sympathizers and fellow travellers amongst the Turkish intelligentsia.[89] Yet even after Montreux and Sa'dabad, Turkish leaders continued to proclaim that they did not consider the Soviet

Union a menacing neighbour, nor did they suspect Kremlin-sponsored communist subversion through the eastern frontier. As the post-war environment became more perilous between 1936 and 1939, both states continued to display a shared determination to isolate the post-imperial space they shared from the Black Sea to the Middle East from the pressures of an international order that was dictated by what they often referred to as imperialism.[90]

3

The End of Soviet–Turkish Friendship

After the Munich Agreement between Britain, France and the Third Reich in September 1938, it became clear that Western Europe would remain hesitant to take action against Nazi aggression. The bitter silence after Germany's occupation of what remained of Czechoslovakia in March 1939 indicated French and British unwillingness to devise a collective security policy against the Anti-Comintern Pact. Soviet foreign policy was therefore adjusted to face the new realities – such as the Jewish diplomat Litvinov's replacement as foreign minister in early May 1939 to facilitate the Nazi–Soviet War negotiations.[1] The transition in Turkish diplomacy during the spring of 1939 was equally remarkable. The wheel had gone full circle, and Turkey established an unequivocal partnership with Great Britain and France.[2] Turkey's annexation of the short-lived Hatay Republic in 1938 bore a disturbing resemblance to Italy's occupation of Albania, and raised question marks in the West, of which the Turks were fully aware.[3] Curbing Italian expansion in the Balkans and cleansing Turkey's blemished reputation after the Hatay incident became an excruciatingly boring dilemma for İnönü, and the immediate result was Turkey's signing of separate agreements with Great Britain and France, which led to a discernible relapse in Soviet–Turkish relations.

But, until the Molotov–Ribbentrop Pact, the Soviet Union continued to be a source of Turkey's security, rather than a threat to it. As annexationist politics swept Europe in 1938, Turks and Soviets sought ways to establish a tangible collective security mechanism that would shield the Black Sea from similar intrusions.[4] The dismemberment of Czechoslovakia by Nazi Germany, disturbing as it was for Turkey, was still more or less remote, and the alarm in regard to an ultimatum to Romania, which followed almost immediately afterwards, proved to be false.[5] But the Italian occupation of Albania in April 1939 touched a more delicate spot.[6] For the greater part of the past two decades, Italy had been the chief enemy in Turkish eyes. By seizing Albania, Rome had become a Balkan power, thereby posing an even more alarming situation for Turks themselves as well as to those Balkan Allies to whom they had treaty obligations.[7] Despite the remilitarization of the Straits in 1936, Turkey's growing concerns over Italian mobilization in the Mediterranean paved the way for mutual assistance agreements with Great Britain and France in May 1939. Turkey's rapprochement with Western powers came at the expense of a predictable apprehension in Moscow.[8] Yet, Turkey's decision was premised on the common understanding in the spring of 1939 that there would soon be the announcement of a triple alliance binding the Western powers to the Soviet Union. Turkish records reveal that between April

1939 and the outbreak of war in Europe, Ankara pursued a quixotic mission of bridging London and Moscow. Only days before the signing of the Nazi–Soviet War Pact, the Soviet ambassador in Ankara had led Turkish diplomats to believe that a mutual assistance treaty was indeed possible.[9]

The Anglo-Turkish declaration of May 1939

Italy's invasion of Albania was a first step in a wider movement for the achievement of the expansionist aims of the Axis Powers, who were acting in collusion. By April 1939, the Turkish government was not able to predict exactly where the next attack would take place; but whenever and wherever it was going to be made – inland Greece, Bulgaria or Poland – the ultimate aim would be the joint domination of Europe by Nazi Germany and Italy.[10] Whichever of these two powers launched the attack, it seemed certain that the other would also be involved. This meant that the next act of aggression by either of the Axis Powers – regardless of the point of first assault – was likely to involve directly or indirectly all the powers bordering on the Mediterranean. In the spring of 1939, Turkey's National Security Service (MAH) was put on full alert against Italian espionage activities in strategic coastal towns of southern Anatolia. The MAH surveilled consular meetings and public receptions hosted by the Italian missions in İzmir and Mersin, and arrested several local handlers of the SIM (Italian Military Intelligence).[11]

The role of public opinion in escalating the Italo-Turkish crisis was quite significant. The dissemination of people's voices through newspaper columns signalled the coming of larger waves of press wars between Italy and Turkey. In the face of exacerbated hostilities, Italy's ambassador in Ankara visited the Turkish Directorate of Printing and Press, offering a mutual state intervention to attune a list of columnists from *Cumhuriyet* and *Il Giornale d'Italia* daily papers, 'who obsessively made inflammatory remarks, hindering the friendly relations between Italy and Turkey'.[12] While the Turkish Minister of Interior later expressed his shared discomfort on this matter, he also added that what disturbed him more was 'the exponential rise in the number of radio shows, broadcast by Turkish speaking Italian anchormen in Rome ... [and that] these programmes were now attracting a substantial audience in the tea houses of Izmir by entertaining the people with this or that Turkish song during public hours'.[13] Mussolini's verbal assurances on the Dodecanese islands proved to be hollow and failed to pacify the Turkish authorities. Bilateral relations rapidly deteriorated after the appointment of Italy's new Consul General to Izmir, Paolo Alberto Rossi, who organized the Fascist Club upon arrival and threw lavish receptions for the city's prominent businessmen, accompanied by recitals and plays performed by Turkish schoolgirls from the Italian Collegiate Institute in Izmir.[14] When Rossi raised the new fascist banner Regno Albanese, relations between Rome and Ankara were irreparably damaged.

In the summer of 1939, some Turkish columnists began to openly question why Italian radio stations were broadcasting Il Duce's propaganda in Turkish. Others suggested that these broadcasts alone would have been sufficient grounds for declaring *casus belli*.[15] Mindful of Turkey's growing distrust of Mussolini, British policy-makers sought to bring Turkey into a regional alliance that included Romania and Greece, constantly reminding Saraçoğlu of his commitments to the Balkan Entente of 1934.[16] Perhaps even more valuable than its naval bases or airfields was Turkey's manpower, which could easily be deployed in neighbouring regions, particularly in the Balkans. In his dispatch to British ambassador Sir Hughe Knatchbull-Hugessen in Ankara on 12 April, Foreign Secretary Lord Halifax wrote: 'His Majesty's Government consider of first importance that the Turkish Government collaborate in any project of common defense [and that] Turkey was much the most important country to us of the countries of south-east Europe, and it was imperative that we should do nothing to queer the pitch with her.'[17] Yet the Turkish Foreign Ministry insisted on a separate Anglo-Turkish mutual assistance agreement against Italy, since the conclusion of a treaty amongst all member states of the Balkan Entente would have strictly binding military obligations against a possible Nazi German attack.

On the eve of war in Europe, however, Turkey's commitment to the Balkan Entente become a recurring problem during the course of Anglo-Turkish negotiations in late April and early May of 1939. Britain was expecting solid assurances from Turkey in case of a German attack on Greece; yet Turkey was wary of openly antagonizing Hitler. During his intermittent meetings with Neville Chamberlain, Turkish Prime Minister Refik Saydam repeatedly said that Turkish policy had thus far been one of complete neutrality designed to keep the country as far as possible apart from international complications.[18] When trouble had spread to the Balkan and Mediterranean regions, however, Turkey had no longer been able to remain aloof without jeopardizing its own security. It was vital for Turkey that all states in the Mediterranean should be able to freely exercise their rights without any encouragement being given to ideas of hegemony. Under these circumstances, the government thought that the safest course to save Turkey from war would be through associating itself with those countries that were united for peace but which would not shrink from war if necessary. For that reason, Refik Saydam asked the National Assembly to approve the association of Turkey and Great Britain in defence of peace and security – an association 'directed against none and nourishing no aims of encirclement', but designed rather to ward off catastrophe of war.[19]

On 12 May 1939, the Anglo-Turkish talks concluded with a joint declaration, in which both parties agreed to oppose any aggression in the Mediterranean. In addressing the Turkish Grand National Assembly, Prime Minister Saydam described how consultations between the two Governments, undertaken as a result of recent disquieting happenings in Europe, had led to the declaration, which he then proceeded to read. After emphasizing the close and cordial nature of Anglo-Turkish relations, Saydam expressed his conviction that the Anglo-Turkish declaration, together with subsequent agreements foreshadowed in it, would help weigh down the scales on the side of peace. The policy of Turkey and its British ally was to keep peace and to attack the rights of no one: 'In pursuit of peace, the Turkish Government would continue to exert every effort; but they would not hesitate firmly to oppose by force of arms any threat to the common rights and interests of Great Britain and Turkey'.[20] Saydam concluded his speech by arguing that equally friendly conversations were proceeding with France, which would lead to the conclusion of an agreement similar to that with

Great Britain. He also added that the closest diplomatic contact was being maintained with the USSR and that Turkish and Soviet views were in complete harmony.

A crowded Assembly listened with close attention to the prime minister's words, manifestly conscious of the importance of the step that was being taken by the government. The British, Soviet and French ambassadors, along with representatives of all Balkan states except Bulgaria, were invited to observe the parliamentary talks and proceedings. Following the prime minister's speech, Saffet Arıkan, former minister of education, rose and emphasized that the joint declaration was not directed against any nation, and that Anglo-Turkish policy aimed at the establishment of peace. Arıkan's speech was followed by an oration from Fethi Okyar, the former Turkish ambassador in London. Okyar posited that Turkey's policy had hitherto been friendly with all nations, and especially with its neighbours, in order to create an atmosphere of peace, in which Turks could devote themselves to internal reconstruction.[21]

But events in Czechoslovakia, Romania and Albania had disturbed that atmosphere, and obliged all nations to take measures for their security and the defence of their frontiers. It was at this juncture that Great Britain, with whom Turkey had long been on friendly terms, proposed joint action against any attempt to disturb peace in the Mediterranean. 'In face of this proposal, and in view of the insecurity everywhere prevailing', argued Okyar in a tone that meant to flatter Britain, 'the Turkish Government could no longer maintain its attitude of neutrality'.[22] By accepting this proposal, Okyar continued, Turkey had ensured peace and security in the Mediterranean: 'Turkey's geographical position, its heroic army and fleet, joined with Britain's strength, could make perpetual peace in the Mediterranean certain.'[23] For Okyar, Turkey's action should not be regarded as hostile to any power, since it was taken in order to protect its frontiers. Because Italy had landed in a small Balkan country (Albania) that ought to belong only to a Balkan people and fortified those islands close to the Turkish coasts, Okyar concluded that: 'Turkey would no longer remain neutral; its interests and England's interests were now the same, namely, to preserve peace, and to prevent Europe and the Mediterranean from passing under the hegemony of one or two States.'[24]

Refik Saydam and Fethi Okyar's speeches at the parliament hinted at the emergence of a common spirit between Turkey and Great Britain – a message that could easily be misread as a pledge for a fully fledged alliance. Nevertheless, İnönü was more cautious. When the Anglo-Turkish declaration was made public the next day, İnonu asked Foreign Minister Şükrü Saraçoğlu to emphasize strongly that Turkey was still 'free of any binding obligations'.[25] A commitment to the British for Greece might have antagonized Nazi Germany, while a similar promise to Romania could have made the Soviet Union very unhappy. While Turkey hoped to pursue cordial relations with its allies in the Balkan Entente, in which Turkey's role would remain unchanged, Britain pushed for a further enlargement of the Entente, with Turkey fulfilling a more useful function as its leader. The lack of consensus between British and Turkish representatives thus postponed a binding agreement of any real substance. There was a prevailing feeling that the Anglo-Turkish declaration should be followed by a strengthening of relations with Soviet Russia, especially in light of the threat posed by Bulgaria, which should be induced (by dint of some pressure by the USSR) to give up its territorial aspirations and to enter the circle of peace.[26]

Potemkin–Saraçoğlu negotiations

By the late spring of 1939, although the Soviets were no longer the only pebble on the Turkish beach, İnönü desperately sought to ensure that the Soviet government still regarded the Turks as their allies. From the onset of Anglo-Turkish negotiations, Saraçoğlu kept the Soviet authorities in loop, informing them about Turkey's position and the course of bilateral talks with Great Britain. During this critical period that tested allegiances, Saraçoğlu's primary objective was to transform Turkey into a diplomatic bridge between the Soviet Union and the Anglo-French bloc. At the time, this seemed like the only viable option for Turkey to avoid an armed conflict and get the others to recognize its quixotic neutrality. On 28 April, two weeks before the Anglo-Turkish Declaration, Maxim Litvinov (soon to be replaced by Vyacheslav Molotov on 3 May) sent V.P. Potemkin, the Vice-Commissar of Foreign Affairs, to negotiate the terms of a non-aggression treaty with Şükrü Saraçoğlu. In fact, the Turkish–Soviet Non-Aggression Pact of 1921 was still in effect. It had been renewed twice – in 1925 and 1935 respectively– and further complemented with a bilateral trade agreement in 1927. Therefore, Potemkin's visit was more about repairing the friendly relations, which had turned sour after the turmoil in the Balkans.

As the Anglo-Turkish talks were being conducted, Potemkin and Saraçoğlu exchanged information with regards to their prospective negotiations, and each expressed the full satisfaction with the correctness and loyalty of the other's government. Potemkin said: 'the Soviet Government applauded Turkish understanding with Britain with regards to the Mediterranean turmoil'.[27] About the Balkans, they equally approved the Turkish attitude, though they thought it to be unduly weak where Romania was concerned. Potemkin emphasized the importance of doing everything possible to solve the Bulgarian and Romanian difficulty, and had promised Soviet support for this. The Soviet Government would use its influence with Bulgaria. Should Turkey decide to declare its support for Romania, it would be delightful for Stalin, Potemkin argued. Both had agreed as to the need for disposing of this question in order to strengthen the position in the Balkans and make it easier to clarify the position of Yugoslavia. The minister for foreign affairs had expressed agreement with the Soviets' point of view on two fronts: first, as regards the possible interpretation of the British guarantee to Poland as applying to attack by Russia; and second, regarding the application of the Polish–Romanian Treaty to all aggressors and not to the Soviets only.[28]

Meanwhile, Saraçoğlu emphasized that the Turkish and Soviet governments should find a way of bringing the British government in, and pointed out the disadvantage of remaining isolated in case of a general war. Potemkin agreed in principle to the advantages of a threefold pact (Britain–Turkey–USSR), but said that he would not like to be approached to join such a pact after the first two had concluded it amongst themselves.[29] Potemkin also assured the minister for foreign affairs that Turkey could always count on material aid from the Soviet Union. He asked the minister whether the Soviets could rely on Turkey's assistance if they joined Romania in a war against Germany. He replied that this would be impossible, unless the Turkish government could be sure of Bulgaria's response.

From the Turkish perspective, the concurrent negotiations with the Soviet Union and Great Britain were exhausting but fruitful. Following the Potemkin–Saraçoğlu talks, *Izvestiia* wrote: 'The declaration between Turkey and Great Britain is a valuable investment in the cause of world peace. [Potemkin] listened with pleasure and approval to the negotiations undertaken with France and England, and with hopes of strengthening the security dialogue between Turkey and the West in Moscow by directly getting involved.'[30] It was agreed that Turkey and the Soviet Union, despite their differences over the current Straits regime, 'shall continue their friendly relations and renew the 1921 bilateral treaty in line with the changing circumstances.'[31] Behind his diplomatic jargon, however, Potemkin's position in Ankara simply reaffirmed the Soviet Union's wait-and-see policy.

At this point, it is crucial to note that unlike the Turks, who had been dutifully informing Molotov about their negotiations with Great Britain, Stalin undermined the chances of a Turco-Soviet pact (which Potemkin had said the Russians 'greatly desired') by not disclosing anything about his ongoing talks with Hitler. It was no secret that the Soviets had been negotiating with Nazi Germany for some time, and the replacement of Litvinov with Molotov as Soviet Commissar for Foreign Relations on 3 May – actually *during* the Potemkin–Saraçoğlu talks – should have signalled to the Turks a reversal in Soviet foreign policy and the coming into being of a Nazi–Soviet pact. On 29–30 April 1939, when Potemkin met with Saraçoğlu and İnönü in Ankara, the Soviet representative had spoken about necessary steps to strengthen Soviet–Turkish cooperation with regards to the crisis in the Balkans in the face of growing fascist movements and Axis pressure. Less than two weeks after this meeting, however, the Soviet ambassador in Ankara, Alexei Terentiev, prepared a comprehensive report for Molotov on Soviet–German talks in Ankara, describing his 'fruitful dialogue' with the new German ambassador, Franz von Papen. According to this report, Terentiev had intermittently met with von Papen beginning with the conclusion Potemkin–Saraçoğlu talks on 1 May until the Anglo-Turkish Declaration of 12 May.[32] Terentiev argued that, in spite of his initial predisposition about von Papen, he now agreed with him, who apparently revealed that 'the Nazis and Soviets should put ideology aside and revive the Bismarckian Russo-German friendship period.'[33]

Relations with Nazi Germany

The Soviet Union and Great Britain were not the only states to get involved in Ankara's diplomatic intrigues in the spring of 1939, and certainly not the only ones trying to win over Turkey to their side. The signing of the Anglo-Turkish Declaration proved an undoubted setback to Nazi Germany. Hitler was acutely aware that İnönü saw a potential enemy in Italy and had been ordering his policy accordingly. The Balkan question therefore posed a tiresome conundrum. On the one hand, the Third Reich had to support the gradual penetration of Axis Powers in the Balkans through Italy, but it also needed to come up with solid assurances that this penetration was not a threat directed against Turks, who had already entered into conversations with the British government and reached a further stage than İnönü would care to tell Hitler.[34]

At this critical conjuncture, on 28 April 1939, Franz von Papen was appointed German ambassador to Turkey with an immediate mission of ending the Italo–Turkish conflict. Serving briefly as Chancellor of the German Reich in 1932 during Hindenburg's presidency and one of Germany's leading political figures, von Papen knew Turkey. Amongst the representatives of all belligerent powers in the crucible of wartime diplomacy in Ankara, few people matched his astute understanding of Turkish politics. This was so much the case that at times he even found himself at odds with Hitler and Ribbentrop, and failed to break Germany's preconceptions about old Turkey and new. Despite his extensive knowledge of Turkey, however, it would have been difficult for the German government to hit upon a more unpopular nominee for their embassy in Turkey.[35]

Franz von Papen's suspicious activities during his previous service in Turkey in 1917 as Chief of the General Staff of the 4th Turkish Army under General Liman von Sanders had never been forgotten and, at least initially, he was heartily distrusted and disliked. Observing the somewhat muted reception given in von Papen's honour upon his arrival, British Ambassador Knatchbull-Hugessen wrote: 'It can safely be conjectured that his reception here was something of a shock to him.'[36] As early as 1934, when von Papen somewhat reluctantly resumed his diplomatic duties in the service of the Third Reich, the Turkish Foreign Ministry received several reports from its diplomatic missions in Europe about von Papen's whereabouts and dealings.[37] On 21 July 1939, İnönü's fears about the new ambassador were confirmed when the Turkish ambassador in Switzerland reported von Papen's trip to Geneva and receipt of 'one million British pounds from a bank account for sponsoring anti-British propaganda in Ankara'.[38] Setting aside Hitler's rationale behind choosing von Papen, from the Turkish perspective, it also seemed incredible that the German Government should not have guessed that Anglo-Turkish negotiations were in an advanced stage. The Anglo-Turkish Declaration was made a fortnight after the arrival of their new ambassador. He and his embassy seemed to have been largely taken by surprise. Herr von Papen was known to have remarked on more than one occasion that he had arrived too late.[39]

Upon his arrival, Turkish intelligence held von Papen's İstanbul residence in Tarabya under close surveillance and reported that, while away from Ankara's eyes, the German ambassador met frequently with his colleagues from the Trabzon Consulate along with the Italian Consul Generals in Izmir and İstanbul, hosting them over prolonged dinner receptions.[40] Some of the intelligence reports go into such detail as describing von Papen's daily mood, when, for instance he was feeling angry, irritated, relaxed or happy.[41] After visiting President İnönü and having a thorough discussion of the general situation in the Balkans, von Papen apprised Ribbentrop that relations with Italy were decisive in determining Turkey's course of action towards a potentially stronger alliance with Britain.[42]

İnönü told von Papen that the mobilization of the Turkish armed forces as a result of Il Duce's speeches in 1935 and before the Abyssinian campaign had cost more than £30 million (Turkish). 'Turkey could not go on affording this,' İnönü added frankly. The occupation force in Albania, which had started with 20,000 men, reached 72,000 men by May 1939 – including heavy artillery, which, according to İnönü, 'was certainly not needed against the Albanians'. Some 100,000 men had been concentrated between Bari and Brindisi. Furthermore, the Italian press continued to describe the Balkan Pact as dead, further convincing Turks of a potential move against Turkey next. Under these circumstances, von Papen stressed the futility of Italy's half-hearted assurances and advised Ribbentrop to convince Count Ciano – Mussolini's son-in-law, who had just arrived in Tirana – to make a substantial reduction of Italian troops in Albania, which was a waste of manpower anyway. Von Papen also asked that consideration be given as to whether Germany's attitude towards the Balkan Pact could be clearly defined, since Turkey was 'well aware that the Dardanelles [could] only be attacked from the landward side and therefore [looked] on the Balkan Pact as a buffer zone, which [needed] to be safeguarded'.[43]

Soon after the signing of the Anglo-Turkish Declaration of 12 May, von Papen argued that if Nazi Germany's position in Turkey were taken over by Britain or France, their relations with the countries that lay beyond Turkey, including Persia, Iraq and the whole Arabian world, would be greatly jeopardized.[44] In von Papen's view, Nazi Germany should have preempted British attempts to win Turkey to its side and suggested the following precautions: first, the reduction of Italian forces in Albania to relieve Turkey of its concerns over the Italian presence in the Balkans; second, a mutual treaty of non-aggression with Ankara; and third, the return of Meis Island (Kastellorizo in the Aegean Sea) from Greece to Turkey, including a number of small islets that remain in the Turkish territorial waters.[45] The German Foreign Ministry did not take von Papen's report seriously. Ribbentrop noted that they counted on: first, the Turks' historical friendship with Germany; second, Turkey's reluctance to endorse a binding agreement with either Britain or the Soviets; and third, Germany's lucrative trade relations with Turkey.[46]

This last point is important since historians paid little attention to the dynamic import-export traffic between Nazi Germany and Turkey during this period, which had a considerable effect on the latter's course of wartime diplomacy between 1939 and 1941. Until 1933, the volume of trade between Turkey and Germany had barely amounted to £3,500,000 sterling per annum.[47] When Hitler came to power, in line with Reich economics minister Hjalmar Schlacht's New Plan, he began implementing a policy of spreading Nazi economic influence in the Balkans. A series of bilateral talks held in Berlin catalysed business with Turkey and ultimately turned the Third Reich into Ankara's main trading partner. The first round of negotiations began on 31 July 1933, two days before Paul von Hindenburg's death, when Turkey's ambassador in Berlin, Kemalettin Sami Pasha, paid a farewell visit to Adolf Hitler and Konstantin von Neurath, the Reich minister of foreign affairs. While there seemed to be mutual differences over Turkey's alliance with the Soviet Union, and Germany's relations with Mussolini, Hitler emphasized the importance of 'ameliorating bilateral ties between the two brothers-in-arms on economic grounds'.[48] Turkey's ambassador, Kemalettin Sami Pasha, was well known to German circles through his acquaintance with Wilhelm II during the Great War and later with Hitler. Thanks to his pro-German reputation, Sami Pasha was able to 'converse in a friendly manner with Hitler', who greeted him with a 'reception more flamboyant than that of Wilhelm II in 1914'.[49]

Upon Neurath's request, the Turkish minister of finance and future president Celal Bayar visited Berlin several times between 1933 and 1939 for trade negotiations. By

1939, despite the slight decrease in Turkey's volume of trade with countries that fell under Nazi occupation, the value of all imports from Germany rose to an astounding £20,946,837 – accounting for 55.3 per cent of all imports into Turkey for that year.[50] Likewise, the level of exports to Germany rose to an unprecedented £11,860,968 (43.75 per cent of Turkey's entire export market).[51] In his report to Viscount Halifax, Ambassador Knatchbull-Hugessen stressed that, while the United Kingdom's share of the import trade showed a slight increase to fourth place, 'Germany improved her usual predominant share even further'.[52] With regard to the export trade, Knatchbull-Hugessen ruefully admitted that, while the United Kingdom registered a slight increase, Germany was again the largest buyer.

With the eruption of hostilities in Europe, Turkey too began to look at Great Britain and France not only as potential allies against Italian revisionism but also as partners to subside Nazi Germany's share in Turkey's foreign trade. İnönü's plea to the British ambassador in Ankara – in almost identical terms to those he had made to the Soviets a few years earlier – is interesting for its note of anxiety. From his perspective, Turkey's trade with Nazi Germany was anything but a healthy relationship, and that 'if Turkey was essential to France and Great Britain, they must free her from this economic slavery'.[53] Indeed, İnönü had received several reports from the Trade Ministry, warning that Nazi companies were buying all sorts of goods in the market for a future dumping option that would lead to predatory pricing in the Turkish market and give the upper hand to Nazi monopolies.[54] The trade minister's report concluded that Nazi traders were stocking large quantities of goods, from raw materials to fruits, tobacco and cereals, in return for war materials which they never delivered on time. Looking at the minutes of İnönü's conversations with Ambassador Knatchbull-Hugessen and his repeated appeals to secure a trade agreement that would counterbalance the Nazis, it is striking to see how Turkey had changed a great deal since the previous World War, when the Ottoman government had been satisfied with strong economic ties with Germany.

The Molotov–Ribbentrop Pact

On 24 August 1939, the news of the Molotov–Ribbentrop Pact thus turned İnönü's national defence strategy upside down. Since most Turkish newspapers employed a government-oriented editorial line, they first tried to put a good face on the pact. Falih Rıfkı Altay of the official gazette *Ulus* wrote: 'The Non-Aggression Pact between Soviet Russia and Germany led everyone to profound amazement. While the ultimate result of all military and political negotiations between Great Democracies and the Soviets turned out to be a doubtful combination, it is not yet time to express conclusive views on this subject.'[55] Yet, once the news soaked into the public psyche, disillusionment became the predominant sentiment. Asım Us of the *Vakit* daily wrote: 'The past decade of European history has taught us that ideological promises and principles come handy in deceiving naïve nations; in practice, there is no belief, principle or ideology that cannot be sacrificed for material advantages. Bearing in mind Stalin's recent alliance with the fascists, Soviet intentions and insincerity becomes crystal clear.'[56] The few newspapers that managed to remain aloof from the government line used much stronger language. Yunus Nadi of the *Cumhuriyet*, for instance, argued: 'The statement of these non-aggressive obligations without any condition or regulation, so openly and unconditionally, is beyond comprehension. Under these circumstances, one is forced to believe that there are hidden motives behind this move. To accept that the Soviets, who split hairs over the little Baltic States, should give the Third Reich freedom of action all along the western and southern frontiers, is not just difficult, but inconceivable.'[57]

With Germany's launch of Operation Tannenberg, on 1 September 1939, Turkey watched with great apprehension as the Wehrmacht's annexed Western Poland and collected detailed reports on the *Einsatzgruppen's* violent march.[58] Yet as far as Turkey's own fate was concerned, the Turkish government was more wary of incurring the active displeasure of Soviet Russia by maintaining their pro-British position after the Anglo-Turkish Declaration in May. Soon after Britain's subsequent declaration of war on Nazi Germany on 3 September, İnönü and Saraçoğlu received the British ambassador for a long meeting so as to better understand Britain's new strategy against the Soviet Union.[59] İnönü expressed strong condemnation of Germany's actions and the folly of it from the Turkish point of view. He seemed quite anxious with regards to Poland's future, but more concerned about the next point of attack and the likelihood of that point being the Balkans. İnönü asked Knatchbull-Hugessen's opinion whether Stalin would remain neutral if, for instance, Italy became belligerent and, if so, would Stalin's attitude be different towards Germany?[60] The British ambassador replied that Stalin's policy would certainly be different if the war did spread to the Balkans, but that it was in the Soviet Union's best interest to remain neutral, at least for the foreseeable future.

After providing İnönü with solid assurances that Great Britain understood Turkey's desire to remain neutral and would provide Turkey with the war materials it needed, Knatchbull-Hugessen went on to outline the British perception of the Molotov–Ribbentrop Pact. The British ambassador was convinced that Nazi Germany's stocks of certain raw materials essential for war purposes – such as copper and chrome ore – were insufficient, and that its oil supply was unlikely to last more than five months under war conditions in Poland.[61] While Knatchbull-Hugessen reluctantly admitted that the conclusion of the Nazi–Soviet War Pact had radically changed the political situation and rendered the position of Poland more difficult, he was persuaded by their intelligence, which suggested that the Germans would be forced to maintain an increasingly large number of troops on the Siegfried Line in the West (a system of forts and tank defences with more than 18,000 bunkers and tunnels, built in 1938), making it impossible for Hitler to bring his blitzkrieg to a successful completion.[62]

As for the Soviet output, Knatchbull-Hugessen argued, 'it [was] difficult to see how Stalin could possibly obtain any material supplies from Baku under war conditions given the poor state of Soviet communications'.[63] Unless, therefore, the Soviet Union was prepared to reduce the standard of living of its own people and to sacrifice its own industry for Germany's benefit, the raw materials Moscow could supply to Berlin would be severely restricted in terms of both quantity and range. Knatchbull-Hugessen underlined the fact that there was also the question of transport, which had always been one of the principal limiting factors in Russian industrial development and trade.

Since most sea routes from Soviet Russia to Nazi Germany, other than those in the Baltic, were shut, much of the material Germany needed from the Soviet Union in its war efforts had to be shipped by rail from the distant south-eastern districts of the USSR. Knatchbull-Hugessen assured İnönü that, as long as the British sea blockade was maintained, neither the Germans nor the Soviets would be able to continue their plans of partitioning Poland.

As for the possibility of Nazi Germany receiving direct military assistance from Russia, the British policy-makers were certain that the Soviet Government's policy would be strictly dictated by absolute security; first, because Stalin could possibly not desire to help Nazi Germany increase its field of domination on the Soviet frontiers; second, because Knatchbull-Hugessen had reason to believe that Stalin's military and naval forces were not capable of any effective offensive; and third, because Stalin no doubt wished to see himself on the winning side. Looking at the minutes of this meeting, it becomes evident how gravely Britain underestimated the German–Soviet scheme in Poland. Chamberlain also miscalculated the repercussions of the Molotov–Ribbentrop Pact on the diplomacy of small states, particularly that of Turkey. İnönü had a much more pessimistic – and perhaps more realistic – picture of the course of war in Europe. As the Wehrmacht marched further into the outskirts of Warsaw, followed by the Einsatzgruppen, İnönü sought to maintain a policy that was still favourably disposed to Britain behind closed doors, but refrained from giving that impression too openly.

At the eruption of hostilities, the Germans were particularly eager to draw Turkey away from its earlier agreements with Britain. In view of this state of affairs, von Papen asked Saraçoğlu to consider whether Turkey would now wish to return to its proven policy of strict neutrality. The foreign minister, taken aback by the latest developments, let von Papen's observations pass unanswered. The ambassador then asked whether Turkey would consider the settlement of all economic agreements in Nazi Germany's favour.[64] With a fair amount of contempt, the foreign minister replied: 'Turkey might be a hundred times weaker than Germany, but it would have to reject a proposal of this kind'.[65] Saraçoğlu explained to von Papen that his government could not simply cancel existing trade contracts with other belligerent parties. If Turks no longer had the opportunity of buying in Germany, then they naturally could not supply Germany either. The Turkish Trade Ministry therefore decided to arrange for the export of that year's harvest to other countries by paying premiums.

Immediately after his meeting with İnönü and Saraçoğlu, von Papen assembled the entire German community in Ankara for a social gathering. Over 800 people accepted the invitation, making a remarkable impression on the Turkish press that, in contrast to the departure of all other foreign nationals, the German Reich citizens appeared inspired and had a strong and unshakable confidence in the future. On 1 September, von Papen requested a third meeting, this time with both İnönü and Saraçoğlu. Referring to the situation which had arisen, von Papen explained how greatly the recently concluded Soviet Pact had changed the balance of power in Europe, and 'into what a regrettable position he had maneoeuvred Turkey by participating in the policy of British encirclement'.[66] İnönü and Saraçoğlu both seemed very resigned and made no comments on von Papen's detailed statements as to why Turkey should revise its foreign policy so soon. İnönü merely broached the question of Turco-German trade relations and the problems arising from Germany's non-delivery of war materials. According to von Papen, the purpose of his latest discussion was to convince them that 'a revision of Turkey's political course had become urgently necessary in Turkey's own interests'.[67]

The gist of İnönü's remarks remained the same; that he most earnestly desired to keep Turkey out of any war; that if Italy were forced to enter the war, Mussolini would not be fighting for Nazi Germany's war aims but only for his own; that Italy's entrance would result in Turkey's vital interests in the Mediterranean being affected; and, consequently, he had little hope that Turkey would be able to avoid fulfilling its obligations in this respect. Franz von Papen tried to ease İnönü anxiety by suggesting that 'if Turkey chose to revert back to its strict neutrality, it would be possible for Hitler to dissuade Mussolini regarding an attack on Turkey'.[68] In conclusion, he asked İnönü to 'at least serve the interest of general peace and those of Turkey at the eleventh hour by using his influence for the final settlement of all problems resulting from Versailles'.[69] He added that neither the Führer nor the Reich would tolerate a further postponement of this long delayed settlement and that in such a general settlement Turkey's position might be greatly improved.

Saraçoğlu–Molotov negotiations in Moscow

The Nazi–Soviet War Pact profoundly disturbed Turkish policy-makers, who, upon hearing Hitler's blunt requests from von Papen, were compelled to design a new strategy from scratch. But even here, it did not seem that the Soviet Union had irreversibly transformed from friend into foe. Stalin had indeed kept Turkey out of the loop during his negotiations with Hitler on the eve of World War II, but, there was still a possibility for an improvement in Soviet–Turkish relations as late as 3 September 1939, when the Soviet leader pleaded with the Ankara government to sign a bilateral pact in defence of the Straits.[70] As Gabriel Gorodetsky aptly put it, Stalin was primarily motivated by realpolitik since the Soviet Union was vulnerable to British predominance in the Mediterranean, and, based on historical experience, he expected the blow to be delivered through the Straits.[71]

It was precisely at this point that İnönü sent Saraçoğlu to Moscow to see whether a new treaty of neutrality and friendship with the Soviets was possible.[72] On 21 September, Saraçoğlu announced his decision to go to Moscow and open up a second round of negotiations with Molotov in order to resolve all issues that remained on the table since the Potemkin Talks. Over the course of the next several weeks, Saraçoğlu embarked on a futile odyssey to rejuvenate Soviet–Turkish relations, while also attempting to avoid exacerbating Anglo-Soviet tensions. Conversely, what Molotov sought to accomplish was simply to turn the disturbing clauses of the Montreux Convention to USSR's advantage.[73]

On 22 September, four days before the opening of Soviet–Turkish talks, the Turkish Foreign Ministry received Moscow's annual report concerning the size of USSR's Black Sea Fleet (*Chernomorskiy Flot*). Article 18 of the Montreux Convention required all Black Sea littoral states to provide non-littoral signatories with an accurate profile of their naval power in the region. Soviet Ambassador Alexei Terentiev's report indicated an alarming increase in tonnage, from 62,678 to 73,290.[74] Until Terentiev's report, Foreign Minister Şükrü Saraçoğlu seemed to have an optimistic view of his mission as an intermediary between Halifax and Litvinov. Yet Halifax was worried about a possible British–Soviet contention over the Straits, perhaps even more so than a Turco–Soviet dispute, which to him seemed 'rather less complicated'.[75] Halifax conveyed Britain's firm position in a meeting with Saraçoğlu – that all parties to the Montreux Convention, including non-littoral ones, were now obliged to dispatch fleets to the Black Sea commensurate with the existing increase in Soviet tonnage.

As early as 22 September, in his letter to Mussolini, Hitler wrote: 'under these circumstances, Turkey would envisage a revision of her previous position', to which Mussolini replied, 'a new strategy on the part of Turkey would upset all strategic plans of the French and English in the Eastern Mediterranean'.[76] Reading German Ambassador von Schulenberg's notes, Ribbentrop got the impression that the Soviet Union tried to exert power on Turkey 'to dissuade her from the final conclusion of assistance pacts with the Western powers'.[77] Britain, on the other hand, saw the Saraçoğlu–Molotov talks as an emergency brake that might prevent Poland from getting further bogged down in its struggles with the Wehrmacht. Despite Britain's earlier prophecies of a potential Nazi–Soviet War collaboration in Poland (which Knatchbull-Hugessen had explained to İnönü on 1 September), Stalin's decision to delay the Polish campaign for two weeks until the Nomonhan victory against Japan in Mongolia, misled the British policy-makers into thinking that the Soviets might remain neutral to the German–Polish war after all.[78]

Six days before the Soviet invasion of Eastern Poland, Halifax asked whether Saraçoğlu could approach the Soviet Government and try to persuade them to send a certain quantity of light and heavy machine guns and ammunition to Poland. Halifax's message read: 'There was no limit to the quantity made available by the Soviets...and any quantity, however small, would be welcome.'[79] Although Halifax probably realized that the Turkish government might hesitate to undertake this invidious task, he nonetheless made it clear that it was in Turkey's best interest that Poland should not be overwhelmed. He thought that Turkey was the only country at the time that could make a friendly enquiry with the Soviet government. Evidently Halifax was also concerned about how the Turks could approach the Soviets without revealing the fact that Polish forces *were* in desperate need of arms (as if the Soviets were unaware). At the very least, Halifax suggested, if the Turkish government themselves felt disposed to sending some light and heavy machine guns and ammunition to Poland through Romania, their expenses would be compensated by Britain 'through some other sources'.[80] He regretfully confessed, however, that he was yet to approach the prime minister with a proposition of this sort. In view of Halifax's grasping at straws during those two weeks between Nazi and Soviet operations in Poland, his actions smack of rank amateurism.

Upon his arrival in Moscow, Saraçoğlu at first thought he was given a very warm welcome and felt positive about the upcoming talks. Soviet newspapers published columns hailing about the foreign minister's arrival, highlighting the fruitful cultural exchange between the two countries. Praising the new generation of Turkish artists, 'which produced works that stood in sharp contrast with their Ottoman predecessors' naïve romanticism', *Pravda* translated and published a series of selected short stories and poems of such young leftists as Sabahattin Ali, Sadri Ertem and Resat Nuri, 'whose realism reflected the virtuous soul of the Turkish peasantry and proletariat and posed a vigorous challenge to the religious retrogressive strand in that country'.[81] But as Saraçoğlu was shunted from opera to football game and boat tours on the Moscow River, his patience was gradually worn down until he refused to go anywhere unless Stalin saw him.[82]

Saraçoğlu's Moscow visit was unquestionably related to the exigencies of war and was a final attempt to return Soviet–Turkish relations to their earlier, friendlier footing. In their private conversations, up until Saraçoğlu's mission, Turkish leaders clearly hoped to maintain a triangular channel between Ankara, London and Moscow.[83] Saraçoğlu's sojourn in Moscow was prolonged because of Ribbentrop's visit for a private round of exploratory talks with Molotov.[84] This seemed unlikely to be coincidence. Saraçoğlu suspected that Molotov's invitation was a ploy to strengthen Moscow's hand in negotiations with Ribbentrop. On the rare occasions he was able to meet with Molotov, Saraçoğlu was vexed by the Soviet Commissar's impudence on the Straits question and by menacing references to occupied Poland as an example of the kind of fate that might befall Turkey.[85] Furthermore, Molotov insisted on a reserve clause that included Nazi Germany in a Soviet pact with Turkey, which Saraçoğlu firmly rejected. During Saraçoğlu's unusually long absence, Turkey's initial faith for a negotiated peace between Nazi Germany and the Anglo-French bloc had quickly faded. On 18 October 1939, President İnönü concluded a tripartite mutual assistance treaty with Great Britain and France, without even waiting for Saraçoğlu's return from Moscow.

On paper, the Soviet–Turkish communiqué signed on 17 October 1939 highlighted 'the positive change that had taken place in bilateral relations, which once again confirmed the strong friendship that existed between the Soviet Union and Turkey, and the shared desire of each government for the maintenance of peace'.[86] But in reality, the Turks were utterly frustrated by Stalin's treatment of Saraçoğlu, who manifested his disdain for the insolence of his Russian counterparts at every opportunity thereafter.[87] The coldness on the part of the Soviets became even more apparent with Stalin's extremely chilly reply to Saraçoğlu's friendly telegram on 2 October.[88] Some scholars suggest that Turkey gradually drifted away from the Soviet Union, as İnönü realized the impossibility of bridging Western powers with the Soviets, leading him to a state of distrust prevailing after the unexpected Nazi–Soviet War Pact. Others favour what Kemal Karpat calls the 'worn-out' Western view of Turkey and Russia as two arch-rivals. According to the latter, Turkey's intrinsic Russophobia was so great that 'she was ready to undertake any sacrifice to guarantee her survival'.[89] In fact, the two states had other, more technical and fundamental problems that ultimately interrupted the talks.

There are competing narratives in Turkish and Soviet accounts as to why the negotiations failed. Predictably, most Soviet accounts blamed Turkey for the failure, while the Turks accused Stalin. The difference in interpretation regarding the events of

October 1939 represents the extension of their irreconcilable policy differences. From the Soviet point of view, the struggle among the ruling circles of Turkey that took place over the course of 1939 was mostly about foreign policy orientation. Soviet historians would later argue that the supporters of the Anglo-French bloc held the upper hand, 'advocating the well-known Munich policy of appeasement' and concentrated all their efforts towards pushing Hitlerite aggression and fascism to the East against the USSR.[90] Conversely, İnönü contended that the Moscow negotiations broke down because the Soviet Government had made demands which ran counter to the two fundamental rules which the Turkish Government had laid down: first, that Turkey should not in any way interfere with the normal working of the Montreux Convention; and second, that Turkey should agree to nothing that would weaken the operation of the treaty which she contemplated with Great Britain and France.[91]

İnönü suggested that the Turkish government might continue to keep up the appearance of negotiations with Soviet Russia, but he evidently did not hope for any results and was utterly disturbed by the breakdown. He said that the Soviet Government, 'having felt themselves obliged in the interests of Germany', made demands that the Turkish government was in no position to accept.[92] Like İnönü, Refik Saydam failed to hide his disappointment about the Moscow talks and indicated that the main reason behind Turkey's negotiations with Russia was the latter's imposition of 'a completely new set of demands, which would jeopardize Turkish national security in the face of growing war pressure'.[93] Upon his return from Moscow, Saraçoğlu confided in Knatchbull-Hugessen about what he really thought went wrong and conveyed İnönü's message on possible outlets to contain the emerging Soviet-Turkish conflict, of which the Balkans now played an important role. Saraçoğlu thought that the Soviet government had hitherto gained 'cheap victories in Poland and the Baltic', but had been severely rebuffed by Finns and Turks.[94] After the break-up of Moscow talks, Stalin might well try to wipe out these two rebuffs by seeking yet another cheap success in Bessarabia. Saraçoğlu suggested that the Turks were inclined to tell the Romanians that, if they resist, 'Turks will render all possible support'. Yet he also added that Turkey's support could not be effective without British and French cooperation. He therefore asked Knatchbull-Hugessen whether the Britain would be prepared to cooperate with the Turks in resisting a Russian advance. Saraçoğlu finally said: 'Do not forget that it is highly probable that if the Russians enter Bessarabia, the Germans might decide to participate via Hungary. If you refuse to help us resist the Russians, we must obviously reexamine the whole position.'[95]

Molotov gave a speech at the Supreme Soviet on 31 October, which more or less encapsulates the Soviet perception of the reasons behind the failure of the Saraçoğlu-Molotov talks. Molotov argued: 'For the negotiations to succeed, Turkey had to comply with two Soviet requests ... First, in the case of war, no belligerent ships are to be allowed into the Black Sea. Secondly, the pact between the Soviet Union and Turkey could not in any way jeopardize Soviet Union's relations with Germany. Turkey declined to comply with these two conditions of the Soviet Union and thus made impossible the conclusion of any Pact.'[96] Looking at these two conditions, it becomes clear that the terms on which Turks sought to negotiate with the Soviets fundamentally opposed those that their own national security relied upon.

Molotov's second condition demonstrates his genuine attempt to dissuade Turkey from joining the Anglo-French Bloc. Hitler and Mussolini had indeed hoped to utilize a potential Soviet-Turkish Pact as a hook to pull Ankara away from the Allies. Much to Hitler's dismay, however, soon after the opening of Soviet-Turkish negotiations, Molotov revealed to the German ambassador that 'in all likelihood a mutual assistance pact with Turkey would not be concluded', for the simple reason that Saraçoğlu strongly objected to any bilateral revision of the treaty signed in Montreux.[97] For Molotov, the signing of a non-aggression pact with Germany on the eve of the war, 'although taken as a necessary precaution', provoked a pointless threat perception in Turkey and was 'blown out of proportion' by the 'reactionary press' in that country. Molotov further suggested 'only a few Turkish newspapers soberly appreciated the efforts of the Soviet Government to bring their country out of political isolation – an isolation that had been created by the Anglo-French imperialists'.[98] The Soviet narrative therefore claimed that England and France, even after the beginning of war, had not given up on their hopes of directing fascist aggression towards the Soviet Union.

From the Soviet point of view, aside from Turkey's demagogic popular press, Turkish diplomats also acted as *agent provocateurs*, disrupting the emerging normalization in Soviet-German relations. For Stalin, this tendency became self-evident particularly in the latter period of Soviet-Turkish negotiations: 'By October 1939,' Stalin remarked, 'the Turkish diplomats radically steered their country towards a Western oriented policy of sabotaging their friendly relations with the Soviet Union'.[99] Soviet newspapers observing the Saraçoğlu-Molotov talks also accused Turkish diplomats of stalling their Soviet counterparts for a treaty of mutual aid. *Pravda*, for instance, claimed that it was only after the conclusion of the Soviet-German Non-Aggression Pact that the Turkish Foreign Ministry responded to Soviet Union's friendly offer to complete the negotiations initiated by Vice-President Potemkin in April and decided to send a delegation under Saraçoğlu to Moscow.[100] A similar article from *Izvestiia* read: 'what the Turkish diplomats merely hoped to achieve at the Moscow negotiations was to gain time for the Anglo-French coalition, which was at war with Germany. They failed to meet the one condition our government asked of Turkey – stopping any belligerent power from entering the Black Sea through the Straits, which the Turks declined, thereby showing us their real intentions and return to old tactics.'[101]

Soviet officials seemed to acknowledge the fact that 'in war conditions, a pact of mutual aid between the two non-warring governments would have undoubtedly strengthened their security and alleviated the danger of military crisis in the Black Sea Region'.[102] Yet they further claimed that such a course of events 'was not at all desirable for England and France whose diplomacy had as its goal the sabotage of the Soviet-German pact'.[103] For this reason, Stalin argued, when the Turkish government began negotiations about an alliance, they were 'less interested in bettering relations with the Soviet Union and more interested in drawing the Soviet Union into that alliance with England and France, whose schemes of Soviet encirclement in the Middle East are well known'.[104]

Indeed, the effects of the Sa'dabad Pact on exacerbating Soviet-Turkish relations were profoundly upsetting for both Turkey and Great Britain. After Saraçoğlu's return from Moscow, Turkey immediately proposed a meeting of the Sa'dabad Powers – the Middle East defence organization established in 1937. Iran cried off, alarmed as to the effect of such a meeting with Britain upon Moscow. There was a certain degree of confusion in Afghanistan and Iraq as well – the latter particularly seemed apprehensive of Soviet intentions. The Iraqi prime minister reportedly advocated an alliance with Turkey to deal with an imminent Soviet threat. İnönü hoped that these conflicting points of view amongst the member states 'would not in any measure weaken the Sa'dabad Pact', which, in the eyes of Turkey, 'formed the best combination under present circumstances and the best foundation on which to build some more solid structure should need arise'.[105]

At the onset of war in Europe, Turkey began looking at the Sa'dabad Pact with a fair amount of pragmatism and sought to use its leadership in the Pact as a bargaining chip during the Anglo-Turkish negotiations. Looking at the correspondence between Halifax and Knatchbull-Hugessen, it is remarkable to see how İnönü's strategy actually proved to be fruitful. In his annual report on Turkey, Knatchbull-Hugessen argued that 'Turkey [was] the deciding factor' among the Pact members, and that, 'in spite of her laicism and treatment of the Caliphate, Turkey still [held] so central and so influential a position among the Moslem countries of the Middle East, both great and small'.[106]

On the domestic level, the worsening of Turkish–Soviet relations over the course of autumn 1939 had a commensurately negative impact on Turkey's perception of socialism and Turkish communists. On 12 December 1939, the minister of education, Hasan Ali Yücel, prepared a detailed report on communist activities among Turkish high-school teachers. The report indicated 'a radical increase in communist propaganda' in most Turkish schools since the outbreak of war, and urged the prime minister 'to take radical measures before the situation gets out of hand'.[107] In response to Ankara's accusations of Soviet-sponsored communist propaganda in Ankara, an anonymous Russian embassy staff member spoke to the Anatolian News Agency and claimed that Stalin and the Soviet government were consciously abstaining from such propaganda abroad.[108] By contrast, the Soviet official claimed, Nazi Germany was doing everything in its capacity to spread fascist ideas in Turkey and elsewhere. Indeed, the Turkish Customs Authority had recently discovered Nazi propaganda pamphlets and copies of Hitler's orations hidden in medicine containers shipped from Germany. The Turkish press was giving substantial coverage to these sorts of news, and the Soviet official had every reason to exonerate Moscow compared to more blatant agitations such as the Third Reich's.[109] But the Turkish ambassador in Kabul reported that 'the Soviets irrefutably reverted back to their imperial policy of anti-British propaganda in Afghanistan', and in collaboration with the Deputy Führer Rudolph Hess, the Soviet diplomatic mission sought to turn tribal allegiances in that country against England, by supporting the former Afghan foreign minister, Gulam Siddikhan.[110] As in Afghanistan, Soviet rapprochement with Nazi Germany, and hence with the aggressive revisionism that Turkey feared, challenged the very logic of Soviet–Turkish friendship and from that point on, bilateral relations steadily declined.[111]

The Tripartite Treaty

After the Red Army had crossed the Curzon Line into Poland, British policy towards Soviet–Turkish relations rapidly changed. The occupation of Kresy marked the beginning of a period, in which Great Britain reverted to its traditional policy of keeping Turkey in fear of Russian aggression in order to preempt the likelihood of a pact between the two – a policy that lasted until the breakout of the Nazi–Soviet War in June 1941. To achieve this, Halifax sought to expedite the conclusion of the long-delayed Anglo-French–Turkish treaty. This was probably the best time for Turkey to use its bargaining chips against Great Britain. Before leaving for Moscow, Saraçoğlu requested from Lord Halifax a credit of £35,000,000 for war materials, a gold loan of £15,000,000 for improving the country's dire economic situation, and £2,000,000 for clearing off the previous year's deficit.[112] Turkey's request was widely criticized in Britain at the time. While the British Cabinet attributed utmost importance to finalizing the terms of the 12 May Declaration in an official mutual-assistance treaty with Turkey, they found Saraçoğlu's request unreasonably high in return for a treaty, which would be rendered inoperable by a suspensive clause for the Balkans. Turkey had been meticulous about the wording of the draft treaty, abstained from any binding obligations for the Balkans' defence, and requested revisions from Britain ad nauseum.

None of the preliminary meetings that had taken place between Britain and Turkey since 12 May 1939 produced a workable draft, due to the latter's continued insistence on an addendum that would free them of any commitments to Greece and Romania. Ambassador Knatchbull-Hugessen had a difficult time explaining to Halifax what exactly Turkey was offering in return for the bullion. Another issue that bothered the British Cabinet was the amount of war materials that Turkey had requested. At a time when the British soldiers themselves urgently needed war supplies, it was unacceptable to give them to Turkey so unconditionally. Nonetheless, the British Cabinet was more convinced than ever that Turkey had to be on Britain's side, even if only in name, rather than side with Nazi Germany. The loan Turkey requested was a high price, but not high enough to pre-empt a potential accession of Ankara into the Axis. Besides, the British clearly understood that with the invasion of Poland there was enormous pressure on the Turkish General Staff, who feared that the defence of Thrace – Turkey's European territory – would not be possible. Thus came into being the Anglo-Franco-Turkish Mutual Assistance Treaty of 18 October 1939, that marked the beginning of a new era, in which Turkey found itself in the midst of war and drifting closer to the Allied encampment – albeit still neutral on paper.[113]

The trilateral treaty was regarded as a major diplomatic victory in Turkey. Yunus Nadi of *Cumhuriyet* wrote that 'during the [ongoing negotiations with the Soviet Union and Great Britain since April] Turkey's entire energy has been directed to avoid doing something that would harm others, especially her neighbours. She has done nothing more than to look to her security'.[114] It is also likely that the failure of the concurrent negotiations with the Soviets compelled the Turks to join the Anglo-French Bloc as soon as possible and at any cost. Receiving both war materials and a substantial gold loan, the Turks secured a treaty aligned with their security interests and foreign policy goals. Turkey would be actively involved only if it were attacked; if its allies were attacked, they simply promised benevolent neutrality.

Ankara's concurrent negotiations with the Soviet Union and Great Britain during the course of April–October 1939 gave a confusing message not only to the rival bidders but also to contemporary historians. Most historical accounts of this period portrayed Turkish diplomats as war profiteers, who were willing to negotiate their price, knowing that all belligerent powers fully appreciated the value of Turkey's strategic position.[115] Selim Deringil, for instance, makes a strong argument that 'the Turks, in their best bargaining tradition, knew they were needed desperately by Britain and thus exploited their position of strength between the two sides'.[116] Deringil further suggests that Turkey 'counted on the possibility of a further deterioration in world affairs' and hoped that 'things would be even more disadvantageous for Britain' on Saraçoğlu's return from Moscow, so that its financial terms might be accepted by the British Cabinet.[117] There is an element of truth in these observations insofar as Turkey indeed managed to capitalize on the contest among warring blocs for its allegiance and emerged fairly jubilant from the gravest world crisis since July 1914. Yet, war profiteering is too strong of a metaphor to explain Turkey's motivations in 1939 and overshadows Turkey's genuine struggle to mediate the growing gap between the West and the Soviet Union.

The conclusion of the tripartite treaty became a source of great apprehension in Germany. Ribbentrop immediately requested a meeting with Ambassador Hüsrev Gerede, warning him that, from the Reich perspective, the entry into force of mutual-assistance pacts with England and France thereby placed Turkey in the anti-Nazi front. Disturbed by Ribbentrop's bullying, the Turkish ambassador vehemently denied this and declared that the treaty was in no way directed against Germany. Ribbentrop replied that it was 'difficult for him to follow this reasoning'.[118] On the contrary, Ribbentrop reiterated, '[he] had the impression that Turkey's policy was chiefly directed against Germany'. In addition, Ribbentrop added, he received reports almost every day to the effect that Turkish policy had taken a predominantly anti-German line and seemed moreover to be very active. The Nazis thought of Turkish policy as an extension of the Foreign Office, 'it seemed at times even more British than Downing Street policy'.[119] The Turkish ambassador had little to say in reply.

In a subsequent meeting with the Turkish foreign minister, von Papen raised similar criticisms and suggested that the Reich government was always prepared to conclude a reasonable trade agreement with Turkey, particularly with regards to chromium transactions. He added that Germany 'could not but consider it an unneutral and therefore unfriendly act should Turkey gave in to British pressure not to deliver any chromium to Germany'.[120] He further suggested that the Führer could understand that Turkey might want to exchange this valuable material for foreign exchange, if possible. Therefore, Nazi Germany was even prepared to deliver war material in payment. Saraçoğlu said that he did not intend to cut the Germans off from the chromium supplies but was only awaiting the result of an investigation of the extent to which the chromium output could be increased in order to make him an offer.[121] Ribbentrop was aware that Saraçoğlu was simply trying to play for time, and found his counterpart's statements on commercial policy disappointing. The fact that Saraçoğlu wanted to do a chromium deal with Nazi Germany that was contingent on the result and investigation of the possibility of increasing the output confirmed the reports that the available supplies and the present output had been, or would be, sold to the Anglo-American camp.[122] Therefore, Ribbentrop asked von Papen to insist on a clear answer as to the truth of these reports or this intention; 'if they [were] true, further negotiations [were] pointless'.[123]

A perilous realignment

In the early days of 1940, a dreadful uncertainty haunted Soviet–Turkish relations. The problem owed more to Stalin's erratic treatment of Turkey's policy of sitting on the fence than anything else. There was hardly a moment in the winter of 1939–40 when serious hope of a permanent improvement in bilateral affairs could be entertained. On 4 January, Halifax drafted a general memorandum on the Soviet–Turkish conflict, in which he argued that 'Soviet ambitions [had] always been Asiatic rather than European', and that the past six months showed more logic and continuity in Stalin's eastern policy than Hitler's. 'With respect to Turkey', he added, 'the influence of tradition on foreign policy may be said to guide the former to a greater extent than the latter'.[124]

By 1940, British foreign policy-makers clearly thought that the real Soviet threat against British interests lay in the Middle East – Turkey, Iran and Afghanistan, with India as the prize – and possibly even further eastwards. From the Turkish perspective, however, it appeared more likely that the next Soviet step would be taken into the Balkans. İnönü was convinced that a Soviet move into Bessarabia, taken with or in spite of Germany, would lead to dire consequences in Bulgaria, spreading the conflict into the mouth of the Danube, thereby bringing the Bosphorus to the brink of war. In less than six months, a vast area of Poland had been seized and the Baltic States had fallen under Moscow's shadow. In November 1939 Stalin had proceeded further: having made clear that Finland was next, he then invaded. İnönü thought that these moves suggested a logical sequence and, if carried out successfully, they could ultimately be expected to reach saturation point in the west, after the recovery of the territories of the former Russian Empire. After all, the Turks regarded the Molotov–Ribbentrop Pact as an alliance, 'which was born out of pure opportunism', illustrating the tendency of revolutionary governments 'to revert to the traditional foreign policy of their predecessors'.[125]

Insofar as a potential Soviet incursion through Southern Caucasus is concerned, the Turkish General Staff created two new army corps in Eastern Turkey and increased their defences on the Soviet frontier. For some time, the General Staff denied that they had moved 'even so much as one man to the eastern front', although the British military attaché in Ankara had good reason to believe from 'other sources' that 'unostentatious precautions' were being taken.[126] This silence on the part of Turkish military authorities was due to the firm policy of avoiding the smallest action likely to offend the Soviet government. By January 1940, however, the minister for foreign affairs informed the British ambassador that Turkish forces in the northeast were being gradually and unobtrusively increased. Even so, it was not until February 1940 that the Turkish General Staff admitted this.

In his dispatch to Halifax, Ambassador Knatchbull-Hugessen noted that the Turkish confession was important, as it constituted proof that things had now reached a different stage, whereby the Turkish government realized that the danger of a Soviet move in the spring was sufficiently concrete to render it necessary for them to set to one side their concerns about offending Moscow. During his private meetings with the British ambassador, Saraçoğlu again admitted that 'in the eyes of the Turkish Government and of the General Staff, Germany [was] regarded as a remoter enemy and their attention was certainly directed towards the Soviet Union'.¹²⁷ In January 1940, İsmet İnönü carried out a number of extensive tours in the northeastern districts, accompanied by General Rauf Orbay – the commanding officer in the Black Sea region.

British policy-makers were acutely aware that wherever the Soviet drive forward would eventually be made – whether in South-Eastern Europe, through North-Western Iran into Iraq, or through Afghanistan in the direction of India – the strategic and geographical position of Turkey was such that it was impossible for the Soviet Union to execute any of these moves without devoting serious consideration to Ankara's reaction. Therefore, it seemed quite clear, both from past experience and from present circumstances, that the most effective safeguard against Soviet designs, wherever aimed, would consist in the development of the utmost strength possible in Turkey. Whether the Soviet threat came from the Balkans, or against Turkey herself, Halifax thought that the advantage of a strong bulwark in Turkey was self-evident both for its own sake and as a centre of attraction for neighbouring countries. 'If the threat came from further east, the stronger Turkey could be made, the greater would be the hope of putting spirit into the other members of the Sa'dabad Pact, and the greater the Soviet need for caution', Halifax claimed.¹²⁸

Whatever the state of Turkish mentality had been in the fall of 1939, when the Saraçoğlu–Molotov talks in Moscow ended abruptly, by the early spring of 1940 there was no doubt that Turkey would react most vigorously against a Soviet fait accompli to establish the USSR as a mistress of the oil fields in Iran and Iraq. If the French and British had been able to secure the Turks a reasonable scale of rearmament, or if Turkey had been able to trust British naval and air support in the Black Sea and Trans-Caucasus, İnönü would have easily regarded a move against Iran and Iraq – its co-partners in the Sa'dabad Pact – as a hostile act and would have taken steps accordingly. It was, in fact, in view of this very contingency that Turkey substantially increased its forces on the eastern frontier; and it was the officially expressed opinion of the Turkish General Staff that the Soviet Union could not dare to undertake a movement against Iran without taking steps at the same time to neutralize the Turkish eastern frontier with powerful forces. This plan seemed to have worked out well, since the Turkish ambassador in Moscow had reported in late 1939 that Russia intended to lie low and recuperate for the time being, and to abstain from further adventure.¹²⁹ Saraçoğlu's own opinion was that Soviet Russia would not be capable of carrying on any outside adventure until the late summer and even then he was doubtful whether she would be fit to do so. He shared this view with Ambassador Knatchbull-Hugessen and reiterated Turkey's confidence in his subsequent meetings during April–May 1940.¹³⁰

Hugessen got an even more confident impression from President İnönü, who described his attitude towards the Soviets quite candidly. He said: 'We do not want to go to war with the Soviets if it can be avoided.' He then went on to point out that their military plans in regard to the Caucasus were still in an embryonic stage, despite the approaching summer. If Turkey did engage in a war with the Soviets, it would be practically alone, as there was no arrangement for Allied help. He referred to the Aleppo conversations, saying that the British had only been prepared to discuss hypotheses. He fully understood this and realized that the British government had in the end been prepared to discuss all possible scenarios. The president then went on to indicate that, in his opinion, the Soviet Union was now standing off from close contact with Nazi Germany. He thought, therefore, that Turkey might still be of some service in drawing Soviet Russia further away from Nazi Germany and bringing her more into line with the Allies.[131]

Ambassador Knatchbull-Hugessen, for his part, was not quite convinced that it would be easy to get the Turks to undertake anything beyond defensive action against Soviet Russia, at all events, until they considered themselves fully equipped and prepared. When Knatchbull-Hugessen returned to what he had previously said about Turkey being at present inadequately prepared and still without organized plans for the Caucasian front, İsmet Pasha had Saraçoğlu translate this remark into Turkish, and immediately replied: 'We must make ourselves strong on land and in the air.' Given all pressing exigencies in France, Ambassador Knatchbull-Hugessen ruefully admitted in his letter to Halifax that İnönü was right, and 'what a pity it [was] that Britain could not commit [itself] to strengthening Turkey's defences.'[132]

4

Of Enemies and Neighbours

Turkish Foreign Minister Şükrü Saraçoğlu was having drinks with colleagues at Karpiç Baba, a famous Georgian tavern in Ankara, when he heard that Nazi Germany had invaded the Soviet Union. It was just after midnight on 22 June 1941, and Saraçoğlu, upon learning of Operation Barbarossa, is reported to have jumped on stage and danced to zeybek tunes until dawn.[1] For anyone unfamiliar with Saraçoğlu's personal scorn for Stalin, such behaviour probably seemed unbecoming.[2] But the foreign minister's reaction was understandable in the context of his most recent trip to Moscow, in September 1939, when he had lobbied in vain for a new Soviet–Turkish alliance. Saraçoğlu's actions were more than a personal vendetta and represented Turkey's position toward the Nazi invasion of the USSR, which many observers found unremarkable at the time. Ernst von Weizsäcker, for instance, later recalled in his Nuremberg prison cell that everyone expected the Turks to 'look on at [the Nazi–Soviet War] with folded arms and legs crossed'.[3] After four centuries of incessant warfare between the Soviet Union's and Turkey's imperial predecessors, it is understandable that von Weizsäcker saw the default nature of the two states' relationship as chronically hostile as inherently destabilizing. But both Soviet and Turkish records demonstrate that antagonism in Soviet–Turkish relations was not a product of natural hostility and that just a few years before the incident in the Georgian tavern, nothing suggested that Saraçoğlu would greet the news of the Nazi–Soviet War War in such transports of joy. His personal frustration with Stalin, after all, had emerged during an attempt to negotiate a Soviet–Turkish pact.

To assume that Turkey's volte-face in its Soviet strategy between the signing of the Molotov–Ribbentrop Pact and Hitler's unleashing of Operation Barbarossa was a logical step in its so-called 'active' diplomacy underestimates Nazi Germany's role in feeding Ankara's panic. In fact, the Nazis were prepared to see Turkey's association with the British and French as a measure born of necessity, and, after some initial concern, they seized the moment. Just after the Molotov–Ribbentrop Pact, on 23 August 1939, Franz von Papen called on the Turkish foreign minister to clarify Berlin's position in the changed circumstances. Alluding to earlier warnings, von Papen expressed his 'profound regret that Turkey was on the wrong side'.[4] The most significant implication of the Nazi–Soviet War Pact was that a blockade of the Axis powers by Britain was now almost impossible and that the balance of power in Europe had shifted in favour of the former. Hoping for a change in Turkish policy, von Papen also met with İnönü to present to him Hitler's 'sincere' view of the situation, 'which had now become entirely to Turkey's disadvantage.'[5] İnönü was greatly distressed by the Nazi–Soviet War Pact, but maintained that Turkey would act in accordance with what it considered to be its vital interests. If the Balkans and the Caucasus were unaffected, İnönü hoped to be able to remain neutral, but he saw no possibility of preventing conflict from spreading to the Black Sea. Ambassador von Papen, who successfully read between İnönü's lines, was now aware that one way of inducing Turkey into a pro-Axis neutrality was to aggravate Ankara's fear of Soviet aggression.

Nazi orchestration of anti-Soviet propaganda

Well acquainted with the ruling circles in his new post, Ambassador Franz von Papen could see that Turkey was not 'wavering between Germany and England like a shopper in the bazaars'.[6] Von Papen understood that Turkey was a silent ally of Great Britain and ultimately desired to see that country emerge triumphant. The Nazi ambassador's allegorical depiction of Turkish diplomacy might appear hyperbolic but it points to the anti-Soviet element that had become central in Turkish politics. After the Saraçoğlu–Molotov negotiations in Moscow, von Papen realized that the idea of a prolonged war was a nightmare for the Turks and that a Soviet threat would eclipse all other considerations. The Nazis were adequately informed about İnönü's persistent management of the country's press to manipulate public opinion and hence devoted efforts to this field.

Of primary concern was the Turkish Left's publication of pro-Soviet articles that might jeopardize relations with Nazi Germany. The Turkish Prime Minister's Office worked in tandem with the Directorate of Press to counter pro-Soviet publications, by either silencing anti-Nazi columns with new censorship laws or by enlisting an equal number of anti-Soviet headlines. In government-sponsored newspapers, for every pro-Allied coverage of the European theatres of war, a corresponding column from the pro-Axis perspective was juxtaposed next to it.[7] In a wide-ranging survey, von Papen informed the Nazi Propaganda Ministry that the official party newspaper, *Ulus*, presented a microcosm of Ankara's attempt to influence the public psyche. *Ulus* had a bi-fold editorial structure, chaired by Ahmet Şükrü Esmer and Falih Rıfkı Atay. While Esmer almost exclusively wrote pieces from a pro-Allied stance, Atay wrote columns more favourable to the Third Reich. Likewise, *Tasvir-i Efkar* and *Cumhuriyet* employed pro-Nazi columns, but were balanced by newspapers like *Yeni Sabah*, *Son Telgraf* or *Vatan*, which adopted a more pro-British discourse.[8]

As did the Turkish government, the Third Reich sought to sideline the pro-Soviet Turkish Left as one of its first tasks. The newspaper *Tan*, whose editor Zekeriya Sertel was a Columbia University alumnus and a socialist, was particularly problematic. Predicting that Nazi–Soviet War war was inevitable, Sertel emphasized the ephemeral nature of the Molotov–Ribbentrop Pact and pushed his newspaper into a vehemently anti-Nazi line.[9] Sertel published columns in *Tan* arguing that the Nazi propaganda service employed cunning tactics that would force the Ankara government to first silence the independent Turkish press and then drive a wedge between Turkey and the Soviet Union. In December 1939, he wrote an open letter to the Turkish government, making a case for 'how Turkey should take measures against Nazi propaganda at home'.¹⁰ He argued that the long-term goals of Nazi propaganda in Turkey were twofold: first, to spread pro-Nazi feelings among Turkey's scientists and academics, who would potentially raise future generations in that fashion; second and more important, to disrupt Turkey's good relations with its allies, primarily with the Soviet Union.

Sertel was right to focus on Nazi organizations in Turkey, for this was a key arm of their propaganda effort. The Auslands-Organisation (AO) set up chapters in Ankara, İstanbul and İzmir, all of which belonged to an umbrella organization led by the Landesgruppenleiter. The organizations subservient to the Landesgruppenleiter served various means, including assisting and sponsoring Nazi-sympathizers to publish local journals and newspapers; aiding anti-Semitic newspapers through various Nazi grants; networking for potential Nazis of Turkish citizenship; preparing regular reports that reflected the mood of the Turkish people vis-à-vis the Third Reich; monitoring bookstores in major neighbourhoods and observing their inventory to understand the reading habits of Turks who purchased foreign-language books; and supplying bookshops with anti-Soviet propaganda materials.¹¹ The İstanbul local chapter was the most influential one in Turkey; its members were also associates of older German social clubs such as the Teutonia Club, the German church, the Deutsches Nachrichtenbüro news agency (DNB), *Türkische Post*, and various German bars in Beyoğlu. The AO sought to manipulate Turkish public opinion by inviting people of interest to social gatherings, plays, balls, and exhibitions.

The Turkish government was by no means unaware of the breadth of Nazi campaign in the country.¹² The archives of the General Directorate of Security demonstrate that Turkish intelligence and security officers were closely monitoring the *Deutsche Schule* as well as several other Nazi institutions, including the *Türkische Handelskammer für Deutschland* and the *Deutscher Orient Verein*.¹³ According to police reports, by 1939, 150 of the *Deutsche Schule*'s 642 students were German nationals, and the school's board of trustees included such influential names as the director of *Deutsche Orientbank*, Paul Burghard, German maritime trading company Deutsche Levantelinie's CEO Karsten Meves, and Ernst Schiller, chief engineer of Wayss und Freytag, which had been commissioned to build weapons factories for the Turkish armed forces. Autonomous institutions also became centres of Nazi cultural propaganda, including the Deutsche Schule in İstanbul. And, indeed, the Third Reich's cultural propaganda in Turkey *did* provide pro-Nazi groups with outlets to express themselves. On the initiative of famous pan-Turkists – including retired Ottoman generals Emir Erkilet, Nuri Killigil (half-brother of the famous Enver Pasha) and Ali İhsan Sabis – a series of anti-Soviet seminars were held in İstanbul and a special anti-Soviet propaganda coordination centre was established.¹⁴ Erkilet and Killigil were frequently in touch with Nazi intelligence operatives in Turkey and were received by Hitler in Berlin after being treated to a tour of the Eastern Front in November 1941.¹⁵ Ali İhsan Sabis, on the other hand, was the chief editor of the *Türkische Post*, which reflected Berlin's official position with financing from a Nazi consortium that included the Deutsche Bank.¹⁶ Until his arrest in February 1944 during the so-called 'Racism-Turanism Trials',¹⁷ Sabis published pamphlets that critiqued the Turkish government's 'appeasement policy' toward the Soviet Union and a wrote an ardently anti-Soviet account of the Wehrmacht's offensive against 'the tyranny of Bolshevism'.¹⁸

Paradoxically, the Turkish Directorate of Press stifled newspapers that challenged the official policy of neutrality, while simultaneously trying to co-opt them to illustrate Turkey's equidistance to both Nazi Germany and the Soviet Union. This proved to be an arduous task. Scores of cables from Turkey's diplomatic missions in Berlin and Moscow demonstrate that Ribbentrop was levying all sorts of accusations against Sertel's *Tan* for exactly the same reasons that Molotov held the *Türkische Post* in contempt. Yet, rather than complying with Nazi or Soviet demands for tighter censorship regulations, the Turkish government effectively pitted opposing newspapers against each other by allowing a certain degree of freedom so long as Ankara's neutrality was not questioned.

In that sense, Turkey was not simply a stooge in Nazi or Soviet machinations. Contrarily, the Ankara government not only profiled pro-Nazi and pro-Soviet media outlets, but also managed to get several agents employed as translators and anchormen at foreign news agencies and radio stations in order to gather counterintelligence.[19] For instance, in order to find out the scope of Nazi propaganda in Turkey, Ambassador Gerede in Berlin personally endorsed a mission in July 1940, when approached by a retired Ottoman medical officer of Syrian descent who had been living in Berlin since the Great War and who offered his services to provide sensitive information from various Nazi circles that he claimed to belong to.[20] The fact that the Turkish government took proactive measures against Nazi propaganda challenges previously established notions that portrayed Turkey as having no agency.

Nazi propaganda means and purposes were ubiquitous and not exclusive to Turkey.[21] But with these institutions at work on the ground, the diplomats of the Third Reich did their best to amplify fears of the Soviet threat among Turkish political elites. When the Red Army marched into Bessarabia and Northern Bukovina, Ernst von Weizsäcker of the Nazi Foreign Office asked for a meeting with Hüsrev Gerede, the Turkish ambassador in Berlin. Weizsäcker insinuated to Gerede that Stalin might soon make a motion to revise the Straits regime. If an agreement was not reached, Gerede was informed that the Soviets might even come up with 'claims to Turkey's frontier provinces in Eastern Anatolia'.[22] Gerede had faith in the Turkish army and cited the Soviets' recent ordeal in Finland to cast doubt on the scenario, and he admitted that the Nazis might be playing on Turkish insecurities vis-à-vis Moscow. But, looking at the sparsely populated frontier towns in Eastern Anatolia, he ruefully admitted that the Soviets' Caucasian forces were far superior in terms of arms and manpower. With the absence of natural defences, such as Finland's ice-covered lakes, Gerede thought that Turkey's Eastern Anatolian plateau would not be able to withstand a potential Soviet offensive in the summer. The tone of these messages from Berlin was unquestionably fearful.

With Italy's entrance into the war in June 1940, the main problem Nazi Germany had to resolve was whether there was still a chance of keeping Turkey out of the war and the necessary means to secure Turkey's neutrality on the eve of the Balkan operations. While some quarters of the German foreign ministry suggested possible scenarios to paralyse Turkey's powers in order to preempt a possible accession to the British alliance, Franz von Papen favoured a different, diplomatic scheme to achieve this. In his dispatch to Ribbentrop, von Papen argued that the Turkish question was of decisive importance for Nazi Germany's fate and course of war in the Mediterranean and the Near East. For von Papen, carrying on war in this sphere of British hegemony without coordination with Turkey 'could rob the German army of final victory despite its heroic efforts'.[23] He got the impression that within Ankara's leading political circles, the desire to keep out of the conflict had grown considerably with the increase in German successes within the first half of 1940. Hence, he suggested that 'this chance should be exploited under any circumstances'.[24] Yet there was still a lingering question in von Papen's mind: would Italy be able to conduct its war against the hegemonic position of Great Britain and France in the Mediterranean without bringing the Balkans and Turkey into its field of operations and without in this way giving up important advantages that would help achieve victory? In von Papen's view, the answer was 'yes'.[25]

Not everyone in Berlin agreed with him. August von Mackensen – the 95-year-old prominent German monarchist who later became a figurehead for the Wehrmacht – thought differently. In von Mackensen's view, the Italian government was not in a position to give Turkey reassuring declarations to that effect. Von Mackensen regarded it as much more likely that Italy, together with the German government, would attempt to exercise strong and intimidating pressure on Turkey, rather than have its hands tied with assurances. Franz von Papen concurred with this observation but added that Turkish–Italian relations were such that any attempt at intimidation by the Italians 'would only achieve the opposite of the desired result'. He knew that Turkey still regarded Italy as a traditional enemy, and that, in spite of its unfavourable military position, Ankara would not hesitate for one moment to go to war against Italy if the latter challenged its national interests.[26] Hence, there remained two possibilities: first, Italy would smash Anglo-French dominance in the Mediterranean singlehandedly and without directly intimidating Turkey; second, it might be necessary to use an imminent Russian military action as a threat against a possible Anglo-Turkish alliance.

By July 1940, the latter clearly seemed like a more viable option. Von Papen thought that Nazi Germany could simultaneously stoke Ankara's dormant fear of Russia and offer on Italy's behalf similar assurances that Britain and France had offered Turkey in 1939 as the price for its accession to the Mutual Assistance Treaty. 'While one might not accord too high evaluation of her military forces', von Papen argued, 'Turkey still remains an extremely unpleasant threat to the flank of any operation against the British Empire in the Near East'.[27] But there was one key obstacle in achieving the desired scenario: Turkey's professedly Anglophile Foreign Minister Saraçoğlu, still peeved at the way he had been treated by Stalin in Moscow last October, but nonetheless willing to pursue an extremely cautious policy towards the Soviets in order not to antagonize them. Franz von Papen was convinced that Saraçoğlu had to go.

Ultimately, the Turkish ambassador in Berlin reported with consternation that his Nazi counterparts persistently inquired about the fate of the Tripartite Agreement between Turkey, France and Great Britain. Now that France seemed on the brink of collapse and Britain was grasping at straws, the Nazis were curious to find out whether Ankara 'felt obliged to assist France in any way, if not in the Balkans then in Syria'.[28] In subsequent meetings with von Weizsäcker, Gerede witnessed a discernible scepticism in his counterpart's references to Turkey's neutrality and urged his government to clarify their position vis-à-vis the Soviet Union, Nazi Germany and the Anglo-French bloc.[29] Gerede's experience was, in fact, only a precursor of what was to come. The Third Reich used these meetings to drive home the connection between diplomacy and public opinion. Ribbentrop instructed von Papen to urge the Turkish government to close down pro-Soviet newspapers and increase the number of pro-Nazi papers.[30] If the Turkish government could not be induced, Ribbentrop suggested that more financial aid could be extended to recruit more pro-Nazi journalists in the Turkish press. The Third Reich's agents were to be given full autonomy with regard to how and where this money would be spent, so long as more editors, columnists, and newspaper owners were brought on the Nazi payroll.[31] The culmination of this ambitious attempt to influence Turkish public opinion was a Nazi-sponsored conspiracy that succeeded in producing serious tension between Moscow and Ankara.

The Massigli Affair

A fortnight after the Nazi occupation of Paris in June 1940, the Deutsches Nachrichtenbüro leaked a telegram sent by the French ambassador in Ankara, René Massigli, to General Maxime Weygand of the French high command in Syria. The DNB claimed the Nazis had discovered a wrecked train wagon between Nevers and Loire, containing thick folders of French cables and sensitive information about Turkey's wartime position. Between 5 July and 12 July 1940, the DNB released Massigli's subsequent telegrams along with several other French reports, which were carefully woven into a coherent scheme that implicated Turkey in an anti-Soviet conspiracy. The coverage of the Massigli Affair in Soviet newspapers and radio broadcasts caused unprecedented tension in Turkish–Soviet relations, feeding Ankara's fear of Moscow's latent revanchism. As the Soviet Union mobilized troops in the Caucasus, the Turkish government watched with trepidation.[32]

The first telegram – dated 14 March 1940 – was René Massigli's summary of a conversation with Şükrü Saraçoğlu about a projected aerial bombardment of Baku and Batumi by the French air force.[33] In his report, the French ambassador informed General Weygand that Saraçoğlu would not create any obstacles in an Allied operation targeting Soviet oil fields. On the contrary, Massigli claimed, the Turkish foreign minister confirmed his assessment of Moscow's vulnerability in the Caucasus. Saraçoğlu was alleged to have revealed a recent cable from the Turkish ambassador in Moscow to the effect that the Soviet Government was anxious regarding their oil refineries and the time it would take to extinguish fires after an aerial bombardment due to the hazardous Soviet methods of extraction. The critical part of Massigli's telegram, and what seemed to truly compromise Turkey's neutrality, was a question Saraçoğlu posed regarding the radius of the French aircraft that would carry out the operation. Upon learning that French aircraft from Syria would have to cross Turkish and Iranian territory to reach Baku, the Turkish minister was reported to have asked, 'Do you then fear a protest from the Iranians?' The French ambassador apparently understood the Turkish government to have tacitly consented to opening their airspace to bomb Soviet territory.[34]

On 6 July, the DNB released Massigli's second telegram, which indicated that in the event of military action against Baku and Batumi, Turkey's neutrality should not be compromised.³⁵ Essentially, Massigli proposed an intricate *mise en scène* to prevent Soviet-Turkish armed conflict. French bombers would fly unnoticed from Jezira to Baku over a mountainous area stretching less than 200 kilometres between Lake Urmia and Lake Van. The proposed flight route was the safest for a covert operation since local villages in this region had become sparsely populated after the Turkish Army's systematic eradication of Kurdish rebels in 1937-8. To allow Saraçoğlu to profess ignorance, Massigli advised against sharing flight routes in advance – 'instead, an apology for airspace violation should be extended to the Turkish government either during or immediately after the operation'. Against a potential armed response from the Soviet Union, Massigli urged Weygand that the Ankara government should appear to be the victim of Soviet aggression and not the instigator of it. Massigli held that Turkey would be less harmed by a fait accompli rather than pre-existing intelligence.

Massigli's second telegram was more detailed than the first, and outlined a naval blockade of the Black Sea trading routes that the Soviets had been using to provide the Nazis with oil, food and other supplies. The French ambassador ruefully acknowledged that Black Sea naval traffic would be impossible to impede without Turkey's physical assistance. Massigli wrote: 'According to the [Montreux] Straits Convention, dispatching our warships and submarines would be possible strictly under the auspices of the League of Nations and only if Turkey feels itself in imminent danger ... At this point, none of these extenuating circumstances have been vocalized by Turkey.'³⁶ Therefore, it seemed quite possible that the Soviet Union would regard any naval undertaking through the Straits as casus belli against Turkey. In other words, Massigli thought that France should be prepared to offer military support to the Ankara government most rapidly, since a Soviet-Turkish War would be inevitable in this scenario. Whatever French and Turkish intent, the telegrams made abundantly clear Turkey's significance for the Soviet Union's security.

On 7 July, the DNB published General Weygand's assessment of Massigli's initial reports. Transmitted to General Gamelin, Commander-in-chief of the French Army, and General Vuillemin, Commander-in-chief of the French Air Force, Weygand's telegram addressed a broad range of issues pertaining to Turkey's neutrality and cautious diplomacy. Weygand indicated that the scope and length of a possible aerial bombardment of Soviet oil fields had been studied thoroughly and that, from a purely strategic perspective, securing Turkey's active collaboration seemed neither plausible nor necessary. Ultimately, the French general strongly urged his colleagues that Turkey should not even be remotely implicated since the violation of Turkish airspace would be too costly an endeavour and that alternative flight plans could be found in order to execute the mission, 'such as for instance those that run parallel to the Aleppo–Nusaybin railway'.³⁷

Exacerbating Turkey's concerns about a hostile Soviet response, the DNB next released transcripts of a communiqué prepared by the French prime minister, Edouard Daladier. Two days before his resignation on 21 March, Prime Minister Daladier's hand-written report showed him desperately trying to contain Nazi-Soviet War collaboration. Daladier's earlier strategy to aid Finland in the Winter War had clearly failed by the time of signing of the Moscow Treaty on 13 March. Therefore, he welcomed Massigli's plan to ease France's troubles in the Western theatre through a two-pronged campaign in the East: against the Nazis on the Black Sea on the one hand, and against the Soviet Union in the Caucasus on the other. In his letter, Daladier instructed the heads of the French army and air force to devise a faster and all-inclusive operation plan against the supply routes between Soviet oil fields and the Third Reich. Daladier also proposed closer cooperation with Great Britain in a joint campaign against the Nazi–Soviet War bloc and suggested that, concurrent with the military operations, the Allies should incite nationalist propaganda among the Muslim peoples of Southern Caucasus. Here, too, Turkey's relevance was clear.

Finally, in the addendum to their 8 July issue, the DNB released a secret protocol between France and Great Britain, which laid out the details of an Allied operation against the Soviet Union through Turkey. According to this latest document, the French and British general staff agreed to establish a joint command centre to destroy 35 per cent of Soviet oil fields in a projected six-day aerial campaign, which would involve six squadrons of 100 aircraft, carrying seventy tons of incendiary ammunition and other explosives.[38] The estimated damage would leave the Nazi–Soviet War Commercial Agreement of February 1940 practically inoperable, easing the Allied war effort on the Western theatre. By the time the DNB published this secret protocol, the Massigli Affair was being discussed at breakfast tables across Europe and the Near East.

The Affair, which transpired only two weeks after the capitulation of France, seemed to be a blatant sign of Turkish aggression against the Soviet Union. A month before his removal from office by the newly formed Vichy government, Massigli drafted a public letter denying all allegations that he had ever requested Turkish permission for French airplanes to fly across Turkish territory to bomb Baku; nor, he stated, had the Turkish minister for foreign affairs ever consented to such an operation.[39] Massigli admitted that he might have prepared a report for General Weygand's eyes only, passed on some casually collected information about Baku, and made certain personal conjectures, but that he could never have informed the French government that Turkey had agreed to permit any operation against Baku, nor had he been authorized to seek such agreement.

Despite Turkey's attempts to put a good face on the scandal, behind closed doors panic overtook İnönü's cabinet. Faik Ahmet Barutçu – the owner of the *İstikbal* daily and Turkey's future deputy prime minister– attested to the Turkish government's fear as the Massigli Affair quickly unfolded. When Barutçu met with Prime Minister Refik Saydam on 6 July, the president's entire inner circle was desperately pondering courses of action that would contain the scandal. They were tormented by bitter radio broadcasts from Moscow, which echoed in every parliamentary meeting room. Barutçu noted that the Soviets were levying all sorts of accusations against the Turks, 'from backstabbing to collaboration in heinous imperialist plots'.[40] Meanwhile, Ambassador Haydar Aktay in Moscow admitted that he was struggling to maintain his composure as Molotov kept bombarding him with questions regarding the content of his conversations with the British and American diplomats.[41] Despite Aktay's best efforts, Molotov was certain that Saraçoğlu was complicit in the Allied scheme and kept asking Aktay whether the Turkish foreign minister had sent him instructions to inquire about Soviet fire-fighting capabilities in Baku.[42]

Members of İnönü's own cabinet also questioned Saraçoğlu's role in the scandal on account of his Anglophile inclinations. Atıf Bey, for example, bluntly told Barutçu that if a Soviet–Turkish war could be prevented by simply replacing Saraçoğlu, the Turkish government should consider sacrificing its foreign minister. Adopting a slightly sanctimonious tone, Atıf Bey added that 'Saraçoğlu had always been rather temperamental, unceremonious and frivolous', that 'by nature he talks too much', and was hence prone to disclosing sensitive information.[43] Amidst threats to his career, Saraçoğlu requested a meeting with the Soviet Ambassador Alexei Terentiev, who had been immediately recalled to Moscow after the scandal. Saraçoğlu urged Terentiev to reassure Moscow that during these critical times, the Soviets should trust Turkey's commitment to benevolent neutrality. Saraçoğlu maintained that the whole plot was von Papen's machination, his principal objective in Ankara being to drive a wedge between Ankara and Moscow by capitalizing on the uncertainties of war and by throwing Turkey under the bus.

Turkey's reaction actually testified to the French cables' authenticity. Ankara's official position was that the Massigli files were genuine, but that the DNB deliberately took them out of context, aiming to implicate Saraçoğlu in an anti-Soviet plot. By giving verbal assurances to the Soviet Union, Turkey hoped to keep things in perspective. Nevertheless, behind Ankara's brave face lay fear of a hostile Soviet reaction. In an urgent communiqué dispatched twenty-four hours after the DNB scandal broke, the Turkish ambassador in Moscow, Ali Haydar Aktay, weighed in on 'the dreadful impact of the Nazi publications', which appeared to him 'a very carefully crafted plot' to sever good neighbourly relations between Ankara and Moscow.[44] Ever since the Soviet victory in Finland, Aktay had been arguing that Stalin was 'pondering measures in the Balkans and in the Caucasus' in order to recalibrate the Soviet Union's southern security corridor, which meant that Romania and Turkey might be adversely affected by new mobilizations.[45] With the outbreak of the Massigli Affair, Aktay admitted that he was 'terrified of what might happen next', now that 'the Nazi scheme provided Stalin with a legitimate excuse to implement new designs on the Turkish border'.[46] In his initial assessment of the situation, Aktay quoted 'reliable sources', arguing that the Soviets felt justified in their suspicions of Turkey's neutrality and emphasized 'how fragile the situation had become'.[47]

Aktay reported with trepidation from Moscow that the Soviet Union had mobilized troops on the Caucasian border, moving 10,000 soldiers to Nakhichevan and Sokhumi from Tbilisi.[48] Countless rumours and an evident surge of anti-Turkish public spirit in Moscow convinced Aktay that 'a re-annexation of Kars, Ardahan and Artvin was in the offing'.[49] Furthermore, the Soviet agents were circulating propaganda materials in Transcaucasia with purposes of mustering an anti-Turkish and anti-Iranian coalition. On 11 July, for instance, the Turkish embassy received unconfirmed stories about the Turkish border patrol's downing of two of the five Soviet reconnaissance planes flying near the Borçka air base in Artvin. While the Turkish government ridiculed such allegations in their internal correspondence, rumours of a revived Soviet interest in Eastern Turkey were growing exponentially. Ultimately, the Turkish government dispatched reinforcements to the Kars–Ardahan border. From Aktay's point of view, even if one assumed that Stalin's invasion of Kars did not seem like a plausible scenario, 'the increased Soviet mobilization towards the Batumi checkpoint after the Nazi plot was petrifying'.[50]

What was more, Aktay feared that control of the Straits now became a prerequisite for Soviet interests since Massigli's telegrams implicated a broader fault line across the Black Sea. From various sources, Aktay gathered that Stalin was concerned about the Soviet Union's southern flank, but now that France had collapsed, his anxiety about Nazi designs in the Black Sea became more pronounced.[51] Hüsrev Gerede, the Turkish ambassador in Berlin, had recently endorsed Ambassador Aktay's forecast and reported that the Nazis also expected Stalin to reinstitute Soviet frontiers back to pre-1914 demarcation lines.[52] Any combination that involved British cooperation with either the Soviet Union or Turkey would have hindered Nazi plans beyond the Straits, and thus Hitler attempted to isolate them simultaneously by releasing Massigli's telegrams. Thus by August 1940, when Ambassador Aktay was recalled for consultations in Ankara, the main source of apprehension in Turkey was the prospect of a new Nazi–Soviet War understanding regarding the fate of the Straits.

Britain's grasping at straws

After the Massigli Affair, İnönü came to the conclusion that he could not expect from Great Britain the help that he had hoped for under the 1939 treaty if Turks were attacked, especially now that France had collapsed. The real pretext for İnönü's fear, however, was in effect based on changing circumstances with the Soviet Union rather than France. By 1939, Turkey could not have risked coming into the war on Britain's side unless Ankara was certain that London could come to its defence in the case of an attack either by Italy in the Aegean or by Germany through Bulgaria. By July 1940, with rumours of Soviet designs on the Straits, Turkey did revert to something of the old imperial attitude, at least in the sense that the Porte's foreign policy had been dictated by the Sultan's fear of Russia. Therefore, it seemed quite possible that Turkey would appeal to Nazi Germany to defend itself against a Soviet attack, just as it had in World War I. Hitler would have had every reason to respond to this appeal. In the first place, as long as the idea of the *Drang nach Osten* persisted in Hitler's mind, the Nazis naturally did not want to have the Bolsheviks established across their path in the Bosphorus; and, second, Nazi Germany would naturally be only too willing to detach Turkey from its existing connection with Great Britain and pose again as the protector of Turkey and the Near East against not merely Soviet but also British domination.

At a time when the Soviet Government were clearly manoeuvring for defensive positions against Germany on all fronts, the question of the Straits was bound to overshadow all other aspects of Soviet–Turkish relations since Stalin had long been known to regard the Montreux Convention with dissatisfaction. Alarmed by a potential Turco-Soviet conflict after the Massigli Affair, which might have exposed Britain's interests in the Middle East within Nazi Germany's reach, Viscount Halifax desperately sought to offer his services as arbitrator. Halifax knew that if İnönü's fear of the Soviets at any moment turned to panic, 'Turkey [could] very well perform a complete volte-face and enter into as close relations with Germany as she entered into with [Britain] last autumn'.⁵³ Winston Churchill's recent appointee, Ambassador Stafford Cripps in Moscow, was given instructions to secure reassurances from Stalin vis-à-vis friendly relations with Turkey with an attempt to preempt a German–Turkish dialogue. In his dispatch to Cripps, Halifax argued that the question was not whether the Turkish government would oppose Britain's wish to approach the Soviets on their behalf for reconciliation, but whether they could prevent the Soviet government from taking the initiative themselves, which would most certainly entail the question of the Straits since they had long been known to regard the Montreux Convention with dissatisfaction.⁵⁴ For Halifax, there were thus two courses open to the Soviet government. Either Stalin would attempt to frighten and weaken Turkey to the point of ceding to Moscow a preponderant share in the control of the Straits; or he would seek to gain some more modest share in that control by friendly negotiation and cooperation with Turkey against an eventual German attack.

Ambassador Cripps was of the opinion that the latter course would be the wiser policy, since the former might defeat its own object by driving Turkey to seek Nazi German protection – 'an eventuality, which Britain also must, in its own interests, do everything possible to avoid'.⁵⁵ Ambassador Cripps, however, warned Halifax that 'a further approach to Soviet Government on lines suggested [would] almost certainly be interpreted by them as *carte blanche*, and [would] encourage them to increase their demands and will create most dangerous dead-lock'.⁵⁶ Far from improving relations, Cripps thought that approaching the Soviet government would under these circumstances have had precisely the opposite effect and precipitated war in the Black Sea. But, either way, Cripps concurred with Halifax, that the Soviet government would undoubtedly aspire to some share in the control of the Straits, particularly after the latest scandal. It was therefore agreed that if the Turkish government were prepared to concede some modification of the convention in favour of the Soviet Union, there was a good chance of bringing about a Turco-Soviet rapprochement, thereby barring Nazi Germany's advance towards Asia Minor and at the same time weaning the Soviet Union off Hitler's influence.

If, on the other hand, the Turks were not prepared for this sacrifice, Cripps said that it would be folly to raise Soviet hopes in vain by promoting Turco-Soviet discussion. Broadly speaking, everyone already knew what Stalin wanted from such discussions, and it was worse than useless to 'bring him out into the open' if they merely 'brought him out on the wrong side'.⁵⁷ Both Halifax and Cripps realized that a renewed and positive refusal to reconsider the Straits regime would simply encourage the Soviet government to adopt a hostile course – with all its dangers for Great Britain. While Great Britain briefly considered a revision of the Montreux Convention to ameliorate Turco-Soviet relations, it soon became clear that Turkey was not disposed to accept a compromise, which did not take fully into account its difficulties for the maintenance of its full sovereignty, and entire political independence and security. In the existing uncertain situation, Halifax decided that it would be almost impossible to make anything more than an ad hoc agreement, and that the elements necessary for any long-term revision of the Straits regime did not, in fact, exist at present.⁵⁸ For Ambassador Knatchbull-Hugessen too, it was unrealistic to expect matters to proceed further without the Soviet government raising the Straits question, which involved the danger of a deadlock if the Soviet requirements went beyond what the Turkish government could concede.

The Turkish government was perfectly alive to this situation, as shown in Şükrü Saraçoğlu's reply to his British counterpart. Saraçoğlu told Halifax that, if the Turks agreed to allow *or* prevent passage of warships through Turkish waters, they would inevitably become the ally of the power to whose warships it allowed passage, and the enemy of the power to whom it refused it. None of the Straits' regimes over the previous 150 years had been strictly deliberated or governed. Although some had lasted for long periods in peacetime, all had been based on the relative strength of the Powers concerned or of Turkey, and they had been upset every time the international equilibrium changed.[59] The arrangements envisioned in 1936 at the Montreux Convention, however, went well beyond covering the contingencies of the moment and, from Turkey's perception, established the best regime possible. Naturally, the last thing Turkey wanted was to compromise its ultimate control over the Straits.[60]

Mindful of Turkey's unyielding attitude, Halifax asked Ambassador Cripps in Moscow to seek an early interview with Stalin to inform him that His Majesty's Government was anxious to do all it could to see a progressive improvement in the relations between Soviet Russia and Turkey, and that it would stand ready to place its services at the disposal of the Soviet government with this object in view.[61] At the same time, Halifax asked Cripps to make it plain that the modification of the Straits regime, to which Stalin had long been referring, was a matter of great difficulty and complexity. For their part the British considered that the most hopeful line of approach lay in the possibility that the Soviet and Turkish governments, in conjunction with the British, might recognize that they all had a common interest in protecting the security of the Straits against the ever-present threat of German and/or Italian aggression. Halifax urged Cripps to avoid making any concrete suggestions in regard to an ad hoc agreement between the two countries for the defence of the Straits, but merely an endeavour to elicit such suggestions from Stalin.

In his response, Cripps told Halifax that it was not possible for ambassadors to see Stalin except on the very rarest occasions; hence, he did not see any chance of another interview with Stalin under the present circumstances.[62] Cripps said that it was almost equally difficult to obtain an interview with Molotov and that he was still waiting for an interview he had requested three times. As for Halifax's attempt to act as middleman in Turco-Soviet negotiations, Cripps was much more averse to such ideas and considered it to be dangerous and unwise for His Majesty's Government to become involved. For Cripps, the most they could safely do was to let each party know that the other was willing to discuss the matter, indicating their own attitude, and then leaving the initiative to one of two parties. In his opinion, it was precisely the form of guarantee to which the Soviet government had persistently taken exception; in other words, the liability of some other country to decide when and how the USSR should be called in to assist. If there were to be any question of joint action by Russia and Turkey to protect the Straits, then the Soviet government would ultimately demand the right to take a full share in deciding whether and how that protection shall be given.

Ambassador Cripps must have been surprised when he finally managed to secure interviews with both Molotov and Stalin in early August to discuss the Turkish problem.

In his first meeting with Molotov, Cripps discovered to his regret that Molotov saw a fundamental deterioration in Soviet-Turkish relations. Molotov asserted that after the latest scandal, Massigli's disclaimers did not suffice to alter the essence of the alleged documents. As far back as early April, the Soviet government had complained of foreign aircraft sorties over Batum. While the Turkish government at first denied that any aircraft had come from Turkish territory, Molotov claimed that the Soviet government saw no substantial undertakings in Ankara 'to adopt measures to prevent flights of this kind in future'.[63] On the contrary, Molotov argued, the Massigli revelations convinced the Russians that the Turks even knew what kind of airplanes were to be flown over.

After his interview with Molotov, Cripps met with Stalin, only to discover that it would be futile to bring about a Turco-Soviet rapprochement. Cripps had initially thought that the Turkish government would welcome Britain's arbitration, and declared that he was prepared to play his part as one of the principal negotiators.[64] Having met Stalin, however, Cripps wrote to Halifax explaining that all his assumptions had proved to be incorrect, and that 'even if [he] could secure another interview with Stalin, to go to him again without a single helpful or concrete suggestion (after six weeks to consider his earlier remark) and with nothing but a request that he should hold forth afresh on his own attitude towards Turkey would merely be an irritant'.[65] Stalin's attitude towards Turkey had already been inspired largely by resentment at the *non possumus* red line adopted by Saraçoğlu when he had been to Moscow in 1939. In view of Massigli's alleged telegrams, Cripps told Halifax that he did not see how he could honestly pretend that the Turkish government were now very much more forthcoming. For Cripps, Britain should not hope to secure a betterment of Turkish government relations with Russia without their cooperation. He therefore suggested that the time had come to make this position quite plain to the Turkish government, and to intimate that failing a more helpful attitude on their part, Britain did not propose to do anything further.

The Massigli Affair and the ensuing crisis illustrate the ambition and limits of Berlin's anti-Soviet propaganda. The logical endpoint of the Massigli Affair and Ankara's fear of Moscow would have been Turkey's accession into the Axis, but Turkey remained neutral until February 1945. Ironically, the heart of Nazi Germany's propaganda success – Russophobia – was also the reason that the Nazi plot failed, for Turkey was not prepared to take steps that would provoke conflict with the Soviet Union. Although the Massigli Affair did not effectively amount to a state of war between Turkey and the Soviet Union, it was the nadir in a relationship that had begun to deteriorate since the Molotov-Ribbentrop Pact. By the same token, the Third Reich understood its limitations but hoped to further capitalize on the rhetoric of this imperial historical legacy. By November 1940, when Molotov and Hitler met in Berlin to discuss the fate of the Straits and the Soviet Union's possible entry into the Tripartite Pact as a fourth power, Nazi Germany managed to force İnönü's hand into mobilizing Turkish regiments in defensive positions on the Caucasian border against the Soviet Union. As the Turkish and Soviet armies moved closer to one another, on more than a few occasions shots were fired across the border.[66]

The Balkan turmoil

Following the heated summer of 1940, fear of Russia clearly came to the forefront of the Turkish mind; but in assessing Stalin's reaction to the Massigli Affair, İnönü decided that the danger was perhaps not as imminent as he had initially assumed. The course of events since the outbreak of war demonstrated that a major axiom of Stalin's policy was to avoid getting bogged down in the Anglo-German conflict as a belligerent on one side or the other, while at the same time doing everything short of that to favour Germany.[67] Japan's accession into the Pact of Steel on 27 September 1940 did not come as a big surprise to Stalin. Yet, the swiftness of the tripartite negotiations between Count Ciano, Adolf Hitler and Ambassador Saburo Kurusu *was* unexpected. The Turkish ambassador in Moscow, who observed Stalin's anxiety when the Pact was announced, contended that Molotov was greatly displeased by the fact that the preamble of the treaty agreement was presented to him only hours before its entry into force. Molotov was apparently taken aback by Ribbentrop's informing the Soviets so late and in such an insolent way. The Turkish ambassador was convinced that Great Britain would most certainly attempt to capitalize on the crisis between the Nazis and Soviets. Indeed, less than twenty-four hours after the signing of the Tripartite Pact, British Ambassador Cripps began lobbying in the Kremlin, trying to convince Molotov that the whole *raison d'être* of the Pact was to ultimately crush the Soviet Union. The Turkish ambassador, who met with Cripps immediately after the latter's meeting with Molotov, was informed that Molotov did not utter a single word during three hours and failed to hide his distress.

In any case, İnönü realized that the Russians would not join in any German pressure on Turkey, for fear of being involved in the war. To fend off Soviet pressure, Turkey thus needed to make it plain that it would resist any German pressure or conspiracy contrary to its policy of non-belligerence. In August–September 1940, suspension of Yunus Nadi's *Cumhuriyet,* arrests of Germans on charges of spying, the impending trial of a well-known German archaeologist on a charge of espionage, and amendments to the law concerning the stay of foreigners in Turkey increased precautions against Fifth Column activities.[68] By November 1940, İnönü was convinced that neither Germany nor the USSR wished to go to war with the other, but a conflict of interests between the two was becoming increasingly likely. This conflict was due to the threat of the growing German influence and the possible military menace in the Balkans; a menace that was of concern to Russia, Turkey and Great Britain.

Addressing the events that transpired since July, İnönü delivered a three-hour speech at the National Assembly in November, the most salient points of which concerned the turmoil in the Balkans. He admitted that Turkey's attitude of non-belligerence made it impossible 'without exception' for belligerents to use Turkish territorial waters and airspace against each other, and that Turkey would continue to make such use 'categorically and absolutely impossible' as long as it took no part in the war.[69] In the midst of global turmoil, there lay ahead 'a long period of suffering for the people of the Balkan Peninsula', with which the Turks shared a common destiny.[70] In view of Axis incursions in the Balkans, the British ambassador in Ankara once again urged London to take action in the Balkans in order to retain Turkey's partnership.[71]

In some quarters of the British parliament, the decision of the Turkish government to remain neutral after France's collapse and Italy's entrance into war inspired doubts as to Ankara's loyalty to the tripartite treaty. These doubts were increased by the refusal of the Turkish government to plainly state their position in the event of an Italian attack on Greece or a Nazi invasion of Bulgaria. But, as British ambassador Knatchbull-Hugessen later confessed in his letter to Eden, the Turkish attitude on these occasions was accepted as indicating a difference of method rather than of actual policy. Furthermore, the British government quickly realized that, in its existing state of unpreparedness, 'Turkey would have been a liability rather than an asset as a belligerent ally', and it was thought advisable not to press the Turkish government too far.[72]

On the eve of the Greco-Italian War, it became more important to weld the Balkan states into the fabric of the dam that Great Britain was now singlehandedly constructing against the Axis. Turkey resumed its conventional role as an intermediary amongst disputing Balkan nations. But there were serious obstacles, which eventually proved to be insurmountable. The main problem was that all the Balkan states distrusted Bulgaria, and none of them seemed inclined to sacrifice much to improve the position.[73] Without Bulgaria, the Balkan formation was insecure but its inclusion could be brought about only by concessions. Gafencu, the Romanian foreign minister, although opposed to any immediate concessions to Bulgaria, did not seem entirely adverse to some ultimate accommodation.[74] By the time Italy entered the war, Saraçoğlu was considering a solution whereby Bulgaria could be brought at once into the Balkan Entente, in return for an undertaking that a settlement of the Dobrudja problem would be made when hostilities were over. It was at least essential that Romania kept the door open.

Nevertheless, as Ambassador Knatchbull-Hugessen later recalled in his memoirs, both Turkey and Great Britain 'were doomed to disappointment'. In a public utterance in August 1940, Georgi Kioseivanov, the Bulgarian foreign minister, restated his country's claims to Dobrudja with more than usual emphasis. This might have been a manoeuvre in internal politics, as Knatchbull-Hugessen claimed, since 'it seems always admissible to make the most outrageous statements on foreign issues, provided they are labeled to be consumed on the premises'.[75] But the result was a serious setback with regards to Romania's position. By September 1940, after Germany had forced Romania to cough up territory to Bulgaria and Hungary as part of the Vienna Award, the Romanian minister would hear of no concessions whatever and never lost an opportunity to say so during his visits to Ankara. Kioseivanov's official visit to the Turkish capital was followed by Romanian foreign minister Gafencu's within a few weeks. Knatchbull-Hugessen had hoped to get an early word with Gafencu, and, above all, to have that word before his Bulgarian colleague could speak to him. Alas, Knatchbull-Hugessen was foiled. When they met and Knatchbull-Hugessen put to him the essential importance of doing something to enable Bulgaria to join the Balkan Entente, he was horrified to find that 'the Bulgarian had already presented him with a *non possumus* in the most categorical terms'. Knatchbull-Hugessen said: '*this* was only to be expected of him'.[76]

In fact, there had been a weak ray of hope in 1940 when the Balkan Entente held another of its annual conferences. Signs of solidarity and cooperation had emerged and rather pointed overtures had been made to Bulgaria, who was kept informed of what passed and given to understand that there was a place ready for her at the Balkan table.[77] Turco-Bulgarian relations, disturbed by misunderstandings caused by Turkish troop concentrations in Thrace, had also been mended and both Saraçoğlu and Menemencioğlu visited Sofia with results which appeared very encouraging.[78] It was thought at this point that useful proof of British interest in Balkan developments could be given by the holding in London of a conference of British representatives in those parts. It was arranged that the British ambassador should also pay a visit to Sofia. His presence might possibly be interpreted as an additional sign of interest, and coming from Turkey, the centre of so much activity in favour of Balkan unity, it might have had some influence. Nevertheless, Knatchbull-Hugessen came away full of fears and doubts and with the uncomfortable sensation that anything which he put down on the credit side must, for that very reason, be due to wishful thinking: 'There was a haunted look in those men's eyes. It was obvious that, if Germany applied the pressure, they knew that resistance would be impossible.'[79]

Before the end of 1940, all hopes for Balkan solidarity had foundered. As Knatchbull-Hugessen asked with a fair amount of contempt: 'How, indeed, could it have been otherwise? If Romania had shown more courage and more public spirit, Bulgaria less passionate nationalism and Yugoslavia less exclusive individualism, things might have been very different.'[80] The situation was exacerbated by disasters suffered by the Allies. Holland, Belgium and France had been overrun within six weeks of the start of May 1940. Some months previously, the Kioseivanov government had fallen in Bulgaria, only to be succeeded by the weak-kneed Bogdan Filov cabinet. After King Boris's descent to Avernus, Filov followed him there at the beginning of 1941. On the Turkish side, while there was clear evidence of a determination not to allow themselves to be hurried into hostilities before they had decided for themselves that the moment had arrived, there had never been any doubt that Turks *would* defend themselves if their vital interests were attacked. As the Balkan turmoil unfolded towards the end of 1940, verbal assurances were given by Saraçoğlu that this determination would cover an attack by any power on Turkey itself, an attack by Bulgaria on Greece or an invasion of Bulgaria by Nazi Germany (which Turkey would regard as aimed equally at herself and Greece), or a Nazi attack on Greece through a non-resistant Bulgaria.[81]

By the end of the year, the condition of the Balkan Entente became profoundly miserable. The good offices established at the Belgrade meeting in February 1940 had proved to be worthless. Romania was in the Nazi pocket, Bulgaria in danger of 'Romanization', Yugoslavia frightened and hesitant. Only Greece and Turkey remained resolved against Axis penetration. On 28 October 1940, Greece shared the same fate of fellow Balkan nations and fell into disarray as a result of Italy's campaign against General Metaxas.[82] Less than two weeks prior to the operation in October 1940, Mussolini arrived at Terni – the centre of Italy's steel industries – where he met with Marshal Badoglio, Count Ciano and the three heads of the General Staff to discuss a possible operation in Greece. The generals unanimously pronounced themselves against it, arguing that the Italian forces in Albania were insufficient and that the Navy did not feel that it could carry out a landing at Prevesa because the water was too shallow.[83] All of Badoglio's talk had a pessimistic tinge and he foresaw the prolongation of the war, and with it the exhaustion of Italy's already meagre resources. Mussolini and

Count Ciano, however, did not agree with the generals. They insisted that, 'from a political point of view, the moment was good'.[84] Greece was isolated and Turkey would not move. Nor would Yugoslavia embark on a risky campaign to save Greece. If the Bulgarians decided to enter the war, Ciano argued, it would be on Italy's side.

On 22 October 1940, the Turkish ambassador in Rome reported that Mussolini 'wanted to attack Greece soon and very vigorously', mainly because he would like the operation to be won at the first clash.[85] If the Italians left the Greeks too much time to reflect and to breathe, Il Duce was sure that 'the English would come and perhaps later the Turks, and the situation would become long drawn out and difficult'.[86] Much to Ciano's dismay, the popular response to the occupation of Greece culminated in the form of widespread armed resistance led by EAM/ELAS. In less than two months, the Greeks broke through Italian lines and, by December, any further military action became impossible. Mussolini called Ciano to the Palazzo Venezia and told him: 'There is nothing else to do. This is grotesque and absurd, but it is a fact. We have to ask for a truce through Hitler'.[87] Ciano later recalled in his memoirs that, upon hearing Mussolini, he thought this was simply impossible because the Greeks would, as a first condition, ask for the Führer's personal guarantee that they would not be attacked further. Ciano also claimed that he would rather put a bullet through his head than telephone Ribbentrop and asked: 'Is it possible that we are defeated?'[88]

When Italy first embarked upon its predatory war on Greece, the British government sincerely hoped that the Turks would try, by their military dispositions and their general attitude, to give the Italian government the impression that they intend to intervene at once in the event of Italy attacking Greece. Despite Ambassador Knatchbull-Hugessen's warnings about the impossibility of inducing Turkey to jeopardize its benevolent neutrality, Halifax counted on Turkey's declaration of war against Italy, which, in his view 'would act as a strong deterrent and thus indirectly contribute to the defence of Greece'.[89] The British government had tried, and failed, to obtain Turkey's support in the case of Italy coming into the war earlier, but on that occasion, the situation had been complicated by the sudden collapse of France. In the event of an Italo-Greek conflict, Halifax instructed Knatchbull-Hugessen to make it very clear to the Turkish government that they would 'consider such a declaration as the acid test of [Turkey's] sincerity'.[90]

Yet Turkish action was confined merely to an assurance to Greece that they could safely remove their forces from the Bulgarian frontier to Albania and that Turkey would patrol the Greek–Bulgarian front. Useful assistance was also afforded in meeting Greek needs for certain supplies. But Turkey felt unable to declare war on Italy or to take any more active measures.[91] As late as November 1940, Britain still regarded it as certain that Turkey would go to war if Bulgaria and Nazi Germany joined Italy's attack on Greece. Ambassador Knatchbull-Hugessen came to this conclusion by looking at Turkish public opinion and the press, which 'appeared increasingly determined and accustomed to the idea that the war was approaching them'.[92] On the other hand, Knatchbull-Hugessen noted, it seemed only natural that 'a Government which finds itself steadily approaching a possible war crisis should hold back and avoid finally committing itself as long as possible'. Meanwhile, Franz von Papen was doing his best to propagate the belief that Nazi Germany wished to ensure peace in the Balkans.

While through von Papen's assurances the Turkish government seemed relieved, in view of the Turkish preparations, and of the attitude adopted, Knatchbull-Hugessen had serious doubts about whether this *'politique de chloroforme'* would be effective.[93]

In fact, Hitler did not really plan to invade Greece until the Greek forces pinned the Italians in the mountains in early 1941. The orders for Operation Marita, the Nazi occupation of Greece, were not issued until it became clear that Mussolini would lose. It was simply unthinkable for Hitler to allow his partner to be defeated. Despite the Nazis' ambiguous philhellenism – nurtured by Hitler's Aryan racialism – his unconcealed plans for Greece were soon realized in major capitals.[94] The Nazi administrators, much to Italy's dismay, confiscated as much as they could from Greece's already inadequate economic resources to support the Wehrmacht in Operation Barbarossa. By the end of May 1941, the Nazis were masters in Greece, Crete, Western Thrace and the islands guarding the Dardanelles, the vital approach to the very heart of Turkey. Mitylene, Chios and Samos fell soon afterwards, their loss intensifying the danger to the Turkish mainland.[95]

In his retrospective analysis of the events that transpired during January–June 1941, Halifax contended that it would be easy to 'condemn Turkey for evading her written obligations', or even for neglecting its own best interests by refusing to cooperate with its Balkan neighbors. 'But', Halifax added, 'Turkey's position was indeed difficult'.[96] In the first place, Soviet Russia, from whom Turkish eyes had never been averted, did not declare its position clearly. In fact, during the heated days of spring 1941, Stalin made advances to Bulgaria, in which the Turkish government detected a threat to itself. Second, as Saraçoğlu pointed out, Turkey was not sufficiently equipped for war. The secret of Turkish hesitation lies in this point. French supplies had failed Turkey in 1940. British supplies, in the face of many demands on Churchill, had not come up to the required quantity. If Turkey had plunged into war to resist German invasion of the Balkans, it would have been quickly overwhelmed. Incidentally, as Halifax later admitted, 'the liability to Britain would have been dangerously heavy'.[97]

Thus ended the long-drawn-out efforts to unite the Balkans in common defence. Perhaps Romania was the most to blame, but Bulgaria could also be regarded as culpable. The treachery of King Boris placed Bulgaria under the Nazis' heel. Athens briefly triumphed over Rome but its victory was brought to naught by Hitler's assistance to Mussolini. Regardless of historians' prosecutorial rhetoric on the subject, the Balkan Pact crumbled between the fingers of its signatories. As far as Turkey's fate was concerned, policy-makers in Ankara seemed unwilling to provide the necessary assurances to their allies in the defunct Balkan Pact. Yet, as the British ambassador correctly defined, it was the fiscal situation in the country, more than anything, along with exhausted local remedies and overdue arms deliveries, that deterred the Turks from implementing their treaty obligations in the Balkans.

The Nazi–Turkish Non-Aggression Pact

Despite the Nazis' best efforts, it was equally impossible to rid İnönü of his doubts that the Third Reich 'was also trying to encircle Turkey by way of Romania, Bulgaria and

Greece'.[98] Indeed, the Nazis were acutely aware that the Straits question was the 'alpha and omega of [Ankara's] policy', and was full of symbolism because it meant 'the preservation of Turkey as a European great power'.[99] Hence, 'as a gesture toward Turkey', Hitler ordered the Wehrmacht to halt troop movements near Turkey's Balkan outpost in Edirne.[100] But with the Axis occupation of Greece, Franz von Papen ruefully admitted that he saw no possibility of change in the very reserved and standoffish attitude of Turkey towards the Third Reich. During the ensuing negotiations, Ribbentrop incessantly pleaded with Ambassador Gerede in Berlin that 'the Führer would welcome it if he could have all Germany's old allies at our side at this time', at least in memory of the hard times experienced together.[101]

In his personal correspondence with Hitler, İnönü repeatedly gave hints that the wartime exchange between Ankara and Berlin would ultimately fall short of a military alliance.[102] Yet, Franz von Papen still believed that some form of accord could be reached through their existing connections with certain members of İnönü's entourage who had always been sceptical about the Kemalist claim that the Soviet Union was somehow different than Tsarist Russia. A suitable candidate for the role was Ambassador Gerede, who was convinced that even the remote possibility of Turkey's entrance into the war on the side of the Allies would provoke Russia's old territorial demands. Gerede thought that since most of Turkey's closest trading partners in the Balkans had now fallen to the Nazis, his government should try to maintain better relations with the Third Reich and increase the volume of trade with Balkan countries as much as possible. Beginning with the early days of 1940, when Turkey's industrial growth rate plunged a critical 50 per cent, Gerede had been urging Ankara to enact new trade agreements with Nazi Germany.[103] Consequently, in the first quarter of 1941, Gerede began negotiating for a new trade agreement with the Nazis.[104]

At the same time, however, the Turkish government was fearful of giving the impression that should the incipient trade talks with Nazi Germany result in a non-aggression treaty, this would be taken as its full integration into the Axis. Mindful of İnönü's stipulations, in his meetings with Saraçoğlu, Franz von Papen often acknowledged that Germany fully recognized Turkey's loyalty to the Anglo-French–Turkish Treaty of 1939, and that Hitler had no desire to oppose this, easing Turkey's anxiety about giving the wrong message. The Turkish government had all the right reasons for being nervous about maintaining trade relations with the Third Reich. This was exactly why Stalin would blame Turkey after the war, accusing İnönü for pursuing a Janus-faced agenda and for hedging bets by maintaining trade relations with both the Allies and the Axis.[105]

But a closer examination of Nazi–Turkish trade reveals a different picture from what the Soviets had in mind – one that involves a distorted trade relationship by all sorts of artificial arrangements, which had long been conducted on a basis that had no relation whatsoever to world prices or to the ordinary laws of international trade. Although a favourable balance of £42,523,778 was achieved in 1940, compared to an adverse balance of £9,140,063 in 1939, the aggregate turnover in 1940 diminished by 26.6 per cent, including 12.5 per cent for exports and 41.7 per cent for imports.[106] Turkey's trade volume in 1940 showed a marked deterioration particularly with regards to Germany, whose share diminished from 50.86 per cent (£60,142,000) in 1939 to a mere 11.73 per cent (£8,083,000) in 1940. The chief reason for Germany's loss of trade was a failure to implement the ad hoc Turco-German Agreement of June 1940, for the reciprocal exchange of goods to a value of £21,000,000.[107]

Despite the radical decline in export volume, much higher values were recorded in 1940 because of a stronger demand from European countries for Turkish products such as wool, cotton, mohair, opium, olive oil, fish, cereals, and dried fruits. Smaller shipments of casings, skins, wool, barley, sultanas, figs, flax and hemp, copper and other minerals were also recorded. The principal reasons for this decline in trade were supply and shipping difficulties due to the international situation, and, to a lesser extent, a restriction on certain imports with a view to economizing Turkey's limited resources in foreign exchange in favour of raw materials.[108] The latter factor led to the conclusion of a series of barter agreements between Turkey and a number of countries as alternative sources of supply including Germany, Italy, Switzerland, Yugoslavia, Romania, Finland, Bulgaria and Sweden. This reorientation of the import trade is reflected in the relative shares of the total import trade secured by the countries supplying Turkey.

Consequently, when Gerede initiated a new round of negotiations with the Nazis in early 1941, Saraçoğlu gave a comprehensive list of Turkish requirements to von Papen regarding a potential new trade agreement with Germany. Yet Saraçoğlu did not seem to think that the Nazis would be able to supply this; and if the negotiations dragged on for a considerable time he proposed to say to von Papen that this state of affairs could not continue and that the negotiations were at an end. He argued that the Turks and Germans should agree upon a list of goods, which could be exchanged without controversy or difficulty. He said that if the Nazis could not come to terms over a reduced list he would then terminate the negotiations altogether. Franz von Papen had pleaded with the utmost insistence for a delay up to a month, if possible, before the payment of the guarantee money deposited in connection with some of the orders for goods and war material from the Third Reich. Saraçoğlu had refused to agree to a month's delay – he had equally refused to agree to a fortnight's delay – but in deference to further appeals he finally agreed to submit the matter to Prime Minister Refik Saydam.

Meanwhile, Gerede reported that he had been approached by a 'prominent Nazi' with the proposal that, if Turkey allowed a certain amount of chromium to go to Nazi Germany (between 10,000 and 20,000 tons), they would supply Turkey with all the goods outstanding. The ambassador had been instructed to reply that he could not act on this unofficial approach; that it was Nazi Germany who had broken off the Turco-German commercial treaty; that if any such proposal was to be put forward it must reach him officially, and he would then pass it on to his government, who would examine it. Saraçoğlu kept the British government informed about this recent development to preempt any misunderstanding. When the British ambassador asked him what would happen next with the Nazi proposal, Saraçoğlu laughed and said that he did not suppose anything could possibly come of it, as Nazi Germany would not be able to supply all the goods.

In spite of Saraçoğlu's cynicism, Turco-German negotiations gained a substantial momentum with Hitler's letter to İnönü on 1 March 1941. Mindful of the Turks' fear of

Axis encirclement, in his letter Hitler 'solemnly informed' İnönü that the German incursions into the Balkans were 'in no way directed against the territorial or political integrity of Turkey'.[109] 'On the contrary,' Hitler argued, 'in memory of that great and fateful common struggle and the subsequent years of suffering', Turkey and Germany should work together to create the necessary conditions 'for a really friendly cooperation' between the two countries.[110] For Hitler, such a partnership would be mutually beneficial because 'the economic development which [was] destined to heal the European wounds after the end of the war would of necessity make close trade partners of Germany and Turkey once more'.[111] Hitler argued that the decisive thing about a potential Turco-German agreement was not that Nazi Germany was interested in selling her industrial products, but was able to make purchases on a very large scale.

Although İnönü's response to Hitler was equally welcoming, it had fewer references to the Ottoman–German imperial alliance and a strong emphasis on Turkey's wish to remain neutral: 'After the last great war, which we fought side by side, and the glories and hardships of which we therefore shared ... Turkey cannot consider her territory and her integrity from the standpoint of political and military combinations between one of the other group of powers and she cannot allow her sacred right to inviolability to be judged from the point of view of the victory of any foreign country'.[112] Put differently, İnönü made it clear that Turkey was determined to oppose any encroachment upon its national domain. The exchange of views, which took place between İnönü and Hitler, thanks to the latter's 'auspicious initiative' certainly contributed toward normalizing Turco-German relations, which had soured after the Massigli Affair.

The Turkish ambassador personally presented İnönü's response to the Hitler government. After the Führer read it, he provided Ambassador Gerede with Nazi Germany's view of the current problems in a lengthy speech. He was impressed with the fact that the communication just handed to him was greatly appreciated in Ankara, and repeated his assurances that the Reich had no territorial interest in the areas in question, 'any more than in Bulgaria, Rumania or Greece'.[113] Hitler claimed that Germany was 'perhaps the only state' that could truthfully say that of itself. He gave Ambassador Gerede the impression that it was extremely unpleasant for Germany to have to resort to military intervention in the Balkans as this was, after all, 'contrary to the fundamental strategic principle of concentrating all forces upon a single objective'.[114] He added that Germany would not have sent a single soldier if the Italo–Greek conflict had been confined to these countries alone.

In this connection, Hitler then referred to the conversations during Molotov's recent visit to Berlin in November 1940, when Germany had attempted to draw Russia into the Axis combination against Britain. Molotov had thereupon immediately brought up the Dardanelles problem, which would provide for the stationing of Russian garrisons in Bulgaria, close to the Straits. In passing, Hitler told Gerede that he had refused Molotov's proposal because he simply did not believe this would be possible and that he did not consider it feasible. He had merely declared that he was prepared to advocate a revision of the Montreux Convention to the effect that the warships of the littoral states of the Black Sea would have the right to exit that waterway via the Dardanelles, while foreign ships would not be permitted to enter. He had taken this positive attitude toward Turkey's interest not for any sentimental reasons, although the memory of the German–Turkish comradeship in arms during World War I was still very strong; rather, he had acted from a feeling that it would be against Germany's own interests if anything were to happen to Turkey.[115] It would not be to Germany's advantage to watch any other power establish itself in the Balkans and on the Dardanelles.

Hitler also hinted that Turkey 'had really no interest in Germany's losing the war' and thus seeing the country perish which had been the strongest restraining factor with respect to Turkey's biggest neighbour in the north.[116] By the same token, Hitler contended that Germany had an interest in the continued existence of Turkey as the guardian of the Straits. In other words, Hitler claimed that Germany stood against Soviet Russia, despite the existing Molotov–Ribbentrop Pact, on account of Stalin's stance on the Dardanelles question. The Turkish ambassador, who was visibly gratified, thanked the Führer for his words and promised to do everything in his power to carry on along the road that had now been taken.

Still, the content and tone of Franz von Papen's subsequent meeting with Numan Menemencioğlu in late March 1941 illustrates how Turkish leaders did not attribute too much role to historical conditioning in their relations with Berlin. Menemencioğlu, who would succeed Saraçoğlu as foreign minister in 1942, expressed the great satisfaction of the Turkish government about Hitler's flat rejection of the Russian preliminary condition for accession to the Tripartite Pact, in so far as it involved the right to intervene at the Straits. But he also conveyed to Franz von Papen that in real politics there was no room for 'old friendships and brotherhoods in arms', except for the actual interests which determine the policy of the Reich and of Turkey. Responding to von Papen's repeated remarks that something had to be done by the Turkish Government in order to put Nazi–Turkish relations on a basis of greater trust, Menemencioğlu told him that the Führer's decision not to let the Soviets get to the Straits was 'very wise', and in Nazi Germany's interest as well. With regards to von Papen's concerns about Great Britain, however, Menemencioğlu was much more restrained and told him: 'You know that we are allied with England. We want to keep honourably the few obligations, which we have, and if you, Herr von Papen, now expect a kind of "benevolent neutrality" on the part of Turkey, then I must tell you that such political acrobatics appear hardly possible to me.'[117]

Franz von Papen went on to complain that if Turkey desired a compromised peace in Europe, this was not expressed in the slightest way in her public opinion. The Turkish press demanded the total victory of England and did not have the slightest understanding for the German efforts toward a new order. Thus, public opinion contradicted his statements. 'Certainly,' said Menemencioğlu, 'we do not want much to do with the new order. For us, every state has it right to independence and its own existence.'[118] Menemencioğlu's message was that Turkey knew too little about the aims of the new order propagated by the Axis and the terms which Germany was willing to grant to the conquered and occupied areas. The entire situation left von Papen with the impression that Germany desperately needed to find a treaty instrument to prepare the transition of Turkey to its camp as a 'benevolent neutral'.[119]

In the course of his meetings with Saraçoğlu in April–May 1941, Franz von Papen noticed Turkey's growing concerns about Nazi–Soviet war relations. In accordance with his instructions, von Papen told Saraçoğlu that Berlin–Moscow affairs were entirely regulated, and that they had no problems with respect to Russia. However, von Papen also informed Saraçoğlu that Hitler had taken note of the inexplicable political attitude of Stalin in the case of Bulgaria and Yugoslavia as well as of the fact that very strong Russian forces were mobilized at the frontier of the Reich. Von Papen argued that Germany's primary goal continued to be England's defeat and an attack on the island. Yet he also added that the Germans 'were strong enough to cope with any other eventuality too'.[120] Saraçoğlu interrupted him and said that, since Stalin had resumed the Tsarist policy toward the Balkans and the Straits, Turkey again had to regard Russia as its implacable and greatest enemy. Yet Saraçoğlu argued that if there should be a Nazi–Soviet war clash without an understanding with England having been reached first, then the war would continue for years, and that the Turks were afraid that 'the end of a war weakened by exhaustion and destruction would mean an extensive Bolshevization of Europe'.[121] The critical bit of von Papen's conversation with Saraçoğlu lies here. It was exactly the fear of such a Nazi–Soviet conflict that made the Turkish government inclined to an agreement with Germany. Franz von Papen was convinced that, in order for such a treaty to be concluded, Berlin should swiftly capitalize on Turkey's uncertainty concerning Nazi–Soviet relations.

Reflecting on von Papen's subsequent discussions with Turkish leaders, Ernst von Weizsäcker admitted that they expected a more committed neutrality than the Turks were prepared to give. Although Turkey's fear of Soviet Russia was stronger, after the Massigli Affair, Ankara felt wedged between two colossi. At a time when Great Britain was not in a position to render any tangible support, İnönü was struggling to maintain a neutral stance in the face of what Ribbentrop described as 'an assumed German and an actual Russian threat'.[122] In the end, the Third Reich failed to bring about the sort of pro-Axis neutrality that existed in Spain. But in fanning the flames of Ankara's apprehension, Hitler accomplished his main objective of keeping Turkey as a non-belligerent power malevolently disposed to Moscow. Looking at Hüsrev Gerede's cables from Berlin, it is clear that Franz von Papen masterfully tried to steer Turkish diplomacy into a pro-German neutrality.[123]

While von Papen clearly became the main architect of the Turco-German treaty, bilateral negotiations proceeded with few difficulties. The real problem was regarding the transit of German arms through Anatolia. Negotiations came to a halt on 27 May when Turkey received a British note, which was so full of the most bitter accusations against Turkey that Saraçoğlu told von Papen he would not be surprised if England severed relations with Turkey when the Nazi–Turkish treaty was made public. Thereupon the Turkish cabinet met and decided they were unable to give the Germans any oral assurances about the transit of arms.[124] On his own initiative, von Papen decided to add a secret protocol to the draft Turco-German treaty, whereby the government of the German Reich declared that at the time of the peace negotiations, they would take into account Turkish wishes which in principle related to: rectification of the frontier in Thrace, west of Edirne; the islands in the Aegean near the Turkish coast; and a change to the Montreux Convention regarding the Straits.[125]

On 15 May 1941, İnönü received a detailed report from the Turkish ambassador in Moscow on Nazi–Soviet war affairs (dated 1 May 1941). But before the report was communicated to Ankara, a confidential source (codenamed 'X' by the Turkish embassy staff in Moscow) seized the document and forwarded it to Franz von Papen.[126] In his report, which confirmed von Papen's prognosis, Ambassador Haydar Aktay argued that the military operations of the Germans in the Balkans were far swifter than the Soviet statesmen had imagined. Indeed, Stalin and his people were of the opinion that the Nazis would strain themselves for at least two months in the Balkans and during that time British and American aid would begin to come in sufficient quantities and would win out in the Balkans. But the unexpectedly rapid defeat of the Serbs and the resulting collapse of Greece, which the English were unable to help, had the effect of a cold shower on the leaders in Moscow. As Ambassador Aktay claimed, Stalin – who was one of the factors that had made possible the German victory in Poland by his support of the Germans – showed the same lack of foresight in the case of the French defeat.[127] In Aktay's opinion, Stalin was also the strongest factor in the French defeat 'because of his blind obstinacy'. When the repercussions of the German victory began to shake the walls of the Kremlin, the wake-up call was futile. In Aktay's view, Stalin had expected that Poland would put up a resistance for at least six months, and that France would hold out one or two years. Indeed, Stalin expected that the German and English blockades would last two years and that both belligerents would be exhausted, allowing him to benefit greatly from the situation. All his hopes were dashed, however, and not in the course of a year – but in just a few months. Ambassador Aktay accurately identified Stalin's fear of Nazi Germany, which was casting a greedy eye on Russia. The fact that the Turks were not plunged into the Balkan conflagration caused despair in Moscow. Stalin had believed that the war in the Balkans would be protracted in the event of Turkey's intervention.

At the time, von Papen considered the general political and moral repercussions of a potential bilateral treaty to be of far greater importance than securing the transit of material since such a treaty would appear to the whole world as a signal that the last British ally in Europe now considered Britain's cause as lost. But Ribbentrop was outraged and admonished von Papen for exceeding instructions in discussing his own draft, which would offer guarantees to Turkey without granting Germany concessions in the transit of arms.[128] In a bitter personal letter, Ribbentrop told him that it was 'incomprehensible' to him why von Papen was prepared to arrange a draft of secret protocol regarding Edirne, the islands, and so on, as long as he was not sure of being able to also put through secret clauses regarding the arms transit. Ribbentrop objected, saying that the Turks had stated that they were willing to accept all of Germany's extensive assurances for guaranteeing their interests, without offering them more than the promise to refrain from any aggressive attitude toward the German Reich.

Franz von Papen defended himself and reminded Ribbentrop that İnönü was not willing to make a treaty with Hitler and gradually shift the country's foreign policy toward cooperation with Berlin because the Nazis were issuing Ankara a bill in the future, but because the Turks were 'finally convinced that Hitler has not sold Turkey either to Italy or to Russia'.[129] Like von Papen, the German military attaché in Ankara also claimed that the Turco-German Treaty would have more important repercussions than simply the transit of arms. He passed on a message to Hitler from Asım Gündüz, the head of the Turkish General Staff: 'If Germany crushes Russia, the whole world will be happy and Germany will get her hands on more material than America will be able to deliver to England in 5 years.'[130] In his reaffirmation of the German policy with respect to south-eastern Europe, Hitler welcomed Gündüz's message and noted once more the agreement of Turkish and German views, 'for they [were] animated by the common desire to prevent the war from spreading to the Near East and to restore tranquility to the Balkans'.[131] In a second round of this exchange of letters between İnönü and Hitler it was agreed that, in any case, Turco-German relations would be cemented by a treaty regardless of Russia's or England's reaction.[132]

The Turco-German talks culminated in the form of the Nazi–Turkish Non-Aggression Pact of 18 June 1941.[133] The Pact's stated goal was to save world civilization from the dangers of Bolshevism, one aspect of which was the Soviets' imperialist quest for the Bosphorus and Eastern Anatolia. Four days after the Nazi–Turkish Pact was signed, the Third Reich declared war on the Soviet Union. When Ribbentrop ordered the Nazi ambassador in Moscow, Count Wener von der Schulenburg, to communicate the Third Reich's declaration to Molotov, he gave six reasons for it, one of which pertained to an earlier Soviet proposal to establish military bases on the Straits for Stalin's acceptance of the Four Power Pact.[134] Indeed, on the eve of the Molotov–Hitler meeting in Berlin in November 1940, Molotov *had* handed Schulenburg a draft protocol regarding Soviet conditions for acceptance of the Four Power Pact, which included 'the establishment of a base for land and naval forces of the USSR within the range of the Bosphorus and Dardanelles'.[135] The Nazi declaration of war against the Soviet Union thus proclaimed that competition for influence in Turkey was a crucial part of the Nazi–Soviet relationship.

Among the several fault lines of Russo-Turkish relations, the Straits question always loomed large. A key moment in this century-old dispute transpired on 11 August 1941, when von Weizsäcker advised Ribbentrop to disclose parts of Count Schulenburg's telegram 'as irrefutable proof of Russian designs' on Turkey.[136] Capitalizing on Turkey's historic fear, Ribbentrop followed the advice and shared Molotov's demands in writing with the Turkish ambassador in Berlin on 25 August 1941.[137] The timing and purpose of this disclosure was critical. Two months after the outbreak of the Nazi–Soviet War, Nazi Germany's qualms about Turkey's pro-British tendencies were exacerbated on 10 August 1941 when simultaneous British and Soviet declarations were presented to Turkey in identical terms, each assuring Turkey that they had no aggressive intentions with regards to the Straits. By sharing proof of Molotov's aims in 1940, Ribbentrop challenged the Anglo-Soviet guarantee to Turkey. Ribbentrop told Ambassador Gerede that Hitler's rejection of this demand had been a basic cause of the Nazi–Soviet enmity, precisely because the Führer did not want to let the Bolshevik monster advance any farther. What was more, Ribbentrop's meeting with Gerede took place on the same day that Operation Countenance began, when Great Britain and the Soviet Union invaded Iran. The timing of this disclosure also suggests that it was meant to rekindle Turkey's bitter memories of the Anglo-Russian Entente of 1907.[138]

Exactly when Nazi Germany disclosed Molotov's request is more than a question of chronological order and provides us with a much fuller grasp of Turkey's considerations with regard to the Soviet Union and Nazi Germany after the Massigli Affair. One of the central accounts of this period suggests that Hitler divulged the Soviet request for bases in March 1941, and that this was the principal reason for the Turks' willingness to sign the Non-Aggression Pact with the Nazis on 18 June 1941, before Barbarossa was unleashed.[139] In fact, Turkish records demonstrate that, as early as 18 July 1940, in the immediate aftermath of the Massigli scandal, the Ankara government already anticipated an aggressive Soviet reaction that might target the Bosphorus and Dardanelles.[140] Nazi documents do show that in March 1941 Hitler referred to the Soviet bases in passing as he considered bringing Turkey to a more benevolent neutrality towards Berlin. Hitler insinuated that 'the Russians had spoken about the granting of bases' which no doubt fed Turkey's apprehension, but the context of that conversation was mostly about the closure of the Black Sea to non-Black Sea powers.[141] The Turkish government suspected that by divulging Molotov's request, a fortnight before the Wehrmacht marched into Greece with Bulgaria on its heels in April 1941, Hitler might be offering an ambiguous reassurance to Turkey that the Straits would be off Nazi limits. Indeed, Hitler was informed that just a few days before his meeting with Gerede, Ambassador Aktay in Moscow had been delivered a declaration which showed that 'Turkey could rely on the full neutrality and benevolence of Moscow in case it gets attacked'.[142]

By referring to Molotov's request in passing, Hitler sought to ridicule the Soviet Union's volte-face after the failed talks in Berlin, whereby Stalin decided to improve the Straits regime in direct negotiations with Turkey and not behind her back.[143] Yet, Nazi Germany's anti-Soviet propaganda that it had so carefully cultivated in Turkey found many receptive ears. *Ulus*, the same newspaper that so forcefully denounced the DNB's account of the Massigli Affair, at the same time voiced its support for Nazi Germany's war effort: 'If Germany wins, the Russian world would be divided up and scattered, and the edifice of the Communist International would be forever overthrown.'[144] A number of government leaders also greeted the news of Nazi Germany's attack on the Soviet Union with approval.[145] Şükrü Saraçoğlu, Turkey's foreign minister, who was having drinks with his friends at a Georgian tavern that night, was just one of them. In the remaining years of World War II, Turkish foreign policy went through a number of twists and turns. One thing, however, was fundamentally changed by this period. As the Molotov–Ribbentrop Pact and the ensuing disarray decisively put an end to any Turkish belief in the novelty of the Bolshevik regime, Ankara began to look at Moscow through the lens of history and respond in terms of an older realpolitik. Nazi propaganda played a significant role in that process.

5

The Barbarossa Bubble

In the early days of the Nazi–Soviet War, Turkish diplomats were quite vocal about their hope for Britain's ultimate success, but they also alluded to the need for a strong Germany in the centre of Europe to check Soviet expansion. This was an unusual phased-thinking and during the preliminary talks for the Nazi–Turkish treaty, the Turkish leadership was concerned about the ways in which their attitude might be misconstrued as pro-Axis neutrality. They made it clear that the Turkish government would preclude the smallest possibility for misperception on the part of Great Britain. The Nazis, however, were equally adamant about the wording of the draft treaty and stipulated what they considered to be Berlin's red line: 'The Turkish government must clearly understand that if Turkey cooperates even indirectly with England, with which Germany is waging a life and death struggle, she will automatically place herself against Germany.'[1] Ribbentrop, for instance, was not happy about Menemencioğlu's proposal to include the expression 'Turkey's peace-loving character' in the preamble. For Ribbentrop, the expression 'peace-loving' would be too embellished a description, and was 'even stylistically (*sprachlich*) impossible'.[2] Ribbentrop insisted on replacing that term with 'friendly character' instead.[3] As Ribbentrop's patience wore thin, in a snappy dispatch to Herr von Papen, Ribbentrop reacted against Ankara's insistence on tailoring 'a stronger reference' for Turkey's continued respect to its present commitments, referring implicitly to the Anglo-Turkish Treaty.[4]

A week before the signing of the Nazi–Turkish treaty, it seemed as if Anglo-Turkish relations would remain untroubled; no substantial threat appeared to be in the offing to spoil the mellow atmosphere between London and Ankara, beyond perhaps some chronic problems arising out of Britain's arms shortage. Yet on 18 June 1941 the non-aggression treaty between Nazis and Turks was announced, and four days later, the Nazis invaded Soviet Russia. There is no doubt that these two events were connected and that the signing of the Turco-German Treaty should have signalled something to both Churchill and Stalin.[5] In Moscow, the general mood was even darker. Forty-eight hours before Hitler's war declaration, the Turkish ambassador was invited to a meeting with Molotov, who told Ambassador Aktay that 'the general situation looked very unstable but that the Soviet Union was prepared for any eventuality'.[6] Aktay, however, left the meeting with the impression that Molotov was evidently distressed, despite all his composed responses. For Aktay, Nazi Germany absolutely had to secure guarantees for its southern flank before unleashing Barbarossa. This is why Franz von Papen had hinted that everything 'depended on Turkey's decision to accept or reject the proposed

German treaty'.[7] Put differently, Hitler insinuated that it was Turkey's choice whether the Soviet Union or Turkey would be attacked first. When the Nazi–Turkish agreement became public, Anthony Eden expressed his deep regret that the Turkish government had chosen this moment, of all others, to enter into an economic alliance with Nazi Germany, which had strong and worrying political implications.[8] Eden said that Turkey was under no military pressure from Nazi Germany and that he 'simply did not understand the need for it'.[9] In an emergency meeting with the Turkish ambassador, Eden argued that the crisis in Iraq had been resolved and that matters were going 'surely if slowly in Britain's favour' in Syria, while for the first time they were taking local offensive action against the Nazis in Libya. Hence, Eden acerbically asked 'why now?' and whether the ratification of the treaty could at least be postponed for ten days.[10]

The Turkish ambassador knew only too well that the news of his country's agreement with Germany would shock the British government profoundly. He did not deny Eden's claims, but said that they had done all they could 'to gain time', that delaying the ratification of the treaty could have grave consequences because 'no one knew what the world could witness in the next couple of days' and that he only hoped that 'Britain should not blame Turkey for this'.[11] Eden replied that it was not a question of blame, but of correctly estimating the consequences of the agreement. In Eden's view, the Turkish government should have made it plain and beyond any doubt that nothing in the agreement affected the previous Anglo-Turkish Treaty. In fact, there existed in the preamble of the Nazi–Turkish treaty a clause to that effect, reserving previous engagements; but since the treaty itself was not made public immediately at the time of its signature, the British public was not aware of the preamble and did not quite understand the situation, leaving Eden in a tricky position.

A second meeting took place between Eden and Ambassador Tevfik Rüştü Aras on 26 June 1941. In a pessimistic mood, Aras blamed the Bolsheviks in general, and Molotov in particular, for the Allies' failure to form a Balkan front in the spring. The Turkish government considered that Molotov suffered from 'the Russian disease of ambition to control the Dardanelles'.[12] For Aras, Litvinov had had a much more realistic conception of Turkey's foreign policy: 'It is a great misfortune that he fell from power,' added Aras candidly. He was convinced that Litvinov, Saraçoğlu and Eden himself would have been able to maintain the close collaboration that had always existed between the three nations. Eden emphasized to Aras that he understood Turkey's concerns regarding the Soviet Union, but urged the ambassador that Ankara needed to show its continued loyalty to the Anglo-Turkish Treaty more clearly, bearing in mind the recent reports that appeared in the British press, which put Turkey in a negative light. Eden alluded to another source of apprehension, which was 'the fact that Germany had never yet signed an agreement with any country without finally making a victim of her co-signatory ... Turkey would therefore have to be scrupulously on her guard'.[13] Reflecting on the incipient progress of the Nazi–Soviet War, Aras also expressed his view that the power of the Red Army had been underrated in Britain. Aras argued that the Soviet army's weakness lay in its High Command, but that 'Stalin himself was tough'.[14] Aras was convinced that the Nazis would soon find out that the task at hand – that is, the invasion of the Soviet Union – was much more demanding than they had anticipated.

The Nazi-Turkish trade agreement

Despite Şükrü Saraçoğlu's crass reaction to the outbreak of the Nazi–Soviet War at the Georgian tavern, the tone and content of Turkish diplomatic cables reflected a high degree of pessimism. Secretary-General Numan Menemencioğlu, for instance, received a number of reports from the Turkish ambassador in Berlin, who revealed that since the Red Army was beaten on the Stalin Line, the Russians were now planning to build up a new solid front east of Moscow and that there was talk of '120 new divisions, which the Russians could activate and arm'.[15] From the Turkish perspective, this meant that Nazi Germany's Russian campaign would last much longer than expected. The Wehrmacht would be exposed to the grinding effect of a war on two fronts in winter conditions, the disastrous ramifications of which the Turks knew quite well from history.[16] If carried into reality, Stalin's attempts to force the Germans into lengthy warfare would probably require more German reinforcements (via re-routing the 1st Army) through the Caucasus to save the Wehrmacht from getting bogged down in the Russian winter, thereby dragging the battlefield to the Turkish frontier.[17]

Nazi Germany could see that Turkey's position had been made worse, since a closer association with Great Britain was now impossible given the Anglo-Soviet alliance. Through unleashing Operation Barbarossa, Hitler presented to Churchill one ally as the hereditary enemy of another. In his conversations with Saraçoğlu and Menemencioğlu, von Papen repeatedly capitalized on this anxiety, stressing Turkey's self-evident interest in the elimination of the Bolshevik system, which was 'naturally bound to bring the country over to the side of the German Reich ... though not necessarily on the battlefield'.[18] Franz von Papen reiterated Hitler's respect for İnönü's decision to keep Turkey out of the war and for the existing agreements between Turkey and Great Britain. But the implication was that, as soon as the campaign against the Soviets was victoriously concluded, the Reich would then be in a position to start reorganizing Europe. What this meant for Turkey, of course, was when that moment arrived, İnönü would have to decide whether he wanted to remain 'an appendix to the British–Soviet front'.[19]

It is reasonable to assume that von Papen's message was received with considerable approval in Ankara. In spite of İnönü's anxiety and continued management of the country's popular press, public perception of the Nazi–Soviet War was more favourably disposed to Nazi Germany. Even state-sponsored papers rose to the bait, arguing that 'those on the European Continent, who but recently were at each other's throat, have united to ward off domination by the Kremlin ... Europe has been unified in the mystique of a crusade'.[20] But based on the information he had gathered from Ambassador Gerede in Berlin, Ribbentrop seemed convinced that the Turkish government would try to maintain their neutrality at all costs. Consequently, the Nazis decided to seize the moment and cultivate a corresponding pro-Axis sentiment amongst members of İnönü's close circle.

As a first step, on 11 August 1941, von Weizsäcker inquired whether the question of Soviet designs on the Straits was unequivocally presented to the Turkish government. Although Hitler had mentioned Molotov's request for Soviet bases in passing during his meeting with Ambassador Gerede in March, von Weizsäcker urged Ribbentrop to disclose the minutes of these talks in writing to the Turkish ambassador in Berlin 'as irrefutable proof of the Russian designs'.[21] In a detailed memorandum, Ribbentrop passed von Weizsäcker's instructions to Franz von Papen and suggested that winning Turkey to Nazi Germany's side as a non-belligerent state in the manner desired was feasible only if the Nazis could interest İnönü in the acquisition of new territories, which included border rectifications in Thrace, the Greek islands at the entrance to the Straits, and further acquisitions to the south and east of Turkey at Moscow's expense. Ribbentrop hoped that these conditions would be obtained 'after Russia was definitively smashed in autumn'.[22] Until that time, Ribbentrop conceived of their diplomatic effort in the following terms: first, to strengthen the Turks' confidence that Nazi Germany would never make any territorial demands on them, or pressure them to enter the war on Nazi Germany's side, but that, on the contrary, Hitler would always regard Turkey 'as the historic guardian of the Straits'; and second, to promote and keep alive 'the hitherto somewhat dormant fear of Russian imperialist tendencies'.[23] In short, Ribbentrop argued that Turkey would probably move increasingly into the centre of the international stage in the immediate future, and that it was imperative that Germany maintained 'its friendship with this state forever'.[24] Nor did Ribbentrop see the slightest reason for conflicts between the interests of Turkey and Nazi Germany. On the contrary, he thought that it might even be possible to have Turkey join them in the further course of the war, 'provided Germany found the means to supply arms and assistance in sufficient quantities'.[25]

Nazi Germany's plans to reward Turkey with territorial acquisitions in return for its cooperation is a popular debate in Turkish scholarship. Recently disclosed Turkish records reveal that the Third Reich did indeed entertain such plans as early as August 1941. But the official proposal to Turkey regarding the Greek islands came two years later, in August 1943, when the tide began to turn in Stalin's favour. İnönü responded to the Nazi proposal with the following telegram: 'We would consider repatriating those Aegean Islands that are located in our territorial waters on the condition that such an annexation comes into existence with no strings attached... Otherwise, it is unthinkable to carry out such an action that would potentially result in a dispute between Turkey and Great Britain or Nazi occupied Greece'.[26]

Evidently, in August 1941, Nazi Germany did not want to have Turkey as a belligerent on its side, not at least until the Soviet campaign was successfully brought to an end. The Nazis were lagging behind in delivering the submarines and battleships that Turkey had already paid for, let alone pledging for a future arms supply. Ankara did, however, propose financial assistance and extended a guarantee for buying large quantities of chromium ore after Turkey's existing agreements with Britain expired. What Nazi Germany requested from Turkey in return for the bullion was to impede Soviet naval traffic through the Straits without jeopardizing its neutrality.[27] To achieve this, Ribbentrop invited Gerede to the Reich Foreign Ministry for a second round of talks in late August, when the two exchanged views regarding the course of the war and of the Nazi German offensives in Russia. Ribbentrop summarized the military situation in the east, where Soviet losses had amounted to almost 6 million. Ribbentrop confidently told the Turkish ambassador that the Red Army 'would probably be destroyed and the greater part of European Russia would be occupied'.[28] In any case,

Stalin would be unable to rebuild the Red Army to any significant extent after such blows.

The immediate result of the Ribbentrop–Gerede talks was the arrival of a Nazi delegation in Ankara to rejuvenate Nazi–Turkish trade.[29] Since the termination of the previous commercial treaty in August 1939, a few days before the outbreak of war, several attempts had been made to restore some order into trade relations between Turkey and Germany, yet, nothing satisfactory or permanent had been effected. The Nazi delegation, led by Dr Karl Clodius, successfully concluded a new agreement on 9 October 1941, which provided (in theory) for exchanges on a substantial scale between the two countries. Also known as the 'Clodius Agreement', the new Nazi–Turkish trade agreement attributed a key role to Turkey's deliveries of strategic materials, including chromium ore. During the negotiations in Ankara, Dr. Clodius persistently pressed for Turkish supplies after the new year (8 January 1942), when the original Anglo-Franco-Turkish Chrome agreement was due to expire.[30] Much to Clodius's dismay, by dint of some British pressure, the Turkish government was induced to extend the existing agreement on similar terms for another year, until January 1943. Under the final agreement, however, the Turkish government undertook to let Germany have export permits for 45,000 tons between 15 January and 31 March 1943, another 45,000 tons by the end of the year, and 90,000 tons in 1944, making a total of 180,000 tons for the two years 1943 and 1944. But this further agreement was to be conditional upon the delivery of all war materials to Turkey by Germany as stipulated in the Clodius Agreement.

The Nazi–Turkish Non-Aggression Pact, and the ensuing trade agreement of October 1941, were destined to cast a shadow over Anglo-Turkish relations. In order to repair Turkey's tarnished image, İnönü instructed Ambassador Aras to convey to the British the country's dire financial circumstances, under which he was struggling to build up its defences. Aras explained to Eden that Turkey's local remedies had been totally exhausted, and that Turkish supplies of dollars were 'completely expended'.[31] They had no means of paying for anything more, either here or in the United States, unless Britain could either offer them credit or reduce their defence preparations by supplying arms. Aras communicated Turkey's requests to Eden in an aide-memoire personally drafted by Saraçoğlu. The Turkish foreign minister communicated to Eden that, as a result of the Turkish government's radical economic policies and fiscal measures (the imposition of new taxes, a further increase of direct and indirect taxation, and the floating of internal loans etc.), it had been possible to balance for only six months the extraordinarily high budget of the Ministry of National Defence, which was estimated at £297 million for the year 1941. Simply put, to meet Turkey's defence spending for the latter half of the year, there appeared no remedy except inflation.[32]

Britain's response to the Turkish request for assistance was sharp and gave Aras the impression that for a prospective financial aid agreement between London and Ankara to be concluded, Britain attached utmost importance to the Turkish government refusing the Nazi demand for chromium.[33] Eden made it clear that chromium had become the touchstone of Turkey's good faith towards the Anglo-Turkish alliance. For Eden, the Turkish government and the press might understandably regard it as ironic that a small quantity of chromium should loom so large, but he had no doubt of what

British public opinion would be: 'After all, what was this chromium to be used for?' asked Eden, who then answered himself: 'To make munitions of war to kill our [British] soldiers, of course.'[34] Eden suggested that he had done everything in his power to help Turkey, and would continue to do so, but in return he asked the Turkish ambassador to help him convince İnönü to resolve the chromium problem to Britain's advantage. Aras replied that he understood the position and that the issue was not 3,000 tons of chromium but a moral question. He undertook to do his utmost to persuade his government not to yield on this point in the negotiations. With regards to the United States, however, he did not see how Turkey was to obtain American supplies, since it had 'no more dollars and could not be placed on the lend-lease list'.

The Anglo-Franco-Turkish Chrome Agreement of 8 January 1940 stipulated that the entire available Turkish chromium output, up to the stipulated maximum of 250,000 tons, should be bought in agreed shares by the British and the French governments, respectively.[35] No Turkish chromium was to be exported to any other country except with the consent, in each case, of the said countries. The agreement was valid for two years, but could be extended for a third year on the request of any of the signatories. British Ambassador Knatchbull-Hugessen addressed a note to the Turkish government notifying them of Britain's intention to renew the agreement for the further period of one year. The wording of the agreement was such that this option was to be exercised by the governments of the French Republic and the United Kingdom respectively. But since France disappeared from the agreement to take their share of Turkish chrome output, it was now up to Britain and Turkey to negotiate a revised agreement.

When Eden met Aras in September, Knatchbull-Hugessen still had not received the Turkish government's acknowledgment regarding his note, except for a separate message from Saraçoğlu informing him that the Nazis, in their economic negotiations with the Turkish government, were pressing for the supply of chrome.[36] Therefore, Eden tried to make sure that Aras understood his apprehension. 'Should the Turkish Government not be prepared to renew the chrome agreement unconditionally, or agree to send chrome to Nazi Germany', Eden stated that His Majesty's Government could not but help regarding such action as against the spirit of the Anglo-Turkish alliance. Eden urged Saraçoğlu to recall that after the collapse of France, Great Britain, without hesitation or reference to the legal position, assumed responsibility for the French share of the Arms Credit to Turkey. Naturally, Britain was now expecting Turkey to return the favour, by denying the Nazis to buy chromium from the latter. During the concurrent Nazi–Turkish negotiations in Ankara, Karl Clodius relentlessly pushed to secure all of Turkey's chromium output for the year 1942. Referring to the Anglo-Turkish treaty, Menemencioğlu said that this would be simply impossible before 1943. Clodius objected to Turkey's transfer of France's share of the chromium to Great Britain but he knew well from Nazi intelligence reports that, in fact, Menemencioğlu and Saraçoğlu did the best they could to deliver some chromium to Germany, but ultimately failed to receive British approval. With regard to the political situation, in response to von Papen's remonstrations, Menemencioğlu replied that Turkey still wished to refrain from collaborating with the Nazis, and that, while Turkey had a vital interest in the defeat of Bolshevism, İnönü would not make this public.[37]

Anglo-Soviet occupation of Iran

Following Nazi Germany's execution of Operation Barbarossa in June 1941, another contingency began to shape Turkey's foreign policy toward the Soviet Union. In August 1941, a fortnight after Ribbentrop disclosed the written text of Molotov's demands on the Straits, Great Britain and the Soviet Union set out to invade Iran. For Turkey, the Anglo-Soviet invasion of a neutral neighbour was painfully reminiscent of the Anglo-Russian Entente of 1907. Mindful of the strong parallels between their country and Reza Shah's Iran, first and foremost with regards to the Nazi connection, Ankara's leadership was rightfully concerned. Reza Shah had declared his country's neutrality at the onset of war, but by August 1941, when Operation Countenance was unleashed, Iranian diplomacy was by and large pro-Nazi.[38] Throughout the interwar years, Reza Shah had been one of the largest recipients of German aid. A key region in the Nazi New Order, Iran tried to reduce its dependence on foreign imported goods, such as cotton textiles and war materiel.[39] Generous Nazi loans helped Reza Shah build national textile factories in Tehran as well as other infrastructure facilities and transportation hubs.[40] The Third Reich also promoted its interests by importing Iranian natural resources. The Nazi *Weltanschauung* was very effectively employed as a weapon of propaganda in Iran. To impress the Iranians, the Reich Cabinet had issued a special decree as early as 1936 by which the Iranians were exempted from the restrictions of the Nuremberg Racial Laws as pureblooded Aryans. German authors strove to arouse the sympathy of leading Iranians by drawing parallels among Reza Shah, Hitler, Mussolini and Kemal Atatürk, underlying the role and virtue of the *Führerprinzip*.[41]

Britain and the Soviet Union had become wary of the growing Nazi influence in Iran as early as the mid-1930s but failed to take substantial preemptive measures. When the Wehrmacht began marching east, Britain and the Soviet Union jointly occupied Iran to prevent Nazi encroachment in the area, which could have led to subsequent attacks on the Soviet Union. The Soviet Union desperately needed to safeguard its southern flank, bordering Iran, as well as its oil fields in Baku, which lay in close proximity. Great Britain also needed to protect its strategic oil investments in southern Iran. The chief architect of Operation Countenance was Anthony Eden, who briefly tried diplomatic channels to convince the Iranian authorities to expel the Nazis and sever their ties. Eden's message was such that Britain would, if necessary, support their requests by vigorous action.[42] At first, Molotov seemed indecisive about the effectiveness of a joint operation, and, whether or not such vigorous actions were possible by British forces alone the Chiefs of Staff in London could not say. In Molotov's view, the threat of economic measures against Iran might have sufficed to cause Reza Shah to act. But Eden was dubious about the use of economic sanctions and argued that Iranians knew quite well that 'before the arrival of that hour, they would be rescued by Germans'.[43] After the bitter consequences of the Munich policy of appeasement, Eden was certainly not willing to embark on economic sanctions alone unless he was certain that Britain and the Soviet Union both had the means to implement those sanctions with military action should the need arise.

In view of the anti-Soviet propaganda by the Nazis, Molotov changed his prognosis about Iran and announced that the Soviet Union was under no delusion pertaining to the events in Iran, which required military action.⁴⁴ On 19 July 1941, the Iranian government was asked by both British and Soviet representatives in Tehran to rid their country from Nazi elements on the grounds that they were engaged in activities prejudicial to Iran's status as a neutral state. On 25 August 1941, when the Anglo-Soviet invasion of Iran officially began, the Iranian army spearhead in Transcaucasia was crushed within two hours and, in defiance of Reza Shah's orders, Iranian soldiers laid down their arms without offering any significant resistance to the Anglo-Soviet advance. Having forced Reza Shah to abdicate in favour of his son Mohammed Reza Pahlavi in September, the Allied powers signed a treaty of alliance with Iran and declared that they 'jointly and severally undertake to respect the territorial integrity, sovereignty and political independence of Iran . . . against all aggression on the part of Germany'.⁴⁵ Soviet troops occupied northern Iran, while British troops occupied the south. A neutral zone that included Tehran was placed under Iranian control, and American troops were eventually stationed in 1942 as part of the allied war effort.⁴⁶ It was made clear in this démarche that Iran's independence would be respected only so long as Iran proved capable of defending itself against Nazi Germany, but despite this veiled threat, the Iranians did not take decisive action.⁴⁷ They agreed to keep watch on the Nazis in Iran but refused to expel them immediately on the grounds (which were in fact quite reasonable) that to do so would be a breach of their obligations as a neutral and would lay them open to risk of retaliation from Nazi Germany.

As far as Turkey's fate was concerned, from the onset of Anglo-Soviet negotiations, Anthony Eden considered it desirable not to create the impression among Ankara's ruling elite that Great Britain was returning to the imperial partition policy of the early twentieth century. It was inevitable that the Turks would become nervous when they saw Britain and the Soviet Union putting pressure on Iran under such conditions that were analogous to those from four decades earlier. Eden thought that an early assurance by both Britain and the Soviet Union to Turkey along these lines would do much to prevent that danger. As such, two weeks before the invasion, he instructed Ambassador Cripps in Moscow to convince the Soviets to join Great Britain in a shared declaration signalling their mutual determination to respect and protect the territorial integrity of Turkey.⁴⁸ It seemed to Eden all the more important not to allow the Nazis a free hand with their propaganda in Turkey. The Third Reich had already been making great play with the charge that Britain and the Soviet Union had sinister designs on Turkey. Ambassador Maisky, who appeared to be attracted by the idea, said that he would certainly report Eden's suggestion to his government. He thought it very likely they would agree to take some action on the lines Eden had suggested. In any event, Maisky assured Eden that his proposal would be 'urgently and sympathetically examined'.⁴⁹

Mindful of Turkey's concerns about Iran's fate, and of its own for that matter, Eden and Molotov sought to assure the Turkish government that they fully accept and endorse the Iranian policy of neutrality, and that they had entertained no designs against Iran's political independence or territorial integrity. In a joint communiqué delivered to Saraçoğlu on 14 August 1941, they expressed 'a sincere desire to maintain their existing policy of friendship and co-operation with Turkey which they believe to be in the best interests of both Soviet Russia and the British Empire'.⁵⁰ In a personal letter sent to İnönü, Eden also confirmed Britain's fidelity to the Montreux Convention and assured the Turkish government that they had no aggressive intentions or claims with regard to the Straits. Eden underlined the fact that the United Kingdom, like the Soviet Government, 'is prepared scrupulously to observe the territorial integrity of the Turkish Republic'.[51] While fully appreciating the desire of the Turkish government not to be involved in war, the letter continued: 'His Majesty's Government in the United Kingdom, as also the Soviet Government, would nevertheless be prepared to render Turkey every help and assistance in the event of her being attacked by any European Power'.[52] Likewise, in the preamble to Molotov's letter, the Soviet Union declared that Nazi agents provocateurs had been conducting a malicious anti-Soviet propaganda campaign in Ankara to bring about discord between Stalin and İnönü. Molotov insisted that such hearsay in no way corresponded to the attitude of the USSR, and that, 'if Turkey were in fact attacked and compelled to enter the war for the defense of her territory, she could count on full understanding and neutrality of the USSR on the basis of the non-aggression pact between the two countries'.[53]

Yet from the Turkish perspective, the situation in Iran had far more serious consequences than those imagined by the Soviet and British observers.[54] Despite Turkish policy-makers' resolve in isolating themselves from the broader Middle East theatre, where they would easily get bogged down in the midst of superpower conflict, a massive influx of refugees pouring into Turkey's southeastern provinces from neighbouring countries became a chronic problem. Within days of the Anglo-Soviet invasion of Iran, Ankara faced a surge of 30,000 refugees who required immediate humanitarian aid.[55] The building of refugee camps and supplying the region with fuel, food, vaccines and protection compelled İnönü to rush the ongoing railroad project connecting the Diyarbakır–Elazığ line with the Iran–Iraq border, which put an extra burden on an already strained national economy.[56] By February 1942, the Turkish government seemed to be losing control of the situation: Ankara deployed additional gendarmerie against villages on its border with Iran to block future waves of migration.[57] Turkish intelligence reports indicate that aside from Iranian civilians who migrated to Turkey in the winter of 1942, certain high-ranking officers of the Iranian army, as well as businessmen of Azeri–Turkish origin, had also settled in southeastern Anatolia.[58] Iranian officers and businessmen 'who were quintessentially anti-Soviet and anti-British' sought to propagate 'disturbing' ideas through publishing books, pamphlets and columns.[59] Wary of the various activities around Ankara, the Turkish government consistently banned the circulation of these materials, which they deemed 'perilous to [their] relations with the Soviet Union'.[60]

In any case, the Anglo-Soviet action in Iran did not meet with approval from the Turkish government. Saraçoğlu did not hesitate to express his disapproval of it,[61] clearly due to the anti-Soviet turns in Turkey's general policy. In Ankara, distrust of the Soviet Union was stronger than its trust in Great Britain. With Kurdish activities in Azerbaijan, that distrust grew stronger. It was bad enough (in Turkish eyes) for Iranian Azerbaijan to be in Soviet hands, and even the assurances regarding the temporary nature of this occupation and the promises of evacuation after the war – which were finally embodied in the treaty between Great Britain, the USSR and Iran – did not console the Turkish government.[62] But still more disturbing to them were the reports that the Kurds in those districts were being actively encouraged to seek independence, and even provided with arms with the connivance, if not the active assistance, of the Soviet authorities. This anxiety was aggravated by the appearance on Turkish territory of various spies who appeared to be acting for the Soviets. Several arrests were made in Eastern Turkey and on more than one occasion shots were exchanged.[63]

Not long after the new Shah signed a Treaty of Alliance with Great Britain and the USSR, Turkish soldiers began patrolling the border more attentively, monitoring border crossings near Doğubeyazid, the country's easternmost outpost adjoining Iran. The Third Army was asked to take strict precautions against Soviet espionage in the area, and to monitor potential Soviet agents who might infiltrate through the steep passages of Mount Ararat. Among the numerous reports that were dispatched by Turkish counterintelligence officers to relevant ministries, one of them captures Turkey's discomfort most vividly. In January 1942, four months after the Soviet invasion, a Syrian national of Turkish descent was captured at the Gürbulak checkpoint on the Iranian border and interrogated by the Turkish gendarmerie. The young man (codenamed Halit), who later confessed to being a Soviet spy, confirmed Ankara's fears about Soviet involvement and the convoluted nature of wartime loyalties in the region.[64]

Halit was born in the early 1910s in Ottoman Bayburt (Northeast Anatolia) to a half-Arab, half-Turkish family. He was accepted to the prestigious Ottoman Military School in Aleppo (*Halep Askeri Rüştiyesi*), but decided to drop out and took up driving to make a living. In 1937, Halit encountered the future Syrian prime minister, Cemil Mürdüm Bey (Jamil Mardam) while giving him a city tour in his car. He was appointed as the Aleppo representative of Mürdüm Bey's National Bloc (*Al-Kutlah Al-Wataniyah*) and when the National Bloc won the elections in 1938, Halit asked for an appointment with Cemil Mürdüm Bey to discuss his political career. The meeting between the newly appointed prime minister and Halit proved awkward, when the latter was accused of being a cheap propagandist before being arrested and tortured by the French mandate police. In prison, Halit met two Iraqi mujahedeen, who asked him to smuggle them into Iraq, which he agreed to do after being released from the penitentiary. A few miles off the Iraqi border, Halit and the mujahedeen survived a French police attack with machine guns. As Halit saved his companions' lives, they introduced him to the Grand Mufti of Jerusalem – Muhammad Amin Al-Husayni. The Mufti was an ardent supporter of the Nazi Party, a fierce adversary of the British occupation, and, of course, an enemy of Zionism. Al-Husayni hired Halit as his personal chauffeur, upon which Halit grew more indoctrinaire and more pro-Nazi. After the British occupation of Iraq, when Al-Husayni was exiled and sought refuge in Iran, Halit accompanied him. But a fortnight after the Anglo-Soviet Invasion in 1941, Halit woke up in their Tehran apartment only to realize that the Mufti was nowhere to be found. He later discovered that the Iranian police had secretly arrested the Mufti and sent him into exile in India, on the orders of the British occupiers. In his desperation, Halit sought help to get into Turkey through a car repair shop owner in Tabriz, who apparently took him to the Soviet *rezidentura* rather than to the Turkish border. The Soviets found out about Halit's story and threatened him with extraditing his whole family to the British authorities unless he worked for them and gathered information in Eastern Turkey. Halit acquiesced and consented to reporting to Soviet spies on the following: the number of Turkish planes; the number of Turkish tanks, artillery and anti-aircraft guns; whether or not there were any German soldiers stationed in Turkey; and whether the Turks would be willing to attack Iran. Halit was provided with names of other Soviet local agents in the area and was instructed to make contact with the Soviet consulate in Turkey to share his findings on the above.

One day before his planned mission, Halit saw a chance to evade the Soviet agents tailing him on the streets of Tabriz, and surreptitiously asked a fellow hotel manager to send him across the Turkish border, along with a group of Kurdish smugglers. On the marshes across the Turkish border near Ararat, he spotted a Soviet team looking for him. So he hid in the marshes for twelve hours, with half of his body drenched in freezing water, and later crawled to the Turkish gendarmerie building. The gendarmerie report stated that he was 'half-dead' when the patrol guards found him. The information Halit provided to the Turkish officers revealed that the Soviets were indeed entertaining hostile scenarios and stationing numerous spies in Meskhetia, now that the whole area was deserted after Stalin's deportations.[65]

The plot to assassinate Franz von Papen

In the aftermath of the Soviet occupation of Iranian Azerbaijan, Nazi Germany did revive and propagate the 'evil Russia' trope in Turkey. But Stalin's own blunders, which aggravated Turkish Russophobia, played an equally important role. Halit's story is but one example in Turkish national archives that illustrates Turkey's growing distrust of the Soviet Union. A more significant incident that marred Soviet–Turkish affairs vis-à-vis Nazi Germany occurred a month later, in February 1942, when two agents of the People's Commissariat for Internal Affairs (NKVD), V.V. Pavlov and A.P. Kornilov, were caught in Ankara after an assassination attempt on Franz von Papen.[66] Soviet historians have long claimed that the attempted murder was in fact the work of Nazi Germany's own secret service, and done in order to disrupt Soviet–Turkish relations and provoke Turkey into declaring war on the Soviet Union.[67] With the opening of Soviet archives, however, several Russian monographs have now appeared, eschewing the Russian theory of German conspiracy, and confirmed Franz von Papen's account.[68]

Throughout World War II, neutral Ankara was a hotbed of espionage and international intrigue. Franz von Papen knew that he was under close surveillance by foreign services, most notably the Soviet intelligence. To inquire about von Papen's anti-Soviet propaganda, among other things, Pavel Sudoplatov, chief of the NKVD's 4th Bureau, commissioned military intelligence officers Naum Isaakovich Eytingon, Pavel Vasilievsky and Ivan Vinarov.[69] Eytingon and Vasilievsky's initial reports alarmed Soviet authorities about von Papen's secret plans to disrupt the Anglo-American support for the Soviet war effort. According to these reports, von Papen was using the Vatican's chargé d'affaires in Ankara to cut a deal with the British and American ambassadors.[70] Parallel to these reports, the NKVD was also informed about secret meetings between the American ambassador to the Holy See, Myron Taylor, and Cardinal Angelo Giuseppe Roncalli, who would later become Pope John XXIII. All of this pointed to Germany's designs to isolate the Soviet Union from its coalition with the Anglo-American bloc.[71] Although the mutual exchange between Nazi Germany and the Anglo-American bloc through the Holy See did not really amount to an agreement, von Papen's attempt to use the Catholic Church as an intermediary against the Soviet Union became a source of apprehension in Moscow, and led to Sudoplatov's plot to assassinate von Papen in February 1942.[72] Upon Sudoplatov's instructions, Eytingon hired a 44-year-old İstanbul consular officer, Georgiy Ivanovich Pavlov, and a 34-year-old military attaché Leonid Kornilov to carry out the assassination. Pavlov and Kornilov planted the bomb in a Telefunken radio (presumably to draw attention to the Gestapo) and recruited a 25-year-old Macedonian student from Skopje, Ömer Tokat, who had taken lodgings in a small hotel in Ankara, to kill von Papen.[73] The young man was provided with a pistol, the serial number of which had been scratched off.

On 24 February, at about ten o'clock in the morning, Franz von Papen took his wife out for a stroll at the Embassy Row on Atatürk Boulevard, which to him seemed unusually quiet. Suddenly, they were both hurled to the ground by a violent explosion. Von Papen immediately picked himself up and helped his wife, who, despite being noticeably shaken, made a gesture to indicate that no bones were broken. At first, von Papen assumed that they had set off a mine as he looked around to see two young women, who had been slightly injured.[74] The explosion had broken all the windows for a couple of hundred yards and a crowd quickly begun to gather. Apart from a cut knee and a torn trouser leg, von Papen was unhurt, although he would suffer from temporary hearing loss and concussion. His wife, on the other hand, was completely fine, except for a large bloodstain on her coat, which turned out to come from the assailant, who had been blown to pieces.[75]

Members of the Turkish security service were soon on the spot for a detailed investigation. Within twenty-four hours they solved the riddle. Human remains, including a shoe hanging in a tree, had been found at the scene of the explosion.[76] These clues led the police to Ömer Tokat, who was identified by hotel receptionists Halid Ünsal and Ali Çelik.[77] The trail ultimately led to the Soviet Consulate-General in İstanbul, which was immediately encircled by the Turkish gendarmerie.[78] Despite the Russian ambassador's outraged protests, the embassy building – also on Atatürk Boulevard near von Papen's residence – remained surrounded until the Soviets responded to an ultimatum to surrender Tokats' two accomplices, Abdurrahman Sayma (a medical student) and Süleyman Sağol (a local barber and friend of Tokat) who had taken refuge there earlier and were now suspected of complicity.[79] The Turkish prime minister announced that the incident would be further investigated, 'whatever the political consequences might be'.[80] Saydam said that he 'would not allow Turkey to become the scene of political assassinations'.[81] The investigations and trials lasted several months, and the accomplices were eventually sentenced for their part in the affair.

As it turned out, the would-be assassin, Tokat, and his accomplices, Sağol and Sayma, had been practising pistol shooting for several weeks at the Russian Consulate General in İstanbul.[82] Meanwhile, Pavlov and Kornilov had been observing von Papen's usual route to the office, which he preferred to do by foot at a certain hour every morning, and decided that at 10.00 am they had the best opportunity for attack. In case the student found himself unable to get away after the shooting, he was to pull the pin out of the grenade with which he had been provided.[83] This, he was told, would emit a smokescreen, under cover of which he would be able to escape. The young man must have been over-cautious, and presumably decided to shoot with one hand and set off his bomb with the other.[84] It may be that he exploded it a fraction of a second before firing the shot. At any rate, von Papen later claimed that he had no recollection of hearing a bullet. However, the 'smoke bomb' proved more effective than Tokat had expected and he was blown into pieces. The investigation also proved that the prime conspirators in the plot, Pavlov and Kornilov, tried to flee the crime scene before being caught by the Turkish frontier guards in Erzurum.[85]

Until the investigation got under way, Ankara was full of rumours regarding possible reasons for and organizers behind the attack. At first, it was not clear whether it had been directed against von Papen or the head of the Turkish military, Marshal Fevzi Çakmak, who had passed down the Atatürk Boulevard in his car a few minutes earlier.[86] The Soviets, the British Secret Service and the Gestapo were all suspected of having organized the incident. The fact that the assassin was so well informed about von Papen's walk was at first thought to be the work of British Intelligence, which had set up headquarters across the street from von Papen's private residence, which was kept under constant observation with binoculars. This rumour had also reached the British ambassador, who immediately assured von Papen that 'his people had had nothing to do with the affair'.[87] For von Papen, the Gestapo seemed a distinct possibility, and this suggestion was reinforced by accounts of mysterious telephone calls that various people claimed to have heard.[88] However, all this speculation came to an end very soon, as the Turks pinned the guilt on the Soviets: von Papen himself had had very few doubts as to who the real culprits were. Von Papen was showered with congratulations, and President İnönü and his wife presented von Papen and his wife with a magnificent bouquet of flowers and expressed their regret at this murderous attempt on their lives.

The von Papen assassination trials quickly became breakfast news, with almost every major Turkish daily paper covering details of the conspiracy. *Cumhuriyet* and *Tan* were particularly enthused and found the story appealed to their readership. From Ömer Tokat's love affairs to his Yugoslavian comrades' testimonies, the von Papen assassination plot was scrutinized in great detail in the spring of 1942. Russian news outlets were equally invested in the trials, and mirrored how greatly the Kremlin was perturbed by this blunder. On 6 March, *Pravda* levied harsh accusations against a number of Turkish journalists, who were propagating Nazi fantasies.[89] TASS news agency employed a similar prosecutorial rhetoric and blamed the Turkish authorities for detaining innocent citizens of the Soviet Union rather than going after the real culprits.[90] On 10 April 1942, the Turkish government hired Russian interpreters to provide the defendants with a translation of the indictment and invited Moscow to send forensic experts and legal observers to examine the court findings, including a big jar that contained remaining body parts of Ömer, which was displayed on the front pages of Turkish newspapers the next day.[91]

Upon hearing numerous witnesses, including a factotum and room servant who confessed to seeing Ömer Tokat with Kornilov and Pavlov on at least two different occasions, the two NKVD agents were convicted on 17 June 1942.[92] Both Pavlov and Kornilov repeatedly denied their charges, blamed the Turkish court for falsifying witness statements and claimed that most of the witnesses 'were lying Trotskyists anyway'.[93] 'The Turkish court acted to benefit the Hitlerites', wrote the popular army newspaper *Krasnaya Zvezda*, 'and sentenced two of our innocent citizens to twenty years imprisonment'.[94] *Pravda* published a similar article on the subject and pointed to the continued presence of German spies in Turkey. The article claimed that there were '1,300 fascist agents still operating in Turkey'.[95]

Regardless of the number of Nazi spies in Ankara, the attempted assassination of Franz von Papen undoubtedly gave the Third Reich an upper hand in Ankara's diplomatic intrigues. Von Papen now had a number of legitimate reasons to intensify his anti-Soviet campaign. In his monthly meeting with Şükrü Saraçoğlu, von Papen turned the provocation conspiracy around and blamed the Soviets for impeding Nazi–Turkish friendship by using confiscated Luftwaffe planes against Turkey. The Turkish newspapers were giving considerable coverage to the four Nazi bombers that had been spotted trespassing into Turkish airspace near the Soviet border. Von Papen presented concrete evidence that those planes – one Messerschmidt 109, one Messerschmidt 110, one Junker 87s and another unidentified plane whose pilot had allegedly survived a crash near Kars – were not part of the Luftwaffe, but had been apprehended earlier by Soviets, who had repaired and rearmed them to antagonize the Turks.[96]

SS *Struma* tragedy

The night before Stalin's unsuccessful attempt to assassinate Franz von Papen, on 23 February 1942, a Soviet submarine (ShCh-213) attacked a Turkish steamer (*Çankaya*) in the vicinity of İstanbul's Black Sea coast. When the torpedo missed the *Çankaya*, the submarine surfaced and used its onboard canon to sink it. While this gave additional time for the Turkish sailors to evacuate the ship's passengers into lifeboats and escape, the Turkish government never felt more insecure than it did during the early hours of 24 February.[97] Just when the Turkish authorities began working on a diplomatic note to be delivered to the Soviet ambassador, less than ten hours after the *Çankaya* incident, and minutes before the failed assassination attempt on von Papen, the Soviet submarine ShCh-213 (captained by Lieutenant D.M. Denezhko) torpedoed a second vessel north of the Bosphorus, the SS *Struma*, which was chartered to carry Jewish refugees from Axis-allied Romania to British-controlled Palestine.[98] After a series of engine failures, the SS *Struma* had barely made it half-way through its voyage before anchoring in İstanbul with its 769 Romanian refugee passengers onboard.[99] When this 170-ton former yacht sank, it left behind only one survivor, David Stoliar, making it one of the largest civilian naval disasters of World War II.[100] The menacing naval incidents of 24 February would leave Turkish–Soviet relations irreparably damaged.

Until recently, details surrounding the *Struma* tragedy were often conflicting, or confusing, or both. Only broad factors were recorded: the *Struma* and its passengers sat in İstanbul harbour for ten weeks before the ship was towed back to the Black Sea and set adrift.[101] A mysterious explosion had sunk the vessel, leaving only one survivor. We now know that, after long weeks of arduous waiting on one of the world's busiest waterways, the final straw for the *Struma* came at noon on 23 February. Wary of antagonizing either of the belligerent blocs, particularly the Soviet Union, which had been accusing Turkey of collaborating with the Nazis and of allowing Nazi vessels through the Straits, the Turkish government sent a massive Turkish military tugboat. Its arrival drew passengers to the deck, alarming them. The passengers were still not sure if the *Struma*'s engine was working. The tug's captain had been given orders to take the ship far enough out that it would not return to İstanbul, and the coastguard was on alert in the event that the ship drifted back towards the straits.[102]

Meanwhile the Soviet submarine ShCh-213 was navigating in the vicinity of the entrance of the Bosphorus. In the early hours of 24 February 1942, the submarine placed itself between the Turkish coast and the *Struma*. For many years David Stoliar believed that the *Struma* was torpedoed from batteries located on the Turkish coast, because the *Struma*'s chief mate, Lazar Dikof, saw the torpedo coming from that direction. It seems that Lieutenant Denezhko's submarine accomplished its deadly mission well.[103] When the torpedo hit the ship, David Stoliar, who was asleep just below the deck, was thrown into the air before falling into the water.[104] When he surfaced, he saw that the explosion had completely destroyed the SS *Struma*. Stoliar later estimated that about 100–150 people were still alive and trying to stay afloat among the enormous amount of debris. It was extremely cold and as the day progressed, ever more people disappeared in the freezing waters of the Black Sea. By the evening, Stoliar was alone. The Turkish coastguard station at Şile saw the wreckage in the Black Sea and sent a rowing boat with six sailors, for salvage purposes. By coincidence, they found David Stoliar, who was still alive, floating aside Dikof, the chief mate, who had died, and another corpse.[105] This took place twenty-four hours after the explosion. They took Stoliar to their station, fed him, and told him that he was the only survivor.[106] Two days later, he was taken to the bus station and driven to İstanbul bus terminus, where an ambulance was waiting for him.

As soon as the ambulance had taken Stoliar to the military hospital in Haydarpaşa, Stoliar was wheeled into a room with a policeman at the door. Nobody was allowed in except the doctor and a nurse. Stoliar stayed there for seven days and he was not allowed to communicate with anybody. After seven days of camphor treatment to his legs, hands and arms (suffering from frostbite), the police took him from the hospital to the European side of İstanbul, to the Central Police Station, and incarcerated him on the top floor – the prison floor. He was detained there for seventy-one days. The reason given for his imprisonment was that he was in Turkey illegally, as he did not have the appropriate visa. The *real* reason for it, however, was to keep him away from the army of newspaper correspondents who were struggling to find information about the disaster.

During these seventy-one days in the Central Police Station (or prison, more accurately), Stoliar was at least supplied with plentiful food from a nearby high-end restaurant. The other prisoners, about six of them – German, Bulgarian, Russian, British – were not treated to similar luxury. According to David Stoliar, the Turkish authorities applied to London for a travel document with an entry visa for Palestine. The British Colonial Office refused, but the British Foreign Office overruled that decision and issued him with the necessary documents and visa for Palestine. On his final day in custody, Stoliar was released in the care of Mr Simon Brod, who was then the president of the Jewish community in İstanbul. He took Stoliar to his house, and the next morning dropped him off at the railway station on the Asian side of İstanbul, where a policeman was waiting for them. The policeman and Stoliar boarded the train that took him from İstanbul to Aleppo via Ankara. At the border between Turkey and Lebanon, the policeman gave Stoliar his travel documents and he returned to Turkey, while Stoliar went on to Palestine.[107]

After the *Struma* incident, the material and logistical aid given by Turkey to Jews fleeing to Palestine from Nazi-occupied territories did not come as a surprise to the Nazis, who knew that a group of Turkish diplomats had been helping the Jews either in the form of granting Turkish citizenship retroactively (to former Ottoman subjects now living in Europe) or simply by facilitating their journey from Nazi-occupied zones to Jerusalem.[108] But it would be reasonable to suggest that the Nazis turned a blind eye to this 'problem' mainly because the Turkish government was not particularly sympathetic to the Jewish cause in general and pursued an equivocal policy.[109] As early as the 1930s, when Hitler came to power, a large group of Jewish scholars from the Third Reich had been allowed into Turkey to help modernize the country's higher education system. In a personal letter, Albert Einstein pleaded with the Turkish government 'to allow forty professors and doctors from Germany to continue their scientific and medical work in Turkey'.[110] Likewise, Albert Malche and the prominent Frankfurt pathologist Philipp Schwartz, who established the Notgemeinschaft deutscher Wissenschaftler im Ausland, tried to secure academic posts for the persecuted law and philosophy scholars. Many of these Jewish scholars came from a left-wing Hegelian ideology and left their mark among Turkey's university students and secular intelligentsia in the 1930s.

At the same time, however, Turkish public opinion bred significant anti-Semitic sentiments, which at times corresponded to Ankara's official position towards its own Jewish minority. After the resettlement law of June 1934, for instance, the Turkish government failed to check the pogroms in Eastern Thrace, which were orchestrated by a group of pan-Turkists.[111] Although the government later condemned the violence, approximately 15,000 Turkish Jews fled the country, followed by international protests. Five years later, when Hitler began implementing the Final Solution, Turkey's position toward the Holocaust was equally ambiguous. In 1942, the Turkish government passed the Wealth Tax, which targeted all minority groups, including the Jews. Through taxing minority groups, which included non-Muslim citizens of the republic, Turkey implemented a heavy-handed fund-raising campaign for defence expenditures, which in practice was carried out arbitrarily and in a discriminatory fashion. The Wealth Tax also encouraged anti-Semitic factions who portrayed the Jews, along with Armenians and Greeks, as war profiteers.[112] Nevertheless, during the two-year period in which the Wealth Tax was implemented, the Turkish government also responded positively to international appeals to help displaced Jews, facilitating their safe passage to Palestine. Facing a growing influx of ships entering the Straits from Bulgarian and Romanian ports, the Turkish state regulated their transfer, but seldom allowed them residence permits.[113] According to a prime ministerial report in October 1942, since the outbreak of war in 1939, twenty-one ships had arrived in the port of İstanbul carrying 7,136 Jewish passengers seeking either asylum or transit visas. Of those 7,136 Jews fleeing the Holocaust, 6,084 people were provided with documents and logistical support to go on to Palestine, 893 drowned – 767 in the Struma disaster alone – and only 159 were allowed to stay in Turkey.[114]

After the SS *Struma* disaster, it was not Turkey but Romania that presented a far greater, and somewhat ironic challenge for Hitler. Within a few weeks of ordering the extermination of Europe's Jews in January 1942, a month before the *Struma* incident, Hitler began to worry that Nazi Germany was in danger of being outdone by Romania in terms of implementing the Final Solution and that the whole situation there might deteriorate into bloody chaos. When, for instance, Antonescu proposed sending 110,000 more Jews to concentration camps that were regarded as appalling even by the Nazis, Eichmann asked the Foreign Office in Berlin to order a halt to the Romanian efforts to slaughter the Jews à la Vlad Tepes.[115] The death of 768 Romanian Jews on the SS *Struma* brought untimely and unnecessary public attention to neutral Turkey, and confirmed Eichmann's concerns about the risk of Romania spreading the problem beyond Germany's control.

Great Britain, on the other hand, was thought to be the primary suspect behind the *Struma* tragedy, perhaps even more so than Nazi Germany. For the passengers on the *Struma*, Britain's determination to halt its journey and the resulting political intrigue and gamesmanship would bring disaster, although no one could have known that on the day they were towed into İstanbul harbour. The passengers fully expected that the ship's engine would be repaired, they would receive the promised visas, and they would be on their way to Palestine. They did not factor in the British resistance to their journey. From the moment it arrived in İstanbul, the *Struma* presented a dilemma for the British government. While many British officials, including Winston Churchill, were sympathetic to the plight of European Jews, the British had generally been determined to block illegal immigration to Palestine.

On 20 December 1942, five days after the SS *Struma* arrived in the Bosphorus with engine trouble, the British ambassador met with the assistant secretary of Turkey's Ministry of Foreign Affairs in Ankara. The Turkish official told Knatchbull-Hugessen that the *Struma* was entitled by law to sail through the Straits and the Turkish government could do nothing to stop it. 'If His Majesty's Government would let these immigrants enter Palestine, I will let the ship proceed on its voyage and even assist it,' the Turkish official told the British ambassador. 'His Majesty's Government does not want these people in Palestine and they have no permission to go there,' replied Knatchbull-Hugessen.[116] Looking at Britain's role in the *Struma* incident, it is difficult not to take a dim view. Everything in Britain's diplomatic arsenal was arrayed to stop Jews from reaching the country. The British government would prove itself willing and able to go beyond passive cables and raised voices in Ankara to stop the *Struma* from leaving İstanbul.[117] Its motives were coldly strategic; London did not want to devote even more military resources to keeping a lid on hostilities between Arabs and Jews in Palestine. Even more important, the British did not want to antagonize the Arab populations in the Middle East, who controlled the huge oilfields so vital to the Allied war effort.[118]

Until recently, when the Turkish and Soviet archives were inaccessible, a nagging question loomed over the *Struma* tragedy, as well as the sinking of the fishing vessel *Çankaya* in the vicinity a few hours earlier. If these vessels were sunk by a torpedo fired from a submarine (and David Stoliar's recollection gave credence to this hypothesis), was it a Soviet or a Nazi submarine? Both the Third Reich and the Soviet Union maintained a crowded diplomatic corps and countless spies in Turkey throughout the war, and someone must have known exactly who was on board the *Struma* and to observe their courses of navigation.

The Nazis appeared as the natural culprit behind the attack on SS *Sturma*, since they would have had a reason for attacking a shipload of Jews. And yet there was no sign of Nazi U-boats navigating in that area at that time. While the Soviet Union vigorously patrolled the area with submarines in order to protect their southern flank, to many researchers the suggestion that a Soviet submarine sank a ship full of refugees did not make much sense. The puzzling questions surrounding the *Struma* tragedy were resolved only after the unearthing of Stalin's secret 1941 order to destroy all vessels headed toward Germany in the Black Sea and the discovery of a particular Soviet submarine's logs kept by Lieutenant Denezhko of ShCh-213, which torpedoed the SS *Struma*.[119] As far as Turkey's role is concerned, Prime Minister Refik Saydam was convinced that the Ankara government 'cannot be held responsible for the tragedy since they had done everything in their capacity to assist the Jews on board SS *Struma*'.[120] Two months after the tragedy, in a parliamentary hearing, the prime minister said, in a croaky voice, that 'Turkey cannot and should not be home to people, who are unwanted by others'.[121]

Russophobic neutrality

Until December 1941, the Turkish government entertained hopes of a compromise between the British Empire and the Axis powers. İnönü thought that this could be reached, so long as the United States did not join the other side, which would easily tip the balance. With the ominous incidents of February 1942 and the outbreak of the American–Japanese War after Pearl Harbor, however, İnönü realized that all doors to this option were now closed forever. The immediate consequence of this development was a renewed emphasis on Turkey's unalterable desire to keep out of the war and not to be enlisted by any side for interests that did not affect Turkey. Yet it seemed clear that the entente between the Anglo-American bloc and Soviet Russia determined the contours of Turkish foreign political thought. Turks knew too well from history that their national existence was intrinsically linked to the outcome of the German–Russian war. The fact that Britain decided to reorder Europe against Nazi terror *with* the help of Bolshevik Russia came as a severe shock. The joint Anglo-Soviet assurances to Turkey were regarded as a propagandist measure, in order to support Soviet Russia's fight with every means available.

In Ankara's view, America was strongest of the partners of the Anglo-American bloc. By the same token, the Axis powers could secure a decision in their favour only by smashing the British global empire. Yet İnönü made it quite clear that the destruction of that empire was in no way in Turkey's interest, which required a balance of power in the Mediterranean rather than unlimited Italian domination, which could well have been the consequence of a total victory for the Axis.[122] By January 1942, the other eventuality was a total victory for the Anglo-American bloc, with the help of Soviet Russia. This, in the Turkish opinion, would mean the complete dissolution of Europe, since neither Britain nor the US would have been in a position to check the Russians territorially, or to prevent the bolshevization of a starving, war-exhausted, impoverished Europe.

Consequently, Turkish foreign policy-makers were still focused on finding a compromise, in the event of which they would undoubtedly be prepared at the proper moment to throw their military weight into the mix. İnönü and Saraçoğlu realized that if the Anglo-American bloc sought a decision in Europe, it could find it only on the Russian battlefields. Therein, however, existed a direct threat to the future of Turkey, and, therefore, developments in this theatre caused great apprehension. Franz von Papen was acutely aware of these considerations and argued that 'any attempt to induce Turkey prematurely to take up an active position, whether by demanding her participation in a war or demanding the right of transit for troops through her territory, would inevitably push Turkey over to the other side'.[123] In historical scholarship, the established narrative suggests that Germany put immense pressure on the Turkish government, particularly during 1942, for Turkey to join the Axis. Looking at the correspondence between von Papen and Ribbentrop, it becomes evident that this was not the case. In 1942, Germany pursued a more cautious policy of courting Turkey's allegiance while respecting its neutrality, and was simply waiting for the right moment to request military cooperation.

The necessity of remaining aloof to the war theatre strongly dominated Turkish public opinion (with the exception of pro-Nazi Turanian factions). The government could justify entry into the war only on the grounds of a violation of its sovereign rights. In the highly revealing talk von Papen had with President İnönü in late December, it was repeatedly intimated to him by the president that Turkey was strongly interested in the destruction of the Russian colossus, and that no propaganda or pressure from the Anglo-American side could induce Turkey to do the slightest thing against Nazi interests.[124] Von Papen's following conversations with Menemencioğlu and Şükrü Saraçoğlu again made it clear that they suspected a Russian threat. Von Papen told Ribbentrop that even if the Turkish government were to receive no official confirmation of the territorial demands discussed between Eden and Stalin, 'they would still assume that such demands conformed with the Bolsheviks' actual intentions'.[125] Von Papen, therefore, suggested that it would be desirable for Germany to share all information confidentially with the Turkish government with regard to the Eden–Stalin talks. Von Papen also urged Ribbentrop 'not to do anything which might put Turkey into a morally embarrassing position vis-à-vis its British alliance'.[126] In order for Turkey's trust in Nazi Germany to remain unshaken, he argued that the march of events 'must leave the Turks free to choose for themselves the moment at which they become convinced that the maintenance of their alliance with Britain is incompatible with the safeguarding of their national future'.[127]

In April 1942, mindful of Turkey's growing concerns about the Anglo-Soviet alliance and Nazi Germany's attempts to exacerbate Ankara's anti-Soviet attitude,

Anthony Eden sought to mediate Turco-Soviet relations once again. In his monthly meeting with the newly appointed Turkish ambassador Rauf Orbay, Anthony Eden asked whether the arrival of spring increased Turkey's anxiety with regards to the prolonged warfare at the eastern front.[128] What he really wanted to know was whether Turkey's attitude would become more favourable to the Allied camp in light of Nazi Germany's failure to bring Operation Barbarossa to a successful conclusion. Orbay, in his somewhat evasive reply, suggested that Turkey would seek to maintain its wait-and-see policy with composure, whatever the repercussions might be, and would uphold its previous commitments to Britain. Orbay said that the Turks had had in their long history a variety of governments: 'we had good Sultans, who were great administrators, we had mad Sultans, and we had drunken Sultans – but we had never had a government that broke its word.'[129] The ambassador mentioned to Eden that the Great War had been a tragic and unnecessary interlude in the normal relationship between Great Britain and Turkey. Orbay expressed his firm belief that the reason behind Turkey's integration to the opposing camp in 1914 was due to her fear and suspicion of Russia. 'When Russia joined the Entente in 1905 and 1907,' Orbay claimed, 'Turks immediately began to think that Britain would collaborate with Russia to fulfil the latter's long-cherished ambition of obtaining control of the Straits.'[130] For Orbay, it was the suspicion sown at this time that began the process by which Turkey was led to the side of Germany. The ambassador added that the Turks knew that they had made a terrible mistake, and it was inconceivable that they should repeat the same blunder now. Orbay told Eden that he himself had signed the Armistice at Moudros, and he knew then, while signing it, that it was better for Turkey than 'if she had been victorious, because in that event she would have been quite literally a colony of Germany'.[131]

In spite of Rauf Orbay's mollifying statements, the arrival of spring saw a number of insecurities surface in Turkey, first and foremost being the increased Anglo-Russian collaboration. Mindful of this apprehension, Eden asked Orbay whether Ambassador Knatchbull-Hugessen's recent visit to Moscow had begun to revive in Turkey the old suspicions of Anglo-Russian collaboration. The ambassador replied that it was necessary to distinguish between the Turkish government and Turkish ruling classes and the masses of the people who were inevitably susceptible – to a greater or lesser extent – to Nazi German propaganda. As far as the former were concerned, Orbay said that they were not as afraid of Bolshevik Russia as they had been afraid of the previous Tsarist regime. He also added that the wisest thing Britain had done in this war was to give immediate recognition and friendship to the Bolsheviks as soon as Germany attacked them. But from the point of view of the Turkish people, it was very important not to allow Axis propaganda to get out of control. For Orbay, the Turkish people generally had been much more worried by Sir Stafford Cripps's speech at Bristol, when he referred to the necessity of giving Russia 'inviolable strategic frontiers' than they had been by Knatchbull-Hugessen's visit to Moscow.[132] They were worried because this phrase immediately revived memories of the old Russian desire to control the Straits. They were not in the least worried by the idea of communist expansion. Neither Orbay nor his government were afraid of Russian imperialist expansion, at any rate under the current regime. He was only afraid of it becoming a bogey in Axis propaganda.[133]

Having met Orbay, Eden asked the Soviet ambassador for a meeting on Turkish–Soviet relations.[134] Ambassador Maisky had already been debriefed by Sir Alexander Cadogan, Under-Secretary of the Foreign Office, about Britain's concern with regard to ostensible Russophobia in Turkey, which became apparent after the ominous incidents of February.[135] Eden asked Maisky to urge his government to do something to mitigate the danger of a closer partnership between Germany and Turkey. Maisky said that the Soviet government admitted its mistake in the failed assassination attempt on von Papen, and even reacted strongly to the Soviet press' provocative coverage of the following trials. But he also added that the Turks had handled the matter most unfortunately; Stalin was staggered that the Turkish government had not tried to keep it quiet.[136] Far from keeping quiet, however, the Turkish press had written up the whole matter, and this was what frustrated Stalin most. Maisky told Eden that Saraçoğlu had given Ambassador Vinogradov the impression originally that the whole thing would be handled judiciously, but contrarily the Turks did not pursue this course; instead they had directed a good deal of political criticism against the Soviet Union.[137] Maisky reminded Eden that only Germany could gain from tactics of this kind, and in the circumstances his government maintained that it was natural for the Turkish press to have reacted in this way. Bearing in mind the fact that the Soviet Union was behind the assassination, it is hard to imagine anyone with a thicker skin than Maisky, who also complained that Britain's ambassador in Ankara, Sir Hugh Knatchbull-Hugessen, had been too pro-Turkish in his attitude. In speaking to the Soviet ambassador in Ankara, Vinogradov, Knatchbull-Hugessen appeared to accept the Turkish thesis entirely, and the Soviet ambassador was somewhat put out when Saraçoğlu told him that he had no cause to complain about the Turkish press, since Knatchbull-Hugessen thought its attitude perfectly fair.

Following Stalin's blunders in Turkey during the winter of 1942, Anthony Eden did everything he could to bridge the widening gap in Turkish–Soviet relations. In June 1942, Eden met with Orbay numerous times in the hope of convincing the Turkish government that Turkey's suspicions regarding the Soviet Union had largely been the work of Nazi propagandists. Eden reminded Orbay time and time again that the German campaign seemed to fall into two parts. First, rumours would be spread by the Germans that the Soviet government intended to make a separate peace treaty with Germany. This was obviously intended to sow suspicion between Turkey and the Soviet Union. Second, Germany would offer to supply Turkey with industrial equipment of various sorts; most recently, there had been an offer of a credit to enable Turkey to buy war material, including tanks, from Germany.[138] 'As an ally,' Eden told Orbay, 'England felt justified in putting the Turkish government on their guard against the German maneuvers.'[139] Eden also reminded Orbay that Great Britain had never asked Turkey to take an active part in the war, but had looked to Turkey to serve as a sort of bulwark, 'a protective pad', against German penetration in the Middle East. In other words, as opposed to the established historical narrative, England also did not ask for Turkey's military cooperation in 1942. Neither Germany nor Britain desired to see Turkey as a belligerent power that year.

As late as August 1942, the Turkish General Staff still believed that the capture of Stalingrad would be the key objective of German operations in 1942. The solution of the Russian problem, in Asim Gündüz's estimation, was to push forward northward from Stalingrad in order to cut the railway line between Kuibyshev and Moscow.[140] Gündüz told Ribbentrop that the central and the northern Russian army groups would then have only one railway at their disposal, which was bound to lead to the collapse of these forces.[141] That the Russians had for three weeks thrown their strategically reserves into a hopeless divertive action against the German forces in the central and northern sectors was, in his view, a huge strategic error. In comparison with the complete liquidation of the Russian forces in the central and northern sectors by an operation against Kuibyshev, the operation in the Caucasus was of only secondary importance. In view of this situation, the General Staff was convinced that by the end of 1942, Germany would have so weakened the Russians that they would no longer count as a decisive factor in this war.[142]

On 8 July 1942, the unexpected death of Prime Minister Refik Saydam, who was succeeded by Şükrü Saraçoğlu – a professedly pro-British statesman – caused considerable anxiety in Berlin. Roughly two years after the Massigli Affair, when the Nazis plotted to oust Saraçoğlu as foreign minister, Franz von Papen paid his first official visit to his office as Turkey's new prime minister. In the course of their conversation, which touched upon the general situation in Turkey, von Papen probed Saraçoğlu's views on the Bolshevik question. The prime minister reportedly answered von Papen's question 'both as a Turk and as Prime Minister'.[143] As a Turk, he 'yearned for the destruction of Soviet Russia, which would be an epoch-making deed on the part of the Führer, and which had been the dream of the Turkish people for centuries'.[144] No Turk, not even Hüseyin Cahid Yalçın who wrote for the British, could think differently, argued Saraçoğlu.

Saraçoğlu also told von Papen that the Germans could solve the Russian problem only if they rescued the Russified Turkic national minority regions from Russian influence once and for all, put them back on their feet, and educated them to be willing collaborators of the Axis and foes of Slavdom. Saraçoğlu was aware that the Germans had been entertaining such plans but did not know what the Führer had decided regarding the future constitution of the minority regions. For Saraçoğlu, the overwhelming majority of the inhabitants of these regions belonged to the Turkish race, and Turkey therefore had a legitimate interest in the settlement of this question. Saraçoğlu was of the opinion – and von Papen fully shared it – that a lasting solution of the Russian problem would be possible only if the Nazis enlisted the active co-operation of the minorities in the various parts of the Soviet Union, and if they were educated in a feeling of independence, 'naturally within the framework of German spiritual, economic and military leadership'.[145]

The timing of Saraçoğlu's meeting with Franz von Papen – three days after the Battle of Stalingrad had begun – could account for his geopolitical visions based on racial delineations. The question of emancipating Soviet citizens of Turkic ethnicity to create Turkish satellite states (in Crimea, Azerbaijan and Turkestan) that would be favourably disposed to Nazi Germany, had been an important aspect of Hitler's postwar designs for Eurasia. One might suspect an element of pragmatism in Saraçoğlu's performance in his meeting with Franz von Papen since the odds were in the Wehrmacht's favour by late August. In reality, however, there was no empty phraseology in Saraçoğlu's language. During and before World War II, there was a concerted, if convoluted, effort on the part of the Kemalist establishment to disambiguate Turkism from a racial ideology like Pan-Turanism. Ultimately, there is little doubt that Şükrü Saraçoğlu, much like İsmet İnönü, was opposed to Nazi ideology, but certain Turanian elements found encouragement in the higher reaches of the Turkish state before Stalingrad. For instance, numerous smaller run – but widely influential – journals touting explicitly Pan-Turanist views, including *Çınaraltı, Bozkurt, Atsız Mecmua* and *Orhun*, were untouched by İnönü's censorious hand until after the Nazi defeat at Stalingrad. Only three weeks before his meeting with von Papen, on 5 August 1942, Saraçoğlu had delivered a famous long speech at the National Assembly, when he proclaimed that the Turkish government 'has and will forever belong to Turkism, which was not only a question of blood, but also of conscience and culture'. 'As Turkists,' he said, 'we neither want to be diminished nor do we encourage it; on the contrary, we wish to grow larger and shall ever endeavour in that direction.'[146]

6

Turanian Fantasies

In an age animated by nationalist fervour, the Soviet regime had managed to consolidate its power over the world's largest multi-ethnic, multi-confessional entity. Contemporary scholarship on Soviet nationalities has arrived at a consensus that, sometime in the late 1930s, the 'Great Russian' image reemerged on the Bolshevik periphery. As the new Soviet constitution was promulgated in 1936, declaring the achievement of socialism and legal categories of the 'enemies of the people', Russianness was promoted to a position of *primus inter pares*.[1] Between 1937 and 1939, Stalin focused on peoples of the border regions, who were regarded as more susceptible to provocation by their neighboring ethnic brothers and sisters, and systematically deported nationality groups *en masse*. This was a project to be decisively completed once the Nazi occupation was over.

At times during World War II, the fate of the USSR seemed far from clear. The Soviets ultimately emerged triumphant from their greatest challenge as a union. Of the 30 million Soviet soldiers who served in the Red Army during the conflict, eight million were non-Russians. Behind the frontlines, urban life in virtually every region was transformed by rapid mobilization and mounting war industries unprecedented in Russian history. While Stalinist cultural reforms, collectivization and industrialization had already begun to shape people's lives in the 1930s, it was during the Great Patriotic War that the Soviet citizens identified themselves with the regime under a different rubric.[2] The replacement of internal class enemies (i.e. kulaks, the bourgeoisie) with more vivid and external ones (fascists) provided the Soviet leadership with an opportunity to cement a stronger socialist union between peoples of various ethnic and confessional backgrounds.[3] This is not to suggest that the war had just provided an enemy to fight against. Through bringing men and women of non-Russian peoples into factories, and military units, World War II had put to test the paradoxical relationship between traditional symbols of national identities and a superimposed socialist ideology.

Peoples of the so-called Ural-Altaic race were no exception; Tatars, Kalmyks, Buryats, and Kazakhs were asked to fulfil the brotherhood of nations and the collective socialist ideal by wearing the Red Army uniform, or, in the Nazi-occupied zones, by joining the underground movements and partisan groups. What the war had changed for the Turkic peoples was the criteria on which their allegiance had previously been measured. With the arrival of war, especially for those regions under Nazi occupation, people's loyalty was now determined by the extent of their support for resistance. Each of these groups experienced the war differently; some were occupied; some were not; some collaborated; some did not. Their divergent interests and unique historical ties with Turkey point out the need for a more extensive research at the local level about the fate of Soviet nationalism in the Nazi occupied Turkic realms.

Perhaps no part of the USSR featured a broader range of possible loyalties and choices for self-identification than did Crimea. Among the myths that provided the Tatar foundation narrative with some level of legitimacy and historical relevance, the Great Patriotic War and Stalin's subsequent deportations loomed large.[4] If one seeks to re-conceptualize the Crimean Tatars' experience of World War II not as a post-revolutionary (Bolshevik) addendum, but as a continuum of the Jadidist nationalist agenda, it becomes possible to see the war as the defining moment for the Crimean Tatars (for the Soviets, too, though for mutually exclusive reasons and purposes). A succession of important books has offered new perspectives on Stalin's policy in Crimea, but in existing historiography there are still competing prosecutorial narratives. In Turkish historical scholarship, Stalin's deportation of large nationality groups has been taken to represent an imperial homogenization policy, while Russian historians have focused on what Stalin called 'enemy nations' and sought to explain how Tatars suddenly became traitors.[5]

One important overlooked aspect of Stalin's wartime policy in Crimea is the role of pan-Turkists, who found a reinvigorated zeal in the Tatar cause and facilitated the Tatar–Nazi collaboration. Precisely for this reason, the high rate of collaboration with the Nazis and Turks among the Crimean Tatars brings to mind several intriguing questions about Soviet–Turkish relations: first, was it the Turkish government – as the Soviets later claimed – or pan-Turkist circles in Turkey who collaborated with the Tatars in a vehemently anti-Soviet campaign? Second, if Turkish nationalist circles – governmental or otherwise – had indeed entertained ideas of sponsoring a free Crimean Tatar republic, what was the role of Nazi Germany in bolstering their hopes for the so-called 'grand scheme of Soviet encirclement'? And third, what were the public consequences of Nazi Germany's efforts to orchestrate nationalist and fascist circles in Turkey?

Turkish *Lebensraum*

As in other zones of occupation, the Nazis carried out a sophisticated political agenda in Crimea and found people to cooperate with. Given the complex multi-ethnic multi-confessional structure of the society, they destroyed some and used others for their purposes. For the most part, anyone who had suffered under Stalin's terror helped the Nazis, but there is also a wealth of evidence about people who were included in the Nazi regime 'against their will, by force'.[6] Representatives of the Nazi central command in Crimea believed that of the 12 million inhabitants of the Caucasus, Georgians, Armenians and other Christian groups would not collaborate with the Germans. Meanwhile, the 18 million inhabitants of Turkic heritage and Muslim faith were categorized as anti-Soviet elements. Hence, the Nazis naturally turned to Tatars among other ethnic groups. In return, prominent Tatar intellectuals set up a provisional government, which served the people with a clear-cut programme: the creation of an army, the abolition of Communist activities and the reopening of mosques and courses on the Quran. From the outset, it was clear that Tatar community leaders had been anxiously waiting to seize this moment and remove symbols of Russian rule from Crimean history, replacing them with nationalist ones.[7]

Ever since the annexation of their homeland by Catherine the Great in 1783, deep-rooted anti-Slavic sentiments had been brewing amongst Crimean Tatars.[8] Inspired by Ismail Gaspirali's ideas, and sponsored by the late Ottoman state, their desire for independence came close to realization during the short-lived Tatar National Parliament (*Kurultay*) between 1917 and 1920. But after the defeat of General Wrangel by Nestor Makhno and the closure of the Tatar National Parliament by the Red Army, plans for an independent Crimean state had fallen into abeyance for two decades. The return of the Nazi soldiers in 1941 rekindled hopes not only in Crimea but in Turkey as well, particularly amongst the pan-Turkists and Tatar émigré community. The seizure of Crimea from the Ottoman Empire had had an equally negative impact on the Turkish public psyche, which continued to haunt Russo-Turkish relations until the end of World War I. Turkish nationalists of the late Ottoman Empire dreamed of taking from Russia that part of its territory, which was settled by Turkic-speaking peoples.

Turkish nationalism as ideological construct went through a number of twists and turns in the late imperial period, particularly after the 1908 Revolution, absorbing distinctly Turkish national, linguistic and cultural features. In its formative years, the term 'pan-Turkism' had sometimes been used interchangeably with 'pan-Turanism'. After the Second Balkan War of 1913, which precipitated fully fledged pan-Turanism, the distinction between the two became more discernable. In 1917, the American white supremacist historian Theodore Lothrop Stoddard claimed that the Turanian movement had become a complex hybrid entity following the inclusion of Bulgaria amongst Finno-Ugric and Ural-Altaic groups. In effect, the Turanian group that stretched out from the Danube to Mesopotamia, had a common deadly enemy – Russia – and, in Stoddard's words, 'from a certain point of view, the whole Russian Empire may be conceived as a Slav alluvium laid with varying thickness of a Turanian sub-soil'.[9] Ziya Gökalp, in his *The Principles of Turkism* (1923), made a clear distinction between the often confused concepts – *Turk* and *Turan* – and argued that the former denotes a people (*ulus*) with a homogenous culture and language, while the latter is more equivocal in terms of its cultural and linguistic delineations, and hence may include lands that connect Asia Minor all the way to Uzbekistan and Kirgizstan.[10] Building upon Gökalp's theses, a new Kemalist strand of Turkish nationalism emerged in the early 1920s, which was adopted as an official superstructure, while pan-Turkism was marginalized as a historical nexus.

The champion of the pan-Turkist movement during World War I was the Ottoman war minister, Enver Pasha. One of the architects of the Turco-German alliance, Enver was forced to resign after the Mudros Armistice in October 1918, and escaped into exile in Germany and later in Russia. In the summer of 1921, with the Turkish War of Independence in full swing, Enver decided to return to Anatolia and fight the Greeks. Yet, Mustafa Kemal was determined to prevent Enver's return. Having severed his ties to the Committee of Union and Progress (CUP) and explicitly denounced pan-Turkist ideas, Mustafa Kemal sought to cleanse the country of all the wrongdoings and debauchery, for which he held Enver responsible. In November 1921, after a failed attempt to reorganize the CUP in Batumi, Enver went to Bukhara in the Turkestan ASSR to help the Basmachi rebellion, armed the Mlada Turki and organized a series of counter offensives against the Red Army. Ultimately, Enver failed to ignite the anti-Russian movement he hoped for, and died in a battle against the Bolsheviks near Tajikistan in August 1922.[11]

While most pan-Turkists of Enver Pasha's generation used German imperialism to incite expansionist feelings in Turkey, neither the German *Weltanschauung* nor pan-Turkic ideas played a noticeable role in the ideological life of the Turkish Republic during the presidency of Kemal Atatürk.[12] Nevertheless, Kemalist principles of non-adventurism changed radically during the course of World War II, when the reinvigorated pan-Turkic organizations promulgated propaganda and support of a close political and military relationship with Germany, the seizure of Soviet territories, and the liberation of their brothers including Azeris, Tatars, Uzbeks, Kirgiz, Kazaks and Turkmens.[13] Turkey's rapprochement with Nazi Germany between 1941 and 1943 had radical social consequences from within. Friendly relations with Nazi Germany provided pro-Nazi groups in Turkey with new outlets to express themselves. On the initiative of famous pan-Turkist Ottoman generals – including Emir Erkilet, Nuri Killigil (half-brother of Enver Pasha) and Ali İhsan Sabis – a series of anti-Soviet seminars were held in İstanbul and a special anti-Soviet propaganda coordination centre was established.

Looking at the headlines of Turkish newspapers during this period, it is easy to see why the Soviet officials gained the impression that Turks were reverting to their imperial policy of aggression against the Russians. Most Turkish daily papers spared a substantial space for readers' comments and public forums, which saw opinions from all sorts of ideologies, including those supporting fascist plans to annihilate the Soviet Union. The Turkish government, however, was not sympathetic to the fascist ideology nor did it encourage pan-Turkist circles. Between June 1941 and August 1943, a period when the Turkish government was allegedly leaning towards fascism, İnönü shut down such pro-German papers as *Vatan* (nine times), *Tasvir-i Efkar* (eight times), *Yeni Sabah* (three times), *Akbaba* (four times) and *Son Posta* (four times), as well as numerous other local papers, each closure lasting from three to nine months. These were called 'publications that fundamentally opposed the Kemalist ideology, and the basic principles on which the Republic was established'.[14] In other words, the Turkish government itself sought to curb rather than sponsor anti-Soviet or pro-German views as much as they did pan-Turkist or pro-Communist ones. Put differently, what Saraçoğlu labelled as 'Turkism' (*Türkçülük*) in his 1942 famous parliamentary address, did not fully correspond to the ideological framework of pan-Turkists.

After World War II, a group of Soviet historians claimed that 'many Turkish intellectuals also attempted to downplay the significance of war-time pan-Turkists and their pro-Nazi tendencies on our relations'.[15] In fact, Turkish scholars wrote extensively on the wartime surge of Crimean Tatar migrations and their role in reviving pan-Turkism in Turkey. Türkkaya Ataöv, for instance, argued that there were people 'attracted by the ideas of pan-Turkism and these were mostly peoples of Turco-Tatar origin'.[16] The situation was strictly limited to immigrant and ultra-nationalist elements, rather than a government-sponsored policy as the Soviets claimed. This was so much the case that, when, for instance, the Berlin Academy of Sciences sent an official invitation to Professor Zeki Velidi Togan of İstanbul University in June 1942 to lead an international symposium on Turcology as a keynote speaker, the Turkish Foreign Ministry intervened and politely refused the offer on Togan's behalf 'for health reasons'.[17] Togan was a prominent pan-Turkist from Turkestan and a leader of the Bashkir liberation movement in 1919–20; later, he served as a philologist and historian at Bonn and Göttingen Universities before migrating to İstanbul in the early 1930s.

In fact, the Turkish government kept pan-Turkist circles under tight surveillance and profiled those who worked closely with the Nazis. Despite İnönü's best efforts, however, the further the war progressed towards the areas of Turkish interests, the greater the inducement was for the pan-Turkists to talk with the Nazis about possible scenarios in the Crimean Peninsula and in the Caucasus. Even amongst top-ranking Turkish generals, many were ready to offer their good offices to Hitler and discuss possible scenarios for the post-war order in the Turkic world. Only a few weeks after Hitler's unleashing of Operation Barbarossa, Ali Fuad Erden, head of the Turkish Military Academy, intimated to Franz von Papen that 'Turkey would be much pleased if a federation of the local tribes, which [were] more or less related to the Turks, could be established in the Crimea and Southern Caucasus'.[18] During his frequent meetings with Herr von Papen, Ali Fuad entertained thoughts of a Turkish *Lebensraum* at Soviet Russia's expense. To achieve this, Ali Fuad argued for the creation of two Turkic satellite states in the said regions, and, suggested a third independent Turanian state in the Eastern Caspian Basin as the best possible solution.

Front runners of the Pan-Turkist movement were, perhaps unsurprisingly, retired Ottoman pashas who fought alongside Germany two decades earlier. Among them were prominent characters, such as Emir Erkilet, Ali İhsan Sabis and Nuri Killigil, who were all convinced that Ankara should immediately join the Axis, regain control of the Aegean Islands and embrace their Turkic brothers, liberating them from centuries of Russian enslavement. Pan-Turkists believed that the creation of these Nazi-sponsored buffer states in the Turkic world would also have short-term benefits, relieving Turkey from Soviet pressure while at the same time greatly strengthening Ankara's economic situation. Their central theses ran conveniently parallel to Franz von Papen's machinations. Mindful of Turkey's trepidation vis-à-vis the Soviet Union, von Papen had long been convinced that 'a skillful exploitation' of the pan-Turkists' longing for Crimea's independence could accomplish a great deal toward extricating Turkey from the present dilemma of 'alliance versus friendship' with the Nazis.[19] Von Papen urged Ribbentrop that this should not be misconstrued as a political, let alone military, pressure upon Turkey, but on the contrary 'by slowly bringing psychological influence to bear [with regard to the customary evil Russia image]' and by emphasizing the intrinsic 'Turanian element in Nazi Germany's mission', the Third Reich should capitalize on such sentiments devolving in Turkey.[20]

Nazi Germany and Pan-Turkism

In view of Nazi Germany's initial successes against the Bolsheviks in the fall of 1941, von Papen believed that the pan-Turkist circles in Ankara and İstanbul, along with certain members of the Turkish General Staff, were giving increasing consideration to the fate of their brethren on the other side of the Turkish–Soviet border, especially the Azerbaijani Turks. There seemed to be a disposition in this group to revert to the events of 1918 and to annex Azerbaijan, especially the valuable Baku oil region. To this end, a committee of civilian experts had been formed, composed partly of persons who rendered similar services at the time of the Committee of Union and Progress. The chief responsibility of this circle was to win adherence both at home, among the émigrés from across the border, and abroad, especially in the Azerbaijan part of Iran, for a unification of the new Turkey with the Turk-inhabited regions bordering on it in the east, as far as the Caspian basin. Another long-term plan of the pan-Turkists was to weld the Eastern Turks (the Crimean Tatars, the Volga Turks, the Turkomans etc.) into their own, outwardly independent, East Turkish state, in which, however, the Western Turks would play a dominant political and cultural role as advisers.

It was doubtful, however, whether this scheme conformed to the wishes of the Eastern Turks themselves. In their opinion, the Turks inhabiting Turkey had been 'definitely lost to the true Turkic folk'.[21] Looking at German intelligence reports acquired in Baku, von Papen argued that the Turks of Turkey were regarded as 'nothing but Turkish-speaking Levantines, with whom it [was] desired to have as little to do as possible'.[22] As for the Eastern Turks, the Azerbaijanis did not want to be burdened with them either, and were convinced that these people in no way formed a coherent community, and above all because of their economic backwardness, could not yet have a claim to state independence, and must still go through a long period of evolution. In short, the Azerbaijani revolutionary movement did not regard it as its duty to train these Turks for statehood. Nevertheless, von Papen's confidential agents recommended him that this task should not be left to the Soviets either. Von Papen therefore decided to mobilize the pan-Turkists (despite Azeri reservations) and to make sure that Nazi German organization and experience be the decisive factor in their further development. In von Papen's view, Nazi Germany should attach greater importance to the formation of a strong state on the southeastern flank in order to keep the Soviet Union constantly in check through this roundabout way.

In his dispatch to Ribbentrop in August 1941, von Papen shared the names of other pan-Turkists, who could give momentum to the 'Greater Turkey' movement with Nazi sponsorship.[23] Von Papen was relying on a wide network of 'well-informed confidential agents in Turkey', who communicated to him the names of the following persons: Professor Zeki Velidi Togan (Bashkir), who had been a professor at İstanbul University, but was forced to leave owing to a quarrel with Atatürk, and temporarily resided in Vienna, Halle and Bonn; Ahmet Cafer (Crimean Tatar), who was believed to be 'unreliable' but was supposedly very close to General Wladyslaw Sikorski's Prometheus organization in London.[24] Şükrü Yenibahçeli (Crimean Tatar), who served as Deputy from İstanbul and had been one of the founders of *Teşkilat-ı Mahsusa* (precursor to the National Intelligence Organization) during the War of Independence; and the Turkish ambassador at Kabul, Memduh Sefket, who nearly always followed the government line in his official capacity, but was considered to be a sincere friend of the Eastern Turks.

A notable Tatar leader of the pan-Turkist movement outside Turkey was Mehmed Emin Rasulzade (founder of the famous Musavat Party in Azerbaijan in 1911).[25] He later joined the Polish Prometheus movement, which sought to undermine the Russian Empire and its successor states including the Soviet Union by supporting national independence movements.[26] Resulzade lived on Polish General Staff funds transferred to Switzerland (the so-called 'Josef Pilsudski Fund') even after the fall of Poland in 1939, visited Wladyslaw Sikorski in London on a political mission in 1940, and then lived with other Polish refugees in Bucharest. Resulzade was represented in Turkey by his adjutant, Mirza Bala, who served in the Turkish army after becoming a faithful disciple of his influential teacher.

Meanwhile, the Turkish ambassador in Berlin, Hüsrev Gerede, was lobbying intensely for those nationalities of Turkic ethnic origin, which lived on the fringes of Soviet Russia. Gerede called Ribbentrop's attention to the possibility of 'spreading anti-Soviet propaganda among these Turkic tribes', and 'frankly' expressed the idea that the Caucasian peoples could eventually be united into one buffer state.[27] He also hinted at the land east of the Caspian Sea as a potential homeland. Ribbentrop was surprised to see Gerede's 'rather casual tone of conversation' when bringing up these far-reaching proposals. However, Ribbentrop added that Gerede's remarks were by no means casual, since they agree to a large degree with the statements made by Ali Fuad in a conversation with von Papen. Gerede put his finger on the decisive question by characterizing Baku as a possible capital since it was 'an entirely Turkish-speaking city'.[28]

Nevertheless, Gerede's subsequent meetings with von Weizsäcker and Ribbentrop gave rise to rumours in Berlin's diplomatic corps about a Turco-German pact, which allegedly would permit the passage of German troops through Anatolia. Although both the Turkish foreign minister and his Nazi counterpart immediately denied this gossip, İnönü was very much disturbed by Ambassador Gerede's recent dealings in Berlin as a self-appointed arbitrator. On 21 August, Gerede was called back to Ankara and given instructions not to enter into such discussions any further.[29] After his return to Berlin he emphasized to von Weizsäcker that in fact 'the Turkish government itself had no ambitions outside its present borders, and that his earlier conversations with von Weizsäcker and Ribbentrop had not been of an official nature'.[30]

In reply to von Weizsäcker's question about Turkey's earlier attitude toward the Turkish peoples near the border in the Caucasus and east of the Caspian Sea, Gerede stated emphatically that pan-Turkist ideas were no longer alive among the ruling circles, 'at least none existed in their official rhetoric'.[31] When von Weizsäcker asked him further what position Turkey would take if England should wish to establish a new front in the Caucasus, the ambassador replied evasively that İnönü would be on his guard. Gerede also gave vague answers to von Weizsäcker's further questions about whether the present official policy might change, the situation in Syria, and whether a closer alignment of Turkey with Nazi Germany might be possible (or not) after the collapse of Soviet Russia.

Evidently, the Turkish government decided to refrain from giving the slightest impression that would remind the Soviet Union and Great Britain of yet another

Turco-Nazi collaboration in the latter's yearning for the east. Informed about Turkey's official position on the Turanian question, by early September of 1941, Ribbentrop and von Papen decided to devise a non-governmental channel, which would revive the sleepwalking pan-Turkists to be used as a fifth column in the Soviet borderlands. To this end, the German embassy in Ankara recommended Enver Pasha's half-brother, Nuri Killigil, as the future leader of the pan-Turkist movement. Nuri spent his entire youth under the spell of his brother and fought in the Africa Groups Command of the Ottoman Army in the Great War, later rising to prominence as a decorated general at the Battle of Baku in the Caucasian front in 1918.

His pan-Turkist ideas were reminiscent of Enver Pasha. During the interwar years, he had continued to cherish hopes for a united Turkic world, so much so that he once confessed to a Polish acquaintance from Józef Piłsudski's famous Prometheus circle: 'if the right opportunity presented itself, he would throw away his career and would follow his brother's [Enver's] footsteps, go to Turkestan, to stand at the forefront of the creation of a united Turkic world'.[32] Made shortly before Nuri helped establish the Turkestan Legion of the Schutzstaffel (SS), this confession is quite telling. He suggested that 'if his services were needed in Turkestan', he could immediately dispatch a few dozen men to the region, 'who shall examine the situation there and formulate opportunities'.[33] If he were to be provided with sufficient funds, Nuri was certain that he could muster a substantial paramilitary force, including officers and NCOs from the region and beyond. In the meantime, however, Nuri instructed his counterpart to carry out a rigorous reconnaissance in the region; since it was here that his former staff officers in the Caucasus 'fell into Russian captivity and were later deported to Siberia, where they soon fled to Turkestan and fought alongside fellow Basmachis for a long time'.[34] Due to his previous losses, Nuri became much more cautious and asked for a few months in Afghanistan on the border with Turkestan in order to gauge the situation very carefully. The cost of each fighter was estimated to be around US$1,000 'especially because they would need most of this money for feeding their families back home'.[35] For Nuri, the success of such a plan required first, a commander of his calibre, and second, utter secrecy.

Consequently, Ribbentrop received a letter from von Papen announcing that Nuri Pasha was coming to Germany to attend the Leipzig Trade Fair and would pay a call at the Foreign Ministry.[36] Ribbentrop told Nuri, who was then a prosperous factory-owner in Turkey in his early fifties, that in the areas in which fellow pan-Turkists would be potentially interested, the German Reich economic rather than political motivations. What Turkey was striving for, therefore, 'was certain to meet with German approval from the outset'.[37] Ribbentrop added, however, that the Turkish government was pursuing different ideas in this respect. Hence, Ribbentrop asked Nuri whether he should not first of all exert influence at home. Nuri Pasha conceded this; actually he had been trying to do so for a long time. With regard to his immediate goals in Berlin, Nuri said that he could be useful by advising the Nazi authorities on all questions concerning the Caucasus with which he was thoroughly acquainted – in its geographic, ethnographic, military and economic aspects. Nuri Pasha tried to reassure Ribbentrop that 'once the German advance toward the Caucasus had penetrated beyond Rostov and reached the important trunk railroad line in the vicinity of Armavir', the fate of the

Soviet troops around the Caucasus would be sealed.[38] Nuri claimed that he himself was in a position 'to bring about an uprising of at least 100,000 men in the Caucasus'.[39]

On 11, 18 and 25 September, Nuri met with Ernst Woermann, director of the Politische Abteilung (Political Department). The second of these meetings took place in the form of a lunch together with Ambassador von Papen and Gustav Hilger, Counsellor at the German embassy. In his circular, Woermann later described Nuri as 'the champion of the future Turanian movement'.[40] According to Nuri Pasha, while the younger generation of pan-Turkists wished to create independent states for the Turkic peoples living outside the territory of present-day Turkey, these areas were not to be annexed by Ankara but rather would receive their political direction from Turkey. This involved mainly ethnic groups residing in the territory of the present Soviet Union. Of present Soviet territories, Nuri primarily laid claim to Azerbaijan and Dagestan (not the entire Transcaucasia as some pan-Turkists later claimed); also the Crimea, as well as (by and large) the area between the Volga and the Urals, stretching northwards to the Soviet Tatar Republic, with its capital in Kazan. Essentially, all of ancient Turkestan was encompassed in the area Nuri designated, including the western portion of former Eastern Turkestan. Furthermore, Nuri claimed the northwestern portion of Iran down to Hamadan as being ethnically Turkic, its border running across the top of the Caspian Sea along the old Soviet frontier. Finally, of Iraqi territories, the areas of Kirkuk and Mosul were included, as well as a strip of Syria.[41]

The outline Nuri presented to his Nazi counterparts showed that pan-Turkists essentially desired to reclaim from the Soviets what their Tsarist predecessors had succeeding in claiming in the nineteenth century: Transcaucasia and Turkestan. Although Turkey remained a purely neutral state during Atatürk's presidency (aside from certain frontier rectifications) and had not pursued any objectives outside its national territories, Nuri claimed that this had only been 'a policy of expediency in the mind of Atatürk, the motive of which had been fear of the Soviet Union'. With present Nazi victories and 'the prospect of smashing the Soviet Union', Nuri suggested that such Kemalist motives have disappeared.[42] When reminded of the Turkish government's continued objection to pan-Turkism, Nuri said that the entire Turkish people could easily be won over and that, at the proper moment, 'a government would surely come to power, which would adopt these ideas'. Ultimately, Nuri Pasha hoped to convince Woermann that he was not acting behind the back of the Turkish government; he also said that, on the contrary, before his departure for Berlin he had informed Prime Minister Refik Saydam of his plans. Among his circles in Turkey, Nuri claimed that large portions of the army were in favour of these ideas; in particular, he mentioned the commanding general on the Caucasian front, who was closely related to him, and who could play a decisive role at the proper time.

Evaluating the question whether support for pan-Turkism was in the German interest, Woermann urged Ribbentrop to distinguish between more tactical interests and long-term goals of some practical implementation. As far as Nazi Germany's momentary interests were concerned, it was obvious that Turkey could realize the pan-Turkist ideas only in alliance with Germany. In other words, a Turkey with pan-Turkist orientation would be of natural consequence a Turkey with pro-German orientation. For Woermann, these pan-Turkist ideas at the same time represented a Turkish imperialism at the expense of the Soviet Union, 'therefore to that extent, too, the German game would be played'.[43] Woermann's entire memorandum spoke in favour of orchestrating the pan-Turkist factions, but required careful attention 'bearing in mind the divergent attitude of the present Turkish Government'.[44]

Upon receiving Woermann's report, Ribbentrop agreed in principle to create new Turkic states, which would be satellites of Turkey, but added that each of these potential Turkish satellites should be judged by different criteria. Ribbentrop argued that an actual enlargement of Turkish territory would possibly occur by acquisition of the oil-rich region of Mosul or Transcaucasia through Batum and Baku. He claimed that recovery of the Mosul region should certainly not be encouraged from the standpoint of Nazi Germany's oil interests, but would perhaps be tolerable, 'whereas it would be entirely out of the question to give the area of Batum and Baku into Turkish hands'.[45] Moreover, in Ribbentrop's opinion, there was a decisive difference between the Volga and the Urals intermingled with Turkic peoples, on the one hand, and the area of Turkestan east of the Caspian Sea. For purely German interests, once the Soviet Union was defeated, large areas of the old Russian Empire should come under German and not foreign influence. It would not be in Germany's interest if states were created in Transcaucasia and between the Volga and the Urals 'which would be politically aligned with Turkey and whose attitude would thus depend upon the vicissitudes of the policy of Turkey, who will certainly continue to be wooed by all the powers'.[46] For Ribbentrop, the case of Turkestan was different. If Russia had been decisively weakened while the English had not been driven out of India, English imperialism 'would certainly seek to seize these economically promising areas (cotton) that have only partially been opened up by the Turco-Siberian railway'.[47] Since these areas would not belong to Germany's sphere of influence even in the future (if only on account of their geographic location), Ribbentrop proposed the creation of ethnically Turkic states aligned with Turkey.

Between early September and late October, Nazi Germany carefully mapped out its immediate aims versus long-term goals with regards to bolstering pan-Turkism and decided that, first and foremost, the Soviet prisoners of war from Turkic ethnic origins should be gathered together in a special camp modelled on that established near Wünstorf during World War I. Woermann was tasked with examining whether a separate combat unit for the future Turanian state could be formed from these prisoners of war at a later date.[48] Second, Nuri Pasha's request to have the administration of Nazi-occupied Turkic regions assigned to the relevant indigenous population was granted; Crimea was designated the first of such areas. Third, Nuri Pasha was given authority to lead the pan-Turkists after the establishment of POW camps for ethnic Turks (where he would somehow participate in sifting and organizing the inmates). Finally, if von Papen could confirm the tacit toleration of the Turkish government, Nuri Pasha would establish a central office for pan-Turkist propaganda in Berlin. Ribbentrop also asked Werner Otto von Hentig, who was on duty as a representative of the Foreign Ministry with 11th Army Headquarters, to assist Nuri Pasha and deal with the pan-Turkist questions.

On 28 October 1941, the Oberkommando der Wehrmacht (OKW) began preparations for the separation of the ethnically Turkic and Muslim prisoners of war.[49] Meanwhile, Ambassador von Papen sent a detailed report on Turkey's official position regarding the separation of the ethnic Turkic POWs. Von Papen said that 'the role of Nuri Pasha in the pan-Turkist movement should be strengthened', and suggested that he should participate in organizing the screening of the prisoners of war and in their indoctrination. Ribbentrop was certain that the Turkish government would not have any objections to this, since he had already remarked to Saraçoğlu that Germany was placing Turkic POWs in special camps.[50] With regard to the establishment of a pan-Turkist propaganda office in Berlin under the direction of, or with the participation of, Nuri Pasha, Ribbentrop was more cautious. In a separate letter, dated 31 October, von Papen argued that the Turkish government, which played down pan-Turkist propaganda in its own country, would certainly consider such propaganda 'if carried on from Berlin as very awkward'.[51] Consequently, von Papen suggested that pan-Turkist propaganda should be limited to POW camps only, and to the training of people who might be sent if necessary to the German-occupied areas.

In the early days of November, von Papen set in motion another round of Turco-German talks and approached General Ali Fuad Erden with hopes of rekindling Turanian dreams amongst the young cadets. Ali Fuad was subsequently invited to the Eastern Front for 'an unofficial conversation with the Führer'.[52] Having returned greatly satisfied from his trip to the Führerhauptquartier Werwolf, Ali Fuad asked von Papen to thank Hitler for the courteous reception given him by all military authorities, and said that 'it was beyond all praise, and everywhere [he] was strongly reminded of the comradeship-in-arms of the World War'.[53] Ali Fuad seemed to be particularly grateful for the instructive talks given him at the unit headquarters by officers of the General Staff, particularly on the Battle of Kiev, the sweeping of the Dnieper, etc. He asked von Papen if it might be possible to receive a map of these operations indicating the Russian dislocations so that he might 'use these exemplary historical operations for instructional purposes in the Turkish Military Academy'.[54]

Ali Fuad added that it had been a great experience for him to be personally received by Hitler and to have been given a detailed first-hand account of the operational position. He concluded from what the Führer had said that Hitler intended to reach the Caspian and the Caucasus as speedily as possible. He inferred this particularly from the fact that the 1st Army was being deployed, with heavy forces and in spite of not inconsiderable losses, to conduct the extremely difficult operation in the Crimea, in order to push on from there to the North Caucasus. Otherwise, Ali Fuad added, 'it would have been easier simply to cut off the Crimea, and to continue with the 1st Army the advance on Rostov'. Ali Fuad finally shared his observations on his visit to a Russian POW camp, where many Turco-Tatar prisoners appealed to him to use his influence to secure for them 'better treatment and rations than the Russians'.[55]

Both the Nazis and pan-Turkists found common ground in disseminating anti-Soviet propaganda in Turkey. After his meeting with von Papen, Ali Fuad strove to widen the pan-Turkist network in Turkey through propagating the Hitlerite cause among the military cadres. Perhaps the most resourceful of the active Nazi spies Ali Fuad recruited was General Emir Erkilet, who was also of Tatar origin and an expert on the Eastern Question. Through Ali Fuad and Nuri's connections, Erkilet began communicating with Otto von Hentig, who was in charge of the diplomatic minutiae of Turanian issues.[56] Despite Erkilet's repeated invitations for a meeting in İstanbul, however, von Hentig postponed his trip several times, arguing that he was 'strongly dissuaded by various parties, including semi-official Turkish, from going to Turkey just now'.[57] Von Hentig apologized for not being able to resume their talks but reminded Erkilet that he needed to refrain from giving the slightest cause for biased parties 'to reckon him among the fifth column'.[58] Dismayed by the incessant delays to von Hentig's visit, Erkilet sent a somewhat blunt response and argued that he could not understand 'who these semi-official Turkish parties were', and why they 'strongly dissuaded' von Hentig from coming.[59] Erkilet was convinced that they were wrong and most likely had a malign agenda. He asked von Hentig to grant Nazi entry visas to two leading members of the Crimean Tatar cause in Turkey – Müstecip Ülküsal and Edige Kırımer. 'Following a brief period of indoctrination', these men were to be sent to Crimea and be used there 'for the common Turco-German interest'.[60]

Shattering hopes

Among the accessible sources on the subject, Müstecip Ülküsal's memoirs are particularly helpful in understanding the circumstances under which Crimean Tatars and Turkish nationalists cooperated with the Nazis.[61] When Hitler unleashed Operation Barbarossa, Ülküsal was about to finish his judicial clerkship at the central courthouse in Ankara. Ülküsal's memoirs begin at this juncture, a week after the invasion, when he received a letter from Cafer Seyitahmet Kırımer, who had previously served as foreign minister during the short-lived Crimean *Kurultay* between 1917 and 1919. When Kırımer became the de facto leader of the Tatar Independence Movement, he met Ülküsal and the two worked closely throughout the 1930s, publishing the Turkish nationalist periodical *Emel* (*Desire*). In his letter, Kırımer urged Ülküsal to join him in his visit to Berlin and help him 'negotiate the future of Crimea with the Germans'. Ülküsal devotes substantial space to their incipient plans and heated dialogues during a lengthy train-ride from İstanbul to Berlin. In his second publication on the subject, *Kırım Türk-Tatarları* (*Turco-Tatars of Crimea*), he comes back to this particular episode, which 'set the grounds for most post-war Turco-Tatar periodicals, including the reintroduction of *Emel* in the 1960s'.[62]

The latter half of his memoirs consists of numerous meetings with the German authorities at the Reich Ministry for the Occupied Eastern Territories (Reichministerium für die besetzten Ostgebiete). The most striking aspect of Müstecip Bey's encounters with Ostministerium officials was his deep frustration with Nazi ideology, which excluded Crimea from the civil jurisdiction of Reichskommissariat Ukraine. Ülküsal understood that he was not dealing with 'the same Germans who allied with their *Ataman* [Tatar national leader] against the Bolsheviks in 1918'.[63] In the first weeks of the occupation, the Nazi forces had set up '14 Tatar battalions (4,000 soldiers) to hunt down the Soviets hiding in the mountains. . . while the villagers welcomed the German soldiers, providing them with food and shelter ever since they arrived'.[64] In return for their good will and services, what they received was 'a few insincere excuses for not being able to send the much needed grain and medicine to Crimea due to insufficient transportation vehicles'.[65] Clearly, Ülküsal and Kırımer felt deep resentment at the

Nazis' handling of the Tatar question. Ülküsal ruefully admitted that, after spending nearly four months in Berlin, holding numerous meetings with the Nazis, translating thousands of German propaganda materials into Crimean Turkish, and quarrelling bitterly with fellow Turkic leaders over purposes and priorities, they had gained 'nothing but empty gestures and despair'.[66]

Ülküsal's longing for independence becomes clear in his diary entries between January–April 1942, where he frequently praised the popular wartime newspaper *Azat Kırım (Independent Crimea)*. *Azat Kırım* is an invaluable source for any researcher seeking to recover the voices of the Crimean Tatars wedged between Nazi Germany and the Soviet Union. First published on 11 January 1942, in Akmescit (Simferopol) using the Cyrillic alphabet, *Azat Kırım* was circulated twice a week in major Crimean cities. The first image that strikes the reader is the *Tarak Tamga*, which used to be the official insignia of the Crimean Khanate, now placed between the words *Azat* and *Kırım* on the front page. Most columnists gradually replaced the Cyrillic alphabet with Latin, which used to be the official alphabet of the Crimean ASSR between 1927 and 1937, until its abolishment by Stalin as 'a nationalist counter-revolutionary symbol'.[67] They emphasized the need for 'a large-scale re-Latinization campaign'.[68] The ultimate goal was to revive and reinstate the 'Gaspirali Language' as the official Crimean Tatar language.[69]

Most political columnists dealt with common themes in their writings, such as the operations of the German army, the significance of the Muslim Tatar committees for unity, and the urgent need to 'crush the Soviet dragon's head'.[70] Aside from using a highly nationalist discourse, most articles published in *Azat Kırım* conjured up images of the dreadful ordeal Crimea had suffered under the Soviets and called for close cooperation with Hitler – 'the saviour of nations from atheist colonizers'.[71] At times, it contained a summary of the events section in German *(Die befreite Krim)*, and published advertisements for state-sponsored German-language classes as well as career pages for Tatar girls seeking to work as German translators. There was frequent coverage of theatre and music festivities organized to entertain the wounded German soldiers.[72] In brief, *Azat Kırım* sheds light on several crucial anecdotes that defined the country's historical trajectory and people's daily lives during the War. Echoes of Crimean Tatars' wartime daily lives also found a great deal of attention in pan-Turkist newspapers and journals.

One of the key figures to facilitate Ülküsal and Kırımer's connections in Berlin was Ambassador Hüsrev Gerede, who was an ardent supporter of German militarism. Throughout his tenure in Berlin, on more than a few occasions, Gerede made his pro-Nazi tendencies quite explicit. In January 1942, he was invited to write an essay for the New Year's edition of *Zeitschrift für Politik*, where he made a case as to why Prussian military education had been a natural fit for the soul of the common Turkish soldier.[73] Gerede sought to explain his strong feelings about the Prussian fighting spirit by facilitating student exchange programmes between Turkish and German war academies; these would closely monitor Turkish cadets' performance and everyday lives upon their arrival in Berlin. Occasionally, Gerede would become excited and dispatch thick dossiers to Ankara, outlining possible ways to strengthen the bond between these two nations that had fought together in the Great War. More often, however, his reports reflected a bitter disillusionment with the incoming Turkish cadets, 'who did not properly represent the Turkish character, and, rather than paying attention to their training, got involved in scandalous affairs with German women, gambling, and other forms of debauchery'.[74]

Nevertheless, most people in İnönü's close circle did not really enjoy reading Gerede's theses on the Turkish cadets and the Prussian military education, nor did they share his enthusiasm for further Turkish–German convergence. On the contrary, Gerede's unequivocal diplomatic sondage in Berlin became riskier when the war progressed into areas closer to Turkey and remaining neutral became an even more excruciating enterprise. Not being able to negotiate the subject with Hentig in his official capacity, Gerede designated a certain 'Dr Harun', who had been a professor at the Berlin Institute of Technology (TUB), as his agent.[75] In his message to Ernst Woermann the same day, von Hentig argued that Dr Harun was inquiring about the German attitude toward Pan-Turkism. Dr Harun conveyed to von Hentig messages from Ambassador Gerede and the Turkish chief of staff, Fevzi Çakmak. Von Hentig suggested that, based on Dr Harun's words, both Gerede and Çakmak had declared 'their great interest in this question', and that 'the Turanian question could be a basis on which to build relations between Germany and Turkey'.[76]

As late as June 1942, days before the German victory in Sevastopol, Dr Harun paid a reciprocal visit to von Hentig, claiming to be a confidential agent of the Turkish chief of staff Marshall Fevzi Çakmak. Nazi reports indicate that, according to Dr Harun, Çakmak strongly favoured Turkey's entrance into the war and told Dr Harun that it was almost unavoidable. Dr Harun told Hentig that 'it may happen at any moment, and will as soon as the Turkish army possesses sufficient arms'. Dr Harun further suggested that the Turkish advance 'would be in the direction of Baku, through the Iranian uplands'.[77] With reference to the 'Turan' question, Harun told von Hentig that he had received assurances from Turkish parliamentary circles and from Marshal Cakmak that, contrary to official declarations and probably also to reports from the new Turkish ambassador, a 'Greater Turkey' movement not only existed in Ankara but was steadily growing in strength and importance.[78] Harun alleged that the true state of affairs was revealed, among other things, by the fact that the President had ordered the deletion of all foreign words from the Constitution. Dr Harun assured Hentig that what was envisaged was not the conquest of these lands by Turkey, but rather the creation of a federal state, similar to the Bismarck Reich. It was to include, besides Anatolia, the Caucasus and the Turkic peoples east of the Volga.[79]

In fact, by mid-1942, there seemed to be a fair amount of bewilderment on the part of the Turkish government about the Turanian question. On 28 June 1942, İnönü replaced Gerede with Saffet Arıkan – the former minister of national defense. On several occasions Ambassador Gerede had been reproached by the İnönü government for being too 'Germanophile', and one of the alleged reasons for his recall was a public utterance leaning too far in this direction.[80] Years later, when Gerede compiled his memoirs, he moaned about the unceremonious way in which he was dismissed. With a fair amount of irony, he argued that the absence of an official excuse behind his recall from the Third Reich, 'at a time when he established a close partnership with the Nazi regime', gave him 'sufficient hints about the undemocratic and dictatorial leanings of the İnönü government'.⁸¹ When paying his farewell visits to the Nazi authorities, Gerede met with Hitler, who shared his regret about Gerede's dismissal and explained to him 'how the German Army will soon destroy the Russians, probably before summer's end'.⁸² This episode haunted Gerede throughout his remaining years in the diplomatic service; so much that, eighteen years after his recall, when he met Franz von Papen at a 1960 social event in Ankara, Gerede asked him whether he was privy to the actual reasons for his dismissal. Von Papen responded with confidence that 'it was the British Ambassador [Knatchbull-]Hugessen who asked Foreign Minister Saraçoğlu to jettison Hüsrev Gerede'.⁸³

Regarding the appointment of Saffet Arikan as the new Turkish ambassador in Berlin, Soviet newspapers initially circulated rumours of 'the continued pro-Nazi sentiments in Ankara', and labelled Arikan as 'another well-known Germanophile'. Having made Arıkan's acquaintance in Ankara, Knatchbull-Hugessen shared a detailed report on Arikan's personality and political leanings with the Soviet ambassador in Ankara, arguing that it was 'most improbable that the Turkish government would wish to send another pro-Nazi Ambassador to Berlin', and that depictions of Arikan as a Germanophile were 'simply erroneous'.⁸⁴ On the contrary, Saffet Arıkan was a realist and an opportunist who would play the government policy of the moment, whatever it was. By nature, he was alert and resourceful. Although he certainly had an admiration for German drive and capacity for organization, he was essentially pro-government and ostensibly in sympathy with the Allied cause. Saraçoğlu had confidentially suggested to Knatchbull-Hugessen that the Turkish government had anticipated increasing pressure from Berlin, and wished to keep a strictly neutral representative in Berlin. Until Ambassador Gerede's recall, İnönü had split hairs about ambassadorial appointments, tried to send the right person to the right post, and laboured hard to maintain harmonious bilateral affairs with each warring camp. But his tolerance grew shorter with Germany's vain attempts to turn the table by propagating Pan-Turkism in Turkey through semi-official channels.

During the latter half of 1942, Nazi Germany gradually abandoned the idea of inducing Turkey towards a closer friendship through promises of a Turanian state, due to von Papen's realization that İnönü entertained no such desire, and that orchestration of pan-Turkist groups would not be enough to pressurize the Turkish government. Von Papen, who engineered the star-crossed Turanian bridge between Turks, Tatars and Germans, quietly warned Ribbentrop and Woermann that replanting Pan-Turkism in Ankara had been overambitious. Nevertheless, von Papen was still certain that Turkey could not remain indifferent to anything the Nazis were doing in Crimea, and therefore urged Woermann to inform the İnönü government about Nazi Germany's drive towards Crimea during the ongoing Battle of Sevastopol.

Based on von Papen's reports from Ankara, on 23 January 1942, Woermann sent new directives to Lieutenant General Walter Warlimont, who had recently joined Field Marshal Erich von Manstein's 11th Army (Army Group South) in the Battle of Sevastopol.⁸⁵ In a message that arrived during the heated days of the Crimean campaign, Woermann told Warlimont that 'Turkic interest outside Turkey proper ... ceased to evoke interest', and that a Turkish desire for territorial increment in Crimea had thus far not been intimated'.⁸⁶ Clearly the Nazis realized that pan-Turkist groups which advocated the formation of an outwardly independent Turkish satellite state in Crimea (as well as in the North Caucasus and Eastern Turkestan), had failed to recruit more allies from the İnönü government. Since the Turkish government did not expect to receive any advantages without offering compensation in return, Woermann argued that it seemed questionable whether 'bearing in mind the price involved, Turkey's participation in the war [was] desirable at all'. From that moment in January 1942 onwards, the object of Nazi Germany's negotiations with Turkey was to ascertain how far Turkey was prepared to stretch the concept of benevolent neutrality and thereby make it easier for the Germans to carry the war successfully into the Soviet heartland.

To keep the pan-Turkist spirit alive, General Ali İhsan Sabis made an explicit call for Turkey to enter the war on the side of the Axis, arguing that 'such an action would not expand but contain the theatre of war'.[87] In January 1943, Sabis published a personal account of the first four years of World War II, projecting that 'the Nazis would indubitably emerge triumphant from their life and death struggle against Bolshevism [upon which] it would be impossible for the Anglo-American coalition to advance any further'.[88] In his badly timed book, Sabis suggested that 'the Anglo-American coalition would ultimately succumb to Hitler's *Lebensraum* plans and would end up withdrawing their troops from North Africa before the summer [of 1943]'.[89] When the publisher received the final draft of his manuscript, Stalin had already encircled the German 6th Army and started a counter-offensive – Operation Little Saturn – expanding the Soviet-controlled area in eastern Ukraine until Kharkov and Rostov. By January 1943, it was too late to remove the book's final chapter, in which Sabis argued that 'upon further Nazi victories against the Soviet Union, Hitler would resume his operations against England ... and the British government would be left with no other option but a Great Retreat from the Island, establishing a new base in Canada to continue the war effort'.[90] His clumsy prophecies aside, Sabis's central argument reflected the mindset of many pan-Turkists.

General Emir Erkilet, for instance, published a similar monograph targeting Bolshevism. In his retrospective analysis of Turkish foreign policy during World War II, Erkilet questioned the contradiction between Anglo-American interests before and after Stalingrad. His book began with a rhetorical question: 'When British and American leaders executed their plans to defeat Germany so unconditionally, did it not occur to them that the Bolsheviks would conveniently claim the victory and utilize it as the triumph of communism over capitalism?'[91] In a similar vein to Ali İhsan Sabis, Emir Erkilet predicted that a Soviet reversion to Tsarist imperialism was inevitable and that Moscow would soon 'absorb Iranian Azerbaijan, put pressure on Shatt al-Arab, Bolshevize Mongolia and Chinese Turkestan, and control northern China with a proxy Chinese communist army'.[92] Under these circumstances, Erkilet argued that Moscow would soon play the Armenian card in connection with Turkey and would 'provoke the Armenians to take over Eastern Anatolia for the greater Soviet Union'.[93] Of the many propaganda instruments at the Bolsheviks' disposal, Erkilet claimed that pan-Slavism would be the most convenient one to find in the playbook of the now-defunct Tsarist Russia.[94] Although Turkish leaders did not share the underlying pan-Turkism in Erkilet's or Sabis's discourse, they soon came to appreciate some of their forebodings about the post-war international order and adopted a similar rhetoric in their dealings with British and American diplomats regarding post-war Soviet designs.

Pan-Turkists' attempts in Berlin to adumbrate İnönü's eradication of Turanian adventurism at home proved futile. From numerous talks in the Ostministerium, Franz von Papen got the impression that neither Ribbentrop nor the Reichsminister Rosenberg favoured plans for the creation of an independent Crimean state under German protection.[95] As to the Crimean Tatars, von Papen learned that it had already been decided not to grant them self-government. In fact, Rosenberg even contemplated removing Tatars from Crimea and making the latter a purely German region. This plan was dropped, chiefly because of the technical difficulties involved in its execution. It was decided that Crimea would be administered by a Commissariat-General, under the direction of Gauleiter Frauenfeld.[96] As for the leading representatives of the Crimean émigrés in Berlin, such as Ülküsal and Kırımer, they were deeply disappointed. Franz von Papen referred in his report that their discontent had considerably increased over the summer of 1942 not for personal reasons alone, such as Rosenberg's refusal to allow them in the Ostministerium as advisers, but because the Nazi schemes implied a darker future in the offing.

The price of collaboration

Between the fall of 1941, when the Wehrmacht (together with Romanian troops) began the invasion of Crimea, and the Soviet army's recapturing of the peninsula in the spring of 1944, Reichskommissariat Ukraine (RKU) carried out a systematic programme of eradicating symbols of Russian and Soviet rule. Particularly after July 1942, when the Axis captured its main target – Sevastopol – Hitler changed tack, and rather than entertaining Tatar hopes of *Azat Kırım*, insisted on turning much of Southern Ukraine into a district (the so-called 'Gotenland') directly connected to the Third Reich. In much the same way that Tsarist Russia renamed Crimean cities (from Akmescit to Simferopol), the RKU changed their names to German, such as Simferopol to Gotenburg and Sevastopol to Theodorichshafen. By the time Stalin ordered the Crimean Offensive to reclaim the peninsula in April 1944, most street signs in Simferopol, which advertised the achievements of 1917, had been given new names in a spirit that was alien to the Soviets, such as Hobt Straße or Park Straße.[97] In less than five weeks (8 April to 12 May 1944), when the Red Army's 4th Ukrainian Front launched a series of offensives against the Wehrmacht and Romanian formations, the Soviet Union successfully forced the Axis forces to evacuate the peninsula.

Two weeks before the Soviet victory, Lavrenty Beria addressed the State Defense Committee (GKO) in a letter dated 1 May 1944, where he described an intricate plan to eradicate all Nazi collaborators from Crimea.[98] This was an addendum to an earlier document that had been sent by the NKVD on 25 April, when the operational forces of NKVD-NKGB-Smersh arrested '4,206 representatives of the anti-Soviet element out of which 430 spies have been exposed'.[99] Beria's letter revealed further arrests in the follow-up operations undertaken by the NKVD troops to secure the rear from 10–27 April, when 5,115 people were apprehended. Among the number of arrested were '55 agents of the German Reconnaissance, 266 traitors of the motherland and 363 persons engaged in aiding and abetting the enemy'.[100]

Looking at Beria's letters, it would be fair to suggest that in its early stages, NKVD operations focused on targeting organized Turkic and Muslim groups. Beria noted that among the total number of arrests, 449 were members of the Muslim Committee. Led by Abbas Ismailov and Batal Batalov, this organization actively promoted fascist propaganda among the Tatar youth, gathered volunteer groups and recruited personnel for various cadres of the future Tatar Republic. Beria asserted that almost every Muslim committee was subsidized by the Nazis and had a spy network. After the defeat of the German army in Stalingrad, for instance, 'the Tatar Muslim committee gathered 1 million rubles from Turkey alone for aiding the Germans'.[101] They propagated the slogan 'Crimea for Tatars only' and 'spread rumours about the unification of Crimea to Turkey after the War'.[102]

Likewise, Beria noted that the Nazis founded a Tatar National Centre, representatives of which came from Turkey in order to befriend Crimean young people. One particular Stanov was arrested by partisans and apparently confessed that 'in 1943 he was met by the SD [*Sicherheitsdienst*] for spy work and was given the task of spreading espionage agents and creating a local institution of spies'.[103] While Beria's initial correspondence with the NKO between early April and late May deals almost exclusively with the arrests of Muslim Tatars, by 19 May 1944, he was convinced that other nationalities residing in Crimea should be deported as well; the list included Bulgarians, Greeks and Armenians.[104] Aside from the deportation of Crimean Tatars from their homeland, upon Beria's order, the NKVD carried out the formidable task of identifying and isolating all anti-Soviet elements. The investigation of forested regions not only targeted the apprehension of Crimean Tatars who were hiding from deportation but also other deserting and bandit elements including '12,075 Bulgars, 14,300 Greeks, and 9,919 Armenians'.[105] Beria's subsequent letters in the Lubyanka include further information about where these people live and how exactly they collaborated during the Nazi occupation.

Several letters were exchanged between Beria and Stalin, showing that a significant portion of the Tatar populace was believed to have actively participated in supplying the Nazi army with bread, food, medicine and arms. The Tatars were accused of cooperating with the Germans in an attempt to identify and arrest soldiers of the Red Army and Soviet partisans. In return for the help they had given to the Germans, they received a so-called 'certificate of security' (*okhrania svidetelstvo*) whereby the identity and property of the collaborators were protected by the Nazi army. The violation of *okhrania svidetelstvo* could result in execution. Aside from Tatars, the Greeks and Bulgarians, who lived primarily in coastal regions, were also believed to have collaborated with the German forces through the mutual trade and transportation of goods. Finally, the Armenian national committees 'with the support of new immigrants that arrived from Berlin and İstanbul' were reported to have actively participated in an 'independent Armenia propaganda'.[106] In conclusion, the NKVD considered it desirable to carry out the deportation from the Crimea 'all Tatars, Bulgarians, all Greeks and all Armenians'.[107] Further evidence from these letters shows that Beria's instructions were immediately seconded by the NKO and put into action.

By 4 July 1944, the deportation from Crimea of all peoples including Tatars, Bulgarians, Greeks and Armenians had been completed: 'In total 225,009 people were deported; among those the numbers were the following: 183,155 Tatars; 12,422 Bulgarians; 15,040 Greeks; 9,621 Armenians; 1,119 Germans; 3,652 other nationalities.' All Tatars were transported to the following places: 'in the regions of the Uzbek SSR 151,604 people; in the regions of the RSFSR, in accordance with the decree of the GOKO May 21, 1944, 31,551 people ...The rest [were] on their way to the Bashkir ASSR, Mariyskii SSR, Kemerovskii, Molotovskii, Sverdlovskii, Kirovskii oblasts of the RSFSR and the Gruievskii ASSR of the Kazak SSR.'[108] A significant portion of the resettled peoples (*spetspereselentsy*) that were capable of work were incorporated into work in agriculture in kolkhozes and sovkhozes as well as in lumber industry and other relevant industries.

In 1945, Moscow declared that the entire Crimean peninsula had been 'emancipated' from the Nazi menace.[109] On 30 June 1945, the Crimean ASSR was liquidated and later awarded to the Ukrainian SSR. But Crimean Tatars were clearly not the only people that suffered from Stalin's purges. Kalmyks, for instance, faced a tragedy of similar proportions. In 1943, only five out of the thirteen *Ulusi* of the Kalmyk ASSR were under the Nazi occupation. An important role in Stalin's decision to deport them was played by the news that the 110th Kalmyk cavalry division surrendered to the Germans en masse. On 27 December 1943, the Kalmyk ASSR was liquidated as an administrated unit and its territory incorporated into the Astrakhan and Stalingrad oblasts. Kalmyk names of all *Ulusi* and their centres were replaced by Russian ones.[110] Soon after the deportations, the former Deputy Representative of the Sovnarkom of the Kalmyk ASSR, Khakhaev, wrote a personal letter to Stalin about the excessive measures taken against their nation. This is one of the many letters sent by the local authorities of various ASSRs to Moscow, including the Crimean ASSR:

> The deportation of the Kalmyks was completely unexpected for most us. We considered it necessary to purge the Kalmyk territory of all bastards (*svoloshi*) since we knew exactly then the *Kalmyki* would be liberated. Yet, it is unclear to us why you decided to deport all Kalmyks including the 40,000 innocent people. Surely, it was possible to deport and send to punitive labor the ten to fifteen thousand guilty ones who were associated with banditry and German fascism. In my opinion, the absolute majority of Kalmyks who turned out to be traitors of their *rodina*, were not persuaded by ideas but their betrayal resulted from their backwardness and the fact that they were subject to provocation and agitation by the Germans. Surely there were mistakes by our bureau too but it is about time to get over it. Autonomy needs to be granted back so that the entire Kalmyk *narod* can wash itself with honest labor and get rid of the stain of honest betrayal. The burden of guilt for honest Kalmyks should not be so heavy just because among us it turned out there were bastards.[111]

Khakhaev was trying to warn Stalin that such a universal deportation might give grounds for 'elements of nationalism in the future in the East'.[112] Aside from the fascinating clues on what was to come after 1991, this succinct document captures virtually every aspect of Stalin's deportations, which targeted many other oblasts and autonomous republics. It explains to readers exactly how the USSR was perceived at the local level and why a mutually enforcing suspicion emerged between the centre and the periphery after the war.[113] As the NKVD letters of correspondence demonstrate, the Soviet leadership was convinced that the Tatars or Kalmyks would be assimilated easily into the Kazakh and Uzbek worlds, while their homelands would be renamed, given a new history and absorbed by other, ostensibly more reliable, nations.[114] But the reality could not be farther from Beria's assessment. For fifty years, the Crimean Tatars proved to be strongly attached to their ethnic and confessional identities and forged their own foundation narrative, more popularly known as *Sürgün* (Exile).

Regarding the fate of the pan-Turkists after Stalingrad, they quickly fell out of favour and began to be perceived as a subversive ideology, which bred antagonism within society against the Kemalist variant of Turkish nationalism. Gradual amendments were made to the Criminal Code (Articles 141 and 142), which now prescribed a death penalty for both the socialists and pan-Turkists. Promoting racist propaganda became punishable by law and the government made it very plain that the pan-Turkists were not welcome. By 1944, as the pan-Turkist agitation for Turkey's involvement in the war reached a cul-de-sac, another prominent pan-Turkist, Nihal Atsız, published an open letter to Prime Minister Saraçoğlu in his magazine *Orhun*, levying all sorts of accusations against the government, including aiding and abetting communists and Soviet sympathizers in his entourage.[115] Atsız singled out the left-leaning Turkish minister of education, Hasan Ali Yücel, and blamed him for harbouring pro-Soviet intellectuals, such as the famous writer Sabahattin Ali. Thus began the famous Racist-Turanian Trials of 1944, which led to street protests and communal unrest in large metropolitan areas.[116] The government responded to the civic unrest by arresting all major pan-Turkists, including Zeki Velidi Togan, Nihal Atsız, Reha Oğuz Türkkan and several other officers, including General Hüseyin Erkilet and First Lieutenant Alparslan Türkeş, who would become the future leader of pan-Turkism.[117] When the police raided the suspects' apartments, they found documents that revealed the existence of secret societies, German support for the pan-Turkists and a possible coup conspiracy against the government. In September 1944, forty-seven pan-Turkists leaders were tried and many of them found guilty as charged. The list included almost all of the leading pan-Turkist personalities, with sentences ranging from two to ten years. Ironically, the trials of pan-Turkists turned out to be counterproductive for the government, since the court proceedings were public and afforded the defendants a good deal of publicity.[118]

Ultimately, the failure of Nazi Germany's Turanian propaganda prevented the coming into being of a silent Nazi–Turkish alliance similar to that in Spain. Nevertheless, in fanning Sovietophobia in Ankara, Nazi policy-makers accomplished their main objective of keeping Turkey as a benevolent non-belligerent power favourably disposed to Berlin against Moscow, and forced İnönü's hand into mobilizing Turkish regiments in defensive positions on the Caucasian border against the Soviet Union. The unspoken agreement between the Nazi and Turkish governments with regards to the latter's wartime neutrality caused a great apprehension amongst the pan-Turkist circles, who were still convinced that without Turkey's entrance into war on Nazi Germany's side, their dreams of realizing the Turanian network against Soviet Russia would hardly be possible. Even after Germany's abandonment of post-war Turanian schemes, a number of pan-Turkists continued to serve as meddling intermediaries in Berlin, repudiating allegations that İnönü ultimately discarded the Turkish *Lebensraum* idea.

Looking at the objectives of Nazi activities in Turkey, it would be fair to suggest that feeding Turanian fantasies had a broader goal than merely gaining Turkey as a belligerent ally. German records demonstrate an intriguing dynamic in the dispute between Ribbentrop and Ambassador Franz von Papen about the pan-Turkists' role in the Nazi–Soviet war. In response to von Papen's attempts to further incite the idea of a Turkish *Lebensraum*, Ribbentrop instructed von Papen to refrain from language that could be misconstrued as a implying a military alliance, as Nazi Germany's sole objective was to guarantee Turkey's neutrality.[119] But Ribbentrop's instructions did not indicate a lack of ambition. Nazi propaganda in Turkey also aimed to strengthen the ideological and economics links between Berlin and Ankara. The effects of these efforts outlived Nazi Germany's defeat, for Russophobia continued to be a defining feature of Turkish foreign policy long after 1945.

7

When the Hurlyburly's Done

As Mark Bernes portrayed in his poignant songs of victory (*pesni pobedy*), millions of Soviet soldiers died in World War II. The Battle of Stalingrad was heavy with symbolism for any rank-and-file Ivan, as they turned into snow-covered cranes (*zhuravli*) in Rasul Gamzatov's famous poem.[1] Defence of the motherland meant something more than the number of cannons fired against the Hitlerite apocalypse in Europe. To accomplish Vasily Chuikov's pyrrhic victory alone, more than half a million Soviet soldiers were killed in action in January 1943.[2] The story of Stalingrad is one of imprudence, mercilessness and disaster; and it is revealing in a number of ways. On the German side, the most striking aspect of this battle lies in the confusion of its aims and purposes, particularly the muddle between political beliefs and their consequences. Nazi troops in Stalingrad were in complete moral disarray and quickly realized that the objectives of subjugating the Slavs, and defending Europe from Bolshevism through a pre-emptive strike, had proved counterproductive.

From the Turkish perspective, Stalingrad was a clever Soviet trap into which the Wehrmacht had been enticed by deliberate withdrawals.[3] The consequences of Hitler's defeat were crystal clear from the onset. Turkish sympathy swung decisively towards the Atlantic powers, while Nazi–Turkish relations became more neutral and colder. The Soviets were acutely aware that the deterioration in Nazi–Turkish affairs owed more to Turkey's 'realization of the serious successes of Soviet troops in the battle on the Volga by the early months of 1943', when İnönü changed 'his prognosis relating to the country of victors'.[4] The Nazis seemed to have the same impression. Three weeks after the advance of the Red Army in late February 1943, the Nazi Consul General in İstanbul spoke to the *Cumhuriyet* daily and said that in their official statements Turkey's leaders appeared to be on the side of the Reich in its 'fated march against Soviet Russia', but that recently it had became more obvious that Ankara was seriously concerned about the possibility of a Soviet victory and 'might roll the dice for Great Britain at any moment'.[5]

Indeed, Turkish official opinion became more vocal over the prospect of Soviet expansion after Stalingrad. The westward advance of the Red Army and its tacit acceptance by the British led to the surrender of Eastern Europe and the Balkans to the Soviets. It was thought that, if Great Britain did not have the courage or strength to oppose Soviet Russian designs at a future date, Poland would be eventually forced to make the best terms it could with Moscow, that Romania was already condemned, and that Greece would rapidly follow suit. Despite their scepticism and distrust, Turkish officials did not get beyond the stage of passive pessimism, remained silent with regards to their own orientation, which they repeatedly claimed to be 'rapidly establishing', and merely confined themselves to croaking with alarm about the future.[6]

During the greater part of the period under review here, roughly between February 1943 (Soviet victory in Stalingrad) and August 1944 (the end of Nazi–Turkish diplomatic and trade relations), the problem before the Turkish government was finding the right moment to fulfil their treaty obligations to Great Britain and enter the war. After the Tehran Conference in November 1943, İnönü quickly realized that Stalin did not relish a large-scale arming of Turkey – since an adequately equipped Turkish army acting in tandem with the Allies could get in its way in the Balkans. Stalin had shown almost no enthusiasm for Churchill's proposal for a Turkish–American lend-lease agreement. Nevertheless, as Turkish policy-makers began to realize that the end of the war would not bring about a return to the antebellum status quo, they decided to adjust themselves and their national interests to a new build-up before it was too late.

Ultimately, Turkey's entrance into war on the side of the Allies occurred in three stages: the first was immediately after the Adana meeting between Churchill and İnönü in January 1943, when the Turks moved closer to Great Britain, while still anxious not to become implicated in the Allies' over-optimistic interpretation of Ankara's attitude; the second occurred after the Second Cairo Conference in December 1943, following a sharp reaction from Great Britain when Turkey's manifestations of neutrality were slightly modified; and the third took place after a rapprochement with the American government in the summer of 1944, when Turkey cut off all political and trade relations with Nazi Germany.

Beginning with the Churchill–İnönü talks in Adana in January 1943, Turkey's wartime position was repeatedly called into question by Great Britain. As Ankara delayed its entry into the war, London made its dissatisfaction more explicit. In his conversations with the Secretary of State Anthony Eden, the Turkish ambassador frequently complained that Eden had coupled Turkey's name on a number of occasions with those of Spain and Portugal as 'neutrals'.[7] Eden took the opportunity to urge that in due course, Turkey should sit at the peace table as an ally that had fought in the war, adding that the time might soon come when, without active belligerency, Turkey would still be able to provide facilities that might shorten the war. In addition to Britain's grievances as to the open advocacy of neutrality, the question of Turkey's position in the post-war world turned upon two factors: its position vis-à-vis the victorious powers; and its relations with the Soviet Union.

Turkish policy-makers rivalled Hamlet in their indecisiveness, because Great Britain did not truly appreciate Turkey's chronic mistrust and fear of Soviet Russia, which, in return poisoned Anglo-Turkish relations. War-related problems and Turkey's revived Russophobia rendered only one safe course for Turkey to enter the war: to align itself with the United Nations before Soviet dissatisfaction found expression. Turkey's point of view was diametrically opposed to Great Britain's. Whenever British policy-makers proposed Ankara's alignment with Moscow, the Turkish government responded that Turkey's participation or non-participation in the war would have had no effect whatsoever on Soviet policy. If Turkey were to fight, it would merely weaken itself and increase the danger of becoming a satellite of Russia – like Poland. In some ways, Great Britain understood Turkey's thinking and admitted that 'she had to keep her powder dry against the day when Russian imperialism will inevitably revive', but the Turks' fear of Russia, in the British view, was never completely justified.⁸

After Ankara failed to convince London about an imminent Russian threat, two interrelated desiderata shaped Turkey's diplomacy in the latter half of 1944 and early 1945. First, if there were a danger of the defeated countries becoming 'Bolshevik or Slav', as Saraçoğlu put it, Turkey needed to be 'closely associated with the [future] United Nations and its prospective collective security system'; and second, if Russia were at any time to menace European peace after the war, Turkey needed a closer and stronger ally than Britain.⁹ This latter security concern, arising mostly out of Britain's disdain for Turkey's Russophobia, prompted the incipient Turkish–American rapprochement throughout the heated days of 1944.

Apart from its general desire to prevent itself from post-war Soviet aggression, Turkey also strove to prevent neighbouring Middle-Eastern states from becoming a threat to its national security through Soviet influence in those countries. It was no secret that to Turkey, the Arab world had long been, as the British ambassador put it, 'something between a joke and a nuisance' since the Great War.¹⁰ But Turkey's established policy of isolationism towards the Middle-East theatre was largely shaken after the Adana Conference in early 1943 in the face of its deteriorating relations with the Soviet Union. Turkey's direct interest in the Middle East was largely occupied with the presence of Kurdish tribes located on both sides of its southern and eastern frontiers. The British ambassador aptly noted in his 1944 report that 'the Kurds had little reason to love the Turks', while some Turkish Kurds were 'pathetically loyal' to the Ankara government. Yet, in real terms, the emergence of incipient Kurdish movements in Soviet Azerbaijan became a source of apprehension.¹¹

The Turkish government kept a watchful eye on movements in Tabriz after the Anglo-Soviet invasion in 1941, but seemed to have been duly assured that there was in no sense an imminent threat to Turkish interests arising out of British presence.¹² Ankara had probably been casting a suspicious eye on some of the activities of British experts in connection with the 'Kurdish Question', but the Turks felt more disturbed than ever due to the Soviet involvement. Turkey was convinced that the Russians were, once again, planning to exploit Kurdish grievances against Turkey, just as their forefathers had earlier in the century. Ankara was uneasy about the Kurdish problem so much that, when, for instance, the Iraqi government proposed to appoint an Iraqi Kurd as its envoy in Ankara, Menemencioğlu confessed to Halifax: 'If they had only proposed an Arab, or even a Christian, but not a Kurd.'¹³

Turkey's relations with the Allies reached another critical juncture after the Adana Conference, and provoked serious concern among the Turkish policy-makers who now began to perceive the Soviet presence in Iran with extreme anxiety and contempt. The Turkish government was particularly concerned about Iranian Azerbaijan because, apart from its substantial Turkish population and geographic proximity to the historically disputed provinces between Russia and Turkey, the region was now conveniently exposed to Kurdish disturbances with a potential Soviet aegis in the offing. The distressing wake-up call for the government came from the 9th Army Corps in October 1943. In his regular inspection tour of the Erzurum Garrison, the Chief of General Staff stumbled upon numerous pamphlets posted on mosques, coffee houses and public buildings. Written in broken Turkish, these pamphlets appeared to be the work of the Revolutionary Fedayeens of Kars and Erzurum, and called for an imminent Kurdish uprising.[14]

In the course of his annual opening speech delivered at the National Assembly, İnönü took the opportunity to condemn in severe tones 'the spiteful propaganda' emanating from the eastern provinces. He also alluded to disturbing rumours of public discontent regarding the government's allegedly insufficient measure of assistance furnished to the population throughout the war and alleged disregard of looting and disorder.[15] That some such rumours had in fact been circulated is confirmed by the British reports, from which it seems clear that the Kurds were playing upon religious feelings of the population, 'propagating the likelihood of another barbarous repression of the Kurds', and that 'the President of the Republic is considered to be a bringer of bad luck'.[16]

In view of this contingency, the Chief of General Staff increased the number of gendarmerie forces patrolling the border and gradually strengthened Turkish military line on the eastern frontier with new reinforcements.[17] Receiving orders to suppress the slightest grouping against the Republican regime, the 3rd Army raided a small band of Kurdish guerillas in Dersim, where the leaders of the Demenan tribe were killed and

Figure 7.1 Winston Churchill and Anthony Eden are greeted by Turkish Foreign Minister Şükrü Saracoğlu in Yenice, Adana (now in Mersin). Churchill was reportedly in high spirits and energetic about leaving London and visiting Casablanca, Adana and Cyprus in the winter of 1943. His main goal was to encourage Turkey to join the Allied war effort, and to ascertain whether Cyprus would be a safe place for the first 'Big Three' meeting with Stalin and FDR.

Figure 7.2 İsmet İnönü arrives at the Yenice train station to attend the Adana Conference (30–31 January 1943) with Churchill. With recent Allied victories against Nazi Germany, Britain exponentially intensified its efforts to cajole Turkey into becoming a belligerent. İnönü's refusal to cut diplomatic and trade relations with Nazi Germany until 1944, as well as his rigid insistence on neutrality, would be treated with contempt by both Churchill and Great Britain.

Figure 7.3 Turkish Foreign Minister Şükrü Saraçoğlu with Churchill in Adana, 30–31 January 1943. Churchill was reported to be energetic and high-spirited during the Adana talks, and on his journey back to London via Cyprus, which he regarded as an appropriae venue for the 'Big Three' conference.

their weapons confiscated.[18] Although Kurdish disturbances in the eastern provinces were inconsequential and did not seem to culminate in the form of a significant uprising witnessed previously, İnönü suspected that the Soviets were entertaining the idea of sponsoring Kurds in the region and asked the Directorate of Public Security (*Emniyet Umum Müdürlüğü*) to prepare an extensive report on Soviet activities in Transcaucasia.[19] The report emphasized the Karakabakh and Zangezur regiments of the Red Army, which contained about 100 Kurdish soldiers. 'Few Kurds in these two regiments had known their language but used to speak Azeri Turkish instead', the report concluded, 'yet the Russians have been pursuing a state-sponsored campaign to educate these people in the recently established Kurdology centers in Erevan and Moscow'.[20] It seemed quite clear to the Turkish government that the new Soviet designs in Transcaucasia had completely different goals from the *korenizatsiia* policy of the 1920s, and was becoming much more reminiscent of late imperial Tsarist practices.[21]

From Adana to Cairo

Two days before the Adana meeting, İnönü asked for a comprehensive report that showed the total military assistance Turkey had received from Britain since the beginning of the war. The list included fifty Stuart light tanks, forty Valentine tanks, 176 anti-tank guns, 105 anti-aircraft projectors, eighty-six field guns, fifty-eight mid-size guns, 750 Vickers machine guns and more.[22] At the Adana Conference, Turkey did ask for more tanks and guns given a possible landing in the Dardanelles, in line with Churchill's initial proposal for D-Day, which would save Europe from Hitlerite aggression. The main problem facing the British government before the conference

Figure 7.4 İnönü and Churchill in the train carriage that hosted the Adana Conference.

Figures 7.5 and 7.6 İnönü and Churchill during the Adana Conference.

was establishing a more binding cooperation with the Turkish government. To achieve this, Secretary Eden issued a statement on 1 January 1943, regarding Britain's actual war position and a general expose of their ideas on the subject of a Balkan cooperation. Three weeks later came Winston Churchill's proposal to meet President İnönü privately in Cyprus or wherever the president preferred. In fact, there was a faint glimmer of hope that İnönü would receive Churchill in Ankara officially, but Eden himself admitted that this was quite unlikely. Upon serious deliberation, Turkey informed Great Britain that the Conference would take place in Adana on 30–31 January 1943.

The fact that İnönü brought with him a large diplomatic delegation to Adana was an encouraging sign for Churchill. İnönü was accompanied by Prime Minister Saraçoğlu, Chief of the General Staff Fevzi Çakmak and Foreign Minister Menemencioğlu. The British side had an equally high-ranking profile. Churchill asked an impressive number of officers to participate, including the Chief of the Imperial General Staff Alan Brooke, General Henry Maitland Wilson, Air Marshal Peter Drummond and Commodore John Dundas.[23] The presence of so many of Britain's senior military authorities and still more the fact that, despite a certain degree of secrecy surrounding the Conference, the Turks had no hesitation in including their names on the communiqué, were certainly hopeful signs of a more robust Anglo-Turkish partnership.[24]

The conversations at the Adana Conference mainly covered three stages: present wartime circumstances; the immediate future; and possible scenarios of a post-war order. In order to secure Turkey's ultimate participation in the war on the side of the Allies, Churchill promised large quantities of supplies and technical expertise. These preparations were regarded as a necessary preliminary initiative and an affordable price to pay for Turkey's entrance – either on its own initiative or as a result of a potential Nazi attack. At the very least, Churchill hoped to stretch Turkey's neutrality to any wide extent in Allied interests.[25] He deemed it essential to strengthen Turkey so that it could either defend itself successfully if attacked,. Various hypotheses were put before President İnönü to indicate developments that might affect Turkey's position of neutrality.

Churchill made it perfectly clear that İnönü was entirely free to declare Turkey's own course of action. But he also implied that the promised war supplies would be contingent upon Turkey's entrance into the war. From the British perspective, Churchill did not ask for any immediate undertakings or impossibilities. He did not propose that Turkey enter the war if it did not feel ready, nor did he suggest that Turkey should do so in a way that would require exhaustion of all its local resources and lead to disaster. These assurances, however, were accompanied by a clear message that, if the British government were to fulfill its part in strengthening Turkey's defences, Britain would claim the right to seek Turkey's assistance and 'make a firm proposal [to join London in its war effort] when the moment was right'.[26]

While the Turkish government turned out to be non-committal to any immediate military undertaking, the Adana Conference did produce two tangible results. First, the Turkish chief of staff provided the British Army Corps in Tunisia with a special military unit comprising of eighteen top-ranking officers, three of whom had gained combat experience in World War I.[27] Second, İnönü responded 'frankly and positively' to Churchill's self-appointed mission to mend fences between Turkey and the Soviet Union, arguing that Turkey would be open to any undertaking that would restore bilateral relations between Ankara and Moscow in the spirit of the 1920s and 30s Soviet-Turkish friendship.[28] Churchill also emphasized that even should Nazi Germany not attack Turkey, Turkish interests would still dictate that it should still intervene in the Balkans to prevent anarchy. Without becoming a belligerent, Turkey might at some point consider taking the same position as the United States before the war, by 'a departure from strict neutrality'.²⁹ Thus Turkey might grant permission to use Turkish airfields to bomb Romanian oil fields, the Dodecanese islands and Crete. Churchill also stressed the importance of joining 'the winners' table to assure its security after the war', and added that 'at the end of the war, the United States [would] be the strongest nation and [would] desire a solid international structure'.³⁰

Indeed, when the Adana Conference was held in late January, the United States had just emerged triumphant from Operation Torch – the largest amphibious assault hitherto attempted. Although this was a defining episode for the Allied forces in the Mediterranean basin, Operation Torch has occupied a space of lesser significance in historical memory compared to the more famous D-Day or the Italian operations of Avalanche, Baytown and Slapstick. Repercussions of the African campaign were profound for the Americans. Four US divisions now had combat experience in five variants of Euro-Mediterranean warfare: expeditionary, amphibious, mountain, desert and urban. The inexperienced American troops of 1942 had evolved into probably the most advanced army in the world, which had learned 'the importance of terrain, of combined armies, of aggressive patrolling, of stealth, of massed armor', and which now knew 'what it was like to be bombed, shelled, and machine gunned, and to fight on'.³¹ Commensurate with its improved military capabilities, the United States became exponentially more involved in shaping the new Mediterranean diplomacy and balance of power in southeast Europe.

Immediately after the Adana Conference, the US ambassador in Turkey, Laurence Steinhardt, held a meeting with Menemencioğlu and dispatched a memorandum regarding possible courses of action in Turkey.³² In his report, Steinhardt accurately pointed to the 'non-committal tenor of the official [Adana] communiqué, which was offset by the impressive list of high ranking officials who attended the conference'.³³ For Steinhardt, although the Turkish government had complete trust in the Allied cause, Churchill was missing the real point; that the fear of 'a seizure by Russia of Straits was so deeply rooted in consciousness of all classes' that the Turkish people would probably welcome an entry into the war on the side of Allies 'as assuring active support of the United States against Russian aspirations'.³⁴ In his astute analysis, Steinhardt contended that the Turkish government was already convinced that the Allies would win the war and that it was in its best interest to join sooner rather than later. The most important aspect of Turkey's post-war considerations was not about Germany, but a conviction that Turkey's only salvation from possible Russian aggression lies in such protection as she may be able to obtain from the United States.

Despite an excellent understanding of Turkey's security concerns, the United States did not step up as the main facilitator of Turkey's cooperation with the Allies until 1944. This was mainly due to the decisions reached at the Casablanca Conference between the US and Great Britain, whereby Turkey was to be considered to lie within a military sphere of primary British responsibility. This agreement was limited strictly to military matters and implied no recognition by the American government of any British responsibility in the political and social spheres with regards to Turkey.³⁵ But it was obvious that, after the Adana Conference, there was a certain degree of suspicion on the part of the US whether it had been a good decision to delegate their own responsibilities to the British and let them 'play the cards with Turkey on their behalf'.³⁶

Against this background, Turkey's new foreign minister, Numan Menemencioğlu, went to Cairo on 5 November 1943 to meet with Anthony Eden and secure assurances from Great Britain against a possible Soviet threat.[37] In fact, Winston Churchill had already promised substantial military assistance to strengthen the Turkish army when he met with İnönü during the Adana Conference. Yet for the military supplies to be extended, Churchill emphasized that Turkey should be ready to take action and enter into the war against the Axis.[38] While some British assistance was dispatched in the spring of that year, when Churchill was contemplating on a new Balkan front with Turkey as its spearhead, Turkey found the initial aid quite insufficient to abandon its non-belligerent position. By the end of the year, as Stalin's shadow began to stretch out from Erzurum looming over the Straits, Menemencioğlu went to Cairo and sought to take Eden's pulse as he returned from Moscow.

In Cairo, Menemencioğlu saw a deplorable image of Turkey in Eden's eyes, and that Eden was guided merely by Russian considerations.[39] Britain's need for Soviet cooperation in its war effort against Nazi Germany seemed to have convinced Eden that Turkey was the only suitable offering to appease the gods – in other words, a sacrifice supreme.[40] In response to Eden's repeated appeals for Turkey's acceptance of Allied airbases in Western Anatolia, Menemencioğlu stated that this would amount to a declaration of war and was out of the question unless the danger presented to the Allied war effort was imminent. Naturally, Eden warned Menemencioğlu that Britain

Figure 7.7 İnönü and FDR at the Second Cairo Conference, December 1943. Essentially, this meeting addressed Turkey's potential contributions to the Allied war effort.

When the Hurlyburly's Done 155

Figure 7.8 and 7.9 İnönü with Churchill and FDR at the Second Cairo Conference, December 1943. This meeting marked the start of mounting pressure on İnönü to join the war on the Allies' side.

would cease all military assistance to Turkey if the Ankara government decided not to help their friends at this critical moment. In effect, Menemencioğlu felt that Eden was acting as a mouthpiece for the Soviets, 'particularly with regards to [his] questions vis-à-vis the future of Iran and the current regime governing the Straits'.[41] Eden mentioned that the Soviets also had some expectations from Turkey regarding the Balkan front and that the Turkish army was the only successful force in the region to facilitate an operation to invade Romania. Menemencioğlu said that this option too was unacceptable unless Turkey would be treated as an equal ally and not as a colony or inferior power.

The pressure on Turkey was ramping up when the Big Three held their next meeting, this time at the Soviet Embassy in Tehran on 23 November 1943. Stalin, Churchill and Roosevelt agreed that it would be most desirable if Turkey entered the war on the Allies' side before the end of the year.[42] In return, Turkey was offered Soviet Union's pledge for support.[43] The meeting took place a year after Operation Uranus, when the Red Army had launched its campaign against the German 6th Army flanks and emerged triumphant out of the bloodiest battle in human history. That evening, Churchill presented the ceremonial Sword of Stalingrad to the 'steelhearted' people of the Soviet Union 'as a token of homage from King George VI'.[44] Moved by Churchill's emotional oratory, Marshal Voroshilov rather clumsily let the sword slide out of the scabbard, which clattered on the floor. After lifting the sword to his lips, Stalin kissed it and raised his glass, proposing a salute to the 'swiftest possible justice for all Germany's war criminals'.[45]

Commensurate with the insurmountable casualties of the Red Army, Stalin held the upper hand in Tehran. A sort of bloodguilt was prevalent in the British and American delegations' attitudes, through which Stalin managed to manipulate the Western Allies into unleashing just the sort of counter-attack against Hitler that he had envisaged a year before.[46] The conference in Tehran determined Allied strategy for the rest of the war. Churchill's plan for an invasion through the Balkans was vetoed for sound military reasons and the Western Allies' main effort was devoted to northwest Europe. But with this strategic logic, the fate of the Balkans was left entirely in Stalin's hands.[47]

During the second Tripartite Meeting in Cairo, held four days after Tehran, İnönü met with Roosevelt and Churchill to clarify Turkey's position with regards to the war. He pointed out that the real danger for both Turks and the Allies would be to enter the war without proper preparations.[48] The Cairo Summit represents the peak of the pressure on Turkey, when Churchill played on Turkey's sensitivity regarding the Soviets and made it clear that the only way for the Soviet storm to abate would be declaring war against Germany. If Lausanne was İnönü's first diplomatic victory in his political career, Cairo was probably the last. On the one hand, İnönü's stalling tactics prevailed and the Turkish delegation returned home without giving any pledges for any fixed date of entering the war. On the other hand, the Turks realized that the end of their neutrality was near.

In Cairo, the suggestion that Turkey should enter the war before the end of 1943 was presented to the Turkish government with the arguments that Turkey would thus confer a great benefit on the world in general, and on Russia in particular. Moreover, the British ambassador argued, a favourable decision would place Russo-Turkish relations on a 'sound and friendly footing'.⁴⁹ In reality, the Anglo-Soviet pressure as to the date when Turkey would be required to enter the war was due to the intense Russian desire to shorten the war by every means possible. But the Turkish leaders and diplomats argued that they could not simply go enter the fray out of the blue with no other task than to stand alone in a menacing attitude while doing nothing.⁵⁰

This position was vigorously maintained during the roundtable talks and tripartite meetings held in Cairo on 4-5 December. President Roosevelt told İnönü that 'it would be a pity if Turkey now missed the opportunity [of sitting on the bench with her great friends and allies – the US, Great Britain and USSR] because in a few months, perhaps six, German resistance would be broken ... and it would be dangerous if Turkey now missed her chance of joining the English-speaking peoples numbering, excluding colored races, some two hundred million souls'.⁵¹ As a response, İnönü argued that, throughout the war, 'Turkey had remained anchored to her alliance with Great Britain, and to the ideas later postulated by the United States ... in this decision she had not been moved by any egoistical interest'.⁵² He added that, although Turkey had been seriously considering collaboration with the Allies, and even 'mobilized all her equipment, including those that date back to the Middle Ages', so far the assistance they received from the Anglo-American coalition had been far from adequate. 'What could the Allies give Turkey in two months and what could be carried?', asked İnönü with a fair amount of contempt.

Observing the intense Allied pressure over Turkey in Adana, Tehran and Cairo, the chief of the German Intelligence Service paid an important visit to Naci Perkel, head of Turkey's National Intelligence Service (MAH). The purpose of this meeting was to discuss a possible transfer of the Dodecanese islands from Germany to Turkey. The meeting was arranged by Franz von Papen, who thought that, under existing circumstances, Turkey would never accept such an offer, therefore it would not be appropriate for that offer to be made officially through diplomatic channels. İsmet İnönü, who was in Eastern Anatolia at the time, was informed of this meeting through an urgent communiqué by Şükrü Saraçoğlu.⁵³ Presenting a verbatim record of Perkel's meeting, Saraçoğlu inquired about İnönü's opinion and passed on his own assessment. Given the sensitive nature of the issue, the Turkish leadership agreed that Berlin should first provide them with clarifications on a number of questions:

1. What exactly does Germany mean by *transfer*?
2. What does the term 'islands' constitute in Germany's geopolitical thinking?
3. Will there be any conditions for the transfer and will Turkey be able to exercise its free will on the Islands upon receipt?
4. Could Turkey re-transfer the islands to Britain, for instance?

Ultimately, the Turkish government decided that acquisition of the Islands would be too naïve an adventure to risk Ankara's relations with the Allied powers, at a time when they clearly seemed to be on the winning side.

In the early days of 1944, the Turks' position was such that, although they agreed in principle to enter the war, they could not do so in practice unless they were adequately armed for defence and until a joint military plan of action had been decided. But the talks in Tehran and Cairo were complicated by two suspicions in the Turkish mind. The first was that they were being forced into the war regardless of the consequences to themselves in order to satisfy Russia, and the second was that their acquiescence would be advantageous to Great Britain's air offensives via Turkish bases, regardless of the risks Ankara would run.[54] Little secret could be made of the anti-Soviet aspect of Numan Menemencioğlu's efforts to encourage a strong Balkan bloc. In Cairo, the Soviet ambassador, Vinogradoff, described the whole policy as being aimed at creating a barrier in the Balkans against Russia. Likewise, Saraçoğlu repeatedly advised his British counterparts that they should not only increase Turkish strength against Russia but nurse their own for post-war exigencies. Yet, British policy-makers, with their eyes on pragmatic needs of the day rather than potential post-war emergencies, refused to build up a joint defence against predictable Soviet aggressiveness.

The evolution of US–Turkish relations

As early as the Casablanca Conference of 14 January 1943, significant differences between Roosevelt and Churchill began to surface.[55] Casablanca was the first of the wartime meetings to determine the Allies' wartime policy, the sole purpose of which was to affirm the primacy of the war against Germany and to enshrine a Mediterranean strategy. In Morocco, a war-weary General Eisenhower sought to deal with his well-prepared British counterparts 'with their red-leather folders and cocktails'.[56] In his *An Army at Dawn*, Rick Atkinson argues that no soldier in Africa 'had changed more, grown more, than Eisenhower ... he had learned the hardest lesson of all: that for an army to win at war, young men must die'.[57] While confirming the American determination to punish the Axis without mercy, Casablanca also demonstrated 'the ability of the British to outmaneuver and outmuscle their American allies'.[58] Following the conference, Albert Wedemeyer told the War Department: 'We came, we listened, and we were conquered'.[59] For Atkinson, perhaps Ike shared Wedemeyer's sentiments to some extent, but he kept them to himself, because he realized the inevitability of American dominion in Africa and in Iran and that 'the old imperial order was cracking under the pressure of global war, and the British Commonwealth could not preserve the status quo forever'.[60]

Following a heated period of wartime conferences after Casablanca in 1943 – Adana, Cairo and Tehran – it became clear that the United States and Great Britain swept more than a reasonable share of their strategic differences under the Turkish rug. As early as the Casablanca meeting in January 1943, it was decided that Great Britain should play the leading role where Turkey was concerned, and the United States ambassador made a point to second this strategy. But once a proposal for a lease-lend agreement between the United States and Turkey was made to the Turkish government, İnönü realized the potential benefits of a closer partnership with the Americans. US–Turkish relations, which had remained relatively dormant until 1944 when Churchill's shadow still loomed over Ankara, developed significantly through private bilateral talks held during 1944. Roosevelt was acutely aware that the Soviets preferred a neutral, weak and isolated Turkey; and, therefore, much better appreciated Turkey's concerns about the post-war order.

After the conferences in Cairo and Tehran in December 1943, the British authorities thought that the Turks had gained the impression that only Great Britain was pressing for their entry into the war, and that a much less lenient attitude was held by the United States. In late January 1944, Ambassador Knatchbull-Hugessen tried to persuade his American colleague in Ankara (Ambassador Steinhardt) to open a new round of bilateral Turkish–American talks and try to disabuse the Turks of any such impression.[61] Yet, Steinhardt was dubious about this mission's purposes and thought that the conditions put forward by the Turkish government regarding arms deliveries as a prerequisite for their participation in the war was 'quite reasonable'. Having failed to soothe Turkey's post-war anxiety about Soviet expansionism, Great Britain gradually resorted to stronger means of diplomatic pressure and, ultimately decided to punish Turkey by isolating it from its existing connections with the Western Allies.

As a first step, on 5 February, the British ambassador received instructions directing the immediate departure of the British Military Mission from Ankara to Cairo.[62] All shipments of war materiel to Turkey were suspended and the ambassador was directed to avoid any association including social relations with Turkish officials. No action was taken to suspend commercial shipments to Turkey because of possible retaliation by the Turks with particular reference to chrome. The abrupt departure of the British Military Mission after several weeks of fruitless discussion as to the amount of war material to be delivered to Turkey was designed to impress upon Turkish authorities the extreme displeasure of the British government. Until late spring of 1944, there had been no noticeable change in Anglo-Turkish relations. The British continued their attitude of aloofness, and in return, the Turks adopted an equally distant policy towards the British.

In fact, the United States was equally perturbed by the economic assistance Turkey had provided Germany in 1943 through maintaining previous trade agreements. From the US perspective, bearing in mind the rapidly approaching day of reckoning, it was essential that the enemy should be deprived of all means of resistance.[63] While the US government realized that breaking trade relations with Germany would cause a serious inconvenience to Turkey's economy, they agreed with Britain to the extent that any renewal of previous Turco-German trade agreements or the conclusion of fresh treaties should entail the application to Turkey of blockade measures.[64] This was essentially identical to the British tactic of *mutatis mutandis*.

İnönü was not in a position to survive a potential Anglo-American embargo and agreed to reduce its chromium deliveries to Germany by 4,200 tons per month.[65] This was approximately half the rate at which deliveries had been made during the previous months. He also agreed to substantially *increase* chromium deliveries to the British through Turkey's accessible ports in the Mediterranean (since the Aegean coast would be open to possible Nazi retaliation).[66] The reduction in Turkey's chromium supply to Germany can be seen very clearly if we look at deliveries over previous months: 5,180 tons in November; 6,926 tons in December; 11,294 tons in January; and 6,752 tons in February.[67] On 21 April, at the conclusion of his lengthy address to the National Assembly on the subject of chromium, the minister of foreign affairs, Menemencioğlu, announced the government's decision to cease all shipments of chrome to Germany and other Axis countries effective immediately, and to forbid the further export of chromium from Turkey.[68]

The abrupt action of the Turkish government in publicly announcing the repudiation of its obligation to deliver over 100,000 tons of chromium to Germany, for which the Germans had paid in advance over the past year by the delivery of war materials including tanks, airplanes and so on, made the Germans uneasy. In an aide-memoire dated 28 April 1944, Ambassador Steinhardt informed Roosevelt that von Papen had asked Menemencioğlu whether he should 'pack his bags'.[69] Having announced its intention to discontinue chromium shipments to Germany, Turkey offered between 4,000–5,000 tons of copper to the United States. Coupled with copper, the decision of the Turkish government to boost the volume of chromium shipments to the US was generally regarded as implying that Turkey was now prepared more actively associate itself with the US, rather than Britain, in bringing the war to a speedy conclusion.

The US State Department decided that every effort should be made to capitalize promptly on the spirit behind Turkey's recent chromium embargo. Roosevelt informed Ambassador Steinhardt that the ultimate objective of the US diplomacy henceforward would be to stop all Turkish exports to Germany or Nazi-occupied territories. 'Should this goal prove unattainable in its entirety', Roosevelt wrote in a personal message to Steinhardt, 'the minimum objective should be the complete elimination of all exports of strategic materials to the Axis'.[70] Roosevelt also realized that the wisest tactic would be to negotiate with the Turks on a comprehensive basis, rather than attempt to obtain Turkish agreement item by item. The State Department fully appreciated this new policy, and added the vital necessity of increasing imports into Turkey from Allied sources in order to compensate for expected lost imports from Axis. While Steinhardt agreed in principle with this new strategy, he urged Washington to be careful and 'avoid arousing extravagant Turkish hopes'.[71] He thought that it would be inappropriate to consider negotiating a war trade agreement with Turkey (comparable to those negotiated early in the war with Sweden, Spain, Portugal and Ireland etc.), since that type of agreement proved to be useful when the US was relatively weak.

In his private talks with Ambassador Steinhardt, Foreign Minister Menemencioğlu repeatedly brought up the grave risks that Turkey's national economy was suffering with the substantial reduction in export trade of its most valuable products to Axis countries. Steinhardt admitted that, by requesting a real sacrifice from Turkey in stopping all its exports of strategic materials, Great Britain put the US government in a position where they now assumed a moral obligation to meet Turkey's essential requirements to the fullest extent of their ability. Steinhardt argued that while Great Britain had so far advanced the convenient excuse of 'military necessity' or 'shortage of shipping' for not delivering armaments to Turkey, he asserted that this would no longer appease the Turkish government. He envisaged three substantial benefits which the US could derive out of their improved relations with Turkey: first, the incentive for Turkey to take further steps to cut off all trade with Axis; second, the salutary effect on the other neutrals; and third, the strengthening of the US post-war commercial position in Turkey.[72]

In a private conversation with Secretary of State Cordell Hull, Ambassador Steinhardt said that he could not follow London's reasoning that maintenance of constant pressure on the Turks until the launching of a second front in France (Operation Overlord) constituted a threat to the Germans, now that the Turks had cut all trade relations with that country.⁷³ Steinhardt argued that Germany was fully aware of the pressure Britain had been applying to Turkey since February and of the subsequent chill in Anglo-Turkish relations. 'Quite the contrary', Steinhardt added, 'a sudden cessation of pressure accompanied by a public announcement of an agreement between Britain, the US and Turkey, without disclosing the details, would lead the Germans to believe that the agreement perhaps even transcended anything that might be published regarding the details'.⁷⁴ Steinhardt simply did not understand what the British would gain by telling Numan '*frankly*' that, by rupturing relations with Germany what they sought to achieve was diverting Germany's attention before D-Day.⁷⁵

In outlining the Turkish view, Saraçoğlu seconded Steinhardt's position, asserting that his government did not understand and had been 'hurt' by the British policy of 'sulking' since the departure of the British Mission in February.⁷⁶ He referred to the fact that the Turkish embargo on chromium deliveries to Germany, and Turkey's prohibition of the passage of strategic deliveries to German ships through the Straits, had failed to evoke 'any indication of appreciation from London'. He remarked that when he had sent cordial messages to Eden and Molotov, he even received 'a most cordial reply from Molotov' and yet a very 'frigid' one from Eden. He said that, all in all, his government had come to doubt during recent months whether Britain really did want Turkey to enter the war. In light of the relatively limited amount of war materiel previously requested by the Turks and the abrupt departure of the British Mission, 'could the Turkish government be criticized for wondering whether the British were serious in their request at Cairo that Turkey enter the War?'⁷⁷

In outlining his views as to the part Turkey could play on entering the war, Saraçoğlu stated that the Turkish army could eject the Germans from Bulgaria, observing that he was convinced that within forty-eight hours of the Turkish army entering Bulgaria, the Bulgarians 'would shift over to our side'.⁷⁸ Steinhardt reported that, after speaking with Saraçoğlu, he was now more convinced than ever that the Turkish government was 'not only willing but anxious' to enter the war, and that if Turkey's entry into the war at some time in the near future was deemed desirable for either political or military reasons, this result could be achieved 'if account is taken in London of Turkish susceptibilities'.⁷⁹ Ultimately, the American government was persuaded that by offering Turks additional war materiel in quantities commensurate with the potential military operations, promising them that delivery would be made within the time agreed upon, assuring them of fighter protection and radar for its principal cities, the Turkish government would now undertake to enter the war as of an agreed date.⁸⁰

Blood, sweat and tears

By July 1944, İnönü was convinced that Turkey's entrance into the war had become more than a necessity. Turkey was very much alive to the situation in Europe and realized that with the gradual decline of Nazi menace, the need for Turkey's operational assistance was also diminishing. Churchill was infuriated with İnönü and refused to advance any sort of conversation with him unless he stopped dragging his feet. At this point, one would question why the Turks did not declare war on Nazi Germany unconditionally. It had been over a month since the Allied forces' landing in Normandy and the Turkish government did not even rupture trade relations with Germany beyond existing chromium deals and the transfer of other strategic materials. In an informal meeting with the US ambassador during the American Independence Day reception, Saraçoğlu said that Turkey intended to make the rupture complete.[81] Von Papen would be handed his passports; German diplomats in Turkey would be exchanged for Turkish diplomats in Germany; and all other German nationals would be expelled from Turkey with the exception of a few German professors who have been teaching in Turkish schools for many years whose anti-Nazi sentiments were well known and a few German Jewish refugees.

But even then, Prime Minister Saraçoğlu put forward three conditions a week later: first, Turkey to be treated by Britain as a full Ally and not as a colony nor an inferior country; second, Turkey to receive such assistance as the US and UK may find it possible to grant in connection with the disposal of its export surpluses, which would result from the rupturing of trade relations with Germany and to provide Turkey with the commodities essential to the maintenance of its national economy; and third, Turkey to be provided with such war materials as the US and UK may regard necessary to protect the country from a surprise attack. Saraçoğlu emphasized that the assurances to be requested by the Turkish government should not be regarded as conditions but primarily as a statement of the treatment the Turkish government would expect to receive after having broken off all relations with Germany.

A careful examination of Turkey's prerequisites reveals that the first and second conditions appear more trivial than the third, the ending of which was open to interpretation with regards to who would launch the surprise attack. While a German attack still seemed plausible from Greece, which was liberated by the Allies in October, clearly the Turkish government was more perceptive about a possible post-war Soviet expansion in the Balkans now that Bulgaria was under Stalin's boot and Greece's fate was left undecided. Whether or not Turkey would have declared war on Nazi Germany had Churchill's plan for a landing in Greece passed in Cairo is debatable. But one thing is certain; it was unthinkable for an underequipped Turkish army to march into a war theatre in the face of the advancing Red Army, while Nazi garrisons continued to hold out in the Aegean Islands. On the other hand, İnönü knew that, with or without US military assistance against post-war Soviet designs in the Balkans, any further delays in breaking diplomatic and trade relations with Germany would have pushed Turkey into a diplomatic cul-de-sac.

Turkey's heel-dragging sent confusing signals to Nazi Germany. Two months before Franz von Papen – along with the entire German diplomatic staff – was discarded from his mission, the Turkish naval attaché in Berlin was invited to the German Naval Intelligence Headquarters in Steinplatz. The whole purpose of this meeting was a probe into eventualities regarding the fate of Franz von Papen. Meanwhile, the Nazi naval command was curious to learn whether the Turkish state would be interested in ('obviously as a neutral intermediary') sharing their opinion on the Wehrmacht's safe withdrawal from Crimea.[82] German officers communicated to the Turkish attaché that they were certain that an allied landing was unavoidable, and that it was equally possible that such a landing would be synchronized by a Russian land campaign. The implication here was that Turkey would be negatively affected by this operation. After deliberating on what now appeared to be 'futile German war efforts', the Turkish officer reported that Berlin was most anxiously trying to play the role of the victim of Bolshevik domination rather than the perpetrator of this global conflict. For the Turkish attaché, the most salient points of his meeting with the Germans came towards the end, when a German officer expressed his admiration of how the Turks had handled the Armenian rebels in the previous war, perhaps even more successfully than the Germans' handling of the Jewish question. To this, the Turkish attaché apparently gave a robust response, and sought to explain the diametrically different nature of the Turkish–Armenian conflict in terms of civilians and combatants, and pronounced his disdain for the analogy. Two weeks after this meeting, the Allied forces executed the Normandy landing, which terminated the exchange between Turkey and Germany.

Finally, on 2 August 1944, Turkey cut all diplomatic and trade relations with Nazi Germany. In his parliamentary address delivered at the National Assembly, Prime Minister Saraçoğlu said that for centuries Turkey had been tormented by continuous warfare along with a pitiful sort of clumsiness and lethargy that doomed the late Ottoman Empire's reigning sultans. 'In a country like this,' Saraçoğlu added, 'peace could not simply be construed as opium for the masses, but as a noble dream towards achieving the Republican principles both at home and abroad.' He stressed that this had been the fundamental reason behind Turkey's neutrality since 1939. He added that they finally reached a moment, when accomplishing the same dreams, this time required severing their trade and diplomatic relations with Germany, thereby departing from their non-belligerent status for the sake of national security.[83]

Hours before Turkey's declaration of rupturing all trade and diplomatic relations with Germany, the US ambassador in Moscow met with the Deputy People's Commissar for Foreign Affairs, Andrey Vyshinsky, to feel the Kremlin's pulse.[84] Ambassador Averell Harriman told Vyshinsky that the US considered the break with Germany as the first step toward getting Turkey into the war as a belligerent as agreed at the Second Cairo Conference. Vyshinsky, however, told Harriman that he simply did not believe any useful purpose would be served by such a course of action and remarked that Turkey should 'now be left to its own fate'.[85] The Soviets had evidently now decided to remain aloof from Turkey and refused to recognize that Turkey's break with Germany, or even its entry into the war, would come soon enough to be of real help in the defeat of the Nazis. Under this policy, the Soviets would get whatever benefits the Turkish actions might bring *without* having to honour any obligation made on their part toward Turkey in the peace settlement.

Meanwhile, on 26 August 1944, the Turkish government informed Soviet leaders that it felt it had substantially complied with Allied desires, and that closer collaboration between the two governments was plausible.[86] To this, the Soviet government replied that Turkey's entry into the war would serve no useful purpose and was no longer desired. The Turkish government then proposed a joint statement emphasizing friendly relations between Turkey and Russia, to which the Russians replied that such a statement would add nothing to the treaties already in existence. In response to Ambassador Steinhardt's inquiry as to whether the irritation between Moscow and Ankara could be ascribed to the fact that Turkey was yet to declare war on Nazi

Germany, Prime Minister Saraçoğlu said that since the rupture with Germany, no such official request had been made to the Turkish government by the Soviets.[87] Political analysts in London and Washington DC argued that the chief factor impelling Turkey to act was not Allied urging but fear of Russia and that the moment had passed.[88]

Negotiations for a preliminary lend-lease agreement between the United States and Turkey had already been planned, but ultimately had languished during the first four months of 1944 due to political differences between Britain and Turkey.[89] Though the Anglo-Turkish differences were clarified relatively favourably in April and May, there was further delay in the lend-lease negotiations between the United States and Turkey. In view of the unfriendly nature of Soviet–Turkish relations, İnönü decided to reboot Turkish-American dialogue 'as soon as possible' and tasked the Secretary General of the Foreign Office, Cevat Açıkalın with this mission.[90] In October, Açıkalın informed Steinhardt that he had completed his discussions concerning the proposed mutual aid agreement with the prime minister and various parliamentary leaders, and that Turkey was now ready for a treaty with the US 'more than ever'.[91] After the signing of the lend-lease agreement, İnönü delivered an exhilarating oration at the opening of the new parliamentary year on 1 November 1944. Having outlined Turkey's domestic issues and economic hardships, İnönü asserted that during the course of the past year (1943–4) Turkey had gone through 'a rewarding metamorphosis' and found a reliable new Atlantic ally – 'the United States of America'.[92]

Even after April 1944, when Turkey decided to repudiate its chrome agreements with Germany, the British government repeatedly protested against the passage of small German naval vessels and of armed German transports down the Straits. Consequently, the Turkish government banned the passage of both categories of German ships and applied a strict search of all vessels.[93] In October 1944, the British government resumed the supply of military equipment and notified the Turkish government that it wanted to maintain the Anglo-Turkish Alliance. The Allies had made it clear to the Turkish government that a slight increase in Ankara's chances of UN membership would be both possible and advantageous; but that this was contingent upon an entrance fee – levied in this case in blood, sweat and tears.

Epilogue

At the heart of İstanbul's bustling Taksim Square stands the Republic Monument, which is the usual gathering spot for national celebrations, political rallies and other important events in the city. Juxtaposed against a myriad of similar monuments sporting Kemalist symbols from the early republican period, this one is more elaborate and bears an interesting detail that often goes unnoticed.[1] Designed by the Italian sculptor Pietro Canonica, the monument is thirty-six feet high, weighs over eighty-four tons, and mirrors the birth of the Soviet-Turkish alliance during the 1920s. As a token of gratitude for the guns, grain and gold Lenin had sent to Mustafa Kemal during the Turkish War of Independence, the monument includes the statue of Semyon Aralov, the Soviet ambassador in Ankara, standing in solidarity with Turkey's founding fathers. After 400 years of incessant warfare between the Russian and Ottoman empires, the iconic monument was erected in 1928 at a critical juncture, when Bolsheviks and Kemalists forged an alliance against what they both perceived to be Western imperialism.

Friendly relations between Turkey and the Soviet Union gradually came to an end over irreconcilable differences during World War II, when Stalin accused the neutral Ankara government of betraying Russia's friendship and for hedging bets with both the Allies and the Axis. Contrarily, the Turks blamed Stalin for constantly probing their periphery, now in Iran then in Syria, and for assisting client regimes to gain dominant influence in this historic area of Russian imperial expansion against Turkey. As Turkish and Soviet leaders preoccupied themselves with competing prosecutorial narratives throughout the early Cold War years, bilateral relations remained by and large dormant, with intermittent episodes of outright hostility. Consequently, comrade Aralov disappeared from public memory and became invisible, even when his bronze sculpture loomed over public gatherings and official celebrations.

Looking at Turkey's staunchly anti-Soviet stance during the late 1940s and 1950s, Cold War historians emphasized Stalin's quest to lock in the spoils of war, arguing that the glacial rift that divided Moscow and Ankara suddenly came into being at the Yalta Conference. Indeed, Turkey's symbolic declaration of war against the Axis powers came only in the final days, on 23 February 1945, when the Nazi threat had already dissipated. This was little more than a formality and a step taken simply to comply with the conclusions of the Yalta Conference, which conditioned the declaration of war as a prerequisite for joining the United Nations. As this book demonstrates, however, Soviet-Turkish animosity, exacerbated by a series of crises ever since the

Molotov–Ribbentrop Pact, hardly surprised anyone at Yalta. This is more than a question of chronological order and points to problems in historical literature that has overlooked the underlying Soviet factor, which determined Turkey's foreign policy during and after the war.

Historians who have written on Turkey and World War II almost exclusively argued that the Turks showed themselves 'self-confident and bold negotiators' during the Yalta Conference, and that 'they had real advantages on their side'.[2] Frank Weber, for instance, suggests that Turkish diplomacy during the war, and particularly during the Yalta Conference, was 'a brilliant accomplishment by all standards except those of honesty and integrity . . . Only thirty years later, when they invaded Cyprus did the Turks reveal that, after all, they had been dissatisfied with what that diplomacy had gained for them'.[3] Selim Deringil makes a more nuanced argument in his final chapter, which is acerbically entitled 'The Turkish Gambit', claiming that from 1939 to 1945 not only did Turkey avoid involvement in the war, but 'she was able to influence both warring camps to her favor'.[4] For Deringil, Turkey showed considerable diplomatic skill and resourcefulness during the wartime conferences and led its Anglo-American allies into thinking that Turkey, now truncated and poor, was in a much worse state than it actually was.[5]

A closer examination of the Turkish archives suggests that, seen from Ankara, thousands of kilometres and a mental world away from Washington and Moscow, the future looked far less exciting than it did to contemporary historians. Two interrelated desiderata shaped Turkish diplomacy before the Yalta Conference: first, the country's gloomy economic outlook; and second, the need for foreign military assistance against Soviet expansionism. The decision to request financial and military assistance from Western powers was a fundamental reversal of one of the early republic's keystone principles. Turkish political leaders, in their official rhetoric, frequently justified this reversion with Turkey's accession to the Western collective security alliance – a path, which in their view, Mustafa Kemal too would have taken.

Keeping an army on a war footing cost Turkey 184 million liras in 1939, 220 million in 1940, 280 million in 1941, 313 million in 1942, 400 million in 1943, and more than 500 million in 1944.[6] A British war correspondent aptly noted that ever since the outbreak of war in Europe, there had been a steady increase in Turkish prices of basic commodities – by late 1944, ordinary living costs were 400 to 500 per cent above their 1939 level.[7] For instance, sugar was over 3 shillings a pound; rice was 3 shillings and 3 pence; flour 2 shillings and 9 pence, butter 5 shillings and 6 pence; coffee 9 shillings; and tea 3 shillings a pound.[8] The price of clothes was equally high; a man's suit cost £35, a pair of hand-made shoes between £7 and £10 sterling.[9] The 1944 budget, the largest in Turkish history up until then, was three times that of 1939. It was divided into two parts: the Ordinary Budget, which covered all the normal expenditures of the state, including part of the total expenditure on defence; and the Extraordinary Budget, which covered solely expenditure on defence.[10] In 1944 alone, the Ordinary Budget amounted to 547,573,725 liras (approximately £75,000,000). Of this, about £20,000,000 was dedicated to defence. The Extraordinary Budget, which covered credits demanded periodically during the year for defence, amounted to about another 500 million liras. The total yearly expenditure thus reached about 1,000 million liras.[11] While the minister of finance claimed that they could cover this amount from regular sources of revenue (that is, that no special taxation was needed), this proved to be impossible due to the increase in defence expenditures arising out of the Allies' growing demands for Turkey's participation in the war effort.

The largest share of the defence expenditure was spent on the upkeep of the army. There were 900,000 men permanently mobilized at the end of 1944. This represented over 5 per cent of the total population. The total number of divisions was forty, with an average of 20,000 men to a division.[12] While there was only a single armoured division in 1943, the number of Turkish officers and NCOs that were trained in mechanized warfare increased substantially during the course of 1944. Nevertheless, by the standards of the principal belligerents, the Turkish army was not particularly efficient. Its main asset was the large number of rank and file soldiers, for the most part comprised of peasants, who were loyal to their officers – steadfast, obedient and courageous.

The Turkish air force was regarded as part of the army and was directly controlled by the General Staff.[13] Though numerically small, its fighter squadrons could have probably contributed usefully to the daytime defence of the Turkish cities if they were attacked. Turkish flying instructors had been trained in both Britain and Nazi Germany but, as one American observer noted, in the air force, as in the army, the big challenge lay in ensuring crews and ground staff cared for the machines properly.[14] The Turkish navy, on the other hand, had only a symbolical value. It consisted of a 33-year-old battle cruiser (the former German *Goeben*), two 41-year-old cruisers, and a few destroyers, gunboats, mine-layers, mine sweepers and submarines.[15] Some of the submarines and destroyers were modern British-built vessels and could have had a serious defensive value if efficiently manned. But the Turkish fleet spent most of its time at its base in the Gulf of Izmit, and only occasionally ventured out into the Sea of Marmara for manoeuvres.

Turkey's national debt had also witnessed an enormous increase, shooting up from 620 million in 1939 to about 1,500 million liras in 1945 (approximately £300 million).[16] In other words, it had more than doubled in six years. While Ankara owed nearly all this debt to its own people (following one of the key early republican principles of resisting Western loans), Turkey's mounting internal borrowings ultimately led to domestic political pressure. The gold holdings of the Central Bank increased from 26 to 195 tons during the same period (explained to the public as necessary wartime precautions), but Turkey's currency issue had also increased, from 190 million to nearly 1,000 million liras. Therefore, the most serious affliction that Turkey had to endure, was inflation. In spite of the measures taken to contain it, Turkey's 'ill-organized and ill-conceived' macroeconomics continued its 'tempestuous course', as one Western observer aptly put it.[17] Commensurate with inflation, speculators in every commodity, as well as industrialists and farmers, all waxed fat, leading to gambling, ostentation and the nouveaux riches mushrooming everywhere in the country. In other words, the suggestion that Turkey successfully capitalized on World War II by maintaining trade relations with both belligerent blocs falls at odds with the country's sombre economic outlook on the eve of the Yalta Conference. Moreover, Turkey's desperate need and persistent demand (mostly shunned by Western powers until 1947) for foreign military assistance against the Soviet Union in February 1945, rather contradicts the notion of its allegedly 'crafty' diplomacy.

Mounting Soviet pressure after Yalta

When the Big Three finally met in Yalta at the Livadia Palace on 4 February 1945, there was little room for doubt that Stalin would eventually bring up the Dardanelles question. Built from white Inkerman granite in 1911 in the style of the Italian Renaissance from plans by the architect Krasnov, the New Palace was situated 150 feet above the coast, and, seen from the Castle of Sinop across the Black Sea, it glowed with a daunting aura. Now housing its most important guests ever – and not only since the departure of the Romanovs – the results of the meeting at Livadia would determine much of the post-war international order; and the Turks, who were kept out of the loop, feared that secret protocols regarding the Straits might also be signed in those rooms.

On the eve of the Yalta Conference (4–11 February 1945), both Great Britain and the United States hoped that Stalin would raise no questions regarding the Straits, because in their view, the Montreux Convention had functioned well to date. President Roosevelt indicated that the US would agree to minor changes if Britain or the USSR deemed them necessary. The US Navy and War Departments concurred. Major changes, however, were likely to affect adversely the strategic and political balance in the Balkans and the Near East and would violate Turkey's sovereignty. Bearing in mind the upcoming Dumbarton Oaks Conference, where the UN statute would be formulated, Churchill contended that the UK might also consider taking part in a collaborative attempt to revise the Straits regime slightly, if it were asked to do so.[18]

As expected, towards the closure of the seventh plenary meeting, on 10 February around six o'clock in the evening, Stalin changed the subject from post-war Polish elections to the Montreux Convention. He said that the treaty was now outmoded, recalling that the Japanese emperor had played a big part in that treaty, even greater than that of the Soviet Union. The treaty was also linked with the League of Nations, which was now defunct. Stalin contended that, under the Montreux Convention, the Turks had the right to close the Straits not only in time of war, but if they felt that there was a threat of war. He said that the treaty was made at a time when the relations between Great Britain and the Soviet Union were not perfect, but he did not think now that Great Britain would wish to strangle Russia with the help of the Japanese. The treaty, Stalin said, needed revision; but added that he did not know in what manner it should be revised, nor did he wish to prejudice any decisions. But he made it clear that it was impossible to accept a situation in which Turkey had a hand on Russia's throat.[19]

In his evasive response to Stalin, President Roosevelt said that the United States had a frontier of over 3,000 miles with Canada along which there were no border posts or armed forces. This situation had existed for more than a century and it was his hope that other frontiers in the world would operate in the same way. Churchill engaged more directly with the question and said that Stalin had already reminded them of the Straits question during the Moscow Conference last autumn. He said that the British certainly felt that the present position of Russia, with its great interest in the Black Sea should not be dependent on the narrow exit through the Dardanelles and that if the subject was brought up during foreign ministerial level meetings, Britain would support the Soviet motion. In the meantime, Churchill argued, 'it might be wise to inform the Turks that the matter of revision of the Montreux Convention would be under consideration.[20] Churchill felt that this matter affected the position of Great Britain in the Mediterranean more than it did that of the United States; therefore he proposed a London meeting between the foreign ministers of the three countries. It was agreed that the next meeting of trilateral talks over the Dardanelles problem would be held in London, whereby the Soviet government could reveal its position to the Turks more directly.[21] Although the subject of Turkey's post-war situation did not carry as much weight as, for instance, the Curzon Line or demilitarization of Germany, insofar as Russia's century-old Straits policy is concerned, Stalin appeared more beholden to Tsarist designs in places like Turkey.

On 19 March 1945, Molotov informed the Turkish ambassador in Moscow, Selim Sarper, that the Soviet Union would not renew the 1925 Treaty of Friendship. The Molotov–Sarper meeting in March marked the downswing of a relationship that had begun to deteriorate since the Molotov–Ribbentrop Pact. This was the first time when the Soviet Union directly intimated to the Turks that the post-war international order differed greatly from the interwar period of Turkish–Soviet friendship and that the Kremlin's national security would be revised accordingly. Clearly, the Turks had been expecting a Soviet reaction along these lines for at least several months. Hence when Sarper's phone rang that morning, he was not at all surprised by Molotov's invitation. In fact, it was Sarper himself who asked for a 'sondage' meeting with Molotov a week earlier.

When Molotov agreed to see Sarper, he ruefully admitted that the timing of their meeting had not allowed the Soviets to fully formulate their position. Deputy Foreign Commissar Sergey Kavtaradze had informed Molotov about Sarper's trip to Ankara, which was scheduled to last for at least six to seven weeks, hence Molotov decided to broach the subject sooner rather than wait for Sarper's return in late May. Molotov then presented Sarper a diplomatic note in Russian, communicating the denunciation of the 1925 Turkish–Soviet Treaty. Reading verbatim from the official text, Molotov said that although the Soviet government 'greatly appreciated the friendship between our two nations, cemented by the signatories of 17 December 1925', the said treaty became 'practically inoperable' and was 'in need of substantial revisions' due to 'a fundamental change in circumstances, which transpired during the Second World War'.[22]

Soviet newspapers had already adopted an explicit anti-Turkish tone since the early days of 1945, employing increasingly critical language. The Turkish embassy staff reported with consternation excerpts from *Izvestiia and Pravda* on a daily basis.[23] On 9 April, for instance, *Pravda* accused the Turkish judiciary of abetting the racists in the famous pan-Turkist trials of 1944, claiming that the Turkish courts had released most of the Nazi sympathizers and pan-Turkists who had been convicted of anti-republican propaganda, which was very difficult to reconcile with the official position of the Turkish state: 'these irredentists, who gnawed their teeth and clenched their fists against the Soviet Union, envisaged a Turkic union from the Bulgarian frontier to the Altai Mountains'.[24] Similar criticisms appeared on the front page of *Izvestiia* on 14 May 1945, which targeted state-sponsored newspapers including *Ulus* and *Akşam*. *Izvestiia* argued that while most of the free world celebrated Allied victory in Europe, a widespread feeling of discontent was present among Turkish journalists, who continued to publish anti-Soviet articles with an inflammatory discourse, 'bearing in mind Goebbels's disgusting propagandistic barks'.[25] Soviet newspapers levied similar accusations and held Ankara responsible for abandoning its neutrality and blamed İnönü for granting passage to German military ships through the Straits, the supply of strategic materials to Germany, and espionage activities in Ankara for passing on information about the USSR to the Germans.

Meanwhile, the Soviet ambassador in Ankara absented himself from Assembly hearings and sessions, thereby creating a forum for several American newspapers to debate that Turkey might soon seek US protection against possible Soviet designs on the Straits.[26] Facing a menacing Soviet attitude, İnönü gave a long speech in the National Assembly, outlining the reasoning behind a seemingly protracted period of Turkish neutrality. He said that the Turkish government catergorically refused to be a pawn in the Third Reich's *Drang nach Osten* machinations. When, for instance, both Vichy Syria and the newly founded Axis government in Iraq moved from a policy of subtle innuendos to direct hostility against the Anglo-Soviet bloc in 1941, İnönü said that Turkey stood firm against Nazi Germany and denied all means of transit to these two states through Anatolia. 'We did not allow it; and that was the Turkish contribution to the victory in Europe.'[27] As for Soviet accusations regarding Turkish troop movements, İnönü firmly rejected all of them, arguing that when the Nazis advanced to the banks of the Volga in 1942, Turkey had indeed moved its troops to the eastern Soviet–Turkish border, but rather than jeopardizing Soviet security, this was a precaution that quadrupled the length of Turkey's own defence line, expanding it from Rhodes to Hopa.

On similar occasions after the Yalta Conference, İnönü repeated Turkey's duty to carefully fulfil their contractual obligations in their relations with their large northern neighbour during a period that tested loyalties.[28] During another parliamentary address, for instance, İnönü referred to the Molotov–Ribbentrop Pact, arguing that Turkey had stood its ground and preferred to be neutral at a time when even the Soviets themselves deemed it necessary to shake hands with the aggressor.[29] İnönü urged the Soviets to bear in mind that remaining neutral had been 'a strenuous ordeal' for them and 'required even a greater sacrifice than simply aligning with one or the other bloc'.[30]

Witnessing the growing conflict between Turkey and the Soviet Union, Ambassador Edwin C. Wilson met with the new American president Harry Truman in February 1945 before leaving for Turkey. Wilson told Truman that, given Turkey's ill-equipped army, a serious situation might arise after the Soviet repudiation of the 1925 treaty.[31] If the USSR desired to merely modify the Montreux Convention, the Turks were likely to be reasonable and cooperative, but if it made demands affecting Turkey's independence, they would resist. Wilson argued that the US should support the Turks now that 'Eastern Europe had been lost, and America had interests both in the Middle East, and, more generally, in world security and cooperation'.[32] The president agreed, and said that Turkey might need American assistance sooner rather than later.

To no one's surprise, Ankara and Moscow had been heading for a squabble at least since 19 March 1945, but few anticipated that the second Molotov–Sarper meeting on 7 June that same year would be the last straw.[33] The significance of this meeting is twofold. First, it is clear that the Soviets had meticulously studied the Turkish position since Yalta and adjusted their policy accordingly. Second, in his meeting with Molotov,

Sarper proved to be utterly unprepared when Molotov introduced the issue of territorial claims and spent nearly two hours on border revisions in Eastern Anatolia rather than the Straits question. From the onset of their meeting, Sarper sensed a manifest sullenness in Molotov's mood, who hastily shelved Turkey's proposal for an alliance, which he found intriguing but at too early a stage to negotiate. Molotov said that the Soviet Union had a number of serious geopolitical concerns that needed to be addressed before Soviet-Turkish relations would be cemented with such an arrangement.

The first of these concerns related to the 1921 Treaty, which Molotov thought was enacted at a time when the Soviet Union was weak. When Molotov claimed that 'certain territorial exchanges had been made in 1921 and this situation needs to be fixed', Sarper was caught off guard, and asked if Molotov meant that Turkey's eastern frontier should be subjected to major revisions. Molotov calmly responded, 'yes, I mean this injustice should be revamped before we proceed with anything else'. Animated by a sudden sense of pessimism, Sarper cited Lenin, who once claimed that the Soviets regarded eastern Anatolia as falling within the Turkish sphere of influence. In vein, Sarper tried to substantiate his thesis by giving examples of Soviet-Turkish cooperation in that region a decade earlier, before admitting that he was utterly dismayed by Molotov's remarks: 'What is to be done about this?'

Molotov's answer exemplified the approaching war of nerves. He said that there was almost no harm in revising Turkey's eastern frontier if this would come with the gift of regaining the Soviet Union's trust. 'Look at Poland, for instance', Molotov said, as if he had rehearsed this example. 'We signed an unfavorable treaty with Poland, also in 1921, and have just revised it to attain a long-lasting friendship.'[34] Appalled by Molotov's ultimatum-like tone, Ambassador Sarper scoffed that his government was not prepared to reopen those clauses in the 1921 treaty, which they regarded as freely negotiated. Sarper also told Molotov that he would be unable to discuss any question affecting Turkey's territorial integrity. For Sarper, Molotov's insistence on the similarities drawn between the Polish and Turkish cases was a clear sign of animosity. Brushing the Polish example aside, Sarper said that he could not see a geopolitical justification of the Soviets' sudden interest in Turkey's eastern provinces. Soviet demands over Eastern Anatolia, as Sarper understood it, meant that Moscow preferred 'a sensational diplomacy for its own prestige' and would be willing 'to sacrifice the sympathy of a whole nation'.[35] He made it clear that requests of such bellicose nature would be detrimental to regional politics. But to make matters worse, he anticipated a nationalist backlash in Turkey feeding on dogmatic anti-Sovietism, whose long-standing claims would be justified. When Sarper finished his rant and suggested dropping this conversation, Molotov said that Sarper's grievances were duly noted but that the Soviet position would remain firm.

The heated exchange between Molotov and Sarper got even worse when the subject turned to the elephant in the room. Regarding the current status of the Straits, Molotov argued that the Soviet Union, while facing an existential crisis, had to pay undue attention to its Black Sea defences, mainly due to Turkey's precarious neutrality. Molotov said: 'Perhaps our concerns were unwarranted, and, granted, Turkish diplomacy never caused a material damage to us but we nonetheless cannot surrender the safety of 200 million inhabiting an area surrounding the Straits to Turkey's goodwill.' Skilfully turning the Turkish case around, Molotov added that this was not only a question of goodwill but defence capabilities as well, and that the Turkish government itself attested to the weakness of their defences as grounds for their non-belligerence when their assistance was urgently needed to defeat fascism. The most critical part of the conversation came when Sarper fell into Molotov's trap and hastily said: 'If you are about to broach the issue of a Soviet naval base on the Straits, no government in Turkey would agree to do this, nor will they agree to revise their Eastern frontier.'[36]

Stumbling into the Cold War

The Turkish government grew tired of Stalin's moral allegations, but with rumours of Soviet mobilization on Turkey's eastern border, İnönü knew that it would be a mistake to underestimate Molotov's complaints. The grievances were symptoms of a more fundamental resentment, and it would have been an even bigger mistake to make concessions on any of the particular issues. Molotov's intransigence on the Straits question and border issues had a profound effect on the ensuing communications between Saraçoğlu and Sarper in June 1945.[37] The aftershocks of the Molotov–Sarper meeting were noticeable in Ankara's official response, dated 12 June 1945, when the Turkish government approved Sarper's firm stand but left the door open for negotiations regarding possible minor changes in the Montreux Convention, so long as Great Britain and the US were informed.

The ensuing few months showed that Stalin was not bluffing and that he seriously considered using the Armenian card to annex Turkish provinces in the east around Lake Van. Whether Stalin expected his demands to be met, or used them as part of his 'horse-trading with the West', is debatable.[38] But numerous Armenian diasporas around the world pinned their hopes on the Kremlin's policies.[39] Armenian organizations, including the wealthiest ones in the United States, appealed to Stalin to organize mass repatriation of Armenians to Soviet Armenia – with the hope that the USSR would give them the lands 'reclaimed' from Turkey.[40] And Stalin's provocations against Turkey between late 1945 and early 1946 also included claims made in the names of the Georgian SSR. Stalin tapped into nationalist ambitions in Georgia, which was met with a serious protest from the Armenian SSR. By the same token, Armenia's sudden prominence in Stalin's plans vexed the officials of Georgia. They nurtured their own 'national project', according to which the disputed Turkish provinces were part of Georgian ancestral lands.[41] Lashing out at Armenian claims on 20 December 1945, two Georgian professors published an article on their 'Lawful Demands to Turkey'. The article was addressed to 'world public opinion' to help Georgia regain its 'ancestral lands', which the Turks had been occupying for nearly a millennium.[42]

Ominous reports of Red Army movements, coupled with Georgian and Armenian claims, fuelled nationalist demonstrations around Hagia Sophia and the Blue Mosque in İstanbul. In a crafty move, the Soviet ambassador, S.A. Vinogradov, asked Moscow whether the recent nationalist backlash in Turkey should be presented to the Americans as evidence of a fascist threat. He also suggested that they could be a good pretext for severing diplomatic relations with Turkey and for 'taking measures to ensure our security', which was, of course, a euphemism for military preparations.⁴³ In hindsight, Vinogradov's allegations were not entirely unfounded. Clouds of uncertainty loomed over Turkey, whose concerns about a very real Soviet threat had been falling on deaf ears in London and Washington. A bitter sense of Russophobia was rampant in all segments of society, and this widespread sentiment produced new outlets for anti-Soviet groupings. Right-wing groups were allowed to rally against leftists and minorities, both of whom were targeted as Bolshevik collaborators. Given Stalin's repatriation scheme in Soviet Armenia, leaders of the Armenian community in Turkey were put on the list of usual suspects and subjected to close surveillance.⁴⁴ The Directorate of the Press hired Armenian translators to monitor local newspapers that were circulated amongst the Turkish-Armenian community, and prepared detailed reports about Armenian journalists, poets and activists, including personal stories about their everyday lives. The cultivation of anti-Soviet feelings in the society led to widespread looting and violence. On the morning of 4 December 1945, thousands of İstanbul University students paraded through the city, arriving at the Zekeriya and Sabiha Sertel's publishing house *Tan* (Dawn), which had been fighting against Nazi propaganda in Turkey since the outbreak of the war. The mob proceeded to destroy the printing house and its equipment, and vandalized a few other nearby publishers.⁴⁵

Out of these ferocious hatreds and frantic fears emerged a new mindset in Turkey that was determined to rebuff Stalin's designs at all costs. In response to Soviet allegations of Montreux violations during World War II, Ankara delivered a note to the Soviet government that declared Turkey had 'never allowed war vessels to pass arbitrarily or without proper inspection' during the war. The official response to Soviet requests for a revision of the Straits' regime suggested that 'there might have been a few violations', when this or that Axis vessel forced their way through, but that the number of such occasions would probably not exceed the Allied vessels that did the same through various forms of a fait accompli. Essentially, what the Turkish government was trying to say was that the Soviet government had no legitimate basis to ask for a revision of the Montreux, unless they had other intentions, such as, for instance, revising the Turkish-Soviet Agreement of 16 March 1921, or resurrecting practices of the now deceased Tsarist Empire.⁴⁶

Upon mounting pressure from the USSR in 1946, in the form of two official notes, the Turkish government desperately sought to contain Stalin's demands within the playbook of international law and sent him minutes of previous bilateral negotiations and agreed treaties between Ankara and Moscow.⁴⁷ When this did not work, they tossed relevant pages from Lenin's corpus at the Soviet Union. In June 1946, for instance, the Turkish ambassador in Moscow presented his counterparts parts of a long *Pravda* interview from 1922, where Lenin had outlined his thoughts about the Turkish Straits.⁴⁸ The Turks were evidently showing Stalin that they have not forgotten the Bolsheviks' language and that it was Lenin who argued that 'the Bolshevik experience since 1917 proved that a certain degree of patriotic fulfillment was necessary to cope with larger waves of nationalist upheavals and to preempt imperialist intrigues in countries that succeeded the multi-ethnic empires after the Great War'.⁴⁹ Regarding the Straits' regime, Lenin claimed that the main Soviet goal was to guarantee that no warships would be allowed to pass through, 'neither in peace, nor at war'. 'Consequently', Lenin argued, 'it would be unnecessary and unwise' to continue critiquing the Turks' anxiety about the status of the Straits.

In 1947, shortly after the proclamation of the Truman Doctrine, Cevat Açıkalın, Turkey's former ambassador in Moscow who had also chaired the Turkish delegation to the Montreux Convention in 1936, published an article in the journal *International Affairs*.[50] In his piece, Açıkalın recalled that the Soviet Union's treacherous proposals regarding Turkey had been delivered at an interesting moment when the Conference at San Francisco was meeting to elaborate the Charter of the United Nations, 'whose purpose and principles [were] so eloquently embodied in the document signed on 26 June 1945'. Therefore, 'while it seemed to the world that a ray of hope was at last shining at San Francisco ... a dark and heavy cloud had descended on Turkey'.[51] Açıkalın accused the Soviets of singlehandedly and systematically severing their ties with Turkey, 'the most peaceful nation on earth'.[52] Açıkalın concluded that, beginning with the Montreux Convention in 1936, the Soviets gradually intensified their 'war of nerves', and ultimately circulated propaganda in 1945 for the cession to Soviet Russia of the Eastern Anatolian districts. 'We had once answered "No;" it is still "No;" and it will always be "No"', added Açıkalın bluntly and said: 'Turkey will not allow this new kind of "exclusive friendship" nor relations, which lead to vassalage, nor can she repudiate her relations and ties with other countries'.[53]

In an equally anxious tone, Necmeddin Sadak, who served as the last foreign minister of the post-war İnönü cabinet (1947–50), wrote a personal article for *Foreign Affairs*, explaining the underlying motives that would guide Turkey's staunchly anti-Soviet diplomacy throughout the remainder of the Cold War years. Addressing 'the average American [who] knows very little about Turkey', Sadak argued that prior to 1936, the Turks, who had been obliged to wage war with Russia seven times in the course of 250 years, had sincerely thought that they were finally 'delivered from the nightmare of Muscovite imperialism'.[54] For foreign minister Sadak, it seemed unfortunate that, as the war broke out, Stalin 'too readily fell into the trap' that Hitler and Ribbentrop cunningly designed for Russia, and, even after the Nazi–Soviet war, despite Turkey's desire to renew friendly relations, he 'launched a furious campaign against Turkey without any plausible reason'.[55] Sadak asserted that 'Russia's greatest regret was that Turkey was not occupied first, and then "liberated." Later on, the Red Army would have come to liberate her, as it liberated Poland, the Baltic countries, Rumania, Bulgaria ... A lost opportunity!'[56] Sadak accurately concluded that Turkish–Soviet relations during the period from 1936 to 1945 had gone through an ugly metamorphosis, making it impossible for Ankara to maintain good relations with its northern neighbour.

Beginning with the exacerbated Soviet–Turkish conflict after World War II, Great Britain too realized the need to formulate a new alliance in the Middle East to replace the now defunct Sa'dabad Pact, which had been the only solid structure in the region. During the Anglo-Turkish talks after Yalta, the British government reiterated its hope that the Iranian situation would not in any measure weaken Turkey's commitment to their partnership in the Middle East. It seems clear that the British viewed Turkey's regional power as the deciding factor, noting both how remarkable and how ironic it was that Turkey, 'in spite of her laicism and treatment of the Caliphate, should still hold among the Moslem countries of the Middle East, both great and small, so central and so influential a position'.[57] Turkey, on the other hand, seemed to have accepted her new position, not without a certain degree of amused surprise. Nonetheless, İnönü cherished no desire to turn this influence to practical account in any policy of external expansion. The minister for foreign affairs had, on many occasions, spoken about the benefits which have resulted from the disappearance of the Ottoman Empire, and the fact that Turkey was now left free to develop its own national life for the people, 'now united and homogeneous, without incurring such responsibilities as, for instance, the maintenance of order in Iraq, Syria or Yemen, which in the present European situation would [have been] a disastrous obligation'.[58]

What had once been a meaningful Soviet–Turkish partnership against the 'forces of world imperialism' thus turned into outright hostility in the 1940s and 50s.[59] Stalin's unremitting antagonism toward Turkey, which lasted until his death in 1953, compelled Turkish leaders to seek a stronger alliance with the United States. Turkey's quest for NATO membership ushered in a new era in 1952 amidst major transformations in the country's domestic politics and diplomacy. Heralding the policy of containment, which would remain the essence of America's conduct in the Cold War for the rest of its duration, the March 1947 Truman Doctrine resulted in the delivery of military assistance to Greece and Turkey. Two months after Stalin's death, Khrushchev admitted that Moscow's menacing attempt to coerce Turkey had been a cardinal error.[60] Accordingly, on 30 May 1953, Molotov told the Turkish ambassador that the Soviet Union – 'having reconsidered its position concerning border rectifications and the Straits regime' – was renouncing its earlier demands.[61] At this point, however, Turkey's government was heavily invested in its pro-Western diplomacy, portraying themselves as the gatekeepers of NATO. This was so much the case that the Soviet ambassador in Ankara later remarked in a casual conversation that 'Turkey was acting more royalist than the king'.[62]

It was only after the disastrous Syrian Crisis in 1957 that Turkey adopted a more balanced diplomacy toward the Soviet Union. Claiming to contain communist subversion in the region, Turkey had played a major role in escalating the conflict in Syria, and later felt betrayed when the Eisenhower administration decided to restrain Turkey from provoking an unwarranted war in the Middle East.[63] As Turkey's relations with the United States became more strained over the Cyprus conflict in the 1960s, Turkey once again turned to the Soviet Union. From that point on, and all the way until the end of the Cold War, Moscow was an important partner in Turkey's quest for state-sponsored industrialization.[64]

The relationship between NATO-allied Turkey and the Soviet Union during the 1960s and 70s would constitute a good case-study for political scientists who are interested in the bloc and alliance politics of the Cold War. For historians, however, its significance lies elsewhere. Juxtaposed with the interwar convergence between Ankara and Moscow, renewed cooperation in the 1960s, 70s and 80s suggests that antagonism was not the default mode in Soviet–Turkish exchange. In the broader context of the short twentieth century, the period under review here can be seen as an anomaly in an otherwise cordial relationship. In 1945, in its drive for absolute security, the Soviet

Union pushed Turkey into a terrifying uncertainty, and the resulting decade saw a radical transformation in Turkish strategic thinking. The remaking of post-war Turkey as a solidly pro-Western ally was unsustainable in the long run. Turkey's unduly pro-Western and anti-Soviet direction in the 1950s marked a radical departure from the grand strategy that had guided the republic successfully during the interwar years and was to do so again in the latter half of the Cold War. This book has dealt with an extraordinary period, one in which the twists and turns of world war fundamentally restructured the relationship between Moscow and Ankara. Ultimately, both sides learned from this history and have managed conflict in such a way as to allow Turkey to 'balance' between Russia and the West.

Notes

Introduction

1. Başbakanlık Cumhuriyet Arşivleri [hereafter, BCA] 030.10.59.402.3 (Eastern Patrol Gendarmerie Station to the Ministry of Interior, 27 March 1943).
2. Türk Diplomatik Arşivi [hereafter TDA], TSID 16992881 (Molotov-Sarper Meeting – Minutes, 7 June 1945). An accepted practice for citing the Turkish diplomacy archives has not yet emerged among historians; the TDA archivists stipulated that references be made to digital image identification numbers (TSID).
3. In addition to the direct claims on Turkey, the USSR sought to establish influence in another area that worried Turkey, delaying the evacuation of Soviet troops from Iran. For Turkey's new leaders, the Soviet presence in Iran since 1941 was painfully reminiscent of the Anglo-Russian Entente of 1907.
4. Samuel J. Hirst, 'Anti-Westernism on the European Periphery: The Meaning of Soviet-Turkish Convergence in the 1930s', in *Slavic Review*, 72, 1 (Spring 2013): 32–53.
5. İsmet İnönü, *Söylev ve Demeçleri, TBMM'nde ve CHP Kurultaylarında* (İstanbul: Milli Eğitim Basımevi, 1946), 280–321.
6. See, for example, Zara Steiner, *The Triumph of the Dark: European International History, 1933-1939* (Oxford: Oxford University Press, 2011), 112, 122, 533, 534 and 623.
7. TDA, TSID 5028381 (15th Anniversary of the Soviet-Turkish Friendship Treaty, 24 March 1936).
8. Dilek Barlas and Serhat Güvenç, *Turkey in the Mediterranean during the Interwar Era: The Paradox of Middle Power Diplomacy and Minor Power Naval Policy* (Bloomington: Indiana University Press, 2010), 151.
9. See 'The Lausanne Convention Relating to the Regime of the Straits, July 24, 1923', League of Nations Treaty Series (hereafter LNTS), vol. XXVIII, 117–37.
10. Dilek Barlas, 'Friends or Foes? Diplomatic Relations Between Italy and Turkey, 1923-36', *International Journal of Middle East Studies*, 36 (2004), 231–52, here 231.
11. *Dokumenty vneshnei politiki SSSR* [hereafter *DVP*], vol. 20 (Moscow, 1976), 267 (Conversation with Zekai Apaydın, 14 May 1937).
12. *Kritika*'s "Russo-Turkish Special Issue" included one article that treated the interwar period at significant length: Adeeb Khalid, 'Central Asia between the Ottoman and the Soviet Worlds', *Kritika*, 12, 1 (Winter 2011): 451–76. Another good example, again published in *Kritika*, is Samuel J. Hirst, "Soviet Orientalism across Borders: Documentary Film for the Turkish Republic," *Kritika* 18,1 (Winter 2017): 35–61.
13. Arkhiv vneshnei politiki Rossiiskoi Federatsii [hereafter AVP RF], f. 5, op. 15, pap. 110, d. 86, l. 10 (Internal NKID Correspondence, 28 May 1935).
14. AVP RF, f. 5, op. 15, pap. 110, d. 86, l. 12–13 (Litvinov to Zalkind, 13 June 1936).
15. AVP RF, f. 5, op. 16, pap. 122, d. 112, l. 1 (Zalkind to NKID, 1 March 1937).
16. On the German question in Soviet-Turkish relations see: TDA, TSID 5001797 (Apaydın to Aras, 09 May 1938); TDA, TSID 5000995 (Apaydın to Aras, 16 November 1938); and TDA TSID 5001202 (22 November 1938).

17 Selim Deringil, *Turkish Foreign Policy During the Second World War: An 'Active' Neutrality* (Cambridge: Cambridge University Press, 1989).
18 Türkkaya Ataöv and Frank Weber both offer intriguing glimpses of German-Turkish relations during the Second World War, but neither achieves the breadth of Deringil's work. See: Türkkaya Ataöv, *Turkish Foreign Policy, 1939-1945* (Ankara 1964); and Frank Weber, *The Evasive Neutral: Germany, Britain and the Quest for a Turkish Alliance in the Second World War* (New York: University of Missouri Press, 1979).
19 Weber, *The Evasive Neutral*, 215. Mustafa Aksakal's *The Ottoman Road to War* dispelled a similar historiographical consensus that saw expansionism in the behaviour of an Ottoman leadership that actually believed alliance with Germany was the only solution to a plethora of international threats. Mustafa Aksakal, *The Ottoman Road to War in 1914* (Cambridge: Cambridge University Press, 2008).
20 Selim Deringil's book remains the standard account of Turkish foreign policy during World War II, and it is based primarily on British archival documents. The opening of Russian archives has produced a set accounts about Soviet policy towards Turkey, which received deserved acclaim, helping us understand what Turkish politicians were responding to. For Soviet-focused perspectives, see Jamil Hasanlı, *SSSR - Turtsiya: Ot neytraliteta k kholodnoy voyne* (Moscow: TP, 2008); Gabriel Gorodetsky, *Grand Delusion: Stalin and the German Invasion of Russia* (New Haven: Yale University Press, 1999); Vladislav M. Zubok, *A Failed Empire: The Soviet Union in the Cold War from Stalin to Gorbachev* (Chapel Hill: University of North Carolina Press, 2007). Also see: Nicholas Tamkin, *Britain, Turkey and the Soviet Union, 1940-1945* (London: Palgrave, 2009).
21 BCA 030.10.0.0/168.172.4 (Directorate of Maritime Transportation and Naval Affairs to the Prime Ministry, 14 July 1939).
22 Documents on German Foreign Policy [hereafter DGFP], series D, vol. XII, no. 231, p. 411 (Papen to Ribbentrop, 28 March 1941).
23 Ankara's export of chrome to feed the Nazi war machine led both the Soviet and British governments to levy moral allegations against Turkey. The Turkish government agreed to delivering 180,000 tons of chromium ore in 1943 and 1944, in return for war materials as stipulated by the Clodius Agreement. By dint of some Anglo-American pressure, Turkey agreed to reduce its monthly chromium deliveries by approximately 6,000 tons until its decision to cease all shipments in April 1944. See: Foreign Relations of the United States [Hereafter FRUS], Vol. IV, pp. 1057-1167, *Diplomatic Papers 1943, Near East and Africa* (The Charge in Turkey, Kelley, to the Secretary of State, 16 October 1942).
24 TDA, TSID 138591 (Gerede to Saraçoğlu, 26 June 1940).
25 Hüsrev Gerede, 'Die deutsch-türkischen Beziehungen', *Zeitschrift für Politik, 32, 1* (January 1942), 1-3. Years later, when Gerede compiled his memoirs, he moaned about the unceremonious way in which he was dismissed. Hüsrev Gerede, *Harb İçinde Almanya, 1939-1942* (İstanbul 1994), 41.
26 DGFP, series D, vol. XII, no. 566, p. 913 (von Papen to von Ribbentrop, 29 May 1941).
27 Although President İnönü himself was tacit in his stipulations, and personally considered the Tripartite Pact between England, France and Turkey as 'a necessary evil', certain members of his cabinet, such as foreign minister Şükrü Saraçoğlu and undersecretary Numan Menemencioğlu, were quite vocal in their support for Britain.
28 TDA, TSIDs 11359443; 11359494; 11359513; 11359566; and 11359580.
29 Public Record Office [hereafter FO] 424/285 R6703 G (Halifax to Knatchbull-Hugessen, 5 July 1942).

30 For instance, a recent article by Mercedes Penalba-Sotorrio shows that German Foreign Minister Joachim von Ribbentrop pursued a similar policy of neutrality in Spain. See: Mercedes Penalba-Sotorrio, 'Beyond the War: Nazi Propaganda Aims in Spain during the Second World War', *Journal of Contemporary History* (2018), doi:10.1177/0022009418761214/url: journals.sagepub.com/home/jch (accessed June 2018).
31 DGFP, series D, vol. XII, no. 623, p. 1022 (Ribbentrop to von Papen, 13 June 1941).
32 FO 421/329, R5703/55/44 (Hugessen to Eden, 1 July 1943).
33 Harry S. Truman, *Memoirs: Years of Trial and Hope, 1946–1952* (New York: Signet, 1965), 157.
34 TDA, TSID 5001202 (Apaydın to Aras, 22 November 1938).
35 TDA, TSID 144144 (Ali Haydar Aktay's report to Ankara, 10 July 1940).
36 Exploring the broader ramifications of the Nazi New Order, Jenifer Jenkins makes a similar argument in her recent article, arguing that Iran's real worth for Hitler, much like Turkey's, lay in its quality to serve as a non-belligerent neutral, shielding the Baku and Caspian oilfields from a potential Allied assault. Jenifer Jenkins, 'Iran in the Nazi New Order, 1933–1941', *Iranian Studies*, 49 (5); 727–51, here 741.
37 BCA 30.10.0.0/124.881.6 (Ministry of Foreign Affairs to the Prime Ministry, 24 February 1942).

Chapter 1

1 *Türkiye Mühendislik Haberleri*, 442–43, 2 (2006), 40–2.
2 *Cumhuriyet*, 30 October 1937, 1.
3 İsmail Yıldırım, 'Cumhuriyet Döneminde Demiryollarımızdaki Gelişmeler', unpublished Ph.D. dissertation, Ankara University (1993).
4 Zeynep Kezer, 'The Making of Early Republican Ankara', *Architectural Design*, 80 (1): 40–5.
5 FO 424/282, E2170/135/44 (Loraine to Halifax, 9 April 1938).
6 Eric Hobsbawm, *Age of Extremes: The Short Twentieth Century, 1914–1991* (London: Abacus, 1995), 36.
7 *Ulus*, 30 October 1937, 1.
8 *Atatürk'ün Tamim, Telgraf ve Beyannameleri*, v.IV (1917–1938), 549–52; and Rona Aybay, *Karşılaştırmalı 1961 Anayasası* (İstanbul: Fakülte Matbaası, 1963), 199.
9 See, for instance: Türkkaya Ataöv, *Turkish Foreign Policy, 1939–1945* (Ankara: SBF, 1965); Bülent Gökay, *Soviet Eastern Policy and Turkey, 1920–1991* (New York: Routledge, 2006); and William Hale, *Turkish Foreign Policy since 1774* (New York: Routledge, 2013).
10 "Montrö Boğazlar Sözleşmesi ve Ekleri," *Resmi Gazete* (5 August 1936): 37.
11 DVP, vol.19, 231–32 (Soviet Note on the Turkish Proposal for a Revision of the Lausanne Straits Convention, 22 June 1936); and BCA 030.18.1.2/65.48.14 (Ministry of Foreign Affairs to the Prime Ministry, 10 June 1936).
12 Syria under the French mandate was subdivided into six states, one of which was the Sanjak of Alexandretta that established its capital in Hatay near Antakya (Antioch). See 'The Accord of Ankara', LNTS, vol. LIV, 178–93.
13 Karakhan's primary purpose was actually to introduce a delegation from the Union of Societies of Assistance to Defence and Aviation-Chemical Construction of the USSR (OSOAVIAKhIM). *Rossiiskii gosudarstvennyi arkhiv sotsial'no-politicheskoi istorii*

[hereafter RGASPI], f. 558, op. 11, d. 388, ll. 10–13 (Record of a conversation with Kemal Ataturk, 29 October 1936).
14 Falih Rıfkı Atay, *Çankaya* (İstanbul: Pozitif Yayınları, 2009), 479.
15 RGASPI, f. 558, op. 11, d. 388, ll. 10 (Record of a conversation with Kemal Ataturk, 29 October 1936).
16 Ibid.
17 TDA, TSID 8512277 (Apaydın's report on Atatürk's statement to the Soviets regarding the new Straits regime, 2 November 1936).
18 RGASPI, f. 558, op. 11, d. 388, l. 9 (Stalin to Rosengol'ts, 7 January 1937).
19 *DVP*, vol. 20, 317 (Conversation between Mustafa Kemal and E.F Karskii, 1 June 1937).
20 Samuel J. Hirst, 'Başında Bir Kalpak Olsa: Georgiy Çiçerin, Sovyet Dış Politikası ve Türk İhtilali', *Toplumsal Tarih*, 299 (Kasım 2018): 50–56.
21 Stefanos Yerasimos, *Türk-Sovyet İlişkileri: Ekim Devrimden 'Milli Mücadele'ye* (İstanbul: Gözlem Yayınları), 634.
22 *Hakimiyet-i Milliye*, 24 October 1931.
23 *Milliyet*, 27 October 1931; *Cumhuriyet*, 27 October 1931.
24 TDA, TSID 8745532 (Weekly Bulletin on the Soviet Press from 24 April to 8 May, 22 May 1932).
25 *Akşam*, 27 April 1932; *Cumhuriyet*, 27 April 1932.
26 *Izvestiia*, 1 May 1932; *Pravda*, 1 May 1932; *Krasnaya Zvezda*, 1 May 1932.
27 TDA, TSID 8415200 (Weekly Bulletin on the Soviet Press from 14 May to 21 May, 8 June 1932).
28 In their press statements, both Turkish and Soviet leaders used these keywords frequently. See: TDA, TSID 8745222 (Weekly Bulletin on the Soviet Press from 8 May to 14 May, 28 May 1932).
29 TDA, TSID 9098827 (Tevfik Rüştü to Hüseyin Ragıp, 12 November 1933); and TDA, TSID 10163457 (Letters of Correspondence between İnönü and Molotov, 16 November 1933).
30 TDA, TSID 12846137 (Tevfik Rüştü to Hüseyin Ragıp, 23 October 1933).
31 TDA, TSID 5022407 (Hüseyin Ragıp to Tevfik Rüştü, 31 December 1933).
32 TDA, TSID 823 (Turkish Embassy in Moscow to the Ministry of Foreign Affairs, 8 January 1934).
33 TDA, TSID 4310 (Ministry of Foreign Affairs to the Turkish Embassy in Moscow, 17 January 1934).
34 TDA, TSID 11996 (Ministry of Foreign Affairs to the Turkish Embassy in Moscow, 26 December 1933).
35 TDA, TSID 5069947 (Turkish Embassy in Moscow to the Ministry of Foreign Affairs, 22 August 1935).
36 TDA, TSID 4706 (Tevfik Rüştü to Hüseyin Ragıp, 28 April 1935).
37 TDA, TSID 5842607 (Turkish Embassy in Moscow to the Ministry of Foreign Affairs, 16 February 1934).
38 Dilek Barlas wrote extensively on Italy and Turkey during the Interwar Period. See: Dilek Barlas, 'Friends or Foes? Diplomatic Relations Between Italy and Turkey, 1923–36', *International Journal of Middle East Studies*, 36 (2004), 231–52; also see Dilek Barlas and Serhat Güvenç, *Turkey and the Mediterranean during the Interwar Era: The Paradox of Middle Power Diplomacy and Minor Power Naval Policy* (Bloomington: Indiana University Press, 2010).
39 Barlas, 'Friends or Foes', 232–7.

40 Mevlüt Çelebi, 'Başvekil İsmet Paşa'nın İtalya Seyahati', *Tarih İncelemeleri*, 22, 2 (December 2007), 21–52, here 32.
41 TDA, TSID 5022407 (Ambassador Hüseyin Ragıp to Foreign Minister Tevfik Rüştü Aras, 31 December 1932).
42 BCA 490.1.0.0/605.95.2; and BCA 030.10.0.0/238.608.2 (Miscellaneous Reports on the Italian Royal Army and Navy, 2 November 1935 and 7 July 1935).
43 BCA 030.10.0.0/238.606.15 (Report of the Turkish Military Attaché in Rome, 5 October 1935).
44 British Foreign Secretary Samuel Hoare and French Prime Minister Pierre Laval proposed a secret deal to Italy, which placed large areas of Ethiopia under Italian control. Once the plan was leaked to the media, however, Hoare and Laval were accused of selling out the Abyssinians, and forced to resign. See: A.J. Barker, *Rape of Ethiopia, 1936* (London: Ballantine Books, 1971).
45 BCA 030.10.0.0/219.476.4 (Ministry of Foreign Affairs to the Turkish Embassy in Rome, 2 March 1936).
46 BCA 030.10.0.0/256.720.20 (Ministry of Interior to the Prime Ministry, 23 January 1936).
47 FO 424/280, E 2024/26/44 (Loraine to Eden, 10 April 1936).
48 Ibid.
49 Ibid.
50 *DVP*, vol. 19:: 231–2 (Soviet Note on the Turkish Proposal for a Revision of the Lausanne Straits Convention, 16 April 1936).
51 RGASPI, f. 159, op. 2, d. 19, l. 100 (19 December 1922).
52 *DVP*, vol. 19: 231–2 (Soviet Note on the Turkish Proposal for a Revision of the Lausanne Straits Convention, 16 April 1936).
53 AVP RF, f. 5, op. 16, pap. 112, d. 113, l. 23 (Krestinsky to Karakhan, 13 May 1936).
54 Ibid.
55 FO 424/280 E 4633/26/44 (Lord Stanley to Eden, 21 July 1936).
56 *DVP*, vol. 19: 231–2 (Soviet Note on the Turkish Proposal for a Revision of the Lausanne Straits Convention, 22 June 1936).
57 AVP RF, f. 5, op. 16, pap. 112, d. 113, l. 28 (Stomonyakov to Karakhan, 13 July 1936).
58 *DVP*, vol. 19: 365 (Stomonyakov to Karakhan, 14 July 1936).
59 AVP RF, f. 5, op. 16, pap. 112, d. 113, l. 28 (Stomonyakov to Karakhan, 13 July 1936).
60 Ibid.
61 *DVP*, vol. 19: 326 (Karakhan to Litvinov, 29 June 1936).
62 AVP RF f. 5, op. 16, pap. 122, d. 112, l. 28–9 (Krestinsky to Litvinov, 31 October 1936).
63 Ibid.
64 TDA, TSID 8513398 (Apaydın's record of his conversation with Litvinov, 20 October 1936).
65 *DVP*, vol. 19: 365 (Stomonyakov to Karakhan, 14 July 1936).
66 *DVP*, vol. 19: 315–16 (Litvinov's Statement at Montreux, 23 June 1936).
67 *League of Nations Treaty Series*, vol. 173, 215–41.
68 Ibid.
69 See Articles 19 and 20: *League of Nations Treaty Series*, vol. 173: 215–41.
70 "Montrö Boğazlar Sözleşmesi ve Ekleri," *Resmi Gazete* (5 August 1936): 37.
71 Ibid.
72 Harry Howard, 'The Straits After the Montreux Conderence', *Foreign Affairs* 15, 1 (October 1936); 199–202.
73 TDA, TSID 5071728 (Aras to Apaydın, 26 October 1936).
74 *DVP*, vol. 19: 500–02 (Conversation between Apaydın and Litvinov, 19 October 1936).

75 RGASPI, f. 17, op. 166, d. 566, l. 78-9 (Litvinov's record of his conversation with Apaydın, 25 October 1936).
76 TDA, TSID, 8513398 (Apaydın's record of his conversation with Litvinov, 20 October 1936).
77 Ibid.
78 RGASPI, f. 17, op. 166, d. 566, l. 80-1 (Litvinov's record of his conversation with Apaydın, 25 October 1936).
79 Ibid.
80 *DVP*, vol. 19: 525-6 (Litvinov's Conversation with Apaydın, 28 October 1936).
81 TDA, TSID 17841279 (Apaydın to Aras, 4 November 1936).
82 TDA, TSID 8512277 (Aras to Apaydın, 2 November 1936).
83 *DVP*, vol. 19: 525-6 (Litvinov's Conversation with Apaydın, 28 October 1936).
84 *DVP*, vol. 19: 538-9 (Litvinov's Instructions to Karakhan, 4 November 1936).
85 Ibid.
86 DVP, vol. 19: 539-40 (Karakhan's Telegram to Litvinov, 5 November 1936).
87 FO 424/280 E 6499/5280/44 (Eden to Morgan, 15 October 1936).
88 FO 424/280 E 6712/5280/44 (Morgan to Eden, 25 October 1936).
89 FO 424/280 E 6812/5280/44 (Eden to Morgan, 30 October 1936).
90 Ibid.
91 TDA, TSID 5032572 (Report on Soviet-Turkish Trade, 2 November 1936).
92 Tables are from Celal Bayar's Report on Soviet-Turkish Trade. See: TDA, TSID 9139755 (Celal Bayar's Report, 23 November 1936).

Turkish imports from Soviet Russia, 1930-6

YEAR	AMOUNT (in 1,000 liras)	RATIO (as percentage of total Turkish imports)
1930	10,606	7,19%
1931	7,943	5,78%
1932	5,942	6,91%
1933	3,907	5,23%
1934	3,911	4,51%
1935	4,325	4,87%
1936 (as of September)	3,278	–

Turkish exports to Soviet Russia, 1930-6

YEAR	AMOUNT (in 1,000 liras)	RATIO (as percentage of total Turkish imports)
1930	7,661	5,06%
1931	4,688	3,69%
1932	5,437	5,36%
1933	4,499	4,62%
1934	3,643	3,95%
1935	4,15	4,33%
1936 (as of September)	1,791	–

Soviet reports confirm Turkish figures but indicate that the total volume for 1935 does not include exchange of goods though Kayseri mills or of military equipment and goods. See: AVP RF f.5, op.16, pap.122, d.114, l. 6 (Ministerial Report Foreign Trade with Turkey for 1935, 30 May 1936).

93 TDA, TSID 8512358 (Report on Litvinov's discussion with Ambassador Zekai Apaydın of Atatürk's conversation with Karakhan, 8 November 1936).
94 AVP RF f.5, op.16, pap.122, d.114, l. 6.
95 Türkiye Cumhuriyeti Başvekalet İstatistik Umum Müdürlüğü, *Harici Ticaret Yıllık İstatistik, Memleketer ve Maddeler İtibarile 1936 İthalat-İhracat, Kısım-2* (Ankara 1937).

TURKISH IMPORTS IN 1936

Countries	Value (in Liras)	Amount (in tons)	Percentage in 1936	Percentage in 1935
Germany	41,742,000	163.800	45%	40%
United States	8,993,000	58.700	9,60%	6,90%
United Kingdom	6,103,000	19.800	6,60%	9,80%
U.S.S.R.	5,030,000	67.800	5,40%	4,90%
Czechoslovakia	3,627,000	13.600	3,90%	4,30%
Austria	2,595,000	8.600	2,80%	3,30%
France	2,300,000	9.900	2,50%	4,70%

TURKISH EXPORTS IN 1936

Countries	Value (in Liras)	Amount (in tons)	Percentage in 1936	Percentage in 1935
Germany	60,042,000	328.000	51%	41%
United States	13,419,000	49.800	11,40%	10,00%
United Kingdom	6,356,000	59.900	5,40%	6,40%
Italy	4,345,000	36.100	3,70%	9,90%
Czechoslovakia	4,012,000	8.400	3,40%	3,20%
U.S.S.R.	3,954,000	6.600	3,30%	4,30%
France	3,800,000	51.700	3,20%	3,20%

96 TDA, TSID 5032535 (Apaydın to Aras, 9 November 1936).
97 See S.G. Gross, *Export Empire: German Soft-Power in Southeastern Europe, 1890–1945* (Cambridge 2015), 222–3.
98 Rossiiskii gosudarstvennyi arkhiv ekonomiki [hereafter RGAE], f. 7292, op. 38, d. 309, l. 61 (Karakhan to Voroshilov, 31 December 1936).
99 TDA, TSID 9139755 (Celal Bayar's Report, 23 November 1936).
100 A key aspect of Nazi–Turkish trade was that it occurred without depleting the two countries' foreign currency reserves. As with other countries, the Nazi New Plan aimed to conduct trade agreements with Turkey, which accepted German goods in return. Dilek Barlas, 'Germany's Economic Policy Towards the Balkan Countries in the 1930s: A Case of Great Power Pursuit of Domination in the Peninsula', *Turkish Review of Balkan Studies* 2 (1994/1995): 135–45, here, 138.
101 TDA, TSID 5032535 (Apaydın to Aras, 9 November 1936).
102 In line with Reich Economics Minister Hjalmar Schlacht's New Plan, Nazi Germany pursued a similar economic policy in Iran as a containment strategy toward the Soviet Union. By comparison, Jenifer Jenkins suggests that German imports into Iran in 1941 made up close to 48 per cent of the national total, while Iranian exports stood at 42 per cent. See Jenkins, 'Iran in the Nazi New Order', 728.

103 Türkiye Büyük Millet Meclisi Tutanakları, [hereafter TBMM], d. 6, c. 13, b. 1, s. 106–28 (7 August 1940).
104 AVP RF f. 5, op. 16, pap. 122, d. 114, l. 26 (Apaydın to Stomonyakov, 16 November 1936); and AVP RF f. 5, op. 16, pap. 122, d. 114, l. 24 (Stomonyakov's Diary, 7 November 1936).
105 Adam Tooze, in his book *Wages of Destruction*, refers to the New Plan as a system of National Socialist economic management, which was essential if the Third Reich was to survive a truly global war. Since clearing agreements were vital for the extension of this system to countries such as Turkey, Tooze claims that maintaining a balanced trade account was the primary Nazi objective. If we read İnönü's pleas to the Soviets (and later to Britain) in this context, they become all the more revealing about Turkey's changing political preferences. Tooze, *Wages of Destruction*, 308–09.
106 TDA, TSID 5032066 (Report on Soviet-Turkish Trade Negotiations, 20 December 1936).
107 AVP RF f. 5, op. 15, pap. 122, d. 114, l. 53 (Stomonyakov to Karakhan, 13 December 1936).
108 TDA, TSID 9139755 (Celal Bayar's Report, 23 November 1936).
109 AVP RF f. 5, op. 16, pap. 122, d. 114, l. 21 (Karakhan to Stomonyakov, 29 November 1936).
110 *Rossiiskii gosudarstvennyi arkhiv ekonomiki* [hereafter RGAE], f. 7292, op. 38, d. 309, l. 61 (Karakhan to Voroshilov, 31 December 1936).
111 Türkiye Cumhuriyeti Başvekalet İstatistik Umum Müdürlüğü, *Harici Ticaret Yıllık İstatistik, Memleketer ve Maddeler İtibarile 1937 İthalat-İhracat, Kısım-2* (Ankara 1938).

TURKISH IMPORTS IN 1937			
Countries	Value (in Liras)	Percentage	1936 Total
Germany	48,132,000	42.02	41,742,000
United States	17,295,000	15.13	8,993,000
United Kingdom	7,129,000	6.23	6,103,000
U.S.S.R.	7,092,000	6.21	5,030,000
Italy	6,085,000	5.33	2,260,000
Czechoslovakia	3,006,000	2.53	3,627,000
Egypt	2,451,000	2.15	1,334,000

TURKISH EXPORTS IN 1937			
Countries	Value (in Liras)	Percentage	1936 Total
Germany	50,412,000	36.53	60,042,000
United States	19,203,000	13.92	13,419,000
United Kingdom	9,769,000	7.08	6,356,000
Italy	7,266,000	5.27	4,345,000
Belgium	6,633,000	4.81	1,657,000
U.S.S.R.	6,508,000	4.72	3,954,000
Czechoslovakia	6,093,000	4.41	4,012,000

112 TDA, TSID 5029808 (Report on New Soviet-Turkish Trade Treaty, 25 December 1936); also see RGAE, f. 7292, op. 38, d. 309, l. 20 (Ordzhonikidze to Molotov, 25 December 1936).
113 RGAE, f. 7292, op. 38, d. 309, l. 20 (Ordzhonikidze to NKTP, 14 February 1937); also see TDA TSID 9106721 (Report on Turkstroi Activities, 2 November 1936).
114 RGAE, f. 7292, op. 38, d. 309, l. 54 (Zolotarev to NKTP, 3 June 1937).
115 RGAE, f. 7292, op. 38, d. 309, l. 90 (Stomonyakov to NKTP, 22 March 1937).
116 In fact, as early as 1933, there had been rumours of Turkish-Romanian negotiations about a Black Sea Pact (*Karadeniz Misakı*) between Aras and Nicolae Titulescu. See: TDA TSID: 6940596 (Turkish Embassy in Moscow to Ankara, 15 September 1933); and TDA TSID 6940463 (Turkish Embassy in Moscow to Ankara, 18 September 1933).
117 FO 424/280 E 4434/386/44 (Sir P. Loraine to M. Eden, 26 July 1937).
118 TDA, TSID 5194348 (Report on Tevfik Rüştü Aras and Şükrü Kaya's Moscow Visit, 12 July 1937).
119 *Izvestiia* reference is from the 12 July 1937 report cited above.
120 AVP RF, f. 5, op. 17, pap. 100, d. 135, ll. 3-25 (Anatolii Fillipovich Miller's report on conversations with Turkish representatives, 1 August 1937).
121 AVP RF f. 5, op. 17, pap. 100, d. 135, l. 18.
122 Ibid.
123 TDA, TSID 8570146 (Report on Soviet-Turkish Friendship, 17 July 1937).
124 TDA, TSID 5194348 (Report on Tevfik Rüştü Aras and Şükrü Kaya's Moscow Visit, 12 July 1937).

Chapter 2

1 See, for instance, Yücel Güçlü, 'The Uneasy Relationship: Turkish Foreign Policy Towards the Soviet Union at the Outbreak of the Second World War', *The Turkish Yearbook*, XXVIII, 106-38; and Frank Marzari, 'Western-Soviet Rivalry in Turkey', *Middle Eastern Studies*, 7, 1 (January 1971), 63-79.
2 BCA 030.10.0.0/249.683.2 (Ministry of Defense to the Prime Ministry, 23 September 1937).
3 There are a number of useful sources on the late imperial history of Caucasus, exploring the Ottoman borderlands, but the early republican period has largely been dismissed. See: Alexander Balisteri, 'A Provisional Republic in the Southwest Caucasus: Discourses of Self-Determination on the Ottoman-Caucasian Frontier, 1918-19', in *The Ottoman East: Trans-regionalism, Fluid Identities and Local Politics in the 19th and 20th Centuries*, ed. Ali Sipahi, Dzovinar Derderian, and Yasar Tolga Cora (London: I.B. Tauris, 2016); and Lucien J. Frary and Mara Kozelsky, ed., *Russian-Ottoman Borderlands: The Eastern Question Reconsidered* (Wisconsin: University of Wisconsin Press, 2014).
4 Candan Badem wrote an impressive account of Kars under Russian imperial administration in his *Çarlık Rusyası Yönetiminde Kars Vilayeti* (İstanbul: Bir Zamanlar Yayıncılık, 2010).
5 Michael A. Reynolds, *Shattering Empires: The Clash and Collapse of the Ottoman and Russian Empires, 1908-1918* (Cambridge: Cambridge University Press, 2011), 1.
6 See: Central Intelligence Agency (hereafter CIA), 'The Boundary Between Turkey and the USSR' (CIA-RDP79-00976A000200010005-2), 1-56. Accessed on 16 November 2016 through CIA Records Search Tool (CREST) at the National Archives in College Park, Maryland.

7 'Kars'da İmza Edilen Sular İtilafnamesile Serdarabat Barajının İnşasına Dair Müzeyyle Protokol', *Resmi Gazete* (3 August 1927); and 'Hudut Mıntıkası Ahalisinin Türkiye-Soviyet Hududundan Mürurlarına Dair Türkiye Cumhuriyetile Sosyalist Şuralar Cümhuriyetleri İttihadı Arasında Akdolunan Mukavelenin Tasdiki Hakkında Kanun' *Resmi Gazete* (6 March 1929).
8 RGAE, f. 7292, op. 38, d. 309, l. 38 (Ambassador Zekai Apaydın to Zolotarev, 9 January 1937).
9 RGAE, f. 7292, op. 38, d. 309, l. 39-40 (Zolotarev to Apaydın, 21 January 1937).
10 RGAE, f. 7292, op. 38, d. 309, l. 57-8 (Stomonyakov to Zolotarev, 13 March 1937).
11 RGAE, f. 7292, op. 38, d. 309, l. 47 (Zolotarev to Apaydın, 23 January 1937).
12 RGAE, f. 7292, op. 38, d. 309, l. 52 (Turkstroi Chief Engineer to NKTP, 2 June 1937).
13 One exception is Mehmet Perinçek, who published a collection of Soviet archival documents that deals mostly with the first two Kurdish uprisings. He cites a number of newspapers that reflect on the Soviet public perception of the Dersim uprising. Mehmet Perinçek, *Sovyet Devlet Kaynaklarında Kürt İsyanları* (İstanbul: Kaynak, 2011).
14 AVP RF, f. 4, op. 39, pap. 242, d. 53268, l. 219 (Suritz to Rüştü, 22 April 1927).
15 While Turkish demographic studies on the size Kurdish population in the early to mid twentieth century vary greatly, in 1937, when the Dersim rebellion broke out in Turkey, Soviet reports indicated approximately 1,500,000 Kurds residing in Turkey – 'Kurdy', *Bol'shaia sovetskaia entsiklopediia*, 2nd ed., Moscow, 1953.
16 The Young Turk Revolution of 1908 played a profound role in the destinies of the peoples that comprised the Ottoman Empire, including the Kurds, whose incipient nationalism was cemented during this second constitutional experiment of the late Ottoman state. In the early phase of the revolution, local Kurdish leaders – like many other ethno-religious groups – greeted the constitution with jubilation, and actively engaged in parliamentary affairs, reforming the empire form within. Until recently, the established view was such that, in the aftermath of the counterrevolution of 1909, the Young Turks' brief honeymoon with the Kurds came to an abrupt end, triggering a period of highly centralized programme in the Kurdish-occupied provinces. Recent scholarship, however, suggests that the Kurdish leaders in fact remained loyal to the Ottoman state, and only after it became certain that the empire would not recover did Kurdish nationalism emerge and clash with the Kemalist brand of Turkish nationalism. See: Hakan Özoğlu, *Kurdish Notables and the Ottoman State* (Albany: SUNY, 2004). A similar argument with regards to the Young Turks' relations with the Arabs could be found here: Hasan Kayali, *Arabs and Young Turks* (Berkeley: University of California Press, 1997).
17 Kamal Madhar Ahmad, *Kurdistan During the First World War* (London: Saqi Books, 2001).
18 Notable survey histories on the subject are: Martin van Bruinessen, *Agha, Shaikh and State: On the Social and Political Organization of Kurdistan* (Utrecht: University of Utrecht, 1978); Wadie Jwaideh, *The Kurdish National Movement* (New York: Syracuse University Press, 2006); Nader Entessar, *Kurdish Ethnonationalism* (Colorado: Lynne Rienner, 1992).
19 Two classical monographs on the subject are Robert W. Olson, *The Emergence of Kurdish Nationalism and the Sheikh Said Rebellion, 1880-1925* (Texas: University of Texas Press, 1989); Gerard Chaliand, *The Kurdish Tragedy* (New York: Palgrave, 1994).
20 BCA 30.18.1.2/12.76.17 (Declaration of Martial Law in Eastern Provinces [*Takrir-i Sükun Kanunu*], 23 February 1925).

21 RGASPI, f. 17, op. 166, d. 566, l. 71 (Litvinov to Chicherin, 5 March 1925).
22 TBMM, d. 7, c. 16, b. 82, s. 33 (1 September 1925).
23 See for example, BCA 30.10.0.0/113.771.1 (Directorate of Public Security to İsmet İnönü, 27 December 1931).
24 Relations between Great Britain and Turkey became increasingly tense over the status of the British-occupied province of Mosul, an issue that had been left unresolved at the diplomacy table in Lausanne. When the League of Nations awarded the British mandate in Iraq with Mosul – a crucial *wilayat* that Turkey regarded its own under the National Oath (*Misak-i Milli*) – Mustafa Kemal sought to challenge the decision by sending military forces to the region. The Sheikh Said rebellion, which broke out in the spring of 1925, forced him to abandon his original plan of annexation.
25 For a detailed account of the Khoybun (or Xoybun) see: Rohat Alakom, *Xoybun Örgütü ve Ağrı Ayaklanması* (İstanbul: Avesta, 2011). The Turkish Prime Ministerial Archives recently disclosed several documents pertaining to the Ararat Rebellion. See: BCA 30.18.1.2/12.68.8 (Ministry of Interior to the Ministry of Foreign Affairs, 13 November 1925); BCA 30.10.0.0/113.771.1 (Ministry of Interior to the Prime Ministry, 4 April 1927); BCA 30.10.0.0/112.758.13 (Prime Ministry to the Chief of General Staff, 12 March 1929); and BCA 30.10.0.0/113.771.9 (Ministry of Interior to the Prime Ministry, 16 September 1929).
26 By the early 1930s, Khoybun's activities were not limited to Syria but included Iraqi Kurdistan with active support of the Franch authorities in Damascus. At the League of Nations, French diplomats also lobbied on behalf of Iraqi Kurds' petitions for local autonomy, which became a serious source of apprehension in Ankara in the early days of Turkey's own accession to the League. See BCA 30.10.0.0/113.771.4 (Ministry of Interior to the Prime Ministry, 12 April 1929); and BCA 30.10.0.0/259.741.12 (Ministry of Foreign Affairs to the Prime Ministry, 18 July 1932).
27 AVP RF, f. 4, op. 39, pap. 243, d. 53291, l.6 (Suritz to Karakhan, 2 January 1928).
28 Ibid.
29 AVP RF, f. 4, op. 39, pap. 243, d. 53292, l.28 (Minutes of a Conversation between Suritz and Şükrü Kaya, 19 March 1928).
30 Ibid.
31 From the official Turkish perspective, the time span of the Ararat Rebellion was much longer, from 1926 to 1930, and the Rebellion itself was a series of smaller uprisings, the major ones being: the First Ararat Rebellion (May–June 1926); the Koçuşağı Rebellion (October–November 1927); the Mutki Rebellion (May–August 1927); the Second Ararat Rebellion (September 1927); the Bicar Tenkil Rebellion (October–November 1927); the Resul Rebellion (May–June 1929); the Tendürek Rebellion (September 1929); the Zilan Rebellion (June 1930); and the Third Ararat Rebellion (September 1930). While smaller uprisings did occur intermittently, archival evidence suggests that the Turkish state was forced to mobilize an organized counteroffensive only in 1930, and managed to suppress the previous ones without much effort.
32 Cemil Koçak, *Umumi Müfettişlikler* (İstanbul: İletişim, 2003), 294.
33 TGNA prepared yet another detailed report 'On the Kurdish Question in Dersim' in 1934, drawing attention to possible scenarios of assimilation. BCA 030.10.0.0/110.741.9 (Ministry of Interior to the Prime Ministry, 29 April 1934).
34 The Turks considered them as 'racially Turanian'. BCA 030.10.0.0/115.797.16 (Dersim Military Inspectorship, 27 December 1931).
35 BCA 030.10.0.0/111.743.16 (Tunceli Military Inspectorship to the Prime Ministry, 27 July 1936).

36 Martin van Bruinessen, 'The Suppression of the Dersim Rebellion in Turkey (1937–38)' in George J. Andereopulos (ed.), *Conceptual and Historical Dimensions of Genocide* (Philadelphia: University of Pennsylvania Press, 1994); 141–70.
37 BCA 030.10.0.0/47.302.5 (Prime Ministry to the Office of National Security, 27 December 1937).
38 BCA 030.10.0.0/111.744.2 (Public Inspectorship in Dersim to the Prime Ministry, 8 April 1937).
39 BCA 030.10.0.0/128.920.12 (Ministry of Foreign Affairs to the Prime Ministry, 11 November 1930).
40 BCA 030.10.0.0/112.760.14 (Gendarmerie Command South to the Prime Ministry, 10 August 1931).
41 BCA 030.18.1.2/40.80.015 (Gazi Mustafa Kemal to İsmet İnönü, 12 November 1933).
42 BCA 030.10.0.0/115.799.15 (Ministry of Interior to the Prime Ministry, 16 November 1935).
43 BCA 030.10.0.0/216.775.18 (Turkish Consulate in Beirut to the Ministry of Foreign Affairs, 13 June 1937).
44 AVP RF, f. 5, op. 15, pap. 110, d. 86, l.11 (Internal NKVD Report, 28 May 1935).
45 Ibid.
46 This 73 page intelligence report contains fascinating details: BCA 030.10.0.0/113.773.19 (Ministry of Interior to the Prime Ministry, 10 June 1937); also see BCA 030.10.0.0/263.775.18 (Ministry of Interior to the Prime Ministry, 23 June 1937).
47 BCA 030.10.0.0/115.803.36 (Turkish Consulate in Beirut to the Ministry of Foreign Affairs, 13 September 1937).
48 BCA 030.10.0.0/115.801.10 (Ministry of Foreign Affairs to the Turkish Consulate in Beirut, 5 April 1938). This last diplomatic note clearly signalled Turkey's intention of annexing Alexandretta.
49 For a detailed account of the Sanjak (Hatay) question, see: Yücel Güçlü, *The Question of the Sanjak of Alexandretta: A Study in Turkish–French–Syrian Relations* (Ankara: Türk Tarih Kurumu, 2001); and Sarah Shields, *Fezes in the River: Identity Politics and European Diplomacy in the Middle East on the Eve of the Second World War* (Oxford: Oxford University Press, 2011).
50 BCA 030.10.0.0/263.774.16 (), 14 September 1936).
51 BCA 030.10.0.0/263.772.6 (Ministry of Foreign Affairs to Turkish Embassy in Geneva, 12 December 1936).
52 BCA 030.10.0.0/222.501.15 (Draft Resolution Regarding the Sanjak of Alexandretta, 28 January 1937).
53 BCA 030.10.0.0/222.501.24 (Ministry of Interior to the Prime Ministry, 16 December 1937).
54 BCA 030.10.0.0/223.502.5 (Ministry of Foreign Affairs to Prime Ministry, 5 December 1937).
55 BCA 030.10.0.0/224.510.13 (Ministry of Foreign Affairs to the Prime Ministry, 7 April 1938).
56 BCA 030.10.0.0/224.511.2 (Joint Communiqué signed by the Governments of France and Turkey, 10 July 1938).
57 Stephen Hemsley Langrigg, *Syria and Lebanon Under French Mandate* (New York: Octagon Books, 1972), 238.
58 BCA 030.10.0.0/85.558.13 (Turkish Consulate in Beirut to the Prime Ministry, 02 March 1939).

59 BCA 030.10.0.0/225.515.17 (Turkish Consulate in Beirut to the Prime Ministry, 31 May 1939). The Armenians, on the other hand, constituted the second largest minority of Alexandretta next to Arabs. Under the influence of the Armenian Revolutionary Federation (*Dashnaksutyun*) after the annexation, the Armenian population migrated en masse to Aleppo and Beirut. The newly appointed Turkish mayor of Hatay prepared a report on this issue, indicating that at least one-quarter of the people who migrated to Syrian provinces belonged to the upper middle class, 'therefore, affecting the local economy quite badly'. As for the rest of the people, *Dashnaksutyun* secured from the French government a guarantee of 'health services for the resettled, as well as 4 francs per day for living expenses'. BCA 030.10.0.0/225.515.26 (Ministry of Interior to the Prime Ministry, 1 October 1939).
60 Security considerations aside, some scholars also suggested that there were other political reasons at play behind Turkey's promotion of the Sa'dabad Pact. In the pursuit of becoming an important regional power, Turkey wanted to have a semi-permanent seat on the League Council. See, Mustafa Bilgin, *Britain and Turkey in the Middle East* (New York: Tauris, 2007), 27–30.
61 See, İsmail Soysal, '1937 Sadabad Pact', *Studies on Turkish–Arab Relations*, 3 (1988), 132; and Cameron Watt, 'The Saadabad Pact of 8 July 1937', in Uriel Dann (ed.), *The Great Powers in the Middle East 1919–1939* (New York and London: Holmes & Meier, 1988).
62 Touraj Atabaki and Erik Zurcher (eds.), *Men of Order: Authoritarian Modernization under Atatürk and Reza Shah* (New York: Tauris, 2004).
63 *Atatürk'ün Milli Dış Politikası: Cumhuriyet Dönemine Ait 100 Belge, 1923–1938* (Ankara: Kültür Bakanlığı Yayınları, 1992), 256–61.
64 Ibid., 248.
65 Charles Tripp, *A History of Iraq* (New York: Cambridge University Press, 2007), 30–74, here 63.
66 Ibid., 58.
67 *DVP*, vol.15: 62 (Suritz and Karakhan, 26 January 1932).
68 Ibid.
69 *DVP*, vol.15, 94 (Aras and Karakhan, 7 February 1932).
70 Ibid.
71 TDA, TSID 66049 (Tevfik Rüştü to Hüseyin Ragıp, 28 December 1933).
72 FO 371/21836 (James Morgan to Viscount Halifax, 25 June 1938).
73 A.F. Miller, *Otcherki noveishei istorii turtsii* (Moscow, 1948), 184–5.
74 Hasanlı, *SSSR – Turtsiya*, 32.
75 Mustafa Yılmaz, *Atatürk Dönemi Türk Dış Politikası, 1919–1938* (Ankara, 2003), 586.
76 İnönü was re-elected to a second term of office by the unanimous vote of the Grand National Assembly on 3 April 1939. The death of the founder of Turkey's new regime had naturally been a time of anxiety. Yet, it soon became clear that the political edifice constructed by Kemal Atatürk rested on solid foundations and the nation as a whole was very much alive to its merits. It should be safe to suggest that the transition had been smooth, but there were some changes to Ataturk's cabinet. Refik Saydam succeeded Celal Bayar as prime minister; Tevfik Rüştü Aras (later ambassador in London) was succeeded at the Ministry for Foreign Affairs by Şükrü Saraçoğlu, who had previously served as minister of justice; not long afterwards Fethi Okyar, formerly ambassador in London, became minister of justice. These changes can be adequately explained by İnönü's natural desire to surround himself with his own men; and this desire becomes even more understandable given the estrangement between Atatürk and İnönü during the former's latter years.

77 TDA, TSID 5071728 (Aras-Potemkin Talks, 26 October 1938).
78 AVP RF f. 5, op. 17, pap. 100, d. 135, l. 1-2 (Stomonyakov to Zalkind, 27 July 1937).
79 AVP RF f. 5, op. 17, pap. 100, d. 135, l. 26 (Zalkind to Litvinov, 28 July 1937).
80 TDA, TSID 5000995 (Turkish Embassy in Moscow to the Ministry of Foreign Affairs, 16 November 1937).
81 TDA, TSID 4999348 (Turkish request for extension of Karakhan's diplomatic mission in Ankara, 27 April 1937).
82 TDA, TSID 5001356 (Report on Soviet Reaction regarding İnönü's presidency, 15 November 1938).
83 Ibid.
84 DGFP, series D, vol. XII, no. 545, 722-3 (Memorandum by the Deputy Director of the Economic Policy Department, 29 June 1938).
85 TDA, TSID 5000995 (Apaydın to the Ministry of Foreign Affairs, 16 November 1938).
86 TDA, TSID 5039693 (Stomonyakov to Apaydın, 2 August 1938).
87 TDA, TSID 5001470 (Apaydın to Aras, 3 November 1938).
88 BCA 490.01.0.0/609.111.9 (Report of a Conversation with the Soviet Ambassador in Paris, 11 July 1939).
89 BCA 030.10.0.0/209.425.19 (Report on Communist Propaganda Amongst Turkish Teachers, 7 December 1939).
90 TDA, TSID 5001202 (Apaydın to Aras, 22 November 1938).

Chapter 3

1 Richard Overy, *Russia's War: A History of the Soviet War Effort, 1941-1945* (New York: Penguin, 1998), 34.
2 Secondary literature on Turkish foreign policy between the last days of peace and first days of war rely exclusively on the British archives and are inconclusive. See: Frank Marzari, 'Western-Soviet Rivalry in Turkey, 1939', *Middle Eastern Studies*, 7, 2 (May 1971), 201-20; and Brock Millman, 'Credit and Supply in Turkish Foreign Policy and the Tripartite Alliance of October 1939', *The International History Review*, 16, 1 (February 1994), 70-80.
3 BCA 30.10.0.0/132.855.1 (*Le Petit Parisien's* Interview with President İnönü, 31 May 1939).
4 During the Moscow Talks in the summer of 1937, Turkey and the Soviet Union almost entered into a Black Sea military alliance, which would have granted Soviet vessels privileged passage through the Straits. See: AVP RF f. 5, op. 17, pap. 100, d. 135, l. 19 (Stomonyakov to Zalkind, 27 July 1937); and TDA, TSID 5071728 (Aras-Potemkin talks, 26 October 1938).
5 BCA 30.10.0.0/200.370.3 (Conversation with Romanian Foreign Minister Grigore Gafencu, 8 June 1939).
6 Dilek Barlas, 'Friends or Foes? Diplomatic Relations Between Italy and Turkey, 1923-36', *International Journal of Middle East Studies*, 36 (2004), 231-52.
7 On 9 February 1934, Greece, Turkey, Romania and Yugoslavia concluded the Balkan Entente, whereby the signatories suspended all territorial claims against each other. The Balkan Entente would become an excruciating headache for Turks as the Axis powers challenged the regional status quo.
8 Stalin knew that Turkey's leaders regarded the supremacy of the French and British navies as their most effective shield against Italy. Gorodetsky, *Grand Delusion*, 15.

Notes

9   TDA, TSID 11847604 (Saraçoğlu to Aktay, 30 August 1939).
10 BCA 30.10.0.0/222.495.13 (Report on German–Italian Relations, 11 November 1939).
11 BCA 30.18.1.2/85.114.7; BCA 30.10.0.0/239.610.27; and BCA 30.10.0.0/239.610.39 (Miscellaneous Reports on Italian Espionage, 13 January 1939–31 March 1939).
12 BCA 030.10.0.0/85.558.22 (Directorate of Printing and Press to the Ministry of Foreign Affairs, 10 April 1939).
13 BCA 030.10.0.0/239.611.15 (Ministry of Interior to the Ministry of Foreign Affairs, 8 April 1939). Located on the westernmost tip of Western Anatolia, İzmir was Turkey's second largest city by the 1930s and home to the country's biggest Levantine community of Venetian descent, with a population around 10,000 in the early twentieth century. Source: Rauf Beyru, *Levantenler ve Levantizm* (İstanbul: Bağlam Yayınları, 2000), 51–4.
14 BCA 030.10.0.0/239.610.27 (Ministry of Interior to the Prime Ministry, 17 January 1939); and BCA 490.01.5.1/605.96.5 (RPP Izmir Office to RPP General Secretariat, 24 June 1939).
15 Zekeriya Sertel, *Tan* (10 April 1939), 6.
16 BCA 30.10.0.0/239.611.8 (Report on Italy's Invasion of Albania, 28 April 1939). What was particularly infuriating was the news that the Italian Consulate in İzmir raised the new fascist banner of Regno Albanese.
17 FO 424/283, R2688/G (Halifax to Knatchbull-Hugessen, 12 April 1939).
18 FO 424/283, E 2627/297/44 (Knatchbull-Hugessen to Halifax, 11 April 1939).
19 FO 371/23743, R4035 (The Anglo-Turkish Declaration, 12 May 1939).
20 TBMM, d. 6, c. 2 b. 2, s. 67 (12 May 1939).
21 Ibid., 68.
22 Ibid., 69.
23 Ibid., 70.
24 In his dispatch to Halifax, Ambassador Knatchbull-Hugessen quotes Okyar making a similar statement, See FO 424/283, E 2812/294/44 (Hugessen to Halifax, 28 March 1939).
25 TBMM, d. 7, c. 3, b. 7, s. 118 (13 May 1939).
26 BCA 30.10.0.0/243.642.10 (Note on Bulgaria, 28 May 1939).
27 FO 424/283, C 6688/3356/18 (Hugessen to Halifax, 6 May 1939).
28 Ibid.
29 In his *Wages of Destruction,* Adam Tooze argues that not just Turkey, but Greece, Bulgaria and Yugoslavia also cherished similar hopes of forging a tripartite pact with Moscow and London. This is why all the way until the conclusion of the Molotov-Ribbentrop Pact, they drifted towards London and not Berlin. See Adam Tooze, *Wages of Destruction: The Making and Breaking of the Nazi Economy* (London: Penguin, 2006), 309.
30 *Izvestiia* (1 May 1939).
31 Kamuran Gürün, *Türk-Sovyet İlişkileri, 1920–1953* (Ankara: TTK, 1993), 144.
32 Hasanlı, *SSSR – Turtsiya,* 47.
33 Papen quoted in Hasanlı, *SSSR – Turtsiya,* 48.
34 *DGFP*, series D, vol. VI, no. 259, p. 323 (Circular of Weizsäcker, 18 April 1939).
35 Prior to his diplomatic mission in Constantinople during World War I, von Papen had served as German ambassador in Washington DC but was declared *persona non grata* in 1915 and ultimately expelled from the United States for alleged complicity in the planning of sabotage such as blowing up US rail lines. See: William Shirer, *The Rise and Fall of the Third Reich* (New York: Simon & Schuster, 1960), 164.

36 Knatchbull-Hugessen's notes on Papen's personal details are intriguing: In his annual report on important actors in Ankara at the time, Knatchbull-Hugessen wrote: 'Herr von Papen is extremely pleasant to meet and almost exaggeratedly friendly in manner. I should not be inclined to describe him as a heavyweight: there is a suggestion of dilettantism and superficiality about him, accompanied, however, by a certain artfulness, which may constitute his chief claim to efficiency. He is always ready to discuss present international problems and puts his country's case with remarkable glibness and more dispassionately than some.' FO 424/283, E 5006/111/44 (Halifax to Knatchbull-Hugessen, 13 July 1939).
37 Turkish chiefs of missions in both Vienna and Budapest referred to von Papen's activities in those countries as 'suspicious'. BCA 030.10/221.491.2 (Turkish Embassy in Vienna to the Foreign Ministry, 21 October 1934).
38 BCA 030.10/231.560.12 (Turkish Embassy in Geneva to the Foreign Ministry, 21 June 1939).
39 The Turkish Prime Ministry was fully aware of this sentiment: BCA 030.10/231.560.6 (Ministry of Interior to the Prime Ministry, 17 June 1939).
40 BCA 30.10.0.0/131.939.11 (Intelligence report on Franz von Papen, 7 June 1939).
41 BCA 030.10/231.560.8 (Intelligence Report on Franz von Papen, 22 July 1939).
42 DGFP, series D, vol. VI, no. 315, p. 408 (Papen to Ribbentrop, 3 May 1939).
43 Ibid, 409.
44 DGFP, series D, vol. VI, no. 413, p. 116 (Papen to Ribbentrop, 12 May 1939).
45 Ibid; and Franz von Papen, *Memoires* (Paris: Hammorion, 1953), 289.
46 DGFP, series D, vol. VI, no. 413, p. 544 (Ribbentrop to von Papen, 20 May 1939).
47 Fahir Armaoglu, 'Türkiye'nin Hitler Almanya'sı ile İlişkileri, 1931–1941', in *Çağdaş Türk Diplomasisi Sempozyumu: 200 Yıllık Süreç* (TTK: Ankara, 1997), 297–307 (here, 298).
48 See, BCA 30.10.0.0/231.556.2 (Interview with Adolf Hitler, 31 July 1933).
49 Ibid.
50 TBMM, d. 6, c. 13, b. 1, s. 106–28 (7 August 1940).
51 Ibid.
52 FO 424/282, R 1867/18/44 (Hugessen to Halifax, 9 February 1940).
53 FO 424/284 C13322/1110/55 (Viscount Halifax to Sir H. Knatchbull-Hugessen, 10 September 1939).
54 BCA 030.10.0.0/231.560.3 (Ministry of Commerce to the Prime Ministry, 6 June 1939). After receiving a preliminary report from the General Staff on available food supplies and mass mobilization, on 8 September 1939, Prime Minister Refik Saydam passed a resolution restricting over-consumption of 'essential goods and medicine' in the country. The General Staff's report indicated a justifiable fear of inflation and a jump in imports 'since certain citizens [were] buying fifty bottles of the same medicine instead of one . . . and forty packages of coffee for only a single month's worth', and warned the government that, with the existing consumption level, national supplies would dry up within four months, necessitating further concessions to Germany in return for a trade agreement. Source: BCA 030.0.001/34.204.1 (Prime Ministry, Memorandum on Mobilization and Conscription, 8 September 1939).
55 Falih Rıfkı Atay, *Ulus* (25 August 1939), 3.
56 Asım Us, *Vakit* (25 August 1939), 5.
57 Yunus Nadi, *Cumhuriyet* (25 August 1939), 6.
58 See TDA, TSIDs 143652 and 144299 (Miscellaneous Reports on the Outbreak of War, September 1939).

59 TDA, TSID 161948 (Ministry of Foreign Affairs to the Embassy in London, 3 September 1939).
60 Ibid.
61 FO 424/284 E6246/297/44 (Hugessen to Halifax, 1 September 1939).
62 For the intelligence report Knatchbull-Hugessen mentioned see: FO 424/284 C12134/15/18 (Halifax to Knatchbull-Hugessen, 26 August 1939).
63 Ibid.
64 According to a communication from Colonel General Keitel, Hitler decided that new contracts for deliveries of war material might also be concluded with Turkey. Arms that could potentially be used against Germany were obviously not included. The OKW (Oberkommando der Wehrmacht) therefore agreed to certain deliveries of powder and anti-aircraft predictor equipment. For the war materials to be delivered, however, Turkey had to comply with Hitler's requests regarding the supply of raw materials for Germany's war machine such as copper and chrome ore. This meant that Turkey had to terminate its existing contracts with Great Britain and France since the majority of Turkey's output had already been purchased through earlier trade agreements. See: DGFP, series D, vol. VII, no. 219, p. 233 (Ribbentrop to von Papen, 24 August 1939).
65 Ibid.
66 DGFP, series D, vol. VII, no. 393, p. 390 (von Papen to Ribbentrop, 1 September 1939).
67 Ibid., 391.
68 Ibid.
69 Ibid., 392.
70 *DVP, vol.22*, p.12 (Molotov to Terentiev, 03 September 1939).
71 Gorodetsky, *Grand Delusion*, 15.
72 In fact, the 1925 Soviet–Turkish Treaty of Friendship and Neutrality was still in effect. But in the second half of the 1930s, both Turkish and Soviet leaders found the wording of this early treaty to be too vague and entered into intense negotiations to establish a more contractual and binding treaty, which never materialized. An important round of discussions took place in 1936. RGASPI, f. 17, op. 166, d. 566, l. 78–9 (Litvinov's record of his conversation with Apaydın, 25 October 1936); also see TDA, TSID 8513398 (Apaydın's record of his conversation with Litvinov, 20 October 1936).
73 B.M. Potskhveriia, 'Sovetsko-Turetskie otnosheniya i problema prolivov nakanune, v gody vtoroi mirovoi voiny i poslevoennye desyatiletiya', in L.N. Nezhinsky and A.V. Ignatev, eds. *Rossiia i chernomorskie prolivy, XVIII-XX stoletiia* (Moscow, 1999), 437.
74 BCA 30.10.0.0/219.476.9 (Saraçoğlu to İnönü, 11 May 1939).
75 FO 424/283, R 8880/661/67 (Halifax to Knatchbull-Hugessen, 22 September 1939).
76 DGFP, series D. vol. VII, no.266, p. 281 (Hitler to Mussolini, 22 September 1939).
77 DGFP, series D, vol. VII, no. 175, p. 183. (Schulenberg to Ribbentrop, 28 September 1939).
78 What began as a prolonged series of border skirmishes between the Soviet Union and Japanese Empire in Mongolia turned into decisive battles in Khalkhyn Gol during May–September 1939. Although Nazi Germany began invading Western Poland on 1 September, the Soviet Union decided to postpone the operation and consolidate its forces on the eastern theatre until Gregory Zhukov's successful offensive in Nomohan on September 16. See: Otto Preston Chaney, *Zhukov* (Norman: University of Oklahoma Press, 1971).
79 FO 424/284 C13322/1110/55 (Viscount Halifax to Sir H. Knatchbull-Hugessen, 10 September 1939).
80 Ibid.
81 *Pravda*, 27 September 1939.

82 Feridun Cemal Erkin, *Les relations turco-soviétiques et la question des détroits* (Ankara: Başnur Matbaası: 1968); and Cevat Açıkalın, 'Cevat Açıkalın'ın Anıları: 2. Dünya Savaşı'nın İlk Yılları (1939-1941)', *Belleten, LVI:216* (December 1992), 985-1078.
83 R.S. Burçak, *Moskova Görüşmeleri (26 Eylül-16 Ekim 1939) ve Dış Politikamız Üzerindeki Tesirleri* (Ankara: Gazi Üniversitesi, 1983), 84-7.
84 Jamil Hasanlı offers an extensive account of Saraçoğlu's talks in Moscow based on Soviet records, and eschews the prevalent Soviet argument that it was the Turkish side responsible for the failure of the negotiations. Hasanlı demonstrates that the Soviets had no real motivation to sign a pact with the Turks and essentially decided to remain neutral in case of an Axis operation against Turkey. This explains Molotov's menacing suggestions about the Straits. Hasanlı, *SSSR-Turtsiya*, 53-62.
85 In fact, the granting of Soviet bases had been a subject of friendly negotiations between Ankara and Moscow before 1939, in the framework of Soviet-Turkish plans for joint defence of the Straits in case of naval assault. In return for Soviet assistance, Turkey had offered to close the Straits in case the Soviet Union was attacked. There had even been negotiations for maintaining a Soviet fleet on the Aegean near the port of İzmir. See: *Dokumenty vneshnei politiki SSSR*, vol. 19 (Moscow, 1974), 326 (Karakhan to Litvinov, 29 June 1936).
86 T.C. Dışişleri Bakanlığı Araştırma ve Siyaset Planlama Genel Müdürlüğü, *Türkiye Dış Politikasında 50 Yıl: İkinci Dünya Savaşı Yılları, 1939-1945* (Ankara, 1973), 110.
87 Burçak Rıfkı Salim, *Moskova Görüşmeleri (26 Eylül-16 Ekim 1939) ve Dış Politikamız Üzerindeki Tesirleri* (Ankara, 1983), 84-7. Also see: Derek Watson, *Molotov: A Biography* (Palgrave: New York, 2005), 176.
88 *Pravda*, 2 October 1939; Salim, *Moskova Görüşmeleri*, 87.
89 Kemal Karpat, *Turkey's Foreign Policy in Transition, 1950-1974* (Leiden: Brill, 1974), 3.
90 *DVP*, vol.22: 619; *Voyna i politka, 1939-1941* (Moscow, 1999), 16.
91 BCA 030.01.0.0/42.248.6 (RPP Parliamentary Group Discussions, 17 October 1939).
92 FO 424/284 R9046/661/67 (Halifax to Knatchbull-Hugessen, 18 October 1939).
93 BCA 030.01.0.0/42.248.6 (RPP Parliamentary Group Discussions, 17 October 1939).
94 The conflict between the Soviet Union and Finland that arose in November of 1939 called into action (for good reason) what the USSR called the 'reactionary' Turkish press. From the Soviet perspective, 'more time was devoted to figuring out how to strike a blow against Russia – either through aid to Finland, the bombing of Baku, or the landing of British troops in İstanbul – than the question of how to deal with Germany. (Moiseev, 'SSSR i Turtsiia,' 160.) Even though such scenarios did indeed appear frequently in Turkish columns, the government itself certainly refused to entertain any one of these military provocations against the Soviet Union. Nonetheless, in the face of strong pressure and temptation, such plans contributed to a noticeable deterioration in Soviet-Turkish relations.
95 FO 424/284 R8954/328/37 (Sir R. Hoare to Viscount Halifax, 18 October 1939).
96 V. M. Molotov, *O vneshnei politike Sovetskogo Soiuza: doklad* (Leningrad: Gos. izd-vo polit. lit-ry, 1939), 17.
97 DGFP, series D, vol. VII, no. 219, p. 244 (Schulenberg to Ribbentrop, 11 October 1939).
98 Molotov quoted in P.P. Moiseev, 'SSSR i Turtsiia v gody Vtoroi Mirovoi Voiny (1939-1945)', in E.M. Zhukov, et. al., *SSSR i Turtsiia, 1917-1979* (Moscow: Nauka, 1981), 112-89; here, 157-8.
99 Stalin quoted in Iuri N. Rozal'ev, *K Istorii Sovetsko-Turetskikh otnoshenii* (Moscow: Gospolitizdat, 1958), 231.

100 *Pravda*, 31 October 1939.
101 *Izvestiia*, 9 November 1939.
102 Belinkov and Vasil'ev, *O Turetskom 'Neitralitete'*, 32.
103 Ibid.
104 A.N. Sakharov, 'Voyna i sovetskaia diplomaty, 1939-1941', in *Voproshy Istorii, 8* (1995), 165.
105 TDA, TSID 11847777 (Embassy in London to the Foreign Ministry, 30 December 1939).
106 FO 424/284 R241/17/44 (Sir H. Knatchbull-Hugessen to Viscount Halifax, January 5, 1940). Knatchbull-Hugessen further suggests that 'the abolition of Islam as a State religion has by no means entailed its disappearance as a practiced faith. The mosques are full as ever, and it is safe to say that, below the intellectual stratum, Islam retains its hold on the people of Turkey'.
107 BCA 030.0.010/209.425.19 (Ministry of Education to the Prime Ministry, 12 December 1939).
108 BCA 490.01/609.111.9 (Directorate of Public Security to the RPP General Secretariat, 24 October 1939).
109 BCA 490.01/609.112.5 (Ministry of Interior to the RPP General Secretariat, 11 July 1939).
110 BCA 030.0.010/222.495.10 (Turkish Embassy in Kabul to the Prime Ministry, 12 October 1939).
111 TDA, TSID 161948 (Report on The European War – Political Developments, 30 September 1939). Based on numerous cables received from 25 August through 30 September 1939, the Ministry of Foreign Affairs in Ankara compiled a comprehensive report, pertinently entitled 'The European War'. This 189-page pamphlet not only attests to Turkey's fading hopes of a reconciliation with the Soviet Union, but also casts doubts on previously held views that on the eve of the Saraçoğlu-Molotov Talks, Turkey was unable to ascertain the Soviet Union's position. See for instance: A.L. Macfie, 'The Turco-Soviet Talks of September-October 1939: A Secret German Report', *Balkan Studies*, 2 (1985): 431–42.
112 *Documents on British Foreign Policy, 1919-1939*, [hereafter, DBFP], series 3, volume vii, no. 635, 34.
113 BCA 30.18.1.1/89.111.16 (Ratification of the Tripartite Treaty, 21 November 1939).
114 Yunus Nadi, *Cumhuriyet* (19 October 1939), 5.
115 Frank G. Weber, *The Evasive Neutral: Germany, Britain and the Quest for a Turkish Alliance in the Second World War* (Columbia: University of Missouri Press, 1979), 73–104; Zehra Önder, *Die türkische Außenpolitik im Zweiten Weltkrieg* (Munich: Oldenbourg, 1977), 73; Tamkin, *Britain, Turkey and the Soviet Union*, 33; and Deringil. *Active Neutrality*, 54.
116 Deringil, *Active Neutrality*, 80.
117 Ibid, 84.
118 DGFP, series D, vol. VIII, no. 347, pp. 398-405 (Memorandum by Ribbentrop, 11 November 1939).
119 Ibid, 403.
120 DGFP, series D, vol. VIII, no. 390, pp. 451-6 (Memorandum by Ribbentrop, 27 November 1939).
121 Ibid.
122 DGFP, series D, vol. VIII, no. 408, pp. 475-6 (Ribbentrop to von Papen, 1 December 1939).
123 Ibid.

124　FO 424/284 N103/30/38 (Sir H. Knatchbull-Hugessen to Viscount Halifax, 4 January 1940).
125　TDA, TSID 11847604 (Haydar Aktay in Moscow to Saraçoğlu in Ankara, 30 August 1939).
126　FO 424/284 N103/30/38 (Enclosure in No. 4, Minute by Brigadier A.C. Arnold, Military Attaché, 20 December 1939).
127　TDA, TSID 11847604 (Haydar Aktay in Moscow to Saraçoğlu in Ankara, 30 August 1939).
128　FO 424/284 N103/30/38 (Enclosure in No. 4, Minute by Brigadier A.C. Arnold, Military Attaché, 20 December 1939).
129　TDA, TSID 11847657 (Haydar Aktay to Saraçoğlu, 16 December 1939).
130　FO 424/284 R3126/242/44 (Sir H. Knatchbull-Hugessen to Viscount Halifax, 1 March 1940); and FO 424/284 R4236/316/44 (Sir H. Knatchbull-Hugessen to Viscount Halifax, 1 April 1940).
131　FO 424/284 R4337/4156/67 (Sir H. Knatchbull-Hugessen to Viscount Halifax, 3 April 1940).
132　FO 424/284 R4337/4156/67 (Sir H. Knatchbull-Hugessen to Viscount Halifax, 3 April 1940).

Chapter 4

1　Cemal Madanoğlu, *Anılar, 1911–1953* (İstanbul: Evrim 1982), 302.
2　Not, of course, for those with Nazi sympathies. The Third Reich's Ambassador in Ankara witnessed Saraçoğlu's delight the morning after Barbarossa and reported ecstatically to Berlin. DGFP, series D, vol. XII, no. 670, p. 1080 (von Papen to Ribbentrop, 22 June 1941).
3　Ernst von Weizsäcker, *Memoirs* (Chicago 1951), 255.
4　DGFP, series D, vol. VII, no. 247, p. 260 (von Papen to Ribbentrop, 24 August 1939).
5　DGFP, series D, vol. VII, no. 342, p. 348 (von Papen to Ribbentrop, 27 August 1939).
6　DGFP, series D, vol. XII, no. 566, p. 913 (von Papen to Ribbentrop, 29 May 1941).
7　Cemil Koçak, 'Milli Şef Döneminde Yönetim ve Basın Hayatı', *Kebikeç*, 2 (1995), 149–60, here 153.
8　Among the Turkish newspapers that fell within this spectrum, *Cumhuriyet* probably played the most dubious role. *Cumhuriyet* was established at Atatürk's request in 1924, and its founder, Yunus Nadi, had been the chief editor of the official party newspaper of the Turkish Communist Party – also established by Atatürk. But the Soviets trusted neither Nadi nor his party. In 1926, a Soviet report described him as 'a typical Anatolian bourgeois, overgrown with fat and degenerated into a comprador'. AVP RF f.132, op.11, pap.78, d.33 (Biographical sketches of Turkish journalists, November 1926).
9　*Tan* (20 November 1939), 1–3.
10　*Tan* (9 December 1939), 5; and *Tan* (12 December 1939), 2.
11　In 1957, the CIA prepared a comprehensive list of Turkish nationals known for their pro-Axis sympathies. The report included personal details and wartime dealings as well as their role in Nazi Germany's anti-Soviet propaganda. See: CIA, 'Turks and Neighboring Nationals who were Agents, In Contact, or of Operational Interest to the German Intelligence Service in Turkey' (CIA-RDP81-01043R0035000800004-7),

Notes

171–89. Accessed on 16 November 2016 through CIA Records Search Tool (CREST) at the National Archives in College Park, Maryland.
12 Until Berna Pekesen's recent *NS-Propaganda und die türkische Presse im Zweiten Weltkrieg,* existing literature on Nazi propaganda in Turkey depicted Turkey's leadership without agency. See for instance: Johannes Glasneck, 'Methoden der Deutsch-Faschistischen Propagandatätigkeit in der Türkei vor und während des Zweiten Weltkriegs', *Wissenschaftliche Beiträge* (Saale: Martin-Luther-Universität Halle-Wittenberg, 1966). In her book, published in 2014, Berna Pekesen offers a convincing account of Turkey's position towards Nazi propaganda, where the author successfully eschews the idea that Turkey simply acquiesced in Nazi designs. Berna Pekesen, *Zwischen Sympathie und Eigennutz: NS-Propaganda und die türkische Presse im Zweiten Weltkrieg* (Berlin: Lit Verlag 2014).
13 BCA 33.166.01; 33.166.02; 33.166.04; 33.167.01 and 33.170.01 (Miscellaneous reports on Axis propaganda in Turkey, General Directorate of Security, May-November 1939).
14 *Tan* (8 December 1939), 3.
15 *Dokumenty Ministerstvo inostrannykh del. Germanii, vyp II: Germanskaia politika v Turtsii* [hereafter GPT], 7 (Ribbentrop to von Papen, 10 November 1941), 40.
16 Established by the Weimer Republic's first ambassador to Turkey, Rudolf Nadolny, the *Türkische Post* was the only local daily published in German. But German bookstores in İstanbul sold papers direct from the Third Reich on a daily basis, including *Deutsche Allgemeine Zeitung* and *Volkische Beobachter.*
17 İlker Aytürk, 'The Racist Critics of Atatürk and Kemalism, from the 1930s to the 1960s', *Journal of Contemporary History,* 40 (2): 308–35.
18 Sabis badly timed his book's publication, which was meant to come out in 1942 but was delayed due to Soviet victories against Nazi Germany. Ultimately the book was published with sloppy editing and an apologetic epilogue. See: Ali İhsan Sabis, *İkinci Cihan Harbi* (İstanbul: Tan Basımevi, 1943).
19 TDA, TSID 12940344 (Council General K.A. Payman's Report to Ankara, 15 July 1940).
20 TDA, TSID 15312339, 153122350 and 15314321 (File on Dr. Zeki Haşmet Kiram, 21 February, 27 February and 15 July 1940 respectively).
21 Louis de Jong's *Die deutsche fünfte Kolonne im Zweiten Weltkrieg* (1959) and Peter Longerich's more recent *Goebbels: Biographie* (2010) are useful sources for probing Nazi propaganda efforts in general.
22 TDA, TSID 138591 (Ambassador Hüsrev Gerede to Ankara, 29 June 1940).
23 DGFP, series D, vol. IX, no. 265 (Papen to Ribbentrop, May 17 1940), 364–7.
24 Ibid, 365.
25 Ibid, 367.
26 DGFP, series D, vol. X, no. 197 (Memorandum by Papen, July 20 1940), 257.
27 DGFP, series D, vol. X, no. 197 (Memorandum by Papen, July 20 1940), 257.
28 TDA, TSID 5499943 (Ambassador Gerede's Meeting with Ernst von Weizsäcker, 1 June 1940).
29 TDA, TSID 145303 and 148496 (Ambassador Gerede's Meetings with Ernst von Weizsäcker, 16 June and 18 June 1940 respectively). In one of his meetings with von Weizsäcker, when Gerede provided evasive answers, von Weizsäcker changed tack and complained about Turkish newspapers' negative depictions of Hitler, particularly in the pages of Sertel's *Tan.*
30 TDA, TSID 148484 (Ambassador Gerede's Meeting with Ernst von Weizsäcker, 11 June 1940). Although Ambassador Gerede claimed to 'have done his best in giving

assurances about Ankara's benevolent neutrality towards Berlin' in his official dispatch, he surreptitiously conveyed that some leftist newspapers in Turkey indeed followed 'an unequivocally shallow, gratuitously aggressive, and flamboyantly biased editorial line', and suggested that they might be silenced.

31 TDA, TSID 12941485 (Ambassador Gerede's Report on Nazi Propaganda, 3 June 1940).
32 TDA, TSID 144144 (Ali Haydar Aktay to Şükrü Saraçoğlu, 10 July 1940).
33 Deutsches Nachrichtenbüro (5 July 1940), Ausgabe 710.
34 BCA 30.10.0.0/60.367.14 (miscellaneous reports on the Soviet-Finnish War, 10 April 1940). The date on Massigli's first telegram was just a fortnight after the collapse of the Finnish resistance in the Winter War, when France found itself pondering alternative scenarios to contain the Soviet Union's means of collaboration with the Third Reich. The Turkish ambassador in Stockholm, Agah Aksen, had passed on numerous reports about Finland's fate during the Winter War, categorically urging the Ankara government to regulate their relations with the Kremlin and take extra cautious steps. It was thus plausible that Massigli would consider Turkey 'a great asset if drawn in as a silent ally'.
35 Massigli's second telegram was dated 28 March 1940. Deutsches Nachrichtenbüro, Ausgabe 718.
36 Ibid., Ausgabe 720.
37 Deutsches Nachrichtenbüro (7 July 1940), Ausgabe 721.
38 The communiqué was dated 19 March 1940. Deutsches Nachrichtenbüro (8 July 1940), Ausgabe 723.
39 *Ulus* (7 July 1940), 1.
40 Faik Ahmet Barutçu, *Siyasi Anılar, 1939-1954* (İstanbul: Millyet, 1977), 130-40.
41 TDA, TSID 865429 (Ambassador Aktay's Telegram on Kars, 10-11 July 1940).
42 This confirms Gabriel Gorodetsky's account of the Soviet position toward Turkey in July-August 1940. See Gorodetsky, *Grand Delusion*, 60.
43 Barutçu, *Siyasi Anılar*, 135.
44 TDA, TSID 145331 (Turkish Ambassador in Moscow to the Foreign Ministry in Ankara, 5 July 1940).
45 Hüsrev Gerede, the Turkish ambassador in Berlin, concurred with Aktay's assessment and said that the Straits was the current centre of gravity in Nazi-Soviet relations. TDA, TSID 6844011 (Turkish Ambassador in Berlin to the Foreign Ministry in Ankara, 28 June 1940).
46 TDA, TSID 145331 (Turkish Ambassador in Moscow to the Foreign Ministry in Ankara, 5 July 1940).
47 TDA, TSID 144156 (Ambassador Aktay's *Compte Rendu* on *Pravda* and *Izvestiia*, 5-7 July 1940).
48 TDA, TSID 144144 (Turkish Ambassador in Moscow to the Foreign Ministry in Ankara, 10 July 1940).
49 TDA, TSID 865429 (Ambassador Aktay's Telegram on Kars, 10-11 July 1940).
50 TDA, TSID 144141 (Report on Batumi and Kars, 11 July 1940).
51 TDA, TSID 144144 (Turkish Ambassador in Moscow to the Foreign Ministry in Ankara, 10 July 1940).
52 TDA, TSID 6843977 (Turkish Ambassador in Berlin to the Foreign Ministry in Ankara, 27 June 1940).
53 FO 424/285, R 6676/203/44 (Viscount Halifax to Stafford Cripps, 13 July 1940).
54 FO 424/285 R6676/203/44 (Viscount Halifax to S. Cripps, 15 July 1940).

55 FO 424/285 R6676/203/44 (Sir S. Cripps to Viscount Halifax, 18 July 1940).
56 FO 424/285, R6773/316/44 (Sir S. Cripps to Viscount Halifax, 18 July 1940).
57 FO 424/285 R6676/203/44 (Sir H. Knatchbull-Hugessen to Viscount Halifax, 19 July 1940).
58 FO 424/285 R6830/203/44 (Sir H. Knatchbull-Hugessen to Viscount Halifax, 24 July 1940).
59 For Tsarist Russia's interest in the Straits, see: Ronald P. Bobroff, *Late Imperial Russia and the Turkish Straits: Roads to Glory* (I.B. Tauris: New York, 2006).
60 From the British perspective, Turkey's fears were understandable but groundless; Halifax thought that there seemed to be no definite attempt to upset the Montreux Convention. In fact, some of Stalin's demands were for an interpretation of the convention that would actually contain in its final paragraph the phrase 'in view of the war in Europe'.
61 FO 424/285 R6776/203/44 (Viscount Halifax to Sir S. Cripps, 26 July 1940).
62 FO 424/285 R6776/203/44 (Sir S. Cripps to Viscount Halifax, 28 July 1940).
63 FO 424/285 N6109/40/38 (Cripps to Halifax, 3 August 1940).
64 FO 424/285 R6987/203/44 (Cripps to Halifax, 11 August 1940).
65 FO 424/285 R6830/203/44 (Halifax to Cripps, 13 August 1940).
66 TDA, TSID 179978 (Gerede to Saraçoğlu, 6 November 1940).
67 BCA 30.1.0.0/60.367.16 (Turkish Ambassador in Moscow to PM Refik Saydam, 8 October 1940).
68 BCA 30.18.1.2/92.80.9 (Prime Ministry to the Directorate of Press, 17 August 1940).
69 TBMM, d. 6, c. 6, b. 1, s. 8 (1 November 1940).
70 TBMM, d. 6, c. 6, b. 1, s. 4 (1 November 1940).
71 FO 424/285 R7567/316/44 (Halifax to Knatchbull-Hugessen, 11 September 1940); and FO 424/285 R8186/316/44 (Knatchbull-Hugessen to Halifax, 2 November 1940).
72 FO 424/286 R4368/15/44 (Knatchbull-Hugessen to Eden, 21 February 1941).
73 BCA 30.10.0.0/256.723.6 (Foreign Ministry to the Prime Ministry, 10 September 1940).
74 BCA 30.10.0.0/247.670.1 (Turkish Embassy in Romania to the Prime Ministry, 17 August 1940).
75 Sir Hughe Knatchbull-Hugessen, *Diplomat in Peace and War* (London: John Murray, 1949), 154–64.
76 Ibid., 158.
77 BCA 30.10.0.0/235.583.10 (Tevfik Rüştü Aras's Note on British Foreign Policy in the Balkans, 4 April 1940).
78 TDA, TSID 146753 (Turkish Embassy in Sofia to the Ministry of Foreign Affairs in Ankara, 24 October 1940); and BCA 30.18.1.2/90.40.7 (Turkish Embassy in Bulgaria to the Foreign Ministry, 24 April 1940).
79 Knatchbull-Hugessen, *Diplomat in Peace and War,* 162.
80 Ibid., 164.
81 BCA 30.18.1.2/96.72.3 (Turkish Ambassador in Sofia to the Foreign Ministry, 13 December 1940)
82 Mark Mazower, *Inside Hitler's Greece: The Experience of Occupation, 1941–44* (New Haven: Yale University Press, 2001).
83 Count Galeazzo Ciano, *The Ciano Diaries* (New York: Howard Fertig, 1973), 47.
84 Ibid., 54.
85 Ibid., 63.
86 Ibid.

87 Ibid., 78.
88 Ibid., 93.
89 FO 424/285 R7224/764/19 (Halifax to Knatchbull-Hugessen, 27 August 1940).
90 Ibid.
91 While Turkey abstained from declaring war against Italy to defend Greece, İnönü authorized numerous covert naval operations in the Aegean to send arms, medicine and food to the Greek resistance. A recently declassified document in the Republican Archives provides intriguing details about these operations. (BCA 030.10.0.0/ 179.235.12 (PM Refik Saydam to the Naval Command, 13 November 1941). The most famous of these covert ops was pertinently codenamed 'Kurtuluş' (Independence). BCA 030.10.0.0/117.185.20.1 (Operation 'Kurtuluş', 28 March 1942).
92 FO 424/285 R8697/316/44 (Knatchbull-Hugessen to Halifax, 10 November 1940).
93 Ibid.
94 Mazower, *Inside Hitler's Greece*, 160.
95 TDA, TSIDs 153632, 166866, 173038, 173589, 173598, 173606 (Gerede's Reports on Nazi Invasion of Greece, 13 March 1941 to 5 May 1941).
96 FO 424/285 R8697/316/44 (Knatchbull-Hugessen to Halifax, 10 November 1941)
97 Ibid.
98 DGFP, series D, vol. XII, no. 231, p. 409 (von Papen to Ribbentrop, 28 March 1941).
99 DGFP, series D, vol. XII, no. 154, p. 277 (von Papen to Ribbentrop, 11 March 1941).
100 DGFP, series D, vol. XII, no. 195, p. 338 (Directive of the High Command of the Wehrmacht, 22 March 1941).
101 TDA, TSID 172385 (Gerede to Saraçoğlu, 10 April 1941).
102 DGFP, series D, vol. XII, no. 161, p. 286 (İsmet İnönü to Adolf Hitler, 12 March 1941).
103 BCA 30.01.0.0/232.562.2 (Minister of Finance to the Ministry of Foreign Affairs, 30 May 1941).
104 TDA, TSIDs 142911 (Gerede to Saraçoğlu, 19 March 1941).
105 Iuri N. Rozal'ev, *K Istorii Sovetsko-Turetskikh otnoshenii* (Moscow: Gospolitizdat, 1958), 1–15; and S. Belinkov and I. Vasil'ev, *O Turetskom 'Neitralitete' vo vremia Vtoroi Mirovoi Voiny* (Moscow: Gospolitizdat, 1952), x–xii.
106 FO 424/256 R4369/1426/44 (Knatchbull-Hugessen to Eden, 22 February 1941).
107 Ibid.
108 BCA 30.10.0.0/232.561.7 (Turkish Ambassador in Berlin, Hüsrev Gerede, to PM Refik Saydam, 20 March 1940).
109 DGFP, series D, vol. XII, no. 113, pp. 201–3 (Adolf Hitler to İsmet İnönü, 1 March 1941).
110 Ibid.
111 Ibid.
112 TDA, TSID 11848162 (Gerede–Hitler Meeting Minutes, 14 March 1941); and DGFP, series D, vol. XII, no. 161, p. 286 (İsmet İnönü to Adolf Hitler, 12 March 1941).
113 DGFP, series D, vol. XII, no. 177, pp. 308–12 (Record of Conversation between Adolf Hitler and Turkish Ambassador in Berlin, Hüsrev Gerede, 18 March 1941).
114 Ibid.
115 Ibid.
116 Ibid.
117 DGFP, series D, vol. XII, no. 231, p. 409 (Papen to Ribbentrop, 28 March 1941).
118 Ibid.
119 Ibid.
120 DGFP, series D, vol. XII, no. 514, p. 812–17 (von Papen to Ribbentrop, 13 May 1941).

121 Ibid.
122 GPT, No. 3 (Ribbentrop to von Papen, 17 May 1941), 10.
123 TDA, TSID 172385 (Gerede to Saraçoğlu, 9 April 1941).
124 BCA 30.18.1.2/95.51.10 (Prime Ministry to the Foreign Ministry, 6 June 1941).
125 DGFP, series D, vol. XII, no. 556, pp. 886–9 (von Papen to Ribbentrop, 27 May 1941).
126 DGFP, series D, vol. XII, no. 550, pp. 873–5 (von Papen to Ribbentrop, 15 May 1941).
127 Interesting to note here is that historian Gordon Wright brought up a similar argument in his *The Ordeal of Total War, 1939–1945* (Illinois: Harper Collins, 1997).
128 DGFP, series D, vol. XII, no. 565, pp. 910–12 (Ribbentrop to von Papen, 29 May 1941).
129 Ibid.
130 DGFP, series D, vol. XII, no. 621, p. 1020 (Memorandum by Head of Political Division, 12 June 1941).
131 For the text of Hitler's address, see: *Monatshefte für auswärtige Politik* (June 1941), 449–64.
132 DGFP, series D, vol. XII, no. 622, p. 1021 (İsmet İnönü to Adolf Hitler, 12 June 1941).
133 TDA, TSID 4601229 (Nazi-Turkish Non-Aggression Pact, 18 June 1941).
134 DGFP, series D, vol. XII, no. 659, p. 1063 (Ribbentrop to Schulenburg, 21 June 1941).
135 DGFP, series D, vol. XI, no. 404 (Schulenburg to the Nazi Foreign Office, 25 November 1940).
136 DGFP, series D, vol. XIII, no. 193, p. 304 (von Weizsäcker to Ribbentrop, 11 August 1941).
137 TDA TSID 172385 (Gerede to Saraçoğlu, 25 August 1941).
138 By the same token, the news of the Molotov–Hitler meeting in Berlin caused an equally disturbing anxiety in Iran that swept Turkey at the time. Although existing rumours in Iran were paradoxical – that in return for a free hand in the Dardanelles, Germany was offering Russia an equally free hand in Iran – public perception of the Berlin meeting in both countries were unequivocally anti-Soviet. See Jenkins, 'Iran and the Nazi New Order', 741.
139 Bruce Kuniholm, *The Origins of the Cold War in the Near East: Great Power Conflict and Diplomacy in Iran, Turkey and Greece* (Princeton 1980), 27.
140 TDA, TSID 11584331 (Ambassador Hüsrev Gerede to Ankara, 18 July 1940).
141 TDA, TSID 11848208 (Gerede to Saraçoğlu, 17 March 1941).
142 DGFP, series D, vol. XII, no. 177, pp. 308–12 (İsmet İnönü to Adolf Hitler, 12 March 1941), here p. 310.
143 Here too, Turkish records confirm Gorodetsky's assessment about changing motives behind the Stalin's attempt to secure an agreement with Turkey after Molotov's failed negotiations with Hitler in Berlin. See Gorodetsky, *Grand Delusion*, 76.
144 *Ulus* (11 July 1941), 2.
145 Doğan Avcıoğlu, *Milli Kurtuluş Tarihi* (İstanbul 1995), 156.

Chapter 5

1 *GPT*, 7 (Ribbentrop to von Papen, 9 June 1941), 25–8.
2 Ibid., 28.
3 Ibid.
4 *GPT*, 8 (Ribbentrop to von Papen, 13 June 1941), 30–1.

5 Knatchbull-Hugessen ruefully admitted this later: FO 421/326 R1471/24/44 (Hugessen to Eden, 5 February 1942).
6 TDA, TSID 142850 (Aktay–Molotov Meeting Minutes, 19 June 1941).
7 DGFP, series D, vol. XIII, no. 125 (von Papen to Ribbentrop, 18 July 1941), 174.
8 TDA, TSID 136177 (Aras–Eden Meeting Minutes, 18 June 1941).
9 FO 424/286 R6258/1934/44 (Eden to Knatchbull-Hugessen, 18 June 1941).
10 Ibid.
11 Ibid.
12 FO 424/286 R6539/236/44 (Eden to Knatchbull-Hugessen, 26 June 1941).
13 Ibid.
14 Ibid.
15 TDA, TSID 192968 (Ambassador Gerede to Saraçoğlu, 5 July 1941).
16 TDA, TSID 11359443 (Report on 'The Outbreak of War', 22 June 1941).
17 This perspective is also reflected in Soviet historical scholarship: A.Y. Bezugolniy, 'Ni Voyni, Ni Mira', *Voenno-istoricheskii arkhiv*, No. 5 (May 2003), 67–73; and N.I. Tyuleneva, 'Teni Proshlogo', *Voenno-istoricheskiy arkhiv*, No. 5 (May 2003), 23–8.
18 DGFP, series D, vol. XIII, no. 193 (von Weizsäcker to Ribbentrop, 11 August 1941); 304.
19 Ibid., 306.
20 *Ulus* (July 11, 1941), 2.
21 DGFP, series D, vol. XIII, no. 193 (von Weizsäcker to Ribbentrop, 11 August 1941); 308.
22 Ibid.
23 DGFP, series D, vol. XIII, no. 194 (Ribbentrop to von Papen, 11 August 1941), 305–11.
24 Ibid., 309.
25 Ibid.
26 BCA 030.01.0.0/40.240.19 (İnönü's Telegram to the Foreign Ministry, 26 September 1943).
27 DGFP, series D, vol. XIII, no. 227 (Ribbentrop to von Papen, 22 August 1941), 354–8.
28 DGFP, series D, vol. XIII, no. 238 (Ribbentrop to von Papen, 25 August 1941), 373.
29 BCA 30.1.0.0/30.179.4 (Diplomatic Correspondence Regarding Turco-German Chrome agreement, 20 September 1941).
30 BCA 30.1.0.0/17.96.6 (Memorandum on German–Turkish and Anglo-Turkish Chromium Trade, 17 July 19.
31 FO 424/286 R8394/139/44 (Eden to Knatchbull-Hugessen, 12 September 1941).
32 BCA 30.1.0.0/48.309.10 (Budget Framework for the Ministry of National Defense Between 1939 and 1944).
33 BCA 30.1.0.0/235.585.10 (Robert Mackay's Report on Anglo-Turkish Relations, 17 September 1941).
34 Ibid.
35 FO 424/286 R8597/179/44 (Eden to Knatchbull-Hugessen, 23 September 1941).
36 FO 424/286 R9849/236/44 (Eden to Knatchbull-Hugessen, 24 September 1941).
37 DGFP, series D, vol. XIII, no. 367 (von Papen to Ribbentrop, 29 September 1941); 589–94, here 593.
38 For a comprehensive account on the origins of the Iranian crisis see: Jamil Hasanlı, *SSSR - Iran: Azerbaidzhanskii Krizis i Nachalo Kholodnoi Voiny* (Moscow: Geroi Otechestvo, 2006). For Iranian–Soviet relations before 1941, see: Miron Rezun, *The Soviet Union and Iran: Soviet Policy in Iran from the Beginnings of the Pahlavi Dynasty*

until the Soviet Invasion in 1941 (Geneva: Institut Universitaire de Hautes Etudes Internationales, 1981).
39 A useful source for Iran's relations with Nazi Germany is Jenkins, 'Iran and the Nazi New Order', 741.
40 Hasanlı, *SSSR i Iran,* 23.
41 Rezun, *The Soviet Union and Iran,* 186.
42 FO 424/286 E 3995/3444/34 (Eden to Cripps, 19 July 1941).
43 FO 424/286 R 7615/112/441 (Eden to Halifax, 8 August 1941).
44 Hasanlı, *SSSR i Iran,* 121.
45 United Nations, *Treaty Series,* vol.93, 290–6.
46 American service troops, who eventually numbered more than 30,000, began to arrive in the latter part of 1942. This force, the Persian Gulf Command, did not formally participate in the occupation, as it had arrived under British auspices after it was decided that the United States should assume primary responsibility for the supply route through Iran. T.H. Vail Motter, *The United States Army in World War II: The Persian Corridor and Aid to Russia* (Washington: Office of the Chief of Military History 1952), 155; George Lenczowski, *Russia and the West in Iran, 1918–1948: A Study in Big Power Rivalry* (Ithaca: Cornell University Press, 1949), 273; and Edward M. Mark, 'Allied Relations in Iran, 1941–1947', in *The Wisconsin Magazine of History,* 59, 1 (Autumn, 1975), 51–63.
47 Joan Beaumont, 'Great Britain and the Rights of Neutral Countries: The Case of Iran, 1941', *Journal of Contemporary History,* 16, 1 (January, 1981); 213–28.
48 FO 424/286 R 8154/112/44 (Eden to Cripps, 10 August 1941).
49 FO 424/286 E 3995/3444/34 (Eden to Cripps, 19 July 1941).
50 FO 424/286 E 3995/3444/34 (Eden to Cripps, 19 August 1941).
51 TDA, TSID 11499359 (Soviet Memorandum to the Turkish Government, 25 August 1941).
52 Ibid.
53 Ibid.
54 TDA, TSIDs 121846, 121848 and 121849 (Consular Reports on the Operation Countenance, 30 August 1941).
55 BCA 30.10.0.0/212.439.5 (Ministry of Interior to the Prime Ministry, 23 August 1941).
56 Expediting the construction of the railroad project ultimately cost 10 per cent more than the estimated 35,000,000 lira. Source: BCA 30.18.1.2/94.70.8 (Ministry of Interior to the Prime Ministry, 28 August 1941); and BCA 30.10.0.0/55.366.3 (Ministry of Interior to the Prime Ministry, 27 August 1941).
57 BCA 30.18.1.2/97.125.9 (Ministry of Interior to the Prime Ministry, 2 February 1942).
58 BCA 30.10.0.0/262.763.32 (Ministry of Interior to the Prime Ministry, 3 April 1942).
59 BCA 30.10.0.0/100.648.11 (Intelligence Report on Anti-Soviet Propaganda in Eastern Provinces, 31 January 1942).
60 BCA 30.18.1.2/99.56.2 (Prime Ministry to the Directorate of Printing and Press, 27 June 1942).
61 TDA, TSID 109877449 and 19887466 (Saraçoğlu's Meeting Minutes with the British Ambassador, 27 August and 1 September 1941).
62 TDA, TSID 10987642 (Aras–Eden Meeting Minutes, 22 August 1941).
63 FO 421/326 R1471/24/44 (Knatchbull-Hugessen to Eden, 5 February 1942).
64 BCA 030.10.100/648.11 (3rd Army Inspectorate to the Ministry of Foreign Affairs, 31 January 1942).

65 BCA 030.10.100.649.5 (Third Army Inspectorate to the Ministry of Foreign Affairs, 12 June 1942).
66 BCA 30.10.0.0/232.561.19 (Ministry of Internal Affairs to the Prime Ministry, 24 February 1942).
67 S.G. Chuev, 'Kavkazskaya Karta Germanii', *Voenno-Istoricheskiy Arkhiv*, No. 1 (2004), 39; and Y. Gorkov, *Gosudarstvennyi komitet oborona postanovliaet*, 1941–1945 gg. (Moscow, 2002), 287.
68 See Yuriy Baturin, *Dose Razvedchika* (Moskva: Molodaya Gvardiya, 2005); and Z.P. Şharapov, *Naum Eytingon: Karayushchiy mech Stalina* (St Petersburg: Izdatelskiy Dom 'Neva', 2003).
69 Baturin, *Dose razvedchika*, 393–8; and Şharapov, *Naum Eytingon*, 103.
70 V.N. Stepkov, *Pavel Sudoplatov – geniy terrora* (St Petersburg: Izdatelskiy Dom 'Neva', 2003), 131.
71 Pavel Sudoplatov, *Spetsoperatsii: Lubyanka i Kreml, 1930–1950* (Moskva: Olma Press, 1997), 173.
72 Franz von Papen, *Der Wahrheit eine Gasse* (Innsbruck: P List, 1952), 596.
73 *Tan* (March 6, 1942), 1; Baturin, *Dose Razvedchika*, 393–8; and Şharapov, *Naum Eytingon*, 103.
74 *Tan* (25 February 1942), 1.
75 Franz von Papen, *Memoirs* (New York: E.P. Dutton, 1953), 485–90.
76 Ibid.
77 *Cumhuriyet* (26 February 1942), 1–3; and *Tan* (26 February 1942), 2.
78 Z.P. Şharapov, *Naum Eytingon: Karayuşhchiy Mech Stalina* (St Petersburg: Izdatelskiy Dom 'Neva', 2003), 50.
79 Sharapov, *Naum Eytingon*, 62.
80 *Tan* (6 April 1942), 1.
81 Papen, *Memoirs*, 489.
82 Yuriy Baturin, *Dose Razvedchika* (Moskva: Molodaya Gvardiya, 2005), 45.
83 Henry Picker, *Hitlers Tischgesprache im Führerhauptquartier* (Munich: Verlag, 1968), 127–32; see also *Tan* (17 April 1942), 1.
84 Papen, *Memoirs*, 490.
85 Baturin, *Dose Razvedchika*, 408.
86 *Cumhuriyet* (18 June 1942), 4; *Tan* (18 June 1942), 2.
87 Papen, *Memoirs*, 490.
88 Ibid.
89 *Pravda* (6 March 1942), 4.
90 *Pravda* (7 March 1942), 4.
91 *Tan* (10 April 1942), 2.
92 *Tan* (18 June 1942), 1.
93 *Tan* (1 May 1942), 1.
94 *Krasnaya Zvezda* (18 June 1942), 3.
95 *Pravda* (30 August 1942), 1.
96 BCA 30.10.0.0/231.562.11 (Ministry of Foreign Affairs to the Prime Ministry on Soviet Attempts to Impede Turkish-German Relations, 11 June 1942).
97 BCA 30.10.0.0/171.185.21 (Ministry of Foreign Affairs to the Prime Ministry, 24 February 1942).
98 BCA 30.10.0.0/124.881.6 (Ministry of Foreign Affairs to the Prime Ministry, 24 February 1942).

99 Between May 1939 and August 1944, six ships sailed from Balkan ports, carrying a total of 16,797 immigrants. On August 9, 1944, three Turkish ships (*Bülbül, Mefkure* and *Marina*) were commissioned to rescue 400 Jewish passengers off a Romanian ship that had been attacked by a German submarine. The operation was difficult (the Turkish vessels were attacked by three German submarines in the Black Sea) and its success found widespread coverage globally: BCA 030.10.0.0/117.814.3 (Ministry of Interior's Report on the Rescue Operation, 16 August 1944).
100 The publication of Douglas Frantz and Catherine Collins's *Death on the Black Sea* shed new light on the hitherto forgotten story of the *Struma* tragedy. In an eloquently written account, Frantz and Collins unearthed a plethora of new evidence that explored the events that led to the Struma's destruction. See: Douglas Frantz and Catherine Collins, *Death on the Black Sea: The Untold Story of the Struma and World War II's Holocaust at Sea* (New York: HarperCollins, 2003).
101 TDA, TSID 179184 (Ministry of Foreign Affairs to the Ministry of Interior, 22 December 1941).
102 Was it possible the Turks on the tugboat were unaware the *Struma*'s engine did not work? Absolutely not. Recently released Turkish archival evidence suggest that the Turkish coastguard was notified that fixing the engine of *Struma* would require special technical equipment that could more easily be found in the neighbouring port of Şile, where the ship was being towed. BCA 30.10.0.0/124.881.6 (SS *Struma*, 24 February 1942).
103 It is interesting that this submarine, after a crew change, was navigating close to Constanza harbour. In the same year, ShCh213 was torpedoed by a German submarine. In 2008, Romanian divers discovered its wreck at the bottom of Black Sea. They could not identify it because it was completely enveloped in fishing nets. It took two years, and the help of Dutch divers, to penetrate the wreck and identify it.
104 The following account is from my personal e-mail correspondence with David Stoliar, the only survivor of the torpedoed SS *Struma* after it sinking (Washington DC: 16–23 February 2013). David Stoliar passed away on 1 May 2014, at the age of ninety-one.
105 TDA, TSID 178788 (Saraçoğlu to the Turkish Ambassador in Romania, 20 June 1942).
106 At least two documents in the Turkish Diplomatic Archives suggest that David Stoliar was, in fact, not the only survivor of the SS *Struma* tragedy and that there was another – the 23-year-old Medea Solomovich, who was provided with a visa for Palestine by the British Embassy. TDA, TSID 178878 and TSID 178788 (Saraçoğlu to the Turkish embassies in Bucharest and Paris, 20 June 1942).
107 TDA, TSID (MFA Letter to the Turkish Red Crescent Organization, 15 May 1942).
108 BCA 030.10.0.0/110.736.7 (Permits for Jews with Turkish citizenship who are reşiding abroad, 25 November 1940); BCA 030.10.0.0/110.736.12 (Turkish Jews residing in Vichy France, 19 February 1943); BCA 030.10.0.0/232.562.20 (Turkish Jews residing in Vichy France, 21 October 1942).
109 There are competing narratives on Turkey's attitude towards Jews during World War II. See: Stanford J Shaw, *Turkey and the Holocaust: Turkey's Role in Rescuing Turkish and European Jewry from Nazi Persecution During the Holocaust, 1933–45* (New York: Palgrave, 1993); and Corry Guttstadt, *Die Turkei, die Juden und der Holocaust* (Berlin and Hamburg: Assoziation A, 2008).
110 BCA 030.10.0.0/116.810.37 (Albert Einstein to İsmet İnönü, 17 September 1933); F. Neumark, *Zuflucht am Bosphorus: deutsche Gelehrte, Politiker und Künstler in der Emigration 1933–1953* (Frankfurt: Knecht, 1995), 13.

111 BCA 30.10.0.0/110.734.12; 30.10.0.0/110.736.9 and 30.10.0.0/242.634.23 (Consular Reports on the 1934 Thrace Pogroms, 25 August 1934; 12 July 1935 and 20 August 1934).
112 Rıfat Bali, ed., *The Wealth Tax Affair* (İstanbul: Libra, 2012).
113 BCA 30.10.0.0/99.641.7; 030.10.0.0/110.736.5; 30.10.0.0/206.407.31 (Various reports on the Jewish plight to Palestine during World War II, 1939–1941).
114 BCA 30.10.0.0/99.641.13 (Ministry of Interior to the Prime Ministry, 9 October 1942).
115 For a detailed account of Romania and the Holocaust, see: Jean Ancel, *The History of the Holocaust in Romania* (Nebraska: Yad Vashem, 2011).
116 FO 371/32662 (Reasons for the refusal by the Palestine authorities to admit the SS *Struma* refugees on board, Code 48, File 652, Papers 3354–4410).
117 The following documents held in the UK National Archives at Kew answer some important questions about the *Struma* incident: CO 733/446/11 (Illegal immigration: *Struma* ship, PQS, 1942); and FO 371/32662 (Reasons for the refusal by the Palestine authorities to admit the SS *Struma* refugees on board, Code 48, File 652, Papers 3354–4410).
118 Ninian Stewart, *The Royal Navy and the Palestine Patrol* (London: Frank Cass, 2002), 17.
119 The first piece of evidence came in the early 1960s from a German investigator, Jurgen Rohwer, who discovered no indication of German naval activity during the winter of 1942. Rohwer contended that the Germans decommissioned all submarines around the Straits after a dispute with the Turks over the accidental sinking of a Turkish boat. The second piece of evidence came in the early 1980s from Yosef Govrin, an Israeli diplomat and scholar. Govrin was conducting doctoral research on Soviet–Israeli relations at the Hebrew University in Jerusalem, when he came across G.I. Vaneyev's *Soviet Fleet in the Black Sea During the Great Patriotic War* (*Chernomortsy v Velikoi Otechestvennoi voine*). He noticed a reference to the *Struma* in Vaneyev's book and he immediately recognized the ship's name. Despite his instrumental findings, Govrin's hypothesis that the Soviet captain had mistaken the ship for a military transport was incorrect. After the fall of the Soviet Union and the opening of naval archives, Gennadi Kibardin, a Latvian researcher finally discovered the key that solved the *Struma* puzzle and provided the motive. When Kibardin was examining documents about Soviet submarine tactics in World War II, he found Stalin's secret order to destroy all neutral shipping in the Black Sea. It explained why the *Struma* was sunk and why the Çankaya had also been sunk nearby. See: Jürgen Rohwer, *Die Versenkung der Jüdichen Flüchtlingstransporter Struma und Mefkurem Schwarzen Meer* (Frankfurt: Bernard und Graefe, 1964); G.I. Vaneyev, *Chernomortsy v Velikoi Otechestvennoi voine* (Moscow: Voenizdat, 1978); Yosef Govrin, *Israeli–Soviet Relations, 1953–1967* (New York: Routledge, 2002); and 'Doomed from the Start', *Naval History* (February 2004), 46–51.
120 *Tan* (21 April 1942), 1.
121 Ibid.
122 BCA 030.10.0.0/239.613.7 (Foreign Ministry Report on Fascist Italy, 12 January 1942).
123 *GPT*, 16 (Papen to Ribbentrop, 2 January 1942), 49–54.
124 Ibid., 52.
125 Ibid., 53.
126 Ibid.
127 Ibid., 54.

128 Orbay replaced Tevfik Rüştü Aras on February 2, 1942; BCA 30.18.1.2/97.116.10 (Appointment of Rauf Orbay, 2 February 1942).
129 FO 421/327 R2320/403/44 (Eden to Knatchbull-Hugessen, 10 April 1942).
130 BCA 30.18.1.2/98.46.17 (Correspondence Regarding Anglo-Turkish Relations, 17 April 1942).
131 Ibid.
132 BCA 30.18.1.2/98.46.17 (Correspondence Regarding Anglo-Turkish Relations, 17 April 1942).
133 Ibid.
134 FO 421/327 R2730/1266/44 (Eden to Sir A. Clark Kerr, 24 April 1942).
135 Oleg A. Rjeshevskiy, *Stalin i Cherchill: Vstrechi, Besedi, Diskussii, 1941–1945* (Moscow,: Nauka 2004), 15.
136 Rjeshevskiy, *Stalin i Cherchill*, 28.
137 Ibid., 35.
138 FO 421/327 R3717/1429/G (Eden to Knatchbull-Hugessen, 4 June 1942).
139 Ibid.
140 Ibid.
141 *GPT*, 26 (Papen to Ribbentrop, 26 August 1942), 82–6.
142 Ibid.
143 *GPT*, 27 (Papen to Ribbentrop, 27 August 1942), 87–94.
144 Ibid.
145 Ibid.
146 TBMM, d. 6, c. 27, b. 3, s. 21–2 (Şükrü Saraçoğlu's Parliamentary Address, 5 August 1942). The racial turns in Saraçoğlu's premeditated speech had strong parallels with Ziya Gökalp (1876–1924), who established the blueprints of Turkism as an ideological construct in his *The Principles of Turkism* (1923). See: Ziya Gökalp, *Türkçülüğün Esasları* (İstanbul: İlmi Türkçülük Yayınları, 1940).

Chapter 6

1 A major debate in Russian historical scholarship concerns how socialist nationalism was perceived in the Soviet periphery. Terry Martin claims that, in its early phase, the aim was to pursue an indigenization (*korenizatsiia*) programme to promote local leadership in the periphery. Stalin's nationality policy did not adequately address the question of representation at the federal centre, which ultimately led to a 'Great Retreat' from Lenin's 'brotherhood of nations' to Stalin's 'friendship of nations' in the 1930s. In Crimea, for instance, the party sought to promote guidelines for progress through the cohabitation of ethnic culture and nationalism with a socialist content. But this policy was at odds with the industrial and technical elite in the republics, which remained mostly Russian, who were also aggravated by the loss of their privileges. Terry Martin, *The Affirmative Action Empire: Nations and Nationalism in the Soviet Union, 1923–1939* (Ithaca: Cornell University Press, 2001).
2 Recent scholarship draws attention to the Second World War as 'a defining moment of the Bolshevik Revolution'. See: Bruce Grant, *In the Soviet House of Culture: A Century of Perestroikas* (Princeton: Princeton University Press, 1995); Yuri Slezkine, *Arctic Mirrors: Russia and the Small Peoples of the North* (Ithaca: Cornell University Press, 1994); and Amir Weiner, *Making Sense of War: The Second World War and the Fate of the Bolshevik Revolution* (Princeton: Princeton University Press, 2001).

3   Bruce Grant claims that the Second World War 'proved to be a turning point for native peoples in the Soviet world' (Grant, *Soviet House of Culture,* 108). Likewise, Slezkine argues that the war helped Moscow integrate non-Russians into Soviet programmes (Slezkine, *Arctic Mirrors,* 303). In a similar vein, Amir Weiner's seminal *Making Sense of War* focuses on the Vinnytsia region of Western Ukraine, and demonstrates how World War II determined the worldview of the political elite, ordinary people as well as 'the fate of the Bolshevik Revolution' (Weiner, *Making Sense of War,* 16).
4   Amir Weiner makes a similar argument for the Russian side of the story. The author suggests: 'Juxtaposed against other heroic tales, World War II superseded other foundational myths; such as the civil war and the collectivization of the countryside, which were increasingly viewed as distant, irrelevant, and in some cases, too controversial because of their traumatic legacy' (Weiner, *Making Sense of War,* 8).
5   One of the first inclusive Soviet studies on collaboration and purges in Crimea was P.N. Nadinskii's *Ocherki po istorii kryma,* which was published in 1951, covering the entire history of the peninsula and its inhabitants in four volumes. The last volume, published in 1967, deals with the period from 1939 to 1950, focusing exclusively on Crimea under German occupation. But deportations as a subject of serious historical research became available only after the strict censorship laws had been revoked during *glasnost.* In post-Soviet Russian historiography, the first major attempt to explore the history of Crimea in the Great Patriotic War is A.M. Basov's *Krym v Velikoi otechestvennoi voine.* See: P.N. Nadinskii, *Ocherki po Istorii Kryma IV* (Simferopol: Tavria, 1967); and Aleksandr Mikhailovich Basov, *Krym v Velikoi otechestvennoi voine 1941-1945* (Moscow: Nauka, 1987).
6   Basov, *Krym v Velikoi otechestvennoi voine,* 210.
7   Gulnara Bekirova, *Krymskotatarskaya problema v SSSR: 1944-1991* (Simferopol: Odzhak, 2004), 23.
8   Three insightful works in English are: Brian Glyn Williams, *The Crimean Tatars: The Diaspora Experience and the Forging of a Nation* (Boston: Brill, 2001); Hakan Kırımlı, *National Movements and National Identity Among the Crimean Tatars* (New York: Brill, 1996); and Edward A. Allworth, et al., *The Tatars of Crimea: Return to Homeland* (Durham: Duke University Press, 1998). Despite their different agendas, in all three of these accounts, subjugating Crimean Tatar nationalism appears as an exceptionally daunting task for both Imperial Russian, and Soviet, policy-makers. Of particular interest is how these works portray Crimean Tatars as a major reason behind the failure of Soviet *korenizatisiia.* Crimea was indeed a place where *korenizatisiia* became what Terry Martin calls 'a hole in the middle'.
9   T. Lothrop Stoddard, 'Pan-Turanism', *The American Political Science Review,* 11:1 (Feb., 1917), 12-23. Also see: *A Manual on the Turanians and Pan-Turanism* (London: H.M. Stationery Office, 1918).
10 Ziya Gökalp, *Türkçülüğün Esasları* (İstanbul: İlmi Türkçülük Yayınları, 1940), 20.
11 A useful primary source on Enver's final days in Russia is a biography written by his aide, Yaver Suphi. See: Yaver Suphi Bey, *Enver Paşa'nın Son Günleri* (İstanbul: Çatı Kitapları, 2007).
12 Soviet historians also seem to acknowledge this fact. Belinkov and Vasil'ev, *O Turetskom 'Neitralitete',* 179.
13 Moiseev, 'SSSR i Turtsiia', 182.
14 Cemil Koçak, 'İkinci Dünya Savaşı ve Türk Basını', *Tarih ve Toplum,* 35 (November 1986): 29-33.
15 Moiseev, 'SSSR i Turtsiia', 179.

16 Ataöv, *2. Dünya Savaşı*, 152.
17 BCA 030.10/229.542.9 (Foreign Ministry to the German Embassy, 30 June 1942).
18 DGFP, series D, vol. XIII, no. 125 (von Papen to Ribbentrop, 18 July 1941), 174.
19 GPT, 10 (Papen to German Foreign Office, 5 August 1941), 34.
20 Ibid., 35.
21 Ibid., 36.
22 Ibid.
23 GPT, 10 (von Papen to German Foreign Office, 5 August 1941), 35.
24 Cafer also acted as a spy for the Turkish government under the name 'Ahmed Caferoglu'. He was a well-known Turkologist.
25 Mirza-Davud Guseinov, *Tiurskaia Demokraticheskaia Partiia Federalistov 'Musavat' v proshlom i nastoiashchem* (Tiflis [Tblisi]: Izdatel'stvo 'Zakkniga', 1927), 9.
26 Richard Woytak, 'The Promethean Movement in Interwar Poland', *East European Quarterly*, vol. XVIII, no. 3 (September 1984), 273–8.
27 DGFP, series D, vol. XIII, no. 179 (Memorandum by State Secretary, 5 August 1941), 284.
28 Ibid., 286.
29 Ambassador Gerede was ultimately dismissed in August 1942. BCA 030.11.1/156.26.17 (Prime Ministry to the Turkish Embassy in Berlin, 11 August 1942).
30 DGFP, series D, vol. XIII, no. 238, p. 373 (Ribbentrop to von Papen, 25 August 1941).
31 Ibid., 374.
32 Rossiiskii gosudarstvennyi voennyi arkhiv [hereafter RGVA], Ekspozytura № 2 Oddziały II Sztabu Generalnego Wojska Polskiego (Warszawa), 1920–1939," f. 461, op. 2, d. 138. I would like to thank Iurii Chainskyi of Warsaw University for bringing these documents to my attention.
33 Ibid.
34 Ibid.
35 Ibid.
36 DGFP, series D, vol. XIII, no. 298, p. 473 (Memorandum by State Secretary, 10 September 1941).
37 Ibid., 474.
38 Ibid., 478.
39 The number of soldiers Nuri pledged to raise is ironic. In his catastrophic campaign on the Eastern Front, his brother Enver led the same number of soldiers: more than half of them died of starvation and disease at the Battle of Sarikamish, making it one of the most tragic events of World War I.
40 DGFP, series D, vol. XIII, no. 361 (Memorandum by the Director of the Political Department, 26 September 1941), 571.
41 Ibid., 572.
42 Ibid., 573.
43 DGFP, series D, vol. XIII, no. 367 (Papen to Ribbentrop, 29 September 1941), 589.
44 Ibid., 591.
45 Ibid., 592.
46 DGFP, series D, vol. XIII, no. 393, p. 632 (Clodius to Ribbentrop, 10 October 1941).
47 Ibid., 642.
48 According to the information provided by Reichsleiter Rosenberg, the Chief of the Prisoner of War Department of the OKW, they were already considering this issue.

49 DGFP, series D, vol. XIII, no. 431, p. 707 (Memorandum by the Director of the Political Department, 28 October 1941).
50 Ibid., 708.
51 Ibid.
52 GPT, 12 (Papen to Ribbentrop, 10 November 1941), 40–2.
53 After another banquet given in Ali Fuad Erden's honour, von Papen received a similar message from Colonel General Fromm. Ibid., 42.
54 Ibid.
55 Having shared Ali Fuad Erden's reflections, von Papen asked Ribbentrop to comply with Fuad's request and said that it would make a very strong impression on Turkey.
56 During the latter period of World War I, Werner Otto von Hentig served as a diplomat at the German Embassy in Constantinople; therefore he was well informed about Turkey's history and politics. He later became actively involved in the German Youth Movement (*Die deutsche Jugendbewegung*) in the 30s.
57 GPT, 13 (Hentig to Erkilet, 17 November 1941), 43–4.
58 Ibid., 44.
59 GPT, 15 (Erkilet to Hentig, 27 November 1941), 47–8.
60 Ibid., 48.
61 Müstecip Ülküsal, *İkinci Dünya Savaşında 1941–1942 Berlin Hatıraları ve Kırım'ın Kurtuluş Davası* (İstanbul: Kurtuluş Matbaası, 1976), 20.
62 *Emel* became the most cherished journal for future pan-Turkists and was a precursor to future ultra-nationalist periodicals. Müstecip Ülküsal, *Kırım Türk-Tatarları: Dünü, Bugünü, Yarını* (İstanbul: Baha Matbaası, 1980), 23.
63 Ibid., 63.
64 Ülküsal, *Berlin Hatıraları*, 88.
65 Ibid., 65–6.
66 Ülküsal, *Berlin Hatıraları*, 88.
67 Nikolai Deker and Andrei Lebed, *Genocide in the USSR: Studies in Group Destruction* (New York: Scarecrow, 1958), 13.
68 T. Murtaza, 'Hakaret yahut Hakikat', *Azat Kırım 61* (1943): 3.
69 Ismail Gaspirali or Gasprinskii (1851–1914) pioneered the Jadid Movement (*Usul-i Cedid*) in Crimea. His nationalism and ideas on modernization, especially with regard to education and language, inspired a new generation of policy-makers in the Turkic World, transcending the boundaries of the Ottoman State and Central Asia. See: Yavuz Akpınar, *Ismail Gaspirali: Seçilmiş Eserleri* (İstanbul: Otuken, 2005).
70 Memet Yakub, 'İlk Uzum', *Azat Kırım 42* (1942): 4.
71 Y. Ziya, 'Azatlikh Bairagi Altinda', *Azat Kırım 17* (1942): 1.
72 Jemil Abdurashidov, 'Bizim Teshekkurimiz', *Azat Kırım 14* (1942): 2.
73 Hüsrev Gerede, „Die deutsch-türkischen Beziehungen", *Zeitschrift für Politik, 32, 1* (January 1942), 1–3.
74 BCA 30.10.0.0/142.14.8 (Gerede's report about Turkish cadets in Nazi Germany, 10 October 1940); also see Hüsrev Gerede, *Harb İçinde Almanya, 1939–1942* (İstanbul: ABC Matbaası, 1994), 41.
75 Ibid., 42.
76 GPT, 14 (Hentig to Woermann, 17 November 1941), 45–6.
77 GPT, 23 (Conversation between Hentig and Harun, 1 June 1942), 76–8.
78 Ibid., 77.
79 Ibid., 78.

80 BCA 030.11.1/156.26.17 (Prime Ministry to the Turkish Embassy in Berlin, 21 August 1941).
81 Gerede, *Harb İçinde Almanya*, 391–406.
82 Ibid.
83 Ibid.
84 FO 421/327 R4933/480/44 (Hugessen to Eden, 15 July 1942).
85 Andrew Brookes, *Air War Over Russia* (London: Ian Allen Publishing, 2003); and Robert Forcyzk, *Sevastopol 1942: Von Manstein's Triumph* (Oxford: Osprey, 2008).
86 GPT, 17 (Memorandum for General Warlimont with Covering Letter by Woermann, 23 January 1942), 61–4.
87 Ali İhsan Sabis, *İkinci Cihan Harbi* (İstanbul: Tan Basımevi, 1943), 245–6.
88 Ibid., 243.
89 Ibid., 242.
90 Ibid.
91 H. Emir Erkilet, *İkinci Cihan Harbi ve Türkiye* (İstanbul: Kenan Matbaası, 1945), 9.
92 Ibid., 12.
93 Ibid., 25.
94 Ibid., 121.
95 Valdis O. Lumans, *Himmler's Auxiliaries: the Volksdeutsche Mittelstelle and the German minorities of Europe, 1933–1945* (Chapel Hill: University of North Carolina Press, 2000); Johann Kampen and Hans Campen, 'Die deutschen Kolonien in der Krim' in *Heimatbuch der Landsmannschaft der Deutschen aus Russland* (1954).
96 GPT, 25 (Dittmann to Tippelskirch, 5 August 1942), 79–81.
97 Nadinskii, *Ocherki po Istorii Kryma*, 46.
98 An inclusive primary source on the subject is *Lubianka*, which brings light into the actual decision-making process of the *Gosudarstvennyi komitet oborony* (GKO) regarding wartime deportations. *Lubyanka* is the last of a three-volume series published in 2006 from the *Mezhdunarodnyi Fond 'Demokratiia'* (MFD). Overall, the MFD series investigates Stalin's leadership and the establishment of the Soviet punitive system, through which Stalin consolidated his regime. The third volume offers a collection of 337 documents on the 1939–46 period gathered from the archives of the Soviet government and the Communist Party organs. A particularly intriguing section in this book is the 'Special Correspondence between Beria, Stalin, Molotov, and Malenkov' about the work of the operational Chekist group in their purge of anti-Soviet elements from the Crimean ASSR. See V.N. Khaustov and V.P. Naumov, *Lubyanka: Stalin i NKVD-NKGB-GUKR 'Smersh' 1939–Mart 1946* (Moscow: MFD, 2006), 423–79.
99 V. N. Khaustov and V.P. Naumov, *Lubyanka: Stalin i NKVD-NKGB-GUKR 'Smersh' 1939– Mart 1946* (Moscow: MFD, 2006), 423.
100 Ibid., 424.
101 Ibid., 427.
102 Ibid.
103 Ibid., 429.
104 Ibid., 430.
105 Ibid.
106 Ibid., 431.
107 Ibid.
108 Ibid., 432–5.
109 The recently published *Sovietskaia povsednevnost' i Mosovoia soznaniye* is a splendid source that looks at the dissolution of the Crimean ASSR in 1945 and draws

similarities between other deportations under Stalin. AA Livshin and IB Arlov, *Sovietskaia Povsednevnost' i Mossovoe Soznanie, 1939–1945* (Moscow: Rosspen, 2003).
110 Ibid., 410–20.
111 Ibid., 420.
112 Ibid.
113 Ibid.
114 For such details see: GARF f.9401, op.2 (various *dela*).
115 *Orhun* (1 March,1944), 1.
116 *Tan* (7 September 1944), 1.
117 John M. VanderLippe, *The Politics of Turkish Democracy: İsmet İnönü and the Formation of the Multi-party System, 1938–1950* (Albany: SUNY Press, 2005), 108–9.
118 Gavin D. Brockett, *How Happy to Call Oneself A Turk: Provincial Newspapers and the Negotiation of a Muslim National Identity* (Austin: University of Texas Press, 2011), 158.
119 DGFP, series D, vol. XII, no. 623, p. 1022 (Ribbentrop to von Papen, 13 June 1941).

Chapter 7

1 The exact number of Soviet casualties in World War II is a subject of historical debate. The most widely accepted statistics are presented in General Grigoriy Krivosheyev's account. Krivosheyev states that the USSR lost approximately 9 million Soviet soldiers and close to 15 million civilians. See Grigoriy Krivosheyev, *Soviet Casualties and Combat Losses* (London: Greenhill, 1997).
2 Richard Overy, *Russia's War: A History of the Soviet War Effort: 1941–1945* (New York: Penguin, 1997).
3 TDA, TSID 140682 (From the Embassy in Berlin to the Foreign Ministry, 9 February 1943); and TDA, TSID 149537 (Report on the Battle of Stalingrad, 10 January 1943).
4 Moiseev, 'SSSR i Turtsiia', 184.
5 *Cumhuriyet* (23 February 1943), 7.
6 BCA 30.10.0.0/232.563.20 (Report of Colonel Sururi Akalin the Turkish Military Attaché in Berlin, 6 July 1943).
7 FO 421/329, R899/899/G (Eden to Knatchbull-Hugessen, 1 January 1944).
8 FO 421/329, R5703/55/44 (Knatchbull-Hugessen to Eden, 1 July 1943).
9 Ibid.
10 FO 421/329, R6564/55/44 (Knatchbull-Hugessen to Eden, 20 July 1943).
11 Ibid.
12 This is not to suggest that İnönü unequivocally trusted Britain's activities in Kurdish-populated areas. On 14 October 1943, the Turkish intelligence prepared a detailed report on Ambassador Knatchbull-Hugessen's recent trip to the Eastern villages, describing when, where and with whom he met, dined or had tea. Knatchbull-Hugessen was accompanied by his wife and deputy chief of mission E. Peckle and his chauffeur F. Cooper. BCA 030.10.0.0./99.641.16 (Minister of Interior's Report on Knatchbull-Hugessen, 14 October 1943).
13 FO 421/329, R12089/55/44 (Helm to Eden, 23 November 1943).
14 BCA 030.10.0.0/104.676.29 (9th Army Corps to the Ministry of Interior, 25 November 1943).
15 TBMM, d. 6, c. 14, b. 1, s. 8 (11 January 1944).

16 FO 406/82, E 7213/41/65 (Cornwallis to Eden, 25 November 1943).
17 BCA 30.11.1.0/150.32.16 (Prime Ministry to General Staff, 25 November 1943).
18 BCA 030.10.0.0/112.752.2 (3rd Army Inspectorate Headquarters to the Prime Ministry, 15 May 1943).
19 BCA 030.10.0.0/248.678.28 (Directorate of Public Security to the Prime Ministry, 1 November 1942).
20 Ibid.
21 This view is clearly reflected in the 1943 Report of Avni Doğan – the Public Inspectorate for Eastern Provinces. See: 'Umum Müfettişi Avni Doğan Raporu', in Hüseyin Yayman, *Turkiye'nin Kürt Sorunu Hafızası* (İstanbul: DK, 2011), 166–75.
22 TDA, TSID 13705107 (Ministry of Foreign Affairs to the Embassy in London, 28 January 1943).
23 FO 421/329, R899/899/G (Eden to Knatchbull-Hugessen, 1 January 1944).
24 Although the meeting was kept secret until after its conclusion, details were later publicized by Turkish newspapers. See, for instance, *Tan* (2 February 1943), 1.
25 TDA, TSID 16749887 (Ministry of Foreign Affairs to the Ministry of Defense, 24 March 1943).
26 Ibid.
27 TDA, TSID 7716040 (Turkish chief of staff to the Ministry of Foreign Affairs, 25 February 1943).
28 TDA, TSID 11902259 (Ministry of Foreign Affairs to the Embassy in London, 13 February 1943).
29 TDA, TSID 16719534 (Ministry of Foreign Affairs to the Embassy in Washington DC, 29 January 1943).
30 Ibid.
31 Rick Atkinson, *An Army at Dawn: The War in North Africa, 1942–1943* (New York: Henry Holt, 2002), 533.
32 The Foreign Relations of the United States (hereafter FRUS), Vol. IV, pp. 1057–1167, *Diplomatic Papers 1943, Near East and Africa* (Report of Ambassador Steinhardt to the Secretary of State, 3 February 1943).
33 Ibid.
34 FRUS, Vol. IV, pp. 1057–1167, *Diplomatic Papers 1943, Near East and Africa* (Report of Ambassador Steinhardt to the Secretary of State, 4 February 1943).
35 Ibid.
36 FRUS, Vol. IV, pp. 1057–1167, *Diplomatic Papers 1943, Near East and Africa* (Clarification of decisions taken at the Casablanca Conference regarding the respective roles of the United States and British Governments in relations with Turkey, 19 June 1943).
37 TDA, TSID 9966953 (Cairo Negotiations, 5 November 1943).
38 Ibid.
39 TDA, TSID 11258130 (Cairo Negotiations, 6 November 1943).
40 Ibid.
41 Ibid.
42 TDA, TSID 138978 (Report on the Tehran Conference, 11 December 1943).
43 Stalin stated that if Turkey found herself at war with Nazi Germany, and as a result Bulgaria declared war on Turkey or attacked her, the Soviet Union would immediately be at war with Bulgaria. TDA 2999716 (Report on the Tehran Conference, 1 December 1943).
44 Antony Beevor, *Stalingrad* (London: Penguin, 1999), 418.

45 Ibid., 419.
46 TDA, TSID 139019 (Turkish Consulate in Beirut to the Ministry of Foreign Affairs, 14 December 1943).
47 TDA, TSID 147647 (Turkish Embassy in Moscow to the Ministry of Foreign Affairs, 15 December 1943).
48 TDA, TSID 11382382 (Report on the Second Cairo Meeting, 4–6 December 1943).
49 Ibid.
50 TDA, TSID 11409710 (Report on the Second Cairo Meeting, 7 December 1943).
51 FRUS, Vol. IV, pp. 691–700, *The Second Cairo Conference* (First Tripartite Meeting of Heads of Government, 4 December 1943).
52 Ibid.
53 BCA 030.01.0.0/40.240.19 (Saraçoğlu to İnönü, 26 September 1943).
54 TBMM, d. 7, c. 16, b. 1, s. 1–7 (İnönü's address at the National Assembly, 1 November 1943).
55 BCA 30.10.0.0/235.588.3 (Ministry of Foreign Affairs Report on Casablanca and Adana Conferences, 11 February 1943).
56 Ibid.
57 Atkinson, *An Army at Dawn*, 534–5.
58 Ibid., 289.
59 Ibid., 290.
60 Ibid.
61 FRUS, Vol. V, pp. 814–917, *Diplomatic Papers 1944: The Near East, South Asia and Africa* (Report of Ambassador Steinhardt to the Secretary of State, 17 January 1944).
62 Ibid. (5 February 1944).
63 Ibid. (16 April 1944).
64 Ibid. (21 April 1944).
65 BCA 30.18.1.2./105.23.15 (Report on the Revised Turco-German Trade Agreements, 4 April 1944).
66 BCA 30.10.0.0./206.408.6 (Prime Ministry to the Foreign Ministry, 24 April 1944).
67 TBMM, d. 7, c. 13, b. 1, s. 1–10 (4 April 1944).
68 Ibid.
69 FRUS, Vol. V, pp. 814–917, *Diplomatic Papers 1944: The Near East, South Asia and Africa* (Report of Ambassador Steinhardt to the Secretary of State, 28 April 1944).
70 FRUS, Vol. V, pp. 814–917, *Diplomatic Papers 1944: The Near East, South Asia and Africa* (Report of Ambassador Steinhardt to the Secretary of State, 24 April 1944).
71 Ibid. (30 April 1944).
72 Ibid. (29 May, 1944).
73 Ibid. (3 June, 1944).
74 Ibid. (7 June, 1944).
75 Emphasis not mine.
76 BCA 030.01.0.0/11.63.8 (Şükrü Saraçoğlu Parliamentary Address, 2 August 1944).
77 Ibid.
78 Ibid.
79 FRUS, Vol. V, pp. 814–917, *Diplomatic Papers 1944: The Near East, South Asia and Africa* (Report of Ambassador Steinhardt to the Secretary of State, 1 July 1944).
80 Ibid.
81 Ibid. (4 July 1944).
82 BCA 030.01.00/232.563.20 (Turkish Naval Attaché in Berlin to the Prime Ministry, 14 May 1944).

83 BCA 030.01.0.0/11.63.8 (Şükrü Saraçoğlu Parliamentary Address, 2 August 1944).
84 British diplomat Sir Frank Roberts, who served as British chargé d'affaires in Moscow, later described Vyshinsky as 'a quick, clever and efficient [diplomat] who always knew his dossier well'. But Roberts also added that whereas he had 'a certain unwilling respect for Molotov', he had none at all for Vyshinsky. All Soviet officials at that time had no choice but to carry out Stalin's policies without asking too many questions, but 'Vyshinsky above all' gave Roberts the impression of 'a cringing toadie only too anxious to obey His Master's Voice even before it had expressed his wishes'. Sir Frank Roberts quoted in Arkady Vaksberg, *Stalin's Prosecutor: The Life of Andrei Vyshinsky* (New York: Grove Weidenfeld, 1990), 252.
85 FRUS, Vol. V, pp. 814–917, *Diplomatic Papers 1944: The Near East, South Asia and Africa* (Report of Ambassador Steinhardt to the Secretary of State, 30 July 1944).
86 TDA, TSID 88196 (Embassy in Washington DC to the Ministry in Ankara, 19 August 1944).
87 FRUS, Vol. V, pp. 814–917, *Diplomatic Papers 1944: The Near East, South Asia and Africa* (Ambassador Steinhardt to the Department of State, 13 September 1944).
88 TDA, TSID 177030 (Embassy in Washington DC to the Ministry of Foreign Affairs, 14 August 1944).
89 BCA 30.18.1.2/107.99.3 (Appointment of Cevat Acikalin, 2 September 1944).
90 Ibid.
91 Ibid.
92 TBMM, d. 7, c. 14, b. 2, s. 1–7 (1 November 1944).
93 TDA, TSID 138826 (Turkish Embassy in Washington DC to the Ministry of Foreign Affairs, 11 August 1944).

Epilogue

1 Nilay Kan Büyükişliyen, 'Pietro Cannonica müzesi, sanatı ve anıları', *Gençsanat, 73* (September 2000), 10–12.
2 Weber, *The Evasive Neutral*, 218–19.
3 Ibid.
4 Deringil, *An Active Neutrality*, 184.
5 Ibid., 185.
6 TBMM, d. 9, c. 18, b.5, s. 24 (11 June 1945).
7 'Turkey To-day', in *Bulletin of International News*, 21, 9 (29 April 1944), 335–41.
8 Ibid.
9 Ibid.
10 TBMM, d. 9, c. 17, b.4, s. 22 (5 May 1945).
11 Ibid.
12 BCA 30.10.0.0/61.413.16 (Report of the Turkish General Staff regarding deficiencies of the Turkish Army, 6 June 1944).
13 Harp Akademileri Komutanlığı, *Harp Akademilerinin 120 Yılı* (İstanbul, 1968), 26.
14 'Turkey To-day', in *Bulletin of International News*, 21, 9 (29 April 1944), 335–41.
15 Ibid., 46.
16 TBMM, d. 9, c. 18, b.5, s. 24 (11 June 1945).
17 A.C. Edwards, 'The Impact of the War on Turkey', *International Affairs*, 22, 3 (July 1946); 389–400, here 390.

18 Winston S. Churchill, *The Second World War, VI, Triumph and Tragedy* (Boston: Houghton Mifflin Company, 1953), 242; Harry N. Howard, 'The United States and the Problem of the Turkish Straits', *The Middle East Journal*, 1, 1 (1947); 59–72, here 68.
19 TDA, TSIDs 128023,12319390, 156099, and 156116 (Yalta Files, February 1945).
20 FRUS, *The Conferences at Malta and Yalta* (The President's Log at Yalta, Seventh Plenary Session, 10 February 1945), Vol. III, pp. 814–987.
21 Ibid.
22 TDA, TSID 68095 (Turkish Prime Ministry to the Ministry of Foreign Affairs, 21 March 1945).
23 TDA, TSID 144707 (Report on the Soviet Press, 4 April 1945).
24 TDA, TSID 4903865 (Report on *Pravda*, 9 April 1945).
25 TDA, TSID 4903858 (Report on *Izvestiia*, 14 May 1945).
26 *New York Times* (24 February 1945), 1; (28 February 1945), 18.
27 TBMM, d. 8, c. 20, b.1, s. 4 (11 March 1945).
28 TBMM, d. 7, c. 14, b.1, s. 8 (1 November 1945).
29 TBMM, d. 7, c. 19, b.2, s. 16 (15 August 1945).
30 Ibid.
31 FRUS, *The Conferences at Malta and Yalta* (The President's Log at Yalta, Seventh Plenary Session, 10 February 1945), Vol.III, pp.814-987.
32 Ibid.
33 TDA, TSID 16992881 (Molotov–Sarper Meeting, Minutes, 7 June 1945).
34 TDA, TSID 16992896 (Molotov–Sarper Meeting, First Report, 9 June 1945).
35 Ibid.
36 Ibid.
37 TDA, TSID 16992906 (Molotov–Sarper Meeting, Second Report, 9 June 1945).
38 Vojtech Mastny, *Russia's Road to the Cold War* (New York: Columbia University Press, 1979), 289.
39 The story of post-war Armenian repatriation has received considerable attention in recent historical scholarship. Ron Suny, Simon Payaslian and others have offered succinct accounts in their general histories of Armenia and have drawn attention to the significance of this episode. More recently, Susan Pattie, Razmik Panossian and Joanne Laycock have emphasized the need for further investigation. As Laycock claims, the subject has almost exclusively been addressed within the framework of an Armenian tragedy after Stalin's termination of the repatriation programme, when he ordered the deportation of 2,754 Armenian families (12,300 people), who were exiled to the Altay region in 1949, inflicting yet another wound in Armenia's troubled national history.
40 Zubok, *A Failed Empire*, 36–40; and Hassanli, *SSSR – Turtsiya*, 134–49.
41 Zubok, *A Failed Empire*, 40.
42 BCA 030.01/101.634.3 (Press Directorate to the Prime Ministry on Georgian Claims, 7 January 1946).
43 Zubok, *A Failed Empire*, 42.
44 See for instance, BCA 030.01.0.0/101.623.4; BCA 030.01.0.0/101.623.6; BCA 030.01.0.0/101.626.6; and BCA 030.01.0.0/87.573.6.
45 Sabiha Sertel, *Roman Gibi* (İstanbul: Belge, 1987), 304–23; and Zekeriya Sertel, *Hatırladıklarım* (İstanbul: Remzi, 2001), 185–215.
46 BCA 030.01.0.0/60.368.8 (Ministry of Foreign Affairs to the Prime Ministry, 29 January 1946).
47 Ibid.

48 BCA 030.01.0.0/101.624.3 (Directorate of Press to the Prime Ministry, 18 June 1946).
49 Ibid.
50 Cevat Açıkalın, "Turkey's International Relations," *International Affairs,* 23, 4 (October 1947): 477–91.
51 Ibid., 487.
52 Ibid., 489.
53 Ibid., 491.
54 Necmeddin Sadak, 'Turkey Faces the Soviets', *Foreign Affairs,* 27, 3 (April 1949): 449–61.
55 Ibid., 458.
56 Ibid., 459.
57 FO 406/82, E 871/41/65 (Furlonge to Spears, 21 January 1944).
58 TBMM, d. 8, c. 17, b.53, s. 8 (11 April 1945).
59 Litvinov's statement at the Pera Palace, *Cumhuriyet* (26 October 1931).
60 *Khrushchev Remembers: The Last Testament* (Boston: Little, Brown, 1974), 295–6.
61 BCA 30.10.0.0/61.376.17 (Molotov's Note to the Turkish Ambassador in Moscow, 30 May 1953).
62 BCA 30.01.0.0/37.226.7 (Conversation with the Soviet Ambassador, 1955).
63 BCA 30.01.0.0/16.85.4 (Turkish Prime Minister Adnan Menderes's NATO Speech, 16 December 1957).
64 The Soviet Union provided Turkey with financial and logistical support in several important projects, including the Çayırova Glass Factory (1959); the Seydişehir Aluminum Factory (1973); the Aliağa Petroleum Refinery (1972); and the Arpaçay Reservoir (1983).

Bibliography

Archives

Arkhiv vneshnei politiki Rossiiskoi Federatsii (AVP-RF), Moscow.
Başbakanlık Cumhuriyet Arşivleri (BCA), Ankara.
Rossiiskii gosudarstvennyi arkhiv sotsial no-politicheskoi istorii (RGASPI), Moscow.
Rossiiskii gosudarstvennyi arkhiv ekonomiki (RGAE), Moscow.
Rossiiskii gosudarstvennyi voennyi arkhiv (RGVA), Moscow.
The National Archives (TNA), College Park, Maryland.
The Public Record Office (FO), London.
Türk Diplomatik Arşivi (TDA), Ankara.

Newspapers and periodicals

Al-Ahram
Azat Kırım
Cumhuriyet
DNB
Emel
Hakimiyet-i Milliye
Izvestiia
Krasnaya Zvezda
New York Times
Pravda
Resmi Gazete
Tan
Ulus
Vatan

Official publications and document collections

A Manual on the Turanians and Pan-Turanism. London: H.M. Stationery Office, 1918.
Atatürk'ün Bütün Eserleri. İstanbul: Kaynak Yayınları, 1998–2011.
Atatürk'ün Milli Dış Politikası: Cumhuriyet Dönemine Ait 100 Belge, 1923–1938. Ankara: Kültür Bakanlığı Yayınları, 1992.
Atatürk'un Söylev ve Demeçleri. Ankara: Türk Tarih Kurumu Basımevi, 1989.
Cumhurbaşkanları'nın Türkiye Büyük Milli Meclisini Açış Nutukları. İstanbul: Baha Matbaası, 1969.
Documents on British Foreign Policy (DBFP. London: H.M. Stationery Office, 1954.

Documents on German Foreign Policy (DGFP). Berlin: Auswärtiges Amt, 1949.
Dokumenty Ministerstva inostrannykh del. Germanii, vyp II: Germanskaia politika v Turtsii (GPT). Moscow: Gospolitizdat, 1946.
Dokumenty vneshnei politiki SSSR (DVP). Moscow: Politizdat, 1970.
Foreign Relations of the United States (FRUS). Washington DC: GPO, 1952.
The League of Nations: Treaties of Peace, 1919-1923, Vol. II. New York: Carnegie Endowment for International Peace, 1924.
Türkiye Büyük Millet Meclisi Zabıt Ceridesi (TBMM). Ankara: TBMM, 1983.
Türk Boğazları ile İlgili Temel Metinler. Ankara: Dışişleri Bakanlığı Yayınları, 1995.

Memoirs and contemporary publications

Açıkalın, Cevat. 'Turkey's International Relations', *International Affairs*, 23, 4 (October 1947): 477–91.
Aralov, Semen. *Vospominaniia sovetskogo diplomata*. Moscow: 1960.
Arıkoğlu, Damar. *Hatıralarım*. İstanbul: Tan Gazetesi ve Matbaası, 1961.
Atay, Falih Rıfkı. Çankaya: *Atatürk'ün Doğumundan Ölümüne Kadar*. İstanbul: Pozitif Yayınları, 2009.
Yeni Rusya. Ankara: Hakimiyeti Milliye Matbaası, 1931.
Aydemir, Şevket Süreyya. *İkinci Adam: İsmet İnönü*. İstanbul: Yükselen Matbaası, 1966.
Suyu Arayan Adam. İstanbul: Remzi Kitabevi, 1965.
Barutçu, F.A. *Siyasi Anılar, 1939-1954*. İstanbul: Milliyet, 1977.
Cebesoy, Ali Fuad. *Moskova Hatıraları (21/11/1920-2/6/1922)*. İstanbul: Vatan Neşriyatı, 1955.
Chicherin, Georgii. *Istoricheskii ocherk diplomaticheskoi deiatel'nosti A. M. Gorchakova*. Edited by V.L. Telitsyn. Moscow: Liubimaia Rossiia, 2009.
Churchill, Winston S. *The Second World War: VI – Triumph and Tragedy*. Boston: Houghton Mifflin Company, 1953.
Ciano, Count Galeazzo. *The Ciano Diaries*. New York: Howard Fertig, 1973.
Erkilet, H. Emir. *İkinci Cihan Harbi ve Türkiye*. İstanbul: Kenan Matbaası, 1945.
Ertem, Sadri. *Sovyet Rusya Hatıralarım*. İstanbul: Tarih ve Toplum Kitaplığı, 1989.
Gaspirali, İsmail. *Seçilmiş Eserleri*. Istanbul: Otuken, 2005.
Gerede, Hüsrev. 'Die deutsch-türkischen Beziehungen', *Zeitschrift für Politik* 32, 1 (January 1942), 1–3.
Harb İçinde Almanya, 1939-1942. İstanbul: ABC Matbaası, 1994.
Gökalp, Ziya. *Türkçülüğün Esasları*. İstanbul: İlmi Türkçülük Yayınları, 1940.
İnönü, İsmet. *Hatıralar*. Ankara: Bilgi Yayınevi, 1985.
İsmet Paşanın Siyasi ve İçtimai Nutukları, 1920-1933. Ankara: Başvekalet Matbaası, 1933.
İsmet İnönü'nün TBMM'deki Konuşmaları, 1920-1973. Volume 1. Ankara: TBMM Kültür, Sanat ve Yayın Kurulu Yayınları, 1992.
Karabekir, Kazim. *İstiklal Harbımız*. İstanbul: 1969.
Lansere, E. E. *Leto v Angore*. Leningrad: Izdatel'stvo Brokgauz-Efron, 1925.
Madanoğlu, C. *Anılar, 1911-1953*. İstanbul: Evrim, 1982.
Molotov, V. M. *O vneshnei politike Sovetskogo Soiuza: doklad*. Leningrad: Gos. izd-vo polit. lit-ry, 1939.
Nur, Riza. *Dr. Riza Nur'un Moskova/Sakarya Hatıraları*. İstanbul: Boğazi.i Yayınları, 1991.
von Papen, F. *Der Wahrheit eine Gasse*. Innsbruck, 1952.
von Papen, F. *Memoires*. Paris: Hammorion, 1953.

Pavlenko, Petr. *Stambul i Turtsiia*. Moscow: Federatsiia, 1927.
Sabis, Ali İhsan. *İkinci Cihan Harbi*. İstanbul: Tan Basımevi, 1943.
Sadak, Necmeddin. 'Turkey Faces the Soviets', *Foreign Affairs*, 27, 3 (April 1949): 449-61.
Sertel, Sabiha. *Roman Gibi*. İstanbul: Belge, 1987.
Sertel, Zekeriya. *Hatırladıklarım*. İstanbul: Remzi, 2001.
Stoddard, T. Lothrop. 'Pan-Turanism', *The American Political Science Review*, 11, 1 (February 1917): 12-23.
Truman, Harry S. *Memoirs: Years of Trial and Hope, 1946-1952*. New York: Signet, 1965.
Toynbee, Arnold. 'The East after Lausanne', *Foreign Affairs*, 2, 1 (15 September 1923): 84-98.
Ülküsal, Müstecip. *İkinci Dünya Savaşında 1941-1942: Berlin Hatıraları ve Kırım'ın Kurtuluş Davası*. Istanbul: Kurtuluş Matbaası, 1976.
Ülküsal, Müstecip. *Kırım Türk-Tatarları: Dünü, Bugünü, Yarını*. Istanbul: Baha Matbaası, 1980.
Zhukovskii, P. M. *Zemledel'cheskaia Turtsiia*. Leningrad: 1933.

Secondary sources

Ahmad, Kamal Madhar. *Kurdistan During the First World War*. London: Saqi Books, 2001.
Aksakal, Mustafa. *The Ottoman Road to War in 1914: The Ottoman Empire and the First World War*. Cambridge: Cambridge University Press, 2008.
Aleksandr Gerasimovich Dongarov. *Inostrannyi capital v Rossi i SSSR*. Moscow: Mezhdunarodnye Otnosheniia, 1990.
Allworth, Edward A., et. al., *The Tatars of Crimea: Return to Homeland*. Durham: Duke University Press, 1998.
Ancel, Jean. *The History of the Holocaust in Romania*. Nebraska: Yad Vashem, 2011.
Andereopulos, George J., ed. *Conceptual and Historical Dimensions of Genocide*. Philadelphia: University of Pennsylvania Press, 1994.
Arıkan, Zeki. *Tarihimiz ve Cumhuriyet: Muhittin Birgen, 1885-1951*. İstanbul: Türkiye Ekonomik ve Toplumsal Tarih Vakfı, 1997.
Armaoglu, Fahir. 'Türkiye'nin Hitler Almanya'sı ile İlişkileri, 1931-1941'. In *Çağdaş Türk Diplomasisi Sempozyumu: 200 Yıllık Süreç*. TTK: Ankara, 1997.
Aslan, Yavuz. *Mustafa Kemal-M. Frunze Görüşmeleri: Türk-Sovyet İlişkilerinde Zirve*. İstanbul: Kaynak Yayınları, 2001.
Atabaki, Touraj and Zurcher, Erik, eds. *Men of Order: Authoritarian Modernization under Atatürk and Reza Shah*. New York: Tauris, 2004.
Ataöv, Türkkaya. *Turkish Foreign Policy, 1939-1945*. Ankara: SBF, 1964.
—— *İkinci Dünya Savaşı*. İstanbul: İleri Yayınları, 2008.
Atkinson, Rick. *An Army at Dawn: The War in North Africa, 1942-1943*. New York: Henry Holt, 2002.
Avcıoğlu, Doğan. *Milli Kurtuluş Tarihi*, İstanbul, 1995.
Aybay, Rona. *Karşılaştırmalı 1961 Anayasası*. İstanbul: Fakülte Matbaası, 1963.
Aytürk, İlker. 'The Racist Critics of Atatürk and Kemalism, from the 1930s to the 1960s', *Journal of Contemporary History*, 40 (2): 308-35.
Badem, Candan. *Çarlık Rusyası Yönetiminde Kars Vilayeti*. İstanbul: Birzamanlar Yayıncılık, 2010.
Bagirov, Sabit. 'Azerbaijani Oil: Glimpses of a Long History', *Perceptions*, 1, 2 (June 1996): 22-34.

Barkey, Karen, and Mark von Hagen, eds. *After Empire: Multiethnic Societies and Nation-Building: The Soviet Union and Russian, Ottoman, and Habsburg Empires*. Boulder: Westview Press, 1997.
Baran, Zeyno. *Torn Country: Turkey between Secularism and Islamism*. Stanford: Hoover Institution Press, 2010.
Barker, A.J. *Rape of Ethiopia, 1936*. London: Ballantine Books, 1971.
Barlas, Dilek. 'Turkish Diplomacy in the Balkans and the Mediterranean. Opportunities and Limits for Middle-Power Activism in the 1930s', *Journal of Contemporary History*, 40, 3 (July 2005): 441–64.
Basov, Aleksandr Mikhailovich. *Krym v Velikoi otechestvennoi voine 1941–1945*. Moscow: Nauka, 1987.
Baturin, Yuriy. *Dose Razvedchika*. Moskva: Molodaya Gvardiya, 2005.
Beaumont, Joan. 'Great Britain and the Rights of Neutral Countries: The Case of Iran, 1941', *Journal of Contemporary History*, 16, 1 (January 1981); 213–28.
Beevor, Antony. *Stalingrad*. London: Penguin, 1999.
Bekirova, Gulnara. *Krymskotatarskaya problema v SSSR: 1944–1991*. Simferopol: Odzhak, 2004.
Belinkov S., and I. Vasil'ev. *O Turetskom 'Neitralitete' vo vremia Vtoroi Mirovoi Voiny*. Moscow: Gospolitizdat, 1952.
Berkes, Niyazi. *The Development of Secularism in Turkey*. Montreal: McGill University Press, 1964.
Beşikçi, İsmail. *Tunceli Kanunu (1935) ve Dersim Jenosidi*. İstanbul: Belge Yayınları, 1990.
Beyru, Rauf. *Levantenler ve Levantizm*. İstanbul: Bağlam Yayınları, 2000.
Bezugolniy, A.Y. 'Ni Voyni, Ni Mira', *Voenno-istoricheskii arkhiv*, No. 5 (May 2003): 67–73.
Bilgin, Mustafa. *Britain and Turkey in the Middle East*. New York: I.B. Tauris, 2007.
Blake, Kristen. *The US–Soviet Confrontation in Iran, 1945–1962*. New York: University Press of America, 2009.
Bobroff, Ronald P. *Late Imperial Russia and the Turkish Straits: Roads to Glory*. New York: I.B. Tauris, 2006.
Brockett, Gavin D. *How Happy to Call Oneself a Turk: Provincial Newspapers and the Negotiation of a Muslim National Identity*. Austin: University of Texas Press, 2011.
Brookes, Andrew. *Air War Over Russia*. London: Ian Allen Publishing, 2003.
Bruinessen, Martin van. *Agha, Shaikh and State: On the Social and Political Organization of Kurdistan*. Utrecht: University of Utrecht, 1978.
Budak, Mustafa. *Misak-ı Millî'den Lozan'a: İdealden Gerçeğe Türk Dış Politika*. İstanbul: Küre Yayınları, 2008.
Büyükişliyen, Nilay Kan. 'Pietro Cannonica müzesi, sanatı ve anıları', *Gençsanat* 73 (September, 2000), 10–12.
Cagaptay, Soner. *Islam, Secularism, and Nationalism in Modern Turkey: Who is a Turk?* New York: Routldege, 2006.
Chaliand, Gerard. *The Kurdish Tragedy*. New York: Palgrave, 1994.
Chaney, Otto Preston. *Zhukov*. Norman: University of Oklahoma Press, 1971.
Chuev, S.G. 'Kavkazskaya Karta Germanii', *Voenno-Istoricheskiy Arkhiv*, No. 1 (2004): 39–45.
Çelebi, Mevlüt. 'Başvekil İsmet Paşa'nın İtalya Seyahati', *Tarih İncelemeleri*, 22, 2, (December 2007): 21–52.
David-Fox, Michael. 'On the Primacy of Ideology: Soviet Revisionists and Holocaust Deniers (In Response to Martin Malia)', *Kritika: Explorations in Russian and Eurasian History* 5, 1 (Winter 2004): 81–105.

David-Fox, Michael. *Showcasing the Great Experiment: Cultural Diplomacy and Western Visitors to the Soviet Union, 1921-1941*. Oxford: Oxford University Press, 2011.
Debo, Richard. *Survival and Consolidation: The Foreign Policy of Soviet Russia, 1918-1921*. Montreal: McGill-Queen's University Press, 1992.
Deker, Nikolai and Andrei Lebed. *Genocide in the USSR: Studies in Group Destruction*. New York: Scarecrow, 1958.
Deringil, Selim *Turkish Foreign Policy During the Second World War: An Active Neutrality*. Cambridge: Cambridge University Press, 1989.
Deringil, Selim. *The Well-Protected Domains: Ideology and the Legitimation of Power in the Ottoman Empire, 1876-1909*. London: I.B. Tauris, 1998.
Deringil, Selim. '"They Live in a State of Nomadism and Savagery": The Late Ottoman Empire and the Post-Colonial Debate', *Comparative Studies in Society and History*, 45, 2 (April 2003): 311-42.
Dumont, Paul. 'The Origins of Kemalist Ideology.' In Jacob M. Landau (ed.), *Atatürk and the Modernization of Turkey*. Leiden: E.J. Brill, 1984, 25-44.
Edwards, A.C. 'The Impact of the War on Turkey', *International Affairs*, 22, 3 (July 1946): 389-400.
Egorova, N.I. and A.O. Chubaryan. *Kholodnaya Voina, 1945-1965*. Moscow, 2003.
Entessar, Nader. *Kurdish Ethnonationalism*. Colorado: Lynne Rienner, 1992.
Findley, Carter Vaughan. *Bureaucratic Reform in the Ottoman Empire: The Sublime Porte, 1789-1922*. Princeton: Princeton University Press, 1980.
Findley, Carter Vaughan. *Ottoman Civil Officialdom: A Social History*. Princeton: Princeton University Press, 1989.
Findley, Carter Vaughan. *Turkey, Islam, Nationalism, and Modernity: A History, 1789-2007*. New Haven: Yale University Press, 2010.
Forcyzk, Robert. *Sevastopol 1942: Von Manstein's Triumph*. Oxford: Osprey, 2008.
Fox, Annette Baker. *The Power of Small States: Diplomacy in World War II*. Chicago: University of Chicago Press, 1959.
Frantz, Douglas and Catherine Collins. *Death on the Black Sea: The Untold Story of the Struma and World War II's Holocaust at Sea*. New York: HarperCollins, 2003.
Gaddis, John Lewis. *We Now Know: Rethinking Cold War History*. New York: Oxford University Press, 1998.
Gerede, Hüsrev. *Harb İçinde Almanya (1939-1942)*. İstanbul: ABC Yayınları, 2006.
Geyer, Dietrich. *Russian Imperialism: The Interaction of Domestic and Foreign Policy, 1860-1914*. Translated by Bruce Little. New Haven: Yale University Press, 1987.
Gorkov, Y. *Kavkaz vystoyal, Kavkaz pobedil, veterany vspominayut*. Tbilisi, 1973.
Gorkov, Y. *Gosudarstvennyi komitet oborona postanovliaet, 1941-1945*. Moscow, 2002.
Gorlizki, Yoram and Oleg Khleniuk. *Cold Peace: Stalin and the Soviet Ruling Circle, 1945-1953*. New York: Oxford University Press, 2004.
Gorodetsky, Gabriel. *Grand Delusion: Stalin and the German Invasion of Russia*. New Haven: Yale University Press, 1999.
Govrin, Yosef. *Israeli-Soviet Relations, 1953-1967*. New York: Routledge, 1998.
Govrin, Yosef. *Israeli-Romanian Relations at the End of the Ceausescu Era*. New York: Routledge, 2002.
Gökay, Bülent. *Soviet Eastern Policy and Turkey, 1920-1991: Soviet Foreign Policy, Turkey, and Communism*. London: Routledge, 2006.
Gökay, Bülent. 'Turkish Settlement and the Caucasus, 1918-1920', *Middle Eastern Studies*, 32, 2 (April 1996): 45-76.

Göksü, Saime, and Edward Timms. *Romantic Communist: The Life and Work of Nazım Hikmet*. New York: St Martin's Press, 1999.
Gönlübol, Mehmet and Cem Sar. *Atatürk ve Türkiye'nin Dış Politikası*. İstanbul: Milli Eğitim Basımevi, 1963.
Grant, Bruce. *In the Soviet House of Culture: A Century of Perestroikas*. Princeton: Princeton University Press, 1995.
Gross, Stephen G. *Export Empire: German Soft-Power in Southeastern Europe, 1890–1945*. Cambridge: Cambridge University Press 2015.
Guseinov, Mirza-Davud. *Turskaia Demokraticheskaia Partiia Federalistov 'Musavat' v proshlom i nastoiashchem*. Tiflis, 1927.
Guttstadt, Corry. *Die Turkei, die Juden und der Holocaust*. Berlin and Hamburg: Assoziation A, 2008.
Güçlü, Yücel. 'The Uneasy Relationship: Turkish Foreign Policy Towards the Soviet Union at the Outbreak of the Second World War', *The Turkish Yearbook* (XXVIII): 106–38.
Güçlü, Yücel. *The Question of the Sanjak of Alexandretta: A Study in Turkish–French–Syrian Relations*. Ankara: Türk Tarih Kurumu, 2001.
Gürkan, İhsan. 'Turkish Iraqi Relations: The Cold War and Its Aftermath.' In İsmail Soysal (ed.), *Turkish Review of Middle East Studies*. İstanbul: Isis, 1994.
Gürün, Kamuran. *Türk–Sovyet İlişkileri, 1920–1953*. Ankara: TTK, 1993.
Hale, William. 'Ideology and Economic Development in Turkey, 1930–1945.' *Bulletin* (British Society for Middle Eastern Studies), 7, 2 (1980): 100–17.
Hale, William. *Turkish Foreign Policy, 1774–2000*. London: Frank Cass, 2000.
Hanioğlu, Şükrü M. *The Young Turks in Opposition*. Oxford: Oxford University Press, 1995.
Hanioğlu, Şükrü M. *Preparation for Revolution: The Young Turks, 1902–1908*. Oxford: Oxford University Press, 2001.
Hanioğlu, Şükrü M. *A Brief History of the Late Ottoman Empire*. Princeton: Princeton University Press, 2008.
Hanioğlu, Şükrü M. *Atatürk: An Intellectual Biography*. Princeton: Princeton University Press, 2011.
Harris, George. *The Origins of Communism in Turkey*. Stanford: The Hoover Institution, 1967.
Hasanli, Jamil. *SSSR-Turtsiia: Ot neitraliteta k kholodnoi voine, 1939–1953*. Moscow: Tsentr propagandy, 2008.
Hasanli, Jamil. *SSSR–Iran: Azerbaidzhanskii Krizis i Nachalo Kholodnoi Voiny*. Moscow: Geroi Otechestvo, 2006.
Haslam, Jonathan. *Soviet Foreign Policy, 1930–1933: The Impact of the Great Depression*. New York: St Martin's Press, 1983.
Haslam, Jonathan. *Russia's Cold War: From the October Revolution to the Fall of the Wall*. New Haven: Yale University Press, 2011.
Heikal, Mohamed. *The Sphinx and the Commissar: The Rise and Fall of Soviet Influence in the Middle East*. New York: Harper & Row, 1978.
Hemsley Langrigg, Stephen. *Syria and Lebanon Under French Mandate*. New York: Octagon Books, 1972.
Heper, Metin. *İsmet İnönü: The Making of a Turkish Statesman*. Leiden: Brill, 1998.
Hershlag, Zvi Yehuda. *Turkey: An Economy in Tradition*. The Hague: Uigeverij Van Keulen N.V., 1958.
Hirsch, Francine. *Empire of Nations: Ethnographic Knowledge & the Making of the Soviet Union*. Ithaca: Cornell University Press, 2005.
Hirst, Samuel J. 'Anti-Westernism on the European Periphery: The Meaning of Soviet-Turkish Convergence in the 1930s', *Slavic Review*, 72, 1 (Spring 2013): 32–53.

Hobsbawm, Eric. *Age of Extremes: The Short Twentieth Century, 1914-1991.* London: Abacus, 1995.
Howard, Harry N. 'The Straits after the Montreux Conference', *Foreign Affairs*, 15, 1 (October 1936): 199-202.
Howard, Harry N. 'The United States and the Problem of the Turkish Straits', *The Middle East Journal*, 1, 1 (1947): 59-72.
İnan, Yüksel. *Türk Boğazlarının Siyasal ve Hukuksal Rejimi.* Ankara: Turhan Kitabevi, 1995.
Jenkins, Jennifer. 'Iran in the Nazi New Order, 1933-1941', *Iranian Studies*, 49, 5 (2016): 727-51.
Jwaideh, Wadie. *The Kurdish National Movement.* New York: Syracuse University Press, 2006.
Kampen, Johann and Hans Campen. 'Die deutschen Kolonien in der Krim.' In *Heimatbuch der Landsmannschaft der Deutschen aus Russland* (1954).
Karpat, Kemal. *Turkey's Politics: The Transition to a Multi-Party System.* Princeton: Princeton University Press, 1959.
Kayali, Hasan. *Arabs and Young Turks.* Berkeley: University of California Press, 1997.
Kezer, Zeynep. 'The Making of Early Republican Ankara', *Architectural Design*, 80, 1 (2010): 40-5.
Khaustov V. N., and V.P. Naumov. *Lubianka: Stalin i NKVD-NKGB-GUKR 'Smersh' 1939-Mart 1946.* Moscow: MFD, 2006.
Kırımlı, Hakan. *National Movements and National Identity Among the Crimean Tatars.* New York: Brill, 1996.
Kochkin, N.V. 'SSSR, Angliya, SShA i "Turetskii Krizis" 1945-1947 gg', *Novaya i Noveishaya Istoriya*, 3 (2002): 65-75.
Koçak, Cemil. *Umumi Mufettişlikler.* İstanbul: İletişim, 2003.
Koçak, Cemil. 'İkinci Dünya Savaşı ve Türk Basını', *Tarih ve Toplum*, 35 (November 1986): 29-33.
Koptevskii, V.N. *Rossiia-Turtsiia: Etapy torgovo-ekonomicheskogo sotrudinichestva* Moscow: 2003.
Krivosheyev, Grigoriy. *Soviet Casualties and Combat Losses.* London: Greenhill, 1997.
Kuniholm, Bruce. *The Origins of the Cold War in the Near East: Great Power Conflict and Diplomacy in Iran, Turkey and Greece.* Princeton: Princeton University Press, 1980.
Kuruç, Bilsay. *Mustafa Kemal Döneminde Ekonomi.* Ankara: Bilgi Yayınevi, 1987.
Lenczowski, George. *Russia and the West in Iran, 1918-1948: A Study in Big Power Rivalry.* Ithaca, 1949.
Livshin, A.A., and I.B. Arlov. *Sovietskaia Povsednevnost' i Mossovoe Soznanie, 1939-1945.* Moscow: Rosspen, 2003.
Lumans, Valdis O. *Himmler's Auxiliaries: the Volksdeutsche Mittelstelle and the German Minorities of Europe, 1933-1945.* The University of North Carolina Press, 2000.
Malia, Martin E. *Russia Under Western Eyes: From the Bronze Horseman to the Lenin Mausoleum.* Cambridge: Harvard University Press, 1999.
Malia, Martin E. *The Soviet Tragedy: A History of Socialism in Russia, 1917-1991.* New York: The Free Press, 1994.
Mango, Andrew. *Atatürk.* London: John Murray, 1999.
Mardin, Şerif. *The Genesis of Young Ottoman Thought: A Study in the Modernization of Turkish Political Ideas.* Princeton: Princeton University Press, 1962.
Mark, Edward M. 'Allied Relations in Iran, 1941-1947', *The Wisconsin Magazine of History*, 59, 1 (Autumn 1975): 51-63.
Martin, Terry. *Affirmative Action Empire: Nations and Nationalism in the Soviet Union, 1923-1939.* Ithaca: Cornell Unviersity Press, 2001.

Marzari, Frank. 'Western-Soviet Rivalry in Turkey', *Middle Eastern Studies*, 7, 1 (January 1971): 63-79.
Mastny, Vojtech. *The Cold War and Soviet Insecurity: The Stalin Years*. New York: Oxford University Press, 1996.
Mastny, Vojtech. *Russia's Road to the Cold War*. New York: Columbia University Press, 1979.
Mazower, Mark. *Dark Continent: Europe's Twentieth Century*. New York: Vintage Books, 2000.
Mazower, Mark *Inside Hitler's Greece: The Experience of Occupation, 1941-44*. New Haven: Yale University Press, 2001.
Miller, A.F. *Otcherki noveishei istorii turtsii*. Moscow: Gos-politizdat, 1948.
Millman, Brock. 'Credit and Supply in Turkish Foreign Policy and the Tripartite Alliance of October 1939', *The International History Review*, 16, 1 (February 1994): 70-80.
Moiseev, P.P. 'SSSR i Turtsiia v gody Vtoroi Mirovoi Voiny (1939-1945).' In E.M. Zhukov, et. al., *SSSR i Turtsiia, 1917-1979*. Moscow: Nauka, 1981.
Motter, T.H. Vail. *The United States Army in World War II: The Persian Corridor and Aid to Russia*. Washington, 1952.
Nadinskii, P.N. *Ocherki po Istorii Kryma IV*. Simferopol: Tavria, 1967.
Naimark, Norman. *Fires of Hatred*. Cambridge, MA: Harvard University Press, 2001.
Neumark, F. *Zuflucht am Bosphorus: deutsche Gelehrte, Politiker und Künstler in der Emigration, 1933-1953*. Frankfurt: Knecht, 1995.
Nureddin, Vala. *Bu Dünyadan Nazım Geçti*. İstanbul: Remzi Kitabevi, 1969.
O'Connor, Timothy Edward. *Diplomacy and Revolution: G.V. Chicherin and Soviet Foreign Affairs, 1918-1930*. Ames: Iowa State University Press, 1988.
Olson, Robert W. *The Emergence of Kurdish Nationalism and the Sheikh Said Rebellion, 1880-1925*. Texas: University of Texas Press, 1989.
Oran, Baskın, ed. *Türk Dış Politikası: Kurtuluş Savaşından Bugüne Olgular, Belgeler, Yorumlar*. İstanbul: İletişim, 2008.
Oran, Baskın. 'İç ve Dış Politika İlişkisi Açısından İkinci Dünya Savaşında Türkiye'de Siyasal Hayat ve Sağ-Sol Akımlar', *SBF Dergisi*, xxiv, 3 (1969): 227-76.
Overy, Richard. *Russia's War: A History of the Soviet War Effort, 1941-1945*. New York: Penguin, 1998.
Ölçen, Mehmet Arif. *Vetluga Memoir: A Turkish Prisoner of War in Russia, 1916-1918*. Gainesville: University of Florida Press, 1995.
Önder, Zehra. *Die türkische Außenpolitik im Zweiten Weltkrieg*. Munich: Oldenbourg, 1977.
Özoğlu, Hakan. *Kurdish Notables and the Ottoman State*. Albany: SUNY, 2004.
Pekesen, Berna. *Zwischen Sympathie und Eigennutz: NS-Propaganda und die türkische Presse im Zweiten Weltkrieg*. Berlin 2014.
Penalba-Sotorrio, Mercedes. 'Beyond the War: Nazi Propaganda Aims in Spain during the Second World War', *Journal of Contemporary History* (2018): 1-25.
Perinçek, Mehmet. *Atatürk'ün Sovyetlerle Görüşmeleri*. İstanbul: Kaynak, 2005.
Perinçek, Mehmet. *Sovyet Devlet Kaynaklarında Kürt İsyanları*. İstanbul: Kaynak, 2011.
Picker, Henry. *Hitlers Tischgespräche im Führerhauptquartier*. Munich: Verlag, 1968.
Polian, Pavel. *Against Their Will: The History and Geography of Forced Migrations in the USSR*. Budapest: Central European University Press, 2003.
Potok, Chaim. *The Gates of November*. New York: Random House, 1996.
Potskhveriia, B.M. *Turtsiia mezhdu dvumia mirovymi voinami: ocherki vneshnei politiki*. Moscow: Nauka, 1992.
Reynolds, Michael. 'Buffers, not Brethren: Young Turk Military Policy in the First World War and the Myth of Panturanism', *Past and Present*, 203 (May 2009): 137-79.

Reynolds, Michael. *Shattering Empires: The Clash and Collapse of the Ottoman and Russian Empires, 1908-1918.* Cambridge: Cambridge University Press, 2011.
Rezun, Miron. *The Soviet Union and Iran: Soviet Policy in Iran from the Beginnings of the Pahlavi Dynasty until the Soviet Invasion in 1941.* Geneva: Institut Universitaire de Hautes Etudes Internationales, 1981.
Rjeshevskiy, Oleg A. *Stalin i Cherchill: Vstrechi, Besedi, Diskussii, 1941-1945.* Moscow, 2004.
Rohwer, Jürgen. *Die Versenkung der Jüdichen Flüchtlingstransporter Struma und Mefkurem Schwarzen Meer.* Frankfurt: Bernard und Graefe, 1964.
Rozal'ev, Iuri N. *K Istorii Sovetsko-Turetskikh otnoshenii.* Moscow: Gospolitizdat, 1958.
Sakharov, A.N. 'Voyna i sovetskaia diplomaty, 1939-1941', *Voproshy Istorii*, 8 (1995): 165-85.
Salim, Burçak Rıfkı. *Moskova Görüşmeleri (26 Eylül-16 Ekim 1939) ve Dış Politikamız Üzerindeki Tesirleri.* Ankara, 1983.
Şharapov, Z. P. *Naum Eytingon: Karayushchiy mech Stalina.* St Petersburg: Izdatelskiy Dom 'Neva', 2003.
Shaw, Stanford J. *Turkey and the Holocaust: Turkey's Role in Rescuing Turkish and European Jewry from Nazi Persecution During the Holocaust, 1933-45.* New York: Palgrave, 1993.
Shirer, William. *The Rise and Fall of the Third Reich.* New York: Simon & Schuster, 1960.
Shissler, A. Holly. *Between Two Empires: Ahmet Ağaoğlu and the New Turkey.* London: I.B. Tauris, 2002.
Slezkine, Yuri. *Arctic Mirrors: Russia and the Small Peoples of the North.* Ithaca: Cornell University Press, 1994.
Slezkine, Yuri. 'Imperialism as the Highest Stage of Socialism', *The Russian Review*, 59 (April 2000): 227-57.
Sonyel, Salahi. *Turkish Diplomacy, 1918-1923: Mustafa Kemal and the Turkish Nationalist Movement.* London: Sage Publications, 1975.
Sotskov, Lev. *Neizvestniy separatizm: na sluzhbe SD i Abvera.* Moscow, 2003.
Soysal, İsmail. '1937 Sadabad Pact', *Studies on Turkish-Arab Relations*, 3 (1988): 132-45.
Suphi Bey, Yaver. *Enver Paşa'nın Son Günleri.* Istanbul: Çatı Kitapları, 2007.
Steiner, Zara. *The Triumph of the Dark: European International History, 1933-1939.* Oxford: Oxford University Press, 2011.
Stepkov, V.N. *Pavel Sudoplatov - geniy terror.* St Petersburg: Izdatelskiy Dom 'Neva', 2003.
Stewart, Ninian. *The Royal Navy and the Palestine Patrol.* London: Frank Cass, 2002.
Sudoplatov, Pavel. *Spetsoperatsii: Lubyanka i Kreml, 1930-1950.* Moskva: Olma Press, 1997.
Sverchevskaya, A. K. *Sovetsko-Turetskie kul'turnye sviazi, 1925-1981.* Moscow: Nauka, 1983.
Şimşir, Bilal. *Lozan Telgrafları: Türk Diplomatik Belgelerinde Lozan Barış Konferansı.* Ankara: Türk Tarih Kurumu Basımevi, 1990.
Taki, Viktor. 'Orientalism on the Margins: The Ottoman Empire Under Russian Eyes', *Kritika: Explorations in Russian and Eurasian History*, 12, 2 (Spring 2011): 321-51.
Tamkin, Nicholas. *Britain, Turkey and the Soviet Union, 1940-1945.* Palgrave: New York, 2009.
Tripp, Charles. *A History of Iraq.* New York: Cambridge University Press, 2007.
Tooze, Adam. *The Wages of Destruction: The Making and Breaking of the Nazi Economy.* London: Penguin Books, 2008.
Tuna, Mustafa. 'Imperial Russia's Muslims: Inroads of Modernity', Ph.D. Dissertation, Princeton University, 2009.
Tunaya, Tarık Zafer. *Türkiye'de Siyasal Partiler.* İstanbul: Hürriyet Vakfı Yayınları, 1984.
Tyuleneva, N.I. 'Teni Proshlogo', *Voenno-istoricheskiy arkhiv*, No. 5 (May 2003): 23-8.
Uehling, Greta Lynn. *Beyond Memory: The Crimean Tatars' Deportation and Return.* New York: Palgrave, 2004.

Uldricks, Teddy. 'Russia and Europe: Diplomacy, Revolution, and Economic Development in the 1920s', *The International History Review*, 1, 1 (January 1979): 55-83.
Vaksberg, Arkady. *Stalin's Prosecutor: The Life of Andrei Vyshinsky*. New York: Grove Weidenfeld, 1990.
VanderLippe, John M. *The Politics of Turkish Democracy: İsmet İnönü and the Formation of the Multi-party System, 1938-1950*. Albany: SUNY Press, 2005.
Vaneyev, G.I. *Chernomortsy v Velikoi Otechestvennoi voine*. Moskva: Voenizdat, 1978.
Von Hagen, Mark. 'Empires, Borderlands, and Diasporas: Eurasia as Anti-Paradigm for the Post-Soviet Era', *The American Historical Review*, 109, 2 (April 2004): 445-68.
Yalçın, Osman. 'İkinci Dünya Savaşında İsmet İnönü ve Churchill Arasında Yapılan Adana Görüşmesi', *Ankara Üniversitesi Türk İnkılap ve Tarihi Enstitüsü Atatürk Yolu Dergisi*, 47, 1 (Spring 2011): 701-31.
Yayman, Huseyin. *Türkiyenin Kürt Sorunu Hafızası*. İstanbul: DK, 2011.
Yılmaz, Mustafa. *Atatürk Dönemi Türk Dış Politikası, 1919-1938* Ankara: 2003.
Yılmaz, Mustafa and Yasemin Doğaner. *Cumhuriyet Döneminde Sansür, 1923-1973*. Ankara: Siyasal Kitabevi, 2007.
Watson, Derek. *Molotov: A Biography*. Palgrave: New York, 2005.
Watt, Cameron. 'The Saadabad Pact of 8 July 1937.' In Uriel Dann (ed.), *The Great Powers in the Middle East 1919-1939*. New York and London: Holmes & Meier, 1988.
Weber, Frank G. *The Evasive Neutral: Germany, Britain and the Quest for a Turkish Alliance in the Second World War*. New York: University of Missouri Press, 1979.
Weiner, Amir. *Making Sense of War: The Second World War and the Fate of the Bolshevik Revolution*. Princeton: Princeton University Press, 2001.
Westad, Odd Arne. *The Global Cold War: Third World Interventions and the Making of Our Times*. New York: Cambridge University Press, 2007.
Williams, Brian Glyn. *The Crimean Tatars: The Diaspora Experience and the Forging of a Nation*. Boston: Brill, 2001.
Woytak, Richard. 'The Promethean Movement in Interwar Poland', *East European Quarterly*, vol. XVIII, no. 3 (September 1984): 273-8.
Wright, Gordon. *The Ordeal of Total War, 1939-1945*. Illinois: Harper Collins, 1997.
Yerasimos, Stefanos. *Türk-Sovyet İlişkileri: Ekim Devriminden 'Milli Mücadele'ye*. İstanbul: Gözlem Yayınları, 1979.
Zubok, Vladislav. *A Failed Empire: The Soviet Union in the Cold War from Stalin to Gorbachev*. Chapel Hill: University of North Carolina Press, 2009.
Zubok, Vladislav, and Constantine Pleshakov. *Inside the Kremlin's Cold War: From Stalin to Khrushchev*. Cambridge: Harvard University Press, 1996.
Zürcher, Erik-Jan. *The Unionist Factor: The Role of the Committee of Union and Progress in the Turkish National Movement, 1905-1926*. Leiden: Brill, 1984.
Zürcher, Erik-Jan. 'Young Turk Memoirs as a Historical Source: Kazim Karabekir's "Istiklal Harbimiz"', *Middle Eastern Studies*, 22, 4 (October 1986): 562-70.
Zürcher, Erik-Jan. *Political Oppostion in the Early Republic: The Progressive Republican Party, 1924-1925*. Leiden: Brill, 1991.
Zürcher, Erik-Jan. 'The Young-Turks: Children of the Borderlands?', *International Journal of Turkish Studies*, 9, 1-2 (2003): 275-86.
Zürcher, Erik-Jan. *Turkey: A Modern History*. London: I.B. Tauris, 2004.

Index

Açikalin, Cevat 164, 174
Adana Conference (Turkey–Great Britain) (1943) 7, 146, 150–3
Afghanistan, Turkey and 45
Akalın, Şekip 11
Aktay, Ali Haydar
  German–Turkish Non-Aggression Pact (1941), and 99
  Massigli Affair (1940), and 81, 82
  receives Soviet assurance of benevolent neutrality (1941) 98
  report on Nazi–Soviet War affairs (1941) 95
Albania, annexation by Italy (1939) 51, 57
Alexandretta/Hatay, Turkey's annexation of (1937–9) 13, 42, 43–8, 51
Al-Husayni, Muhammad Amin, Grand Mufti of Jerusalem 108
Anglo–French–Turkish Treaty (1939) 64, 67–9
Ankara, Treaty of (1921) 43, 44
anti-Semitism in Turkey 114
Apaydin, Zekai
  purchase of Soviet weapons 49
  Soviet–Turkish Pact talks (1936), and 28
  Straits question, and 26
  trade talks with Soviet Union (1936–7), and 31
Aralov, Semyon 15, 165
Aras, Tevfik Rüştü
  chromium agreement with Germany (1941), and 103
  German–Turkish Non-Aggression Pact (1941), and 100
  Iran, and 46
  Kurdish nationalism, and 39
  Litvinov, and 15
  Moscow talks (1937), and 34, 48
  Near Eastern Non-Aggression Pact, and 46

replacement as Foreign Minister (1938) 49
Soviet visit to Turkey (1933), and 18
Soviet–Turkish Pact talks (1936), and 28
Straits question, and 23, 26
visits Italy (1928) 22
Arikan, Saffet 54, 136, 137
Armenia
  Kurdish insurgency, and 13, 39, 40, 42
  Kurdology Conference (1935) 43
  territorial claims in Turkey 172
Arnshtam, Lev Oskarovich 18
Atatürk. *See* Kemal, Mustafa
Atay, Falih Rifki 74
Atif Bey 81
Atsız, Nihal 142
Azat Kirim (Independent Crimea) (newspaper) 135

Badoglio, Pietro, Marshal 88
Bala, Mirza 129
Balkan Entente (1934) 19, 20, 53, 88
Balkan situation (1940–1) 86–90, 96
Barbarossa, Operation (1941) 7, 73, 99, 101
Barutçu, Faik Ahmet 80
Bayar, Celal 11, 58
Beria, Lavrenty 139
Bernes, Mark 145
Black Sea Straits
  British assurances to Turkey 107
  closure to German ships (1944) 164
  German disclosure of Russian demands for military bases (1941) 97, 101
  growth of Soviet Black Sea Fleet 63
  Hitler–Molotov talks (1940) 93
  Lausanne Convention of the Straits (1923) 3, 24
  Lenin's views on 173

Montreux Convention (1936) 2–4, 25, 27, 63, 84
  Soviet demands over (1945) 1, 171
  Stafford Cripps's speech 118
  Stalin's concerns over 62
  Straits question pre-WWII 22–30
  Turkey's policy 3
  Turkey's remilitarization (1936) 4, 13
  Turkey–Soviet relations (1940–1), and 82–4
  Yalta Conference (1945), and 168
Bosphorus. *See* Black Sea Straits
Brod, Simon 114
Bubnov, Andrei 49
Bulgaria
  Balkan situation (1940–1), and 87
  Pan-Turanism, and 125
  Turkey proposes to invade (1944) 161
  Turkey's relations with (1940–1) 88

Cadogan, Alexander, Sir 119
Cafer, Ahmet 128
Çakmak, Fevzi, Marshall 111, 136, 152
Çankaya, sinking of (1942) 112, 116
Canonica, Pietro 165
Casablanca Conference (Great Britain–United States) (1943) 152, 158
Catholic Church. *See* Vatican
Cemil Mürdüm Bey (Jamil Mardam) 108
Chamberlain, Neville 53
Chicherin, Georgii 15, 25, 27
chromium agreements
  Anglo–Franco–Turkish Chrome Agreement (1940) 104
  Turkey and Germany (1941) 104
  Turkey and Great Britain (1941) 103
Churchill, Winston
  Adana Conference (1943) 7, 146, 150–3
  Casablanca Conference (1943) 158
  military assistance to Turkey 154
  Second Cairo Conference (1943), and 156
  Straits question, and 168
  Tehran Conference (1943), and 150
  Yalta Conference (1945), and 168
Ciano of Cortellazzo and Buccari, Gian Galeazzo Ciano, 2nd Count of 58, 88
Clodius, Karl, Dr. 103, 104

Cold War 172–6
Countenance, operation (1941) 10, 97, 105–9
Crimean Tatars. *See* pan-Turkism
Cripps, Stafford, Sir
  Pact of Steel (1940), and 86
  Straits question, and 118
  Turkey–Soviet relations (1940–1), and 83, 84
Cyprus conflict (1960s) 175
Czechoslovakia, Munich Agreement (1938) 51

Daladier, Edouard 79
Dardanelles. *See* Black Sea Straits
D-Day landings in Normandy (1944) 162, 163
Denezhko, D. M., Lieutenant 113, 116
Dikof, Lazar 113
Dodecanese Islands 23, 157
'Dr Harun' 136

Eastern Anatolia
  Eastern Question pre-WWII 37–50
  İnönü's tour (1940) 71
  Kars, Treaty of (1921) 37
  Kurdish nationalism, and 38–43, 147
  mobilization of Turkish forces (1940) 85
  Ottoman Empire, and 37
  Reform Plan for the East (1925) 39
  Russian Empire's rule 37
  Soviet demands over (1945) 1
  Soviet territorial claims (1945) 171
  Soviet Union returns to Turkey (1921) 37, 171
  Turkey increases defences (1940) 70
  Turkey–Soviet border 37
  Turkey–Soviet economic cooperation 37
  weakness of Turkey's defences 76
Eastern Question. *See* Eastern Anatolia
Eden, Anthony
  Adana Conference (1943), and 146
  Anglo–Soviet occupation of Iran (1941), and 105
  chromium agreement with Turkey (1941), and 103
  German–Turkish Non-Aggression Pact (1941), and 100

German–Turkish trade agreement (1941), and 103
Maisky, and 119
Menemencioglu, and 154
Saraçoglu, and 161
Soviet–Turkish Pact talks (1936), and 30
Straits question, and 24
Turkey's neutrality, and 118
Eichmann, Adolf 115
Einstein, Albert 114
Eisenhower, Dwight D, General 158, 175
Enver Pasha 125, 130
Erden, Ali Fuad, General 127, 129, 133
Erkilet, Emir, General 75, 127, 133, 138, 142
Esmer, Ahmet Şükrü 74
Ethiopia, Italy's invasion of (1935–6) 23
Eytingon, Naum Isaakovich 109

Faisal, King of Iraq 45, 46
Filov, Bogdan 88
France
  Anglo–Franco–Turkish Chrome Agreement (1940) 104
  Anglo–French–Turkish Treaty (1939) 64
  D-Day landings in Normandy (1944) 162, 163
  defeat by Germany (1940) 6, 77, 80, 82, 87, 104
  Franco–Syrian Treaty of Alliance (1936) 44
  Franco–Turkish Friendship Treaty (1938) 44
  Hoare–Laval plan (1935) 23
  Kurdish insurgency, and 42, 43
  Massigli Affair (1940) 9, 78–82
  Munich Agreement (1938) 51
  mutual assistance agreement with Turkey (1939) 51
  Syria's independence, and 43
  Turkey's annexation of Alexandretta/Hatay (1937–9), and 13

Gafencu, Grigore 87
Gamzatov, Rasul 145
Georgian nationalism 172
Gerede, Hüsrev

Anglo–French–Turkish Treaty (1939), and 69
Hitler, and 92, 137
Massigli Affair (1940), and 82
Nazi propaganda in Turkey, and 76
pan-Turkism, and 129, 135
Papen, and 137
pro-Nazism 6, 136
replacement as Ambassador to Germany (1942) 136
Ribbentrop, and 91, 97
talks on German–Turkish cooperation with Ribbentrop (1941) 102
trade talks with Germany (1941) 91, 92
Weizsäcker, and 78
Germany
  Anglo–French–Turkish Treaty (1939), and 69
  Anglo–Turkish Declaration (1939), and 58
  anti-Soviet propaganda in Turkey 9, 67, 74–8, 85, 98, 119, 126, 133, 143
  chromium supplies from Turkey 103, 159
  closure of Black Sea Straits to German ships (1944) 164
  Crimean campaign and occupation (1941–4) 124, 134, 137, 139–43
  declaration of war on Soviet Union (1941) 97
  defeat of France (1940) 6, 77, 80, 82, 87, 104
  encourages Turkish neutrality 61
  invasion of Greece (1941) 90
  invasion of Poland (1939) 60
  invasion of Soviet Union (Operation Barbarossa) (1941) 7, 73, 99, 101
  Iran, and 105
  Massigli Affair (1940), and 9, 78–82, 85
  military assistance to Turkey 6
  Molotov–Ribbentrop Pact (1939) 4, 56, 59–62, 73
  Munich Agreement (1938) 51
  naval discussions with Turkey (1944) 162
  Nazi organizations in Turkey 75
  Non-Aggression Pact with Turkey (1941) 10, 90–8, 99
  Ottoman Empire, and 59, 93, 127, 130

Pact of Steel (1940) 86
promises of territorial acquisitions to Turkey 102
Soviet fear of 4
SS *Struma* sinking (1942), and 115
Stalingrad, Battle of (1942–3) 7, 119, 138, 145
Straits question, and 93, 97, 101
talks on cooperation with Turkey (1941) 102
Tatar nationalism, and (*see* Tatar nationalism)
trade agreement with Turkey (Clodius Agreement) (1941) 101–4, 103
trade talks with Turkey (1941) 91
trade with Turkey during WWII 91, 159
trade with Turkey pre-WWII 30, 49, 58
Turkey cuts relations (1944) 163
Turkey declares war on (1945) 165
Turkey's neutrality, and 6–7, 9, 82, 86, 117
Turkey's pre-WWII relations 11, 56–9
Turkey's view of Stalingrad campaign 120
Vatican, and 109
Gökalp, Ziya 125
Great Britain
Adana Conference (1943) with Turkey 7, 146, 150–3
Anglo–Franco–Turkish Chrome Agreement (1940) 104
Anglo–French–Turkish Treaty (1939) 64
Anglo–Soviet guarantee to Turkey (1941) 97
Anglo–Turkish Declaration (1939), and 51, 52–4, 58
Balkan situation (1940–1), and 86–90
Casablanca Conference (1943) 152, 158
chromium agreement with Turkey (1941) 103
fears of Soviet threat to Middle East 70
German–Turkish Non-Aggression Pact (1941), and 95, 99, 103
German–Turkish trade agreement (1941), and 103
historical relations with Turkey 118

Hoare–Laval plan (1935) 23
increased pressure on Turkey to enter WWII 159, 161
Iraq's independence (1932), and 46
Italian invasion of Greece (1940), and 89
Kurdish insurgency, and 40
Kurdish nationalism, and 39
Massigli Affair (1940), and 80
military assistance to Turkey 6, 150, 154, 159, 164
Molotov–Ribbentrop Pact (1939), and 60
Munich Agreement (1938) 51
Near Eastern Non-Aggression Pact, and 46
occupation of Iran (operation Countenance) (1941) 10, 97, 105–9
occupation of Iraq (1940) 108
postwar relations with Turkey 174
Sa'dabad Pact (Oriental Entente) (1937), and 47
Saraçoglu–Molotov talks (1939), and 63
Second Cairo Conference (1943) 156
Soviet–Turkish Pact talks (1936), and 30
SS *Struma* sinking (1942), and 113, 115
state of Soviet–Turkish relations (1940), and 70
Straits question, and 24, 28, 107, 168
strategy differences with United States 158
Tehran Conference (1943) 150
trade talks with Turkey (1939) 59
Turkey's entry into WWII, and 146, 159
Turkey's fear of Russia, and 8, 146
Turkey's neutrality, and 87
Turkey's remilitarization of the Straits (1936), and 4, 13
Turkey–Soviet relations (1940–1), and 82–5
Yalta Conference (1945) 165, 168–72
Great Terror, Stalin's (1936–8) 48
Greece
Balkan Entente (1934) 22
Entente Cordiale with Turkey (1933) 22
German promises of territorial acquisitions to Turkey 102

Germany's invasion (1941) 90
Italy's invasion (1940) 88
liberation (1944) 162
Turkey's response to Italian invasion of 89
Gündüz, Asim, General 96, 119

Haco Mehmed 43
Halifax, Edward Frederick Lindley Wood, 1st Earl of (Lord Halifax) 59
  Anglo-French-Turkish Treaty (1939), and 68
  Anglo-Turkish Declaration (1939), and 53
  Balkan situation (1940-1), and 90
  Italian invasion of Greece (1940), and 89
  Sa'dabad Pact (Oriental Entente) (1937), and 67
  Saraçoglu-Molotov talks (1939), and 63
  state of Soviet-Turkish relations (1940), and 70, 71
  Straits question, and 63
  Turkey-Soviet relations (1940-1), and 82, 84
Halit (Soviet spy) 108
Harriman, W. Averell 163
Hatay Republic. *See* Alexandretta/Hatay
Hejaz. *See* Saudi Arabia
Hentig, Werner Otto von 132, 133, 136
Hilger, Gustav 131
Hitler, Adolf
  Anglo-Turkish Declaration (1939), and 56
  discloses Russian demands for military bases in the Straits (1941) 98
  ethnic Turks in Soviet Union, and 120
  Gerede, and 93, 137
  German-Turkish Non-Aggression Pact (1941), and 100
  İnönü, and 91, 92, 97
  invasion of Greece (1941) 90
  Molotov, and 93
  Molotov-Ribbentrop Pact (1939), and 56
  Non-Aggression Pact with Turkey (1941) 93, 96
  Operation Barbarossa (1941), and 101

pan-Turkism, and 133
Romania's genocide of Jews, and 115
Sami Pasha, and 58
Saraçoglu-Molotov talks (1939), and 63, 66
Straits question, and 93
Turkey's neutrality, and 7, 9
Hoare-Laval plan (1935) 23
Holy See. *See* Vatican
Hull, Cordell 160

Ibn Saud, King of Saudi Arabia 45
İnönü, İsmet
  Adana Conference (1943) with Churchill 7, 146, 150-3
  Anglo-Soviet occupation of Iran (1941), and 106
  Anglo-Turkish Declaration (1939), and 54
  anti-German cooperation with Soviet Union 4
  army mobilization in Eastern Anatolia (1940) 85
  assassination attempt on von Papen (1942), and 111
  balancing between Great Britain and Germany 6
  Balkans situation, and 86
  becomes President (1938) 49
  chromium exports, and 159
  Eastern Anatolia tour (1940) 71
  entry into WWII, and 146
  fears German encirclement 90
  friendship with Soviet Union as primary goal of foreign policy 3
  German promises of territorial acquisitions in Greece, and 102
  Hitler, and 56, 91, 92, 97
  hopes for compromise between Great Britain and Germany 116
  justifies Turkey's neutrality 170
  Kurdish insurgency, and 40, 148
  lend-lease agreement with United States, and 164
  Litvinov, and 15
  Molotov-Ribbentrop Pact (1939), and 60, 73
  Moscow talks (1937), and 35
  Moscow talks (1939), and 9

Operation Barbarossa (1941), and 101
opposition to Nazism 121
pan-Turkism, and 127, 136, 137, 143
Papen, and 57
post-war cabinet (1947–50) 174
Potemkin–Saraçoglu negotiations (1939), and 55–6
resigns as Prime Minister (1937) 47
Saraçoglu, and 63
Saraçoglu–Molotov talks (1939), and 65
Second Cairo Conference (1943), and 156
Soviet plane crash incident at Kars (1943), and 1
Soviet–Turkish Pact talks (1936), and 28
Stalin, and 19
state of Soviet–Turkish relations (1940), and 71
trade talks with Soviet Union (1936–7), and 32
Turkey's neutrality, and 82
visits Italy (1932) 23
visits Soviet Union (1932) 17
Iran
 Anglo-Soviet occupation (1941) 10, 97, 105–9
 German aid to 105
 Kurdish insurgency, and 42, 147
 modernization policies 45
 Near Eastern Non-Aggression Pact, and 46
 Sa'dabad Pact (Oriental Entente) (1937) 42, 45, 66
 Soviet Union, and 46
 Treaty of Alliance with Great Britain and Soviet Union (1941) 108
Iraq
 admission to League of Nations (1932) 46
 British occupation (1940) 108
 independence (1932) 46
 Kurdish insurgency in Turkey, and 40
 Near Eastern Non-Aggression Pact, and 46
 Sa'dabad Pact (Oriental Entente) (1937) 45
Ismet Pasha 72

Italy
 annexation of Albania (1939) 51, 57
 crisis with Turkey (1939) 52
 Dodecanese Islands, and 23
 enters WWII (1940) 76
 expansionism 3, 13, 22, 52
 invasion of Ethiopia (1935–6) 23
 invasion of Greece (1940) 88
 Kurdish insurgency, and 42
 Pact of Steel (1940) 86
 pre-WWII relations with Soviet Union 19
 pre-WWII relations with Turkey 22
 Syrian nationalism, and 45

Jews
 anti-Semitism in Turkey 114
 German-Jewish scholars in Turkey 114
 Romania's genocide of Jews 114
 Turkey's aid for Jewish migration to Palestine 114
John XXIII, Pope. *See* Roncalli, Angelo Giuseppe

Kalymk people, Stalin's deportation of (1943) 141
Karakhan, Lev
 Balkan Entente (1934), and 20
 concerns over Turkey-Germany trade 31
 execution (1937) 49
 Iran, and 46
 Kemal, and 4
 Litvinov, and 20
 Soviet–Turkish Pact talks (1936), and 29
 Straits question, and 24
 trade talks with Turkey (1936–7), and 33
 Turkey's neutrality, and 4
Kars
 Soviet demands over (1945) 1
 Soviet plane crash incident (1943) 1
 Treaty of (Turkey-Soviet Union) (1921) 37
Karskii, F. 49
Kavtaradze, Sergey 169
Kaya, Şükrü
 Kurdish insurgency, and 41

Moscow talks (1937), and 34, 48
Kemal, Mustafa (Atatürk)
  annexation of Alexandretta/Hatay
    (1937–9), and 43
  death (1938) 11, 49
  Enver Pasha, and 125
  İnönü, and 47
  Lenin, and 165
  Litvinov, and 15
  modernization policies 45
  Mussolini, and 22
  peace policy 12
  Sheikh Said insurrection (1925), and
    40
  Soviet relations, and 3, 13
  Stalin's Great Terror (1936–8), and 49
Khrushchev, Nikita 175
Killigil Pasha, Nuri 75, 127, 130, 132
Kioseivanov, Georgi 87, 88
Kırımer, Edige 134, 139
Knatchbull-Hugessen, Hughe, Sir
  Anglo-French-Turkish Treaty (1939),
    and 68
  Arikan, and 137
  Balkan situation (1940–1), and 88
  chromium agreement with Turkey
    (1941), and 104
  Gerede, and 137
  Halifax, and 53, 59
  İnönü, and 60, 63
  Italian invasion of Greece (1940), and
    89, 90
  Maisky's complaint about 119
  Papen, and 57
  Sa'dabad Pact (Oriental Entente)
    (1937), and 67
  Saraçoglu–Molotov talks (1939), and 65
  Second Cairo Conference (1943), and
    156
  SS *Struma* sinking (1942), and 115
  state of Soviet–Turkish relations
    (1940), and 70, 71
  Turkey's entry into WWII, and 159
  Turkey's neutrality, and 87
  visit to Moscow (1942) 118
Kornilov, Leonid 109, 111
Kurds
  Anglo-Soviet occupation of Iran
    (1941), and 107

Ararat insurrection (1930) 39, 41
Dersim insurrection (1937–8) 42, 43
insurgency in Eastern Anatolia 38–43
Iranian Azerbaijan, in 147
Kurdish State (Khoybun) 40
Kurdology Conference (1935) 43
Mutki insurrection (1925) 41
National Congress (1927) 40
Ottoman Empire, and 39
Sheikh Said insurrection (1925) 39
Soviet policy towards 39–43
Turkey's policy after Adana Conference
  (1943) 147

Lausanne Conference (1922–3) 3, 24
Lausanne Convention of the Straits (1923)
  3, 24
League for National Action (Syria) 45
League of Nations
  Iraq's admission (1932) 46
  Turkey's admission (1932) 3
Lenin, Vladimir 1, 165, 173
Litvinov, Maxim
  Aras, and 15
  Black Sea cooperation with Turkey, and
    49
  Italy, and 20
  Karakhan, and 22
  Kemal, and 49
  Potemkin–Saraçoglu negotiations
    (1939), and 55
  replacement as Foreign Minister
    (1939) 51
  Rüştü, and 22
  Soviet–Turkish Pact talks (1936), and
    28
  Straits question, and 24, 26
  trade talks with Turkey (1936–7), and
    31

Mackensen, August von 77
Maisky, Ivan 106, 119
Malche, Albert 114
Mardam, Jamil. *See* Cemil Mürdüm Bey
Massigli, René 78
Massigli Affair (1940) 9, 78–82, 86
media opinion
  pan-Turkism 135
  in Soviet Union 63, 66, 169

in Turkey 52, 59, 66, 74, 76, 98, 126, 170
Menemencioglu, Numan
  Adana Conference (1943), and 152
  Balkan bloc policy 158
  becomes Foreign Minister (1942) 94
  chromium agreement with Germany (1941), and 103
  Eden, and 154
  Non-Aggression Pact with Germany (1941), and 94, 99
  Operation Barbarossa (1941), and 101
  Steinhardt, and 152
  Turkey's entry into WWII, and 160
military incidents
  growth of Soviet Black Sea Fleet 63
  Soviet airforce flies captured German aircraft into Turkey (1942) 112
  Soviet attack on fishing vessel *Çankaya* (1942) 112, 116
  Soviet attack on SS *Struma* (1942) 10, 112–16
  Soviet plane crash incident near Kars (1943) 1
  Turkey captures Soviet Spy (Halit) operating from Iran (1942) 108
  Turkish mobilization in Eastern Anatolia (1940) 85
Mohammed Reza Pahlavi, Shah of Iran 106, 108
Molotov, Vyacheslav
  Anglo-Soviet occupation of Iran (1941), and 105
  becomes Soviet Foreign Minister (1938) 55
  Cripps, and 84
  Eastern Question, and 171
  German declaration of war (1941), and 97
  German-Turkish Non-Aggression Pact (1941), and 99
  Hitler, and 93
  negotiations with Saraçoglu (1939) 62–7
  Pact of Steel (1940), and 86
  renunciation of territorial demands on Turkey 175
  Saraçoglu, and 161
  Sarper, and 169, 170
  Straits question, and 93, 171

Turkey-Soviet relations (1940–1), and 84
Molotov-Ribbentrop Pact (1939) 4, 56, 59–62, 73
Montreux Convention (1936) 2–4, 14, 25, 27, 63, 84
Munich Agreement (1938) 51
Mussolini, Benito
  crisis with Turkey (1939), and 52
  expansionism 23
  invasion of Greece (1940) 88
  Kemal, and 22
  Saraçoglu-Molotov talks (1939), and 63

NATO, Turkey's membership 175
Nazi Germany. *See* Germany
Nejd. *See* Saudi Arabia
Neurath, Konstantin von 58
newspapers. *See* media opinion
NKVD. *See* Soviet Union

Okyar, Fethi 30, 54
Orbay, Rauf 118
Oriental Entente. *See* Sa'dabad Pact
Ottoman Empire
  Crimea, and 125
  Eastern Question, and 37
  economic failure 31
  Germany, and 59, 93, 127, 130
  Kurds, and 39
  Pan-Turkism, and 125
  partition of 1, 3, 5
  Russian Empire, and 8, 18, 37, 125, 165
  Turkey's benefits from ending of 175
  Turkey's distinctiveness 11, 64, 163

Pact of Steel (1940) 86
Pahlavi dynasty (Iran). *See* Mohammed Reza Pahlavi; Reza Shah Pahlavi
Palestine, Jewish migration to 114
pan-Turkism
  collaboration during German occupation of Crimea (1941–4) 124, 134, 137, 139–43
  deportation of alleged pro-Nazi populations from Crimea 140
  German anti-Soviet propaganda, and 126, 133

Index

German–Tatar collaboration 10
 Germany and 124, 128–34
 ideological development 125
 legacy of German involvement 142
 loss of Turkish support 142
 media opinion 135
 nationalist opnion in Turkey, and 126
 NKVD activity against Tatars 139
 Ottoman Empire, and 125
 Pan-Turanism, and 125
 Pan-Turkism, and 124
 pro-German publications 138
 pro-Soviet loyalty during WWII 123
 Soviet recapture of Crimea (1944) 139
 Stalin's Crimea policy during WWII 124
 Tatar National Parliament (Kurultay) (1917–20) 125
 territorial ambitions in Soviet Union 131
 in Turkey 126
 Turkish scholarship on 126
Papazyan, Balyan 42
Papen, Franz von
 Anglo–French–Turkish Treaty (1939), and 69
 Anglo–Turkish Declaration (1939), and 58
 Balkan situation (1940–1), and 89
 becomes Ambassador to Turkey (1939) 57
 Chancellor of Germany (1932) 57
 encourages Turkish neutrality 61
 expulsion from Turkey (1944) 160, 162
 Gerede, and 137
 German–Turkish Non-Aggression Pact (1941), and 99
 İnönü, and 57
 Molotov–Ribbentrop Pact (1939), and 73
 Nazi propaganda in Turkey, and 78
 Non-Aggression Pact with Turkey (1941), and 91, 94, 95, 96
 Operation Barbarossa (1941), and 101
 pan-Turkism, and 127, 128, 132, 137, 139, 143
 Ribbentrop, and 7, 57
 Saraçoglu, and 77, 120
 Soviet assassination attempt (1942) 10, 109–12

Straits question, and 101
 Terentiev, and 56
 transfer of Dodecanese Islands to Turkey, and 157
 Turkey's entry into WWII, and 160
 Turkey's neutrality, and 6, 74, 76, 95, 117
 Vatican, and 109
 WWI service in Turkey (1917) 57
Pavlov, Georgiy Ivanovich 109, 111
Perkel, Naci 157
Poland
 Germany invades (1939) 60
 Prometheus organization 128, 129
 Soviet Union invades (1939) 63, 67
Potemkin, Vladimir Petrovich 55–6
Prometheus organization 128, 129
propaganda, German anti-Soviet. *See* Germany

Rasulzade, Mehmed Emin 129
relations between Turkey and Soviet Union
 after Stalingrad (1943–5) 10
 anniversary celebrations of Turkish Republic (1936) 13
 anti-German cooperation 4
 Armenian nationalism, and 172
 Black Sea cooperation 49
 buildup to WWII 48–50
 Cold War, and 172–6
 content of current volume 8–10
 cooperation in 1920's 15
 cooperation in late 1930's 49
 Crimean Tatars, and (*see* pan-Turkism)
 decline during 1939–40 67, 70–2
 Eastern Question (*see* Eastern Anatolia)
 ending of friendship 51–72
 ethnic Turks in Soviet Union 120, 123
 evidence for historic enmity 3
 Georgian nationalism, and 172
 German anti-Soviet propaganda, and 7, 67, 74–8, 85, 98, 119, 126, 133, 143
 German–Turkish Non-Aggression Pact (1941), and 99
 Great Britain, and 82–5
 hostility after WWII 165
 hostility as default condition 2, 73, 175

hostility during WWII as anomaly 175
improvement after Syrian Crisis (1957) 175
İnönü becomes President of Turkey (1938) 49
Kemal and Lenin 165
Kurdish nationalism, and 38–43
Massigli Affair (1940) 9, 78–82, 85, 86
media opinion 169
Molotov–Ribbentrop Pact (1939), and 4–5, 59–62, 73
Montreux Convention (1936) 14
Moscow talks (1937) 34, 48
Moscow talks (1939) 9
nationalist demonstrations in Turkey 172
Near Eastern Non-Aggression Pact, and 46
Non-Aggression Pact (1921) 55
Operation Barbarossa (1941), and 73, 99
outbreak of WWII 9
Potemkin–Saraçoglu negotiations (1939), and 55–6
pre-WWII 2, 12, 15–30, 165
Republic Monument in Istanbul 165
Sa'dabad Pact (Oriental Entente) (1937), and 45, 46, 66
Saraçoglu–Molotov negotiations in Moscow (1939) 62–7
Soviet assassination attempt on von Papen (1942) 10, 109–12
Soviet demands in Black Sea Straits and Eastern Anatolia (1945) 1
Soviet mediation between Turkey and Iran (1937) 42
Soviet renunciation of territorial demands 175
Soviet–Turkish Pact talks (1936) 30
Stalin's antagonism towards Turkey 175
Straits question (*see* Black Sea Straits)
Tatar nationalism, and (*see* pan-Turkism)
trade relations pre-WWII 30, 49
Treaty of Friendship (1925) 169
Turkey's attitude to German defeat of Soviet Union 6
Turkey's entry into WWII 145–64, 163

Turkey's fear of Russia 2, 7, 8, 10, 63, 98, 146, 173
Turkey's fears of Soviet advance in Balkans 70
Turkey's neutrality 116–21
Turkey's perspective on prospective Soviet victory 145
Turkey's postwar perspective 173
Turkey's successful balancing between Soviet Union and West 175
Turkish government documents on 5
Yalta Conference (1945) 165, 168–72
. *See also* military incidents
Renda, Abdülhalik 40
Reza Shah Pahlavi, Shah of Iran 45, 105, 106
Ribbentrop, Joachim von
  Anglo–French–Turkish Treaty (1939), and 69
  Anglo–Turkish Declaration (1939), and 58
  declaration of war on Soviet Union (1941), and 97
  Gerede, and 97
  Gündüz's view of Stalingrad campaign, and 120
  Nazi propaganda in Turkey, and 78
  Non-Aggression Pact with Turkey (1941), and 96, 99
  pan-Turkism, and 127, 128, 129, 131, 132, 139, 143
  Papen, and 7, 57
  Straits question, and 101
  talks on German–Turkish cooperation with Gerede (1941) 102
  Turkey's neutrality, and 91, 101, 117
Romania
  Balkan Entente (1934) 22
  Balkan situation (1940–1), and 87
  genocide of Jews 115
  Soviet annexation of Bessarabia and Northern Bukovina (1940) 76
Roncalli, Angelo Giuseppe, Cardinal (Pope John XXIII) 109
Roosevelt, Franklin D. 156, 157, 158, 160, 168
Rosenberg, Alfred 139
Rossi, Paolo Alberto 52
Russian Empire 1, 8, 18, 37, 125, 165

Sabis, Ali Ihsan, General 75, 127, 138
Sa'dabad Pact (Oriental Entente) (1937) 42, 45, 66
Sadak, Necmeddin 174
Sagol, Süleyman 110
Şahin, Mustafa 42
Sami Pasha, Kemalettin 58
Sanjak of Alexandretta. *See* Alexandretta/Hatay
Saraçoglu, Sükrü
   Adana Conference (1943), and 152
   Anglo-French-Turkish Treaty (1939), and 68
   Anglo-Turkish Declaration (1939), and 53
   assassination attempt on von Papen (1942), and 112
   Balkan situation (1940-1), and 87
   becomes Foreign Minister (1938) 49
   becomes Prime Minister (1942) 120
   dislike of Stalin 73
   Eden, and 161
   Gerede, and 137
   German invasion of Soviet Union (1941), and 73, 98
   Massigli Affair (1940), and 78, 81
   Molotov, and 161
   Molotov-Ribbentrop Pact (1939), and 60
   negotiations with Molotov (1939) 62-7
   Non-Aggression Pact with Germany (1941), and 95
   opposition to Nazism 121
   Papen, and 77
   Potemkin, and 55-6
   state of Soviet-Turkish relations (1940), and 70
   trade talks with Germany (1941) 92
   transfer of Dodecanese Islands to Turkey, and 157
   Turkey's entry into WWII, and 161, 162
   Turkey-Soviet relations (1940-1), and 84
   visits Bulgaria (1940) 88
   warnings of Soviet expansionism 158
Sarper, Selim 169, 170, 172
Saudi Arabia, treaty with Turkey (1929) 45
Saydam, Refik
   Anglo-Turkish Declaration (1939), and 53
   death (1942) 120
   Massigli Affair (1940), and 80
   Saraçoglu-Molotov talks (1939), and 65
   SS *Struma* sinking (1942), and 115
Sayma, Abdurrahman 110
Schulenburg, Werner von der, Count 97
Schwartz, Philipp 114
Sefket, Memduh 128
Sertel, Zekeriya 74, 173
Seyit Riza 42
ShCh-213 (Soviet submarine) 10, 112, 116
Sikorski, Wladyslaw, General 128, 129
Soviet Union
   Black Sea interests 34
   deportation of alleged pro-Nazi populations 140
   Eastern Question, and (*see* Eastern Anatolia)
   ethnic minorities 123
   Germany, and (*see* Germany)
   Great Terror (1936-8) 48
   invasion of Poland (1939) 63, 67
   Iran, and 46
   Italy, and (*see* Italy)
   media opinion in 63, 66, 169
   national unity during WWII 123
   NKVD activity 109, 139
   occupation of Iran (1941) 10, 97, 105-9
   recapture of Crimea (1944) 139
   Russianness 123
   Straits question, and (*see* Black Sea Straits)
   Tehran Conference (1943) 150
   Turkey, and (*see* military incidents; relations between Turkey and Soviet Union)
   Yalta Conference (1945) 165, 168-72
   . *See also* Russian Empire
Stalin, Joseph
   Aktay's views on 96
   antagonism towards Turkey 175
   Armenian nationalism, and 172
   Balkan situation (1940-1), and 96
   concerns over Black Sea Straits 62
   Crimean Tatars, and 124
   Cripps, and 84

demands in Black Sea Straits and
  Eastern Anatolia (1945) 1
deportation of Kalymk people (1943)
  141
finances Turkey's industrialisation 19
Georgian nationalism, and 172
Great Terror (1936–8) 48
İnönü's resignation as Turkey's Prime
  Minister (1937), and 47
Kemal, and 14
Kurdish nationalism, and 39
Molotov–Ribbentrop Pact (1939), and
  56
Pact of Steel (1940), and 86
Saraçoglu–Molotov talks (1939), and
  63, 66
Saraçoglu's dislike of 73
Straits question, and 168
Tehran Conference (1943), and 150
territorial demands in Eastern Anatolia
  172
Turkey's entry into WWII, and 146
Turkey's neutrality, and 1, 70, 165
Turkey's Russophobia, and 10
Turkey–Soviet relations (1940–1), and
  83, 84
Yalta Conference (1945), and 168
Stalingrad, Battle of (1942–3) 7, 119, 138,
  145
Steinhardt, Laurence 153, 159, 160, 163
Stoddard, Theodore Lothrop 125
Stoliar, David 112, 113
Stomonyakov, Boris 26, 32
Straits question. *See* Black Sea Straits
Struma, SS 10, 112–16
Sudoplatov, Pavel 109
Suritz, Yakov 39, 41, 46
Syria
  Crisis of 1957 175
  Franco–Syrian Treaty of Alliance
    (1936) 44
  Kurdish insurgency, and 42, 43
  League for National Action 45
  Turkey's annexation of Alexandretta/
    Hatay (1937–9) 13, 42, 43–8

Tatar nationalism. *See* pan-Turkism
Tehran Conference (1943) 150
Terentiev, Alexei 56, 63, 81

Togan, Zeki Velidi 126, 128, 142
Tokat, Ömer 110, 111
Torch, operation (1942) 153
trade
  Turkey and Germany (*see* Germany)
  Turkey and Great Britain (*see* Great
    Britain)
Truman, Harry 170
Truman Doctrine (1947) 175
Turanism. *See* pan-Turkism; Turkism
Türkeş, Alparslan 142
Turkey
  admission to League of Nations (1932)
    3
  Afghanistan, and 45
  Anglo–Soviet occupation of Iran
    (1941), and 10, 105–9
  Ankara, Treaty of (1921) 43, 44
  Ankara Central railway station
    inauguration (1935) 11
  annexation of Alexandretta/Hatay
    (1937–9) 13, 42, 43–8, 51
  anti-communism 49
  anti-Semitism 114
  Balkan Entente (1934) 19, 20, 22, 53
  Balkan situation (1940–1), and 86–90
  Balkans policy (1943–5) 158
  benefits from ending of Ottoman
    Empire 175
  Bulgaria, and 88
  Casablanca Conference (1943), and
    152, 158
  communism in 49, 67, 74
  Crimean Tatars, and (*see* pan-Turkism)
  Cyprus conflict (1960s), and 175
  D-Day landings in Normandy (1944),
    and 162, 163
  economic cost of WWII 166
  entry into WWII 7, 10, 145–64
  foreign trade 30
  Germany, and (*see* Germany)
  government documents on foreign
    policy 5
  Great Britain, and (*see* Great Britain)
  Greece, and (*see* Greece)
  historical relations with Great Britain
    118
  hopes for compromise between Great
    Britain and Germany 116

industrialization 19, 33, 91, 175
invasion of Poland (1939), and 68
Italy, and (see Italy)
Jewish migration to Palestine, and 114
Jewish scholars from Germany, and 114
Kurds, and (see Kurds)
media opinion in 52, 59, 66, 74, 76, 98, 126, 170
Middle East policy after Adana Conference (1943) 147
military expenditure during WWII 166
military strength in WWII 167
modernization policies 45
national debt 167
NATO membership 175
Nazi organizations in 75
neutrality during World War II 5–8
pan-Turkism (see Tatar nationalism)
pre-WWII foreign policy objectives 12
pre-WWII international relations 12
Republic Monument in Istanbul 165
Sa'dabad Pact (Oriental Entente) (1937) 42, 45, 66
Saudi Arabia, and (see Saudi Arabia)
Second Cairo Conference (1943) 156
Soviet Union, and (see military incidents; relations between Turkey and Soviet Union)
Syrian Crisis (1957), and 175
Turkism 121
United States, and (see United States)
Yalta Conference (1945), and 165, 168–72
. See also Ottoman Empire
Turkism. See pan-Turkism

Ubaydin, Cemil 40
Ülküsal, Müstecip 134, 139
Ulus (newspaper) 74, 98
United States
 Casablanca Conference (1943) 152, 158

chromium supplies from Turkey 160
concerns over Turkey-Soviet conflict 170
containment policy towards Communism 175
landings in North Africa (operation Torch) (1942) 153
lend-lease agreement with Turkey 164
postwar relations with Turkey 175
Second Cairo Conference (1943) 156, 157
Tehran Conference (1943) 150
Truman Doctrine (1947) 175
Turkey's relations with 147, 153, 158–61
Turkey's view of 116
Yalta Conference (1945) 165, 168–72
USSR. See Soviet Union

Vasilievsky, Pavel 109
Vatican 109
Vinarov, Ivan 109
Vinogradov, S.A. 119, 172
Voroshilov, Kliment, Marshal 18, 156
Vyshinsky, Andrey 163

Warlimont, Walter, Lieutenant General 137
Wedemeyer, Albert 158
Weizsäcker, Ernst von
 pan-Turkism, and 129
 Straits question, and 76, 101
 Turkey's hostility to Russia, on 73
 Turkey's neutrality, and 77, 95
Weygand, Maxim, General 78, 79
Wilson, Edwin C. 170
Woermann, Ernst 131, 132, 136, 137

Yalta Conference (1945) 165, 168–72
Yenibahçeli, Şükrü 128
Yücel, Hasan Ali 67
Yugoslavia, Balkan Entente (1934) 22
Yutkevich, Sergei 18

www.ingramcontent.com/pod-product-compliance
Lightning Source LLC
Chambersburg PA
CBHW052033300426
44117CB00012B/1798